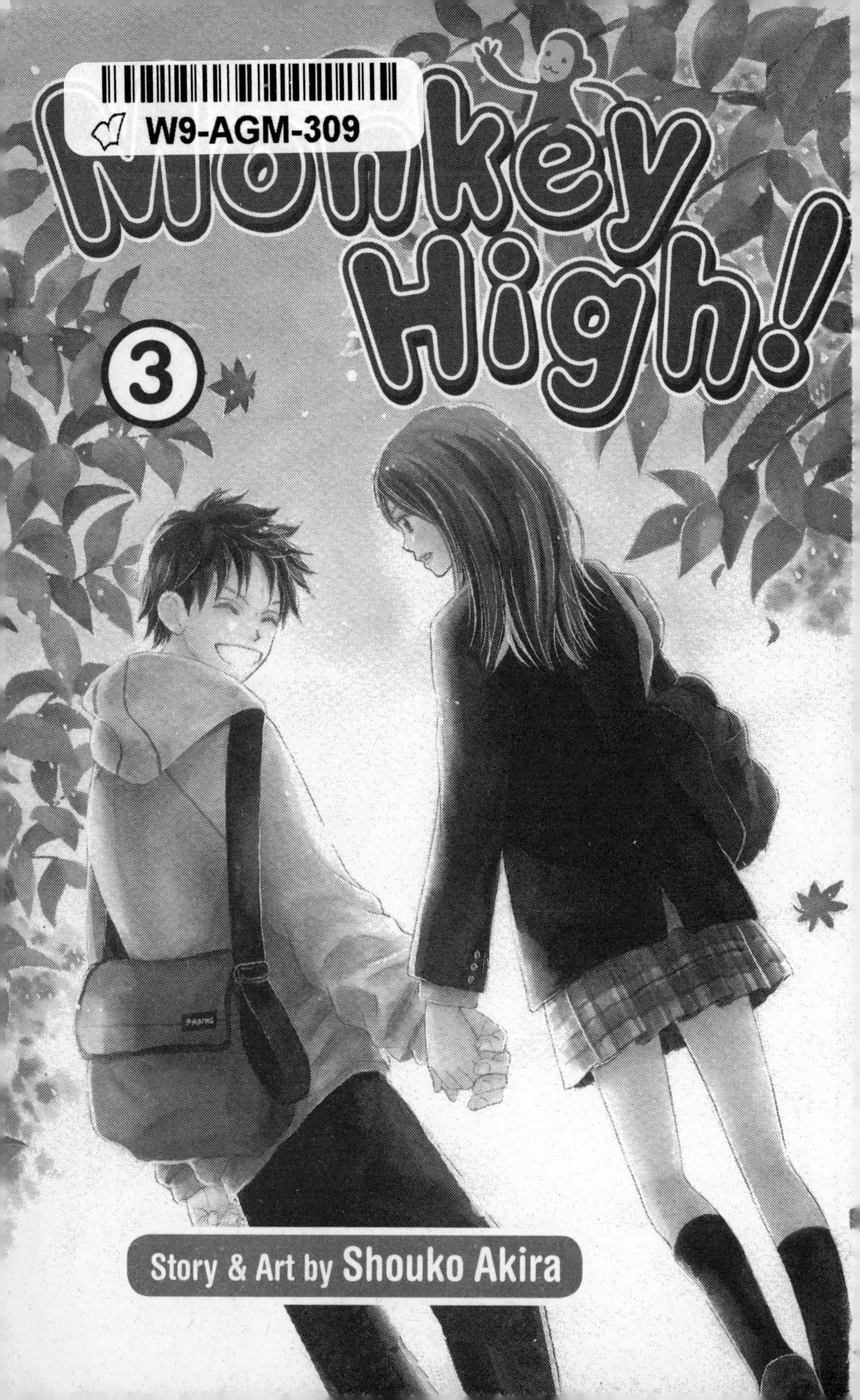
Monkey High!
3
Story & Art by Shouko Akira

Monkey High!

③ CONTENTS

6th Monkey: 2/14 The Chocolate Incident
3

7th Monkey: Happy Birthday
83

8th Monkey: No Dunking in the Game of Love?!
124

9th Monkey: Who'll Be the Student Body President?!
157

Postscript
188

Story Thus Far

Masaru Yamashita
(Nickname: Macharu)

Haruna was forced to transfer to a new school because of her father's involvement in a corruption scandal. She compares her crazy new classmates to a troop of monkeys and attempts to distance herself from them. However, her hard shell begins to melt as Macharu befriends her. After a field trip, the two decide to go out, but...?!

Haruna Aizawa

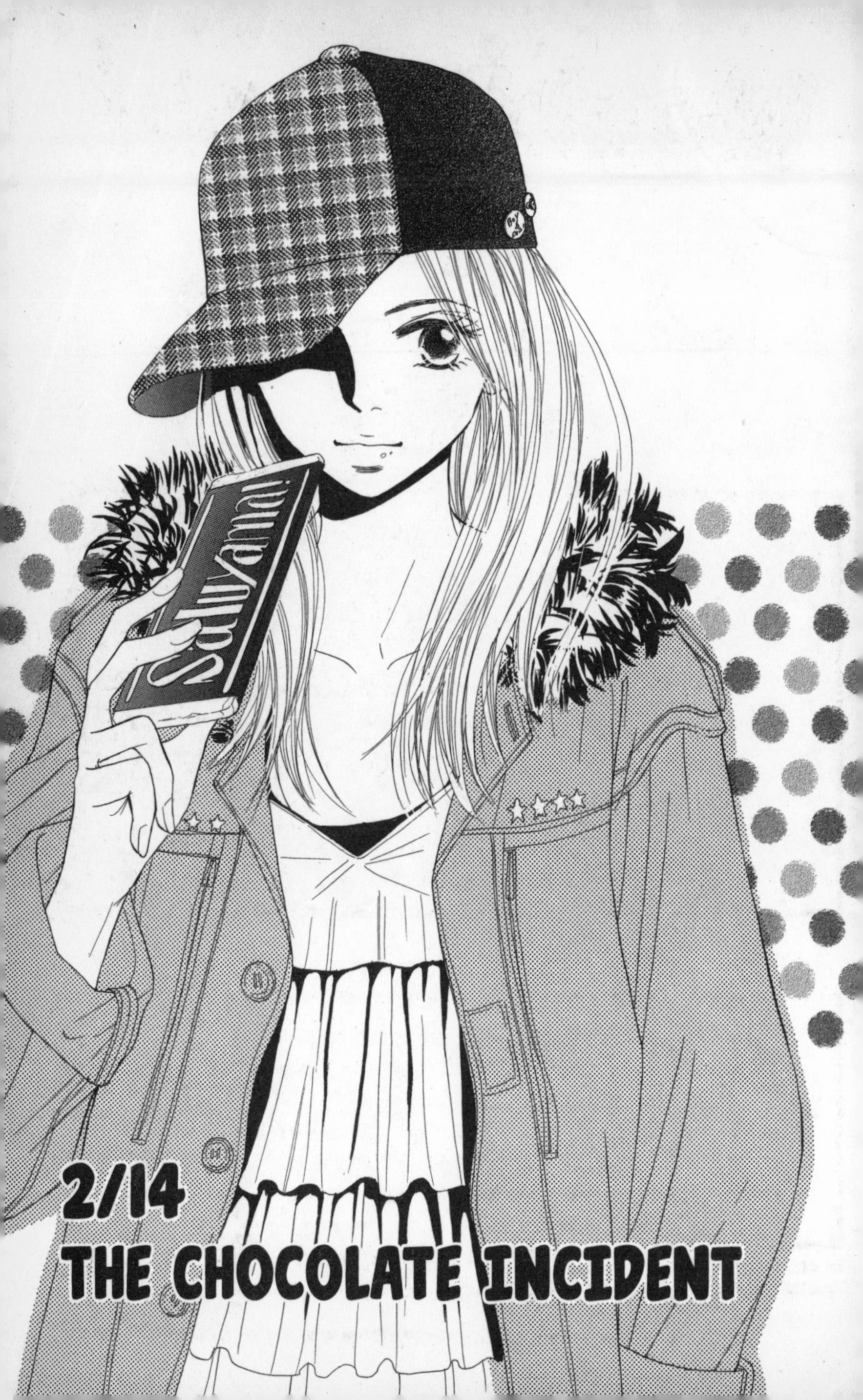

2/14 THE CHOCOLATE INCIDENT

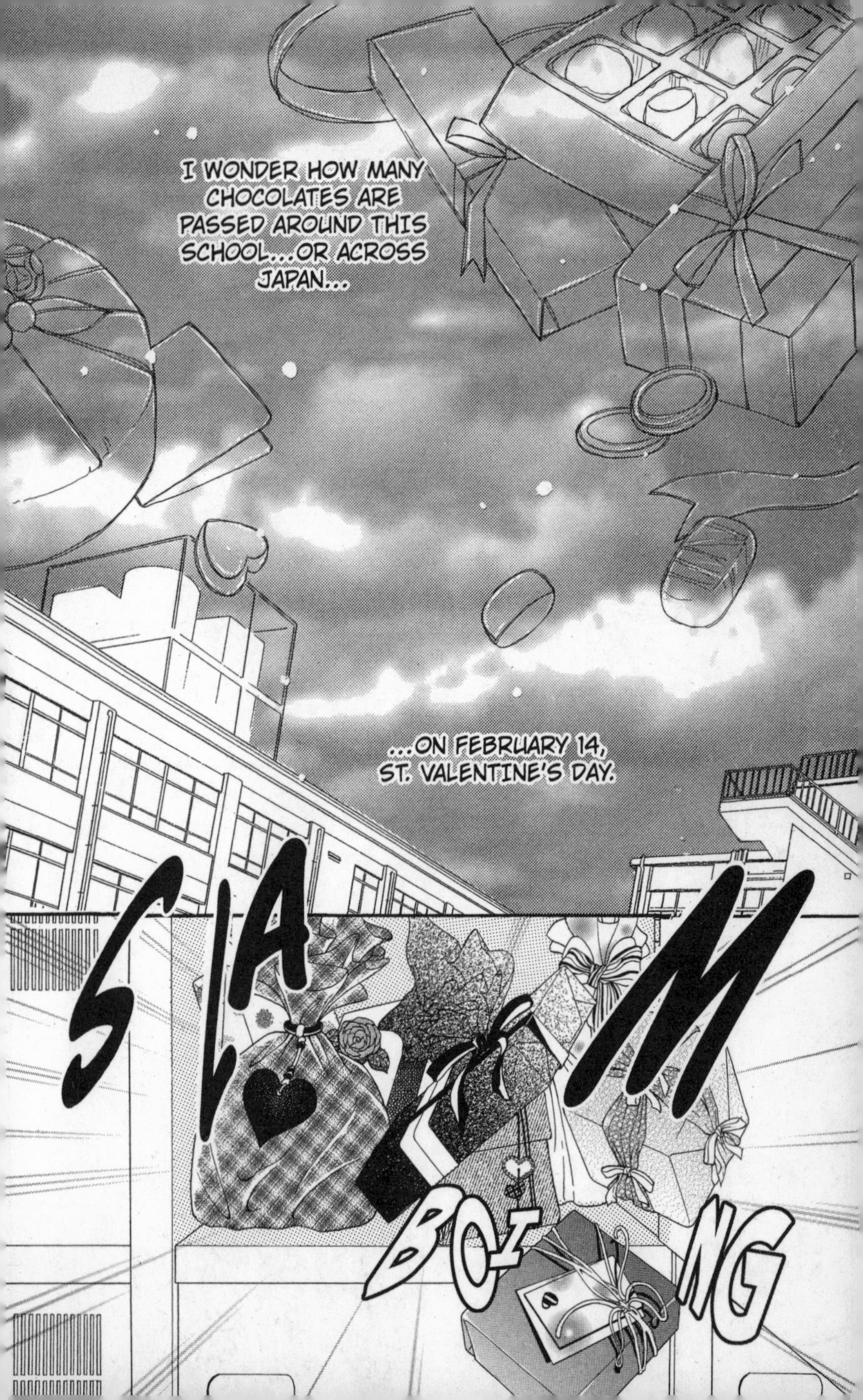
I WONDER HOW MANY CHOCOLATES ARE PASSED AROUND THIS SCHOOL...OR ACROSS JAPAN...
...ON FEBRUARY 14, ST. VALENTINE'S DAY.
SLAM
BOING

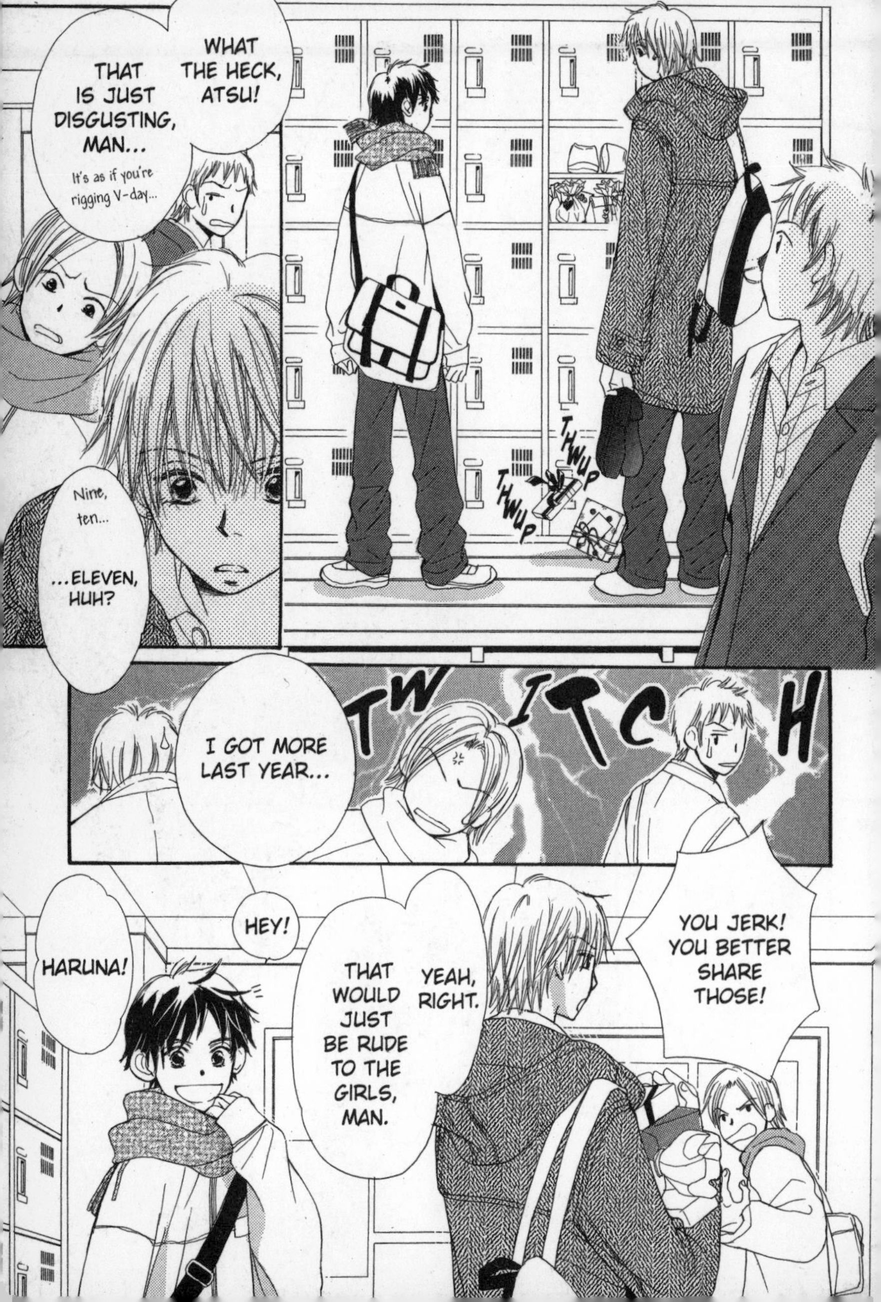
THWUP
THWUP
WHAT THE HECK, ATSU!
THAT IS JUST DISGUSTING, MAN...
It's as if you're rigging V-day...
Nine, ten...
...ELEVEN, HUH?
TWITCH
I GOT MORE LAST YEAR...
YOU JERK! YOU BETTER SHARE THOSE!
YEAH, RIGHT.
THAT WOULD JUST BE RUDE TO THE GIRLS, MAN.
HEY!
HARUNA!

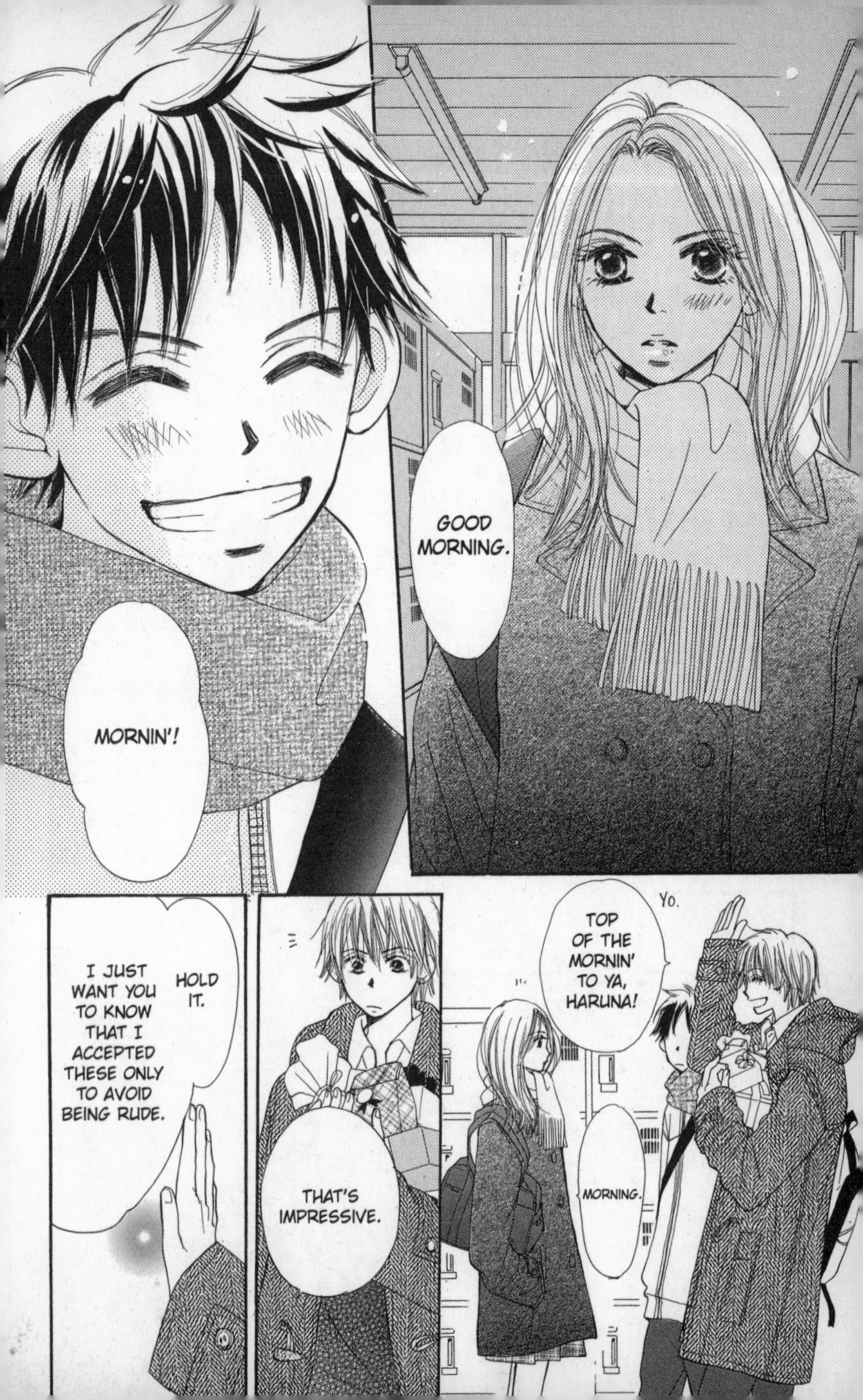
GOOD MORNING.
MORNIN'!
YO.
TOP OF THE MORNIN' TO YA, HARUNA!
MORNING.
THAT'S IMPRESSIVE.
HOLD IT.
I JUST WANT YOU TO KNOW THAT I ACCEPTED THESE ONLY TO AVOID BEING RUDE.

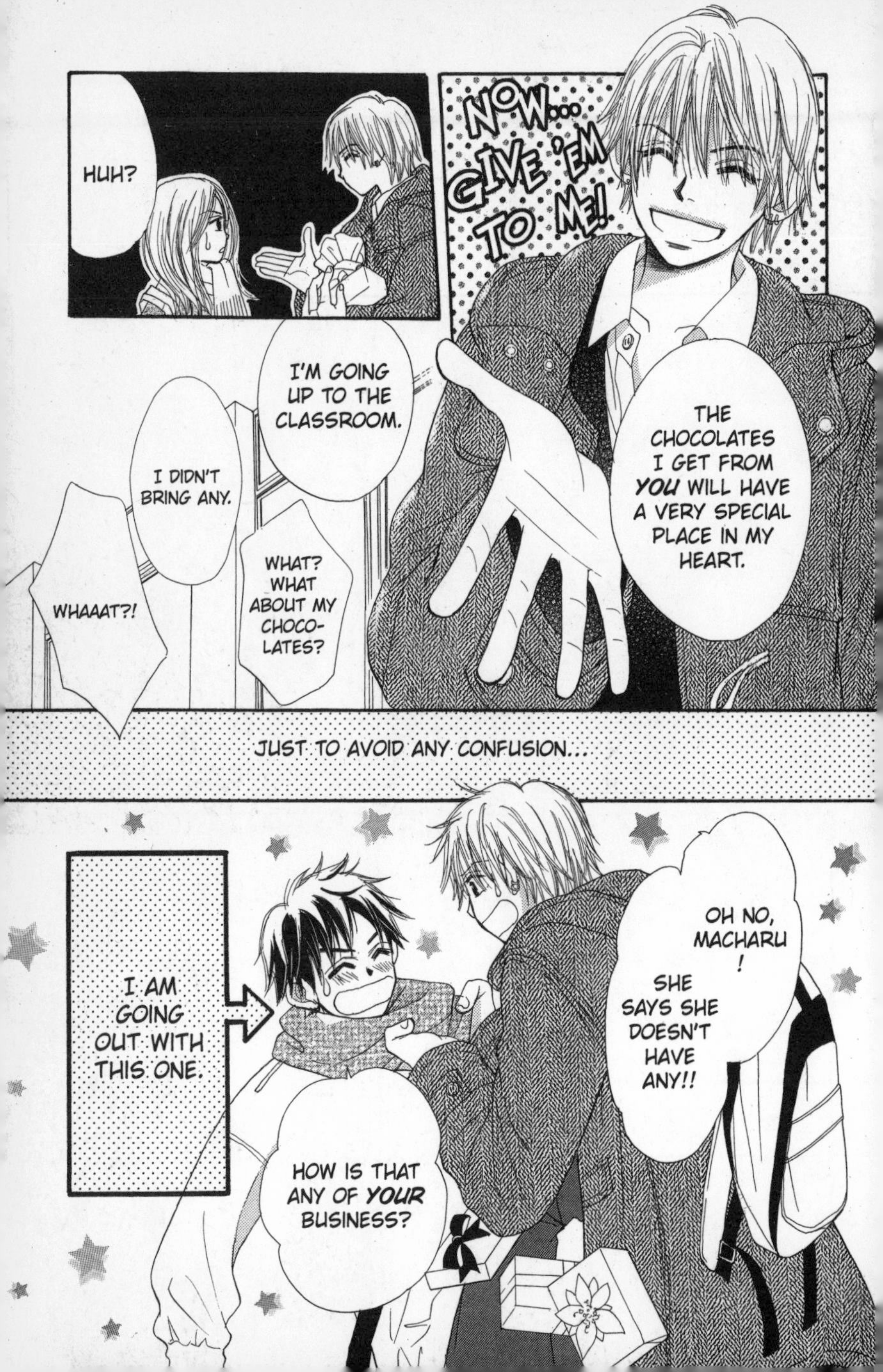
NOW... GIVE 'EM TO ME!
THE CHOCOLATES I GET FROM *YOU* WILL HAVE A VERY SPECIAL PLACE IN MY HEART.
HUH?
I'M GOING UP TO THE CLASSROOM.
I DIDN'T BRING ANY.
WHAT? WHAT ABOUT MY CHOCO-LATES?
WHAAAT?!
JUST TO AVOID ANY CONFUSION...
OH NO, MACHARU!
SHE SAYS SHE DOESN'T HAVE ANY!!
HOW IS THAT ANY OF *YOUR* BUSINESS?
I AM GOING OUT WITH THIS ONE.

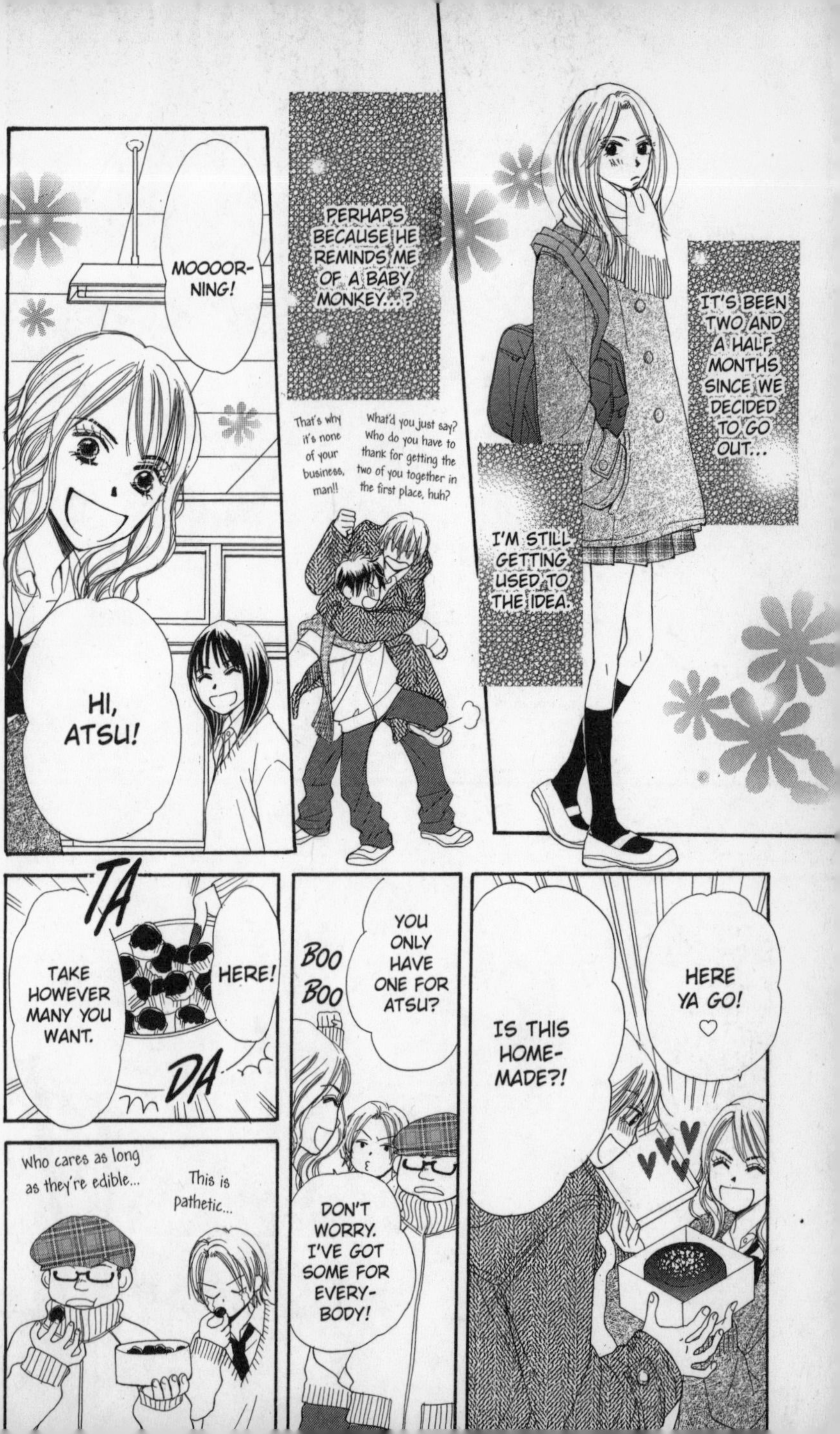
IT'S BEEN TWO AND A HALF MONTHS SINCE WE DECIDED TO GO OUT...
I'M STILL GETTING USED TO THE IDEA.
PERHAPS BECAUSE HE REMINDS ME OF A BABY MONKEY...?
What'd you just say? Who do you have to thank for getting the two of you together in the first place, huh?
That's why it's none of your business, man!!
MOOOOR-NING!
HI, ATSU!
HERE YA GO! ♡
IS THIS HOME-MADE?!
YOU ONLY HAVE ONE FOR ATSU?
BOO BOO
DON'T WORRY. I'VE GOT SOME FOR EVERY-BODY!
HERE!
TA
DA
TAKE HOWEVER MANY YOU WANT.
This is pathetic...
Who cares as long as they're edible...

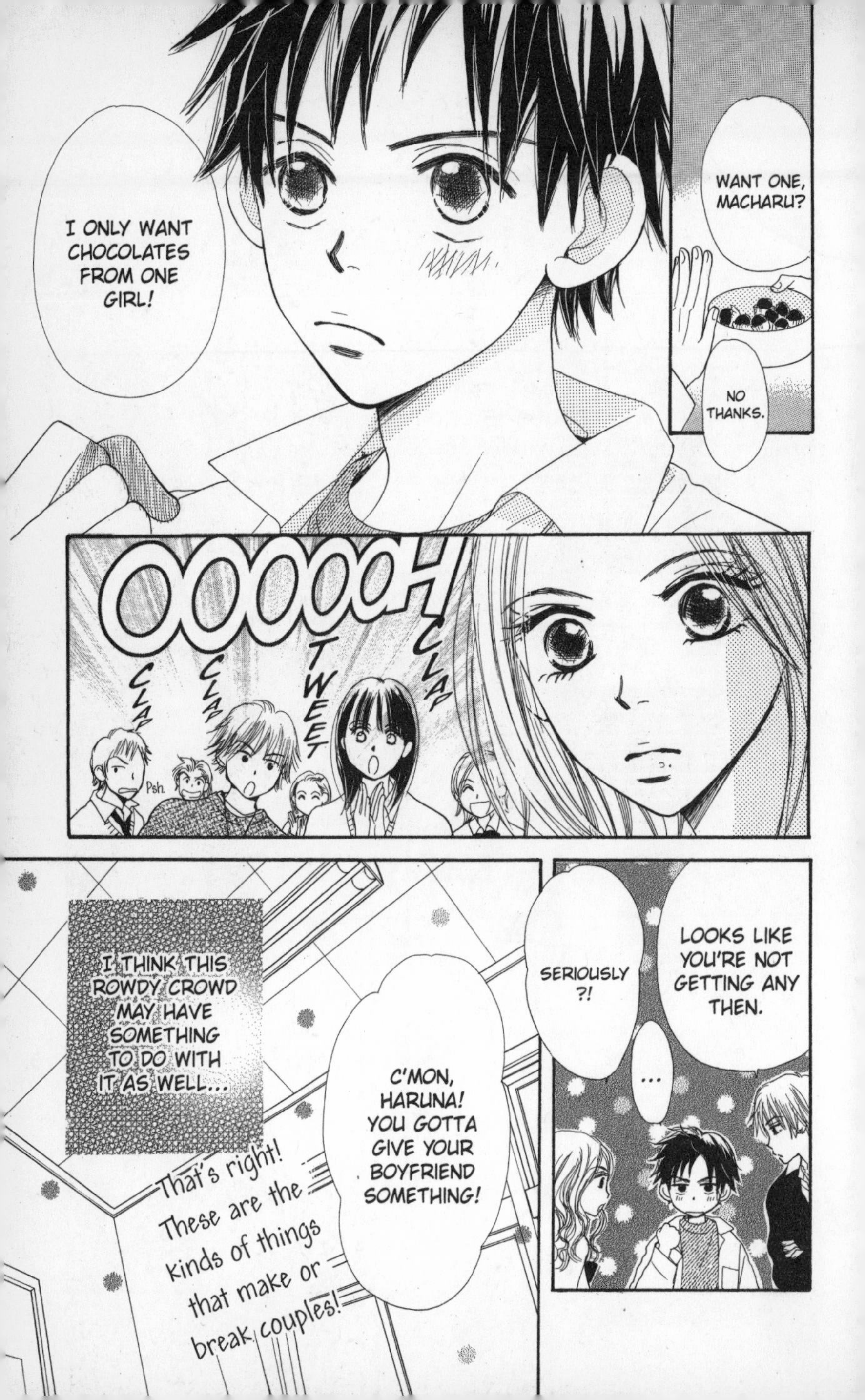
WANT ONE, MACHARU?
NO THANKS.
I ONLY WANT CHOCOLATES FROM ONE GIRL!
OOOOOH
CLAP
TWEET
CLAP
CLAP
Psh.
LOOKS LIKE YOU'RE NOT GETTING ANY THEN.
SERIOUSLY?!
...
C'MON, HARUNA! YOU GOTTA GIVE YOUR BOYFRIEND SOMETHING!
I THINK THIS ROWDY CROWD MAY HAVE SOMETHING TO DO WITH IT AS WELL...
That's right! These are the kinds of things that make or break couples!

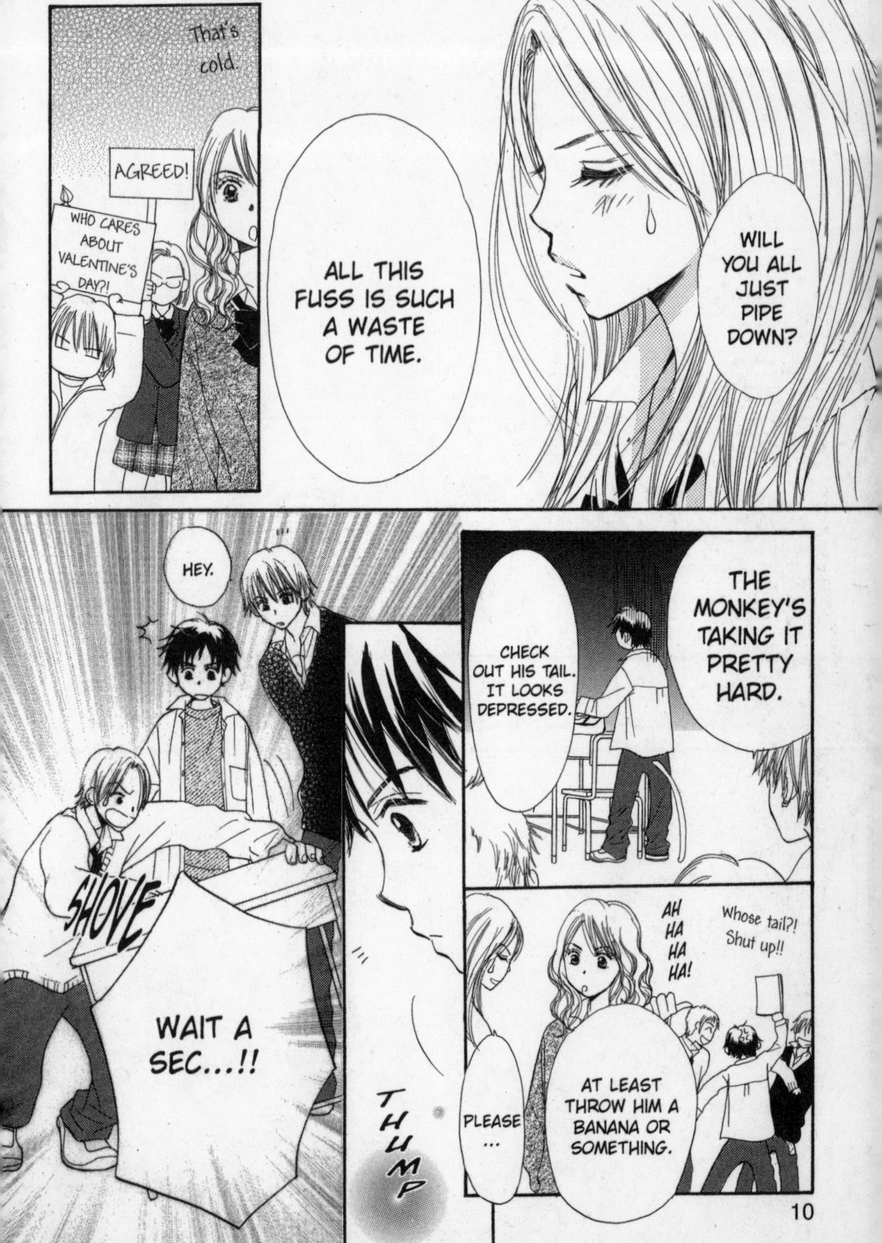
WILL YOU ALL JUST PIPE DOWN?
ALL THIS FUSS IS SUCH A WASTE OF TIME.
That's cold.
AGREED!
WHO CARES ABOUT VALENTINE'S DAY?!
THE MONKEY'S TAKING IT PRETTY HARD.
CHECK OUT HIS TAIL. IT LOOKS DEPRESSED.
Whose tail?! Shut up!!
AH HA HA HA!
AT LEAST THROW HIM A BANANA OR SOMETHING.
PLEASE ...
THUMP
HEY.
SHOVE
WAIT A SEC...!!

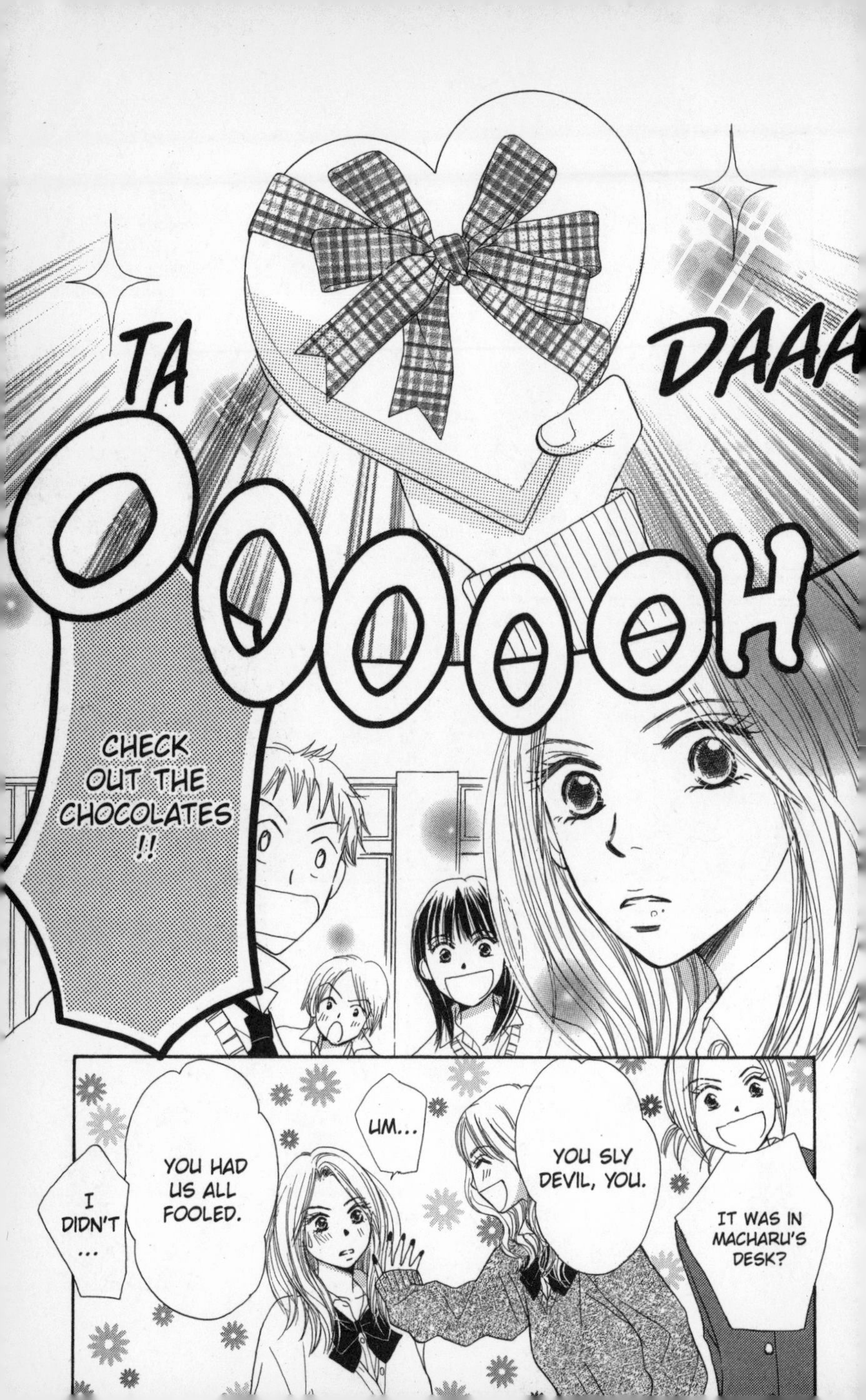
TA DAAA
OOOOOH
CHECK OUT THE CHOCOLATES!!
IT WAS IN MACHARU'S DESK?
YOU SLY DEVIL, YOU.
UM...
YOU HAD US ALL FOOLED.
I DIDN'T...

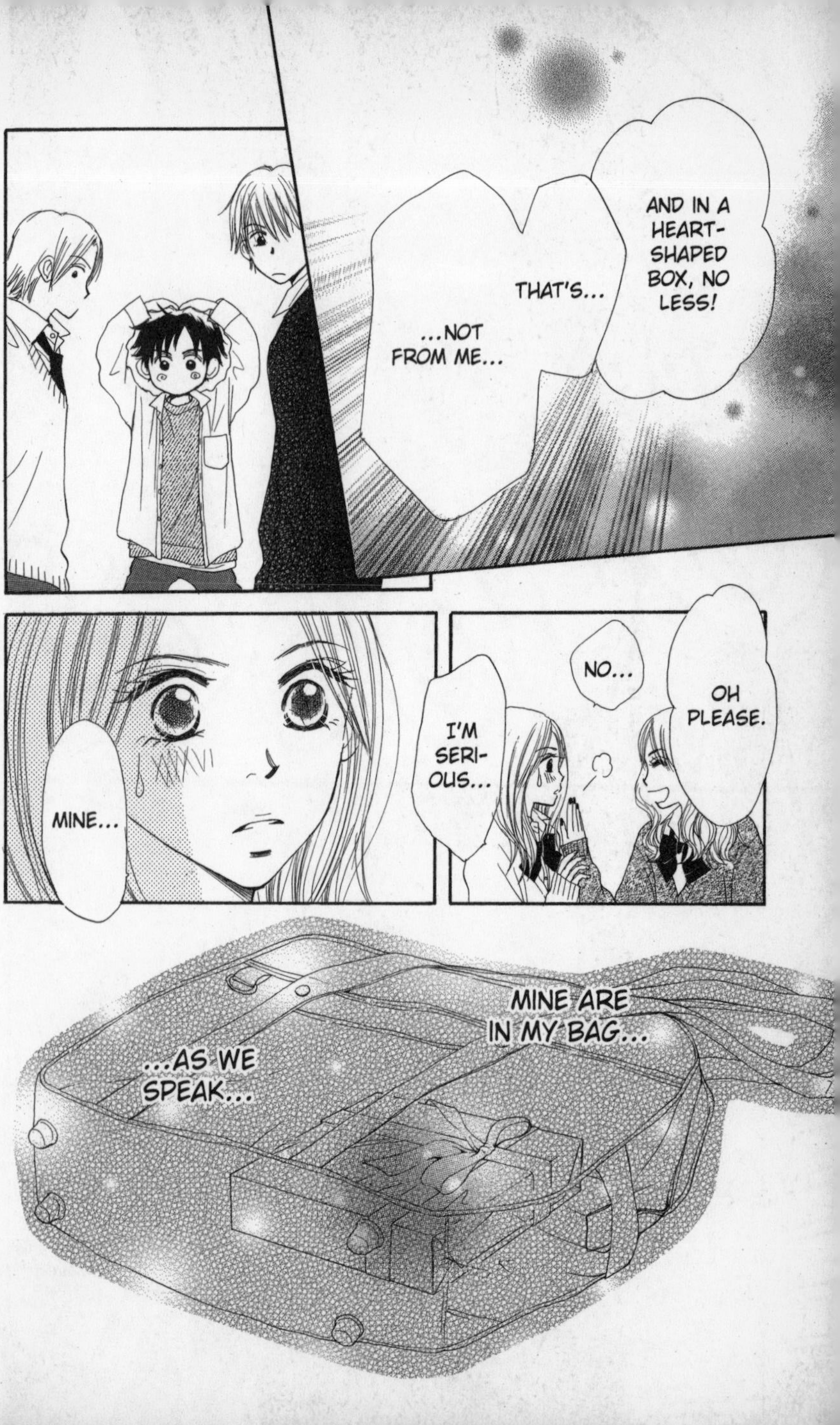
AND IN A HEART-SHAPED BOX, NO LESS!
THAT'S...
...NOT FROM ME...
OH PLEASE.
NO...
I'M SERI-OUS...
MINE...
MINE ARE IN MY BAG...
...AS WE SPEAK...

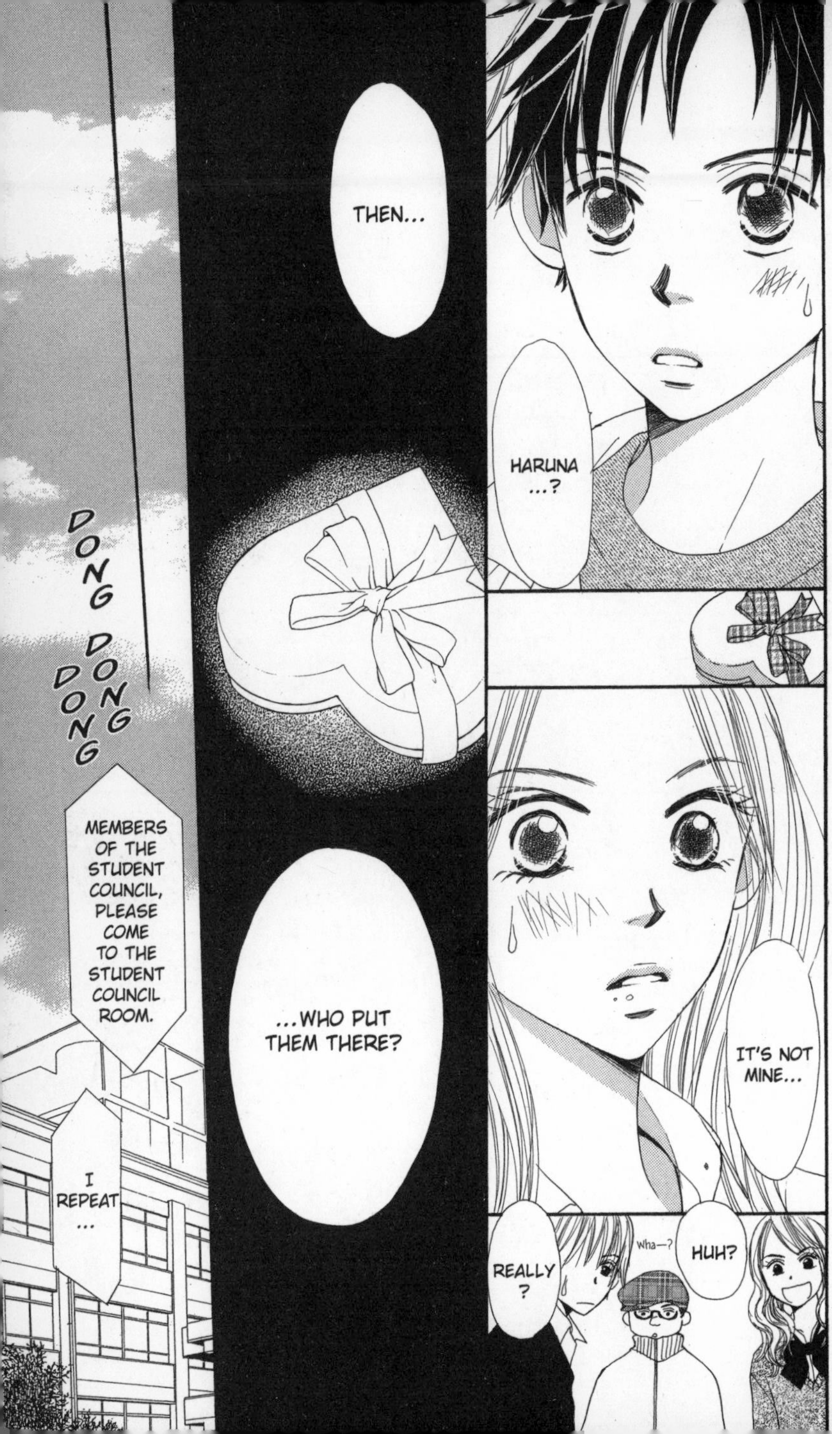
HARUNA ...?
IT'S NOT MINE...
HUH?
Wha—?
REALLY ?
THEN...
...WHO PUT THEM THERE?
DONG DONG DONG
MEMBERS OF THE STUDENT COUNCIL, PLEASE COME TO THE STUDENT COUNCIL ROOM.
I REPEAT ...

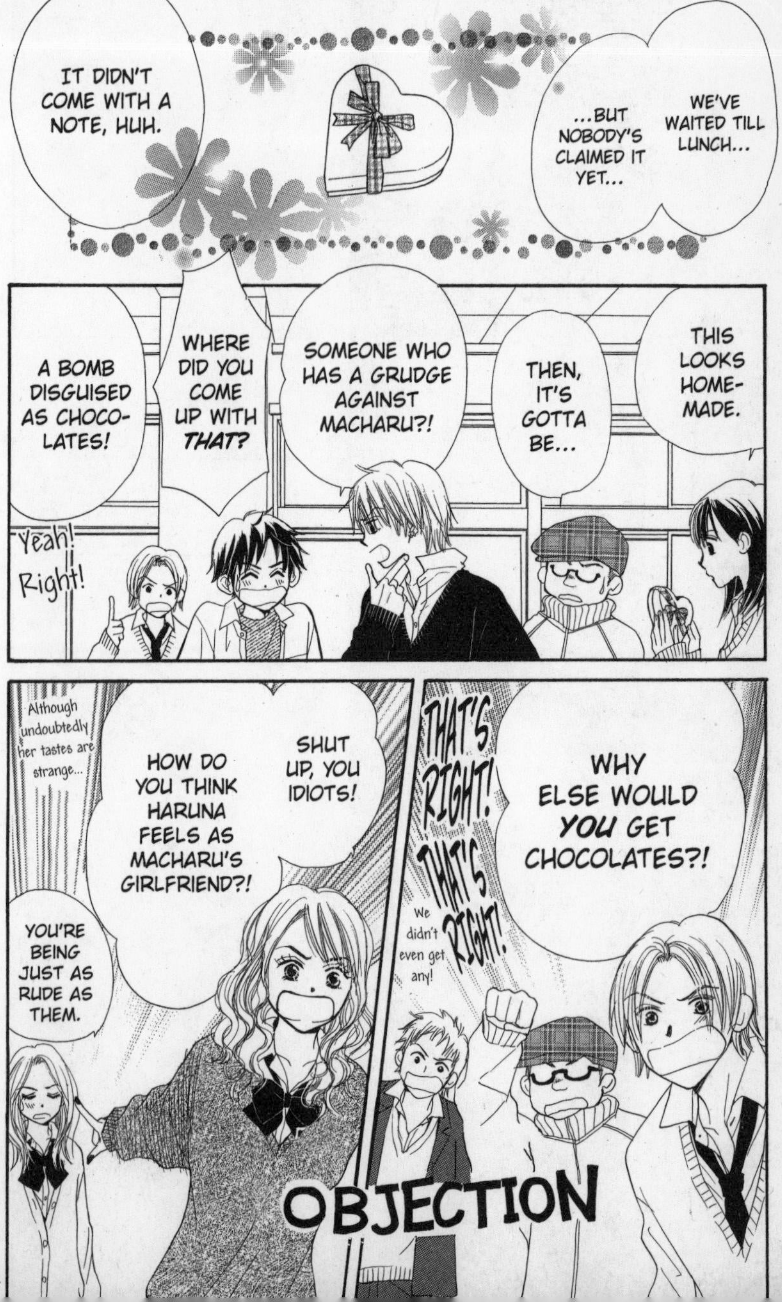
WE'VE WAITED TILL LUNCH...
...BUT NOBODY'S CLAIMED IT YET...
IT DIDN'T COME WITH A NOTE, HUH.
THIS LOOKS HOME-MADE.
THEN, IT'S GOTTA BE...
SOMEONE WHO HAS A GRUDGE AGAINST MACHARU?!
WHERE DID YOU COME UP WITH THAT?
A BOMB DISGUISED AS CHOCO-LATES!
Yeah! Right!
WHY ELSE WOULD YOU GET CHOCOLATES?!
THAT'S RIGHT! THAT'S RIGHT!
We didn't even get any!
SHUT UP, YOU IDIOTS!
HOW DO YOU THINK HARUNA FEELS AS MACHARU'S GIRLFRIEND?!
Although undoubtedly her tastes are strange...
YOU'RE BEING JUST AS RUDE AS THEM.
OBJECTION

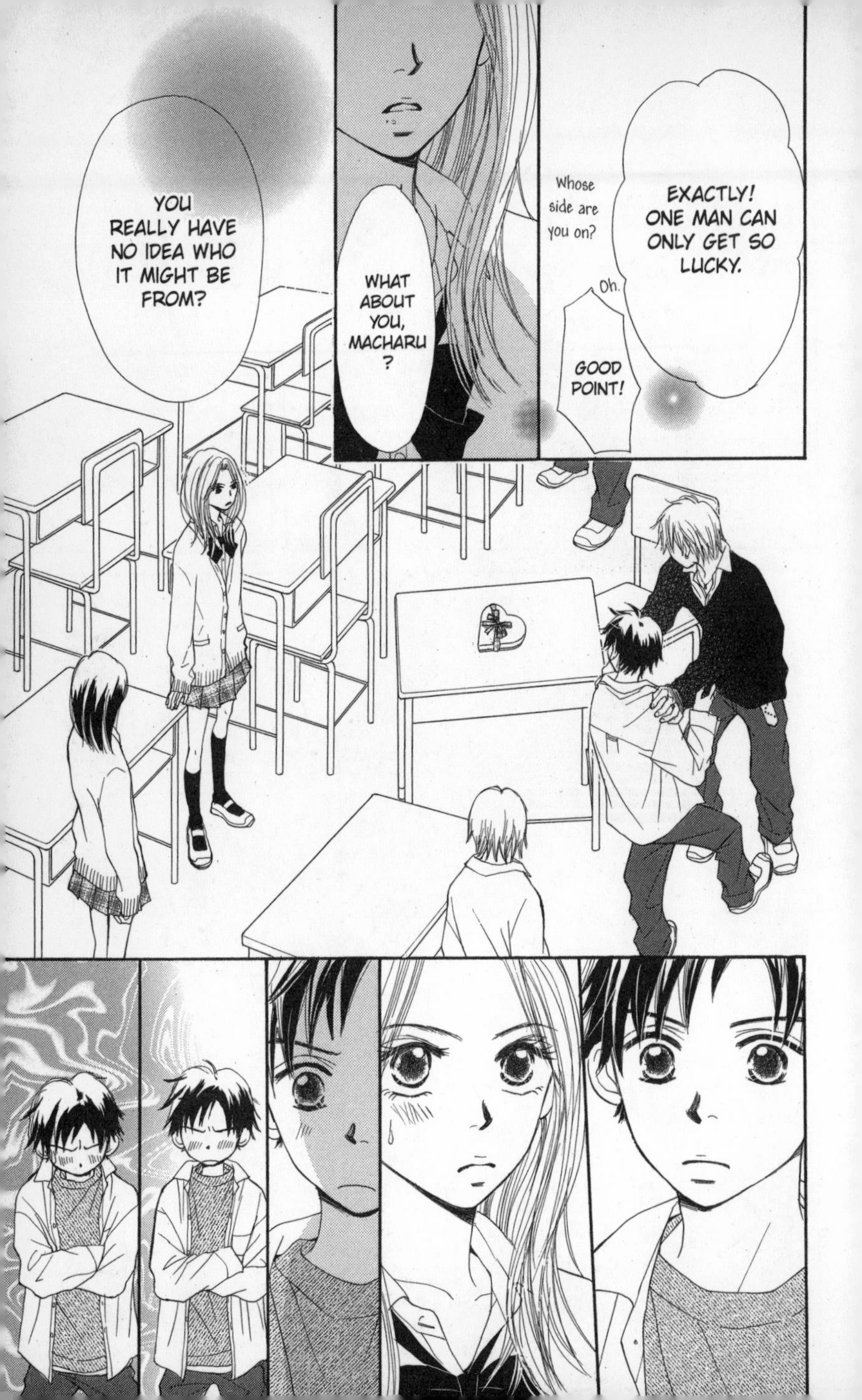
EXACTLY! ONE MAN CAN ONLY GET SO LUCKY.
Whose side are you on?
Oh.
GOOD POINT!
WHAT ABOUT YOU, MACHARU?
YOU REALLY HAVE NO IDEA WHO IT MIGHT BE FROM?

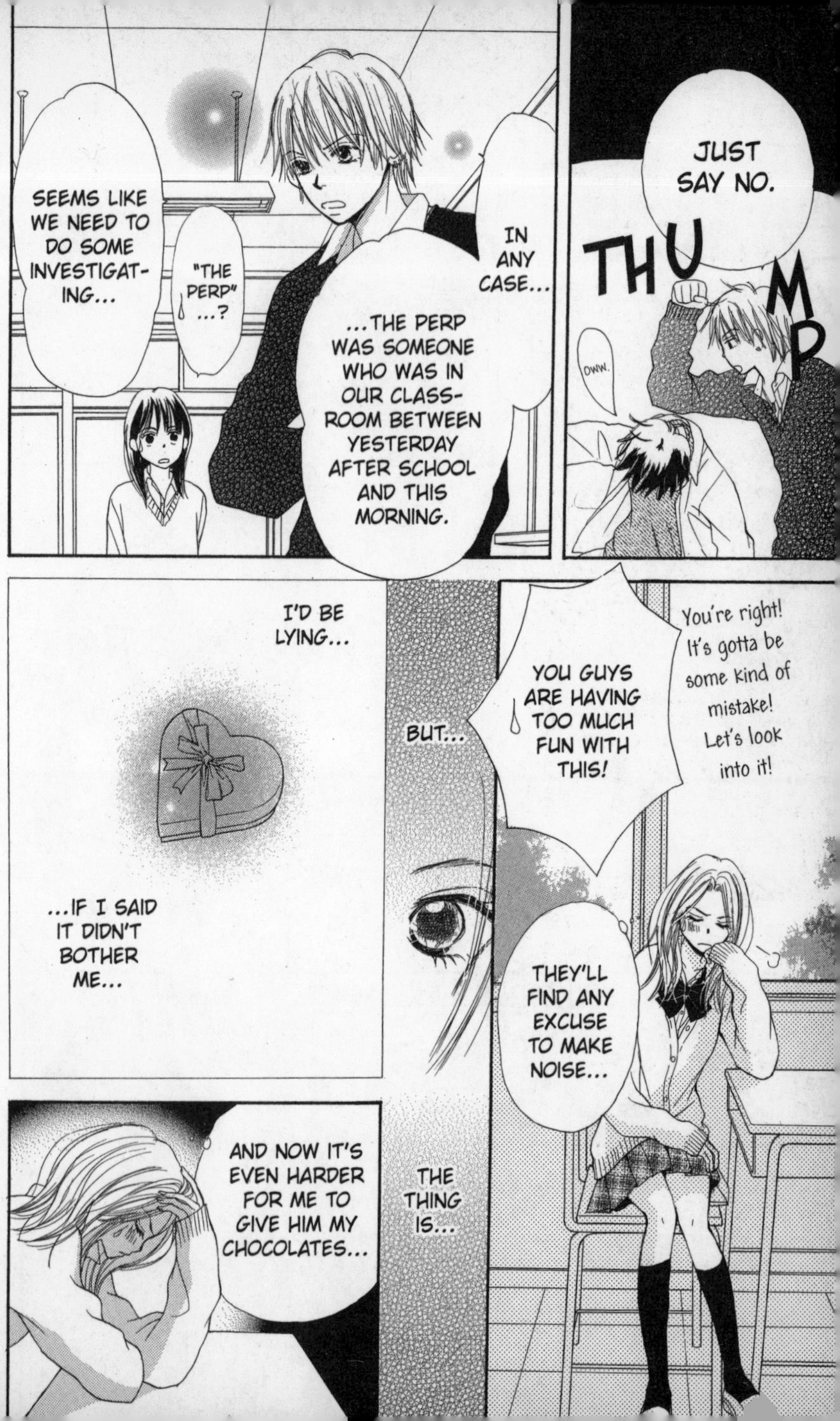
JUST SAY NO.
THUMP
OWW.
IN ANY CASE...
...THE PERP WAS SOMEONE WHO WAS IN OUR CLASSROOM BETWEEN YESTERDAY AFTER SCHOOL AND THIS MORNING.
"THE PERP" ...?
SEEMS LIKE WE NEED TO DO SOME INVESTIGATING...
You're right! It's gotta be some kind of mistake! Let's look into it!
YOU GUYS ARE HAVING TOO MUCH FUN WITH THIS!
THEY'LL FIND ANY EXCUSE TO MAKE NOISE...
BUT...
THE THING IS...
I'D BE LYING...
...IF I SAID IT DIDN'T BOTHER ME...
AND NOW IT'S EVEN HARDER FOR ME TO GIVE HIM MY CHOCOLATES...

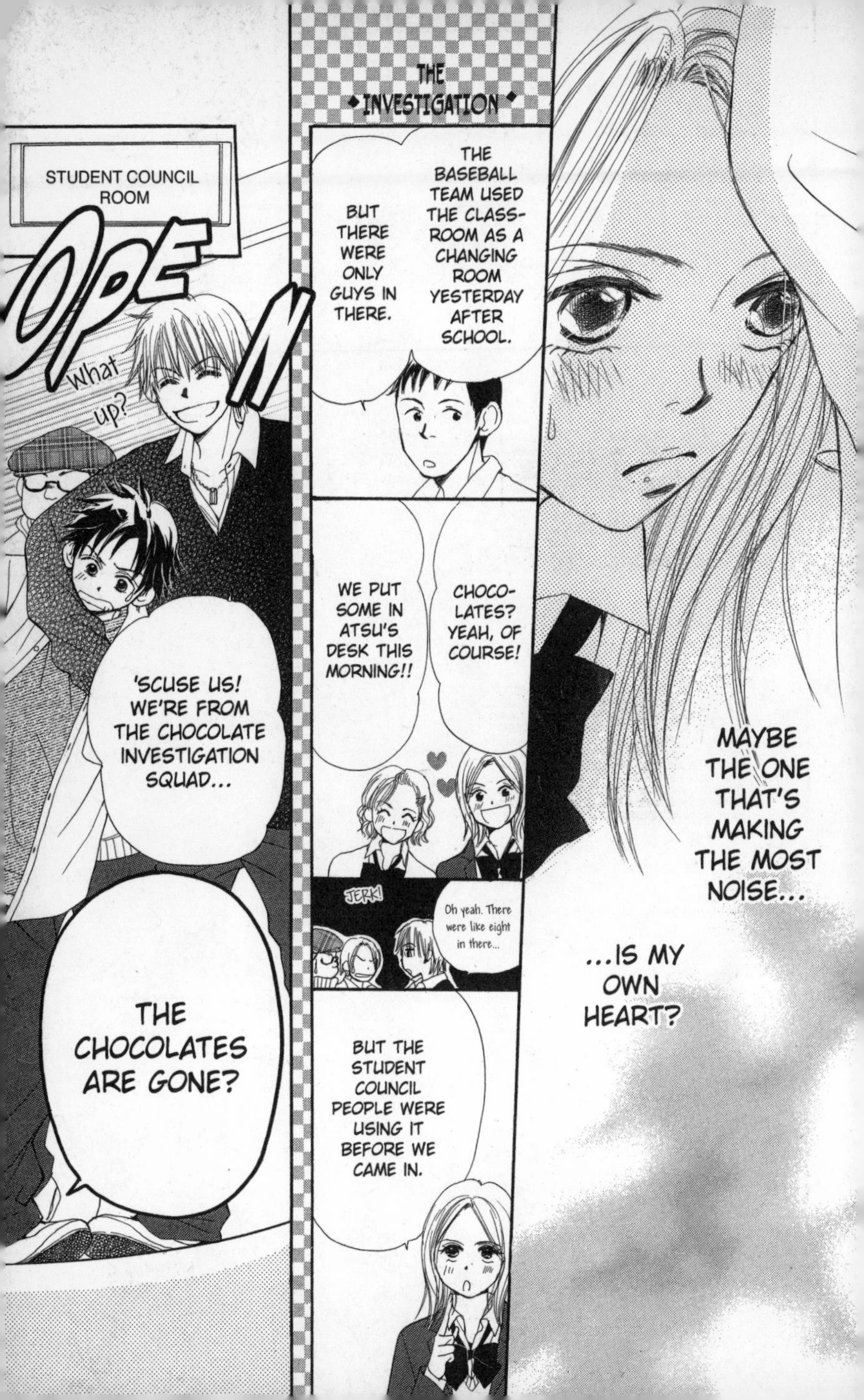
MAYBE THE ONE THAT'S MAKING THE MOST NOISE...
...IS MY OWN HEART?
THE ◆INVESTIGATION◆
THE BASEBALL TEAM USED THE CLASS-ROOM AS A CHANGING ROOM YESTERDAY AFTER SCHOOL.
BUT THERE WERE ONLY GUYS IN THERE.
CHOCO-LATES? YEAH, OF COURSE!
WE PUT SOME IN ATSU'S DESK THIS MORNING!!
Oh yeah. There were like eight in there...
JERK!
BUT THE STUDENT COUNCIL PEOPLE WERE USING IT BEFORE WE CAME IN.
STUDENT COUNCIL ROOM
OPEN
What up?
'SCUSE US! WE'RE FROM THE CHOCOLATE INVESTIGATION SQUAD...
THE CHOCOLATES ARE GONE?

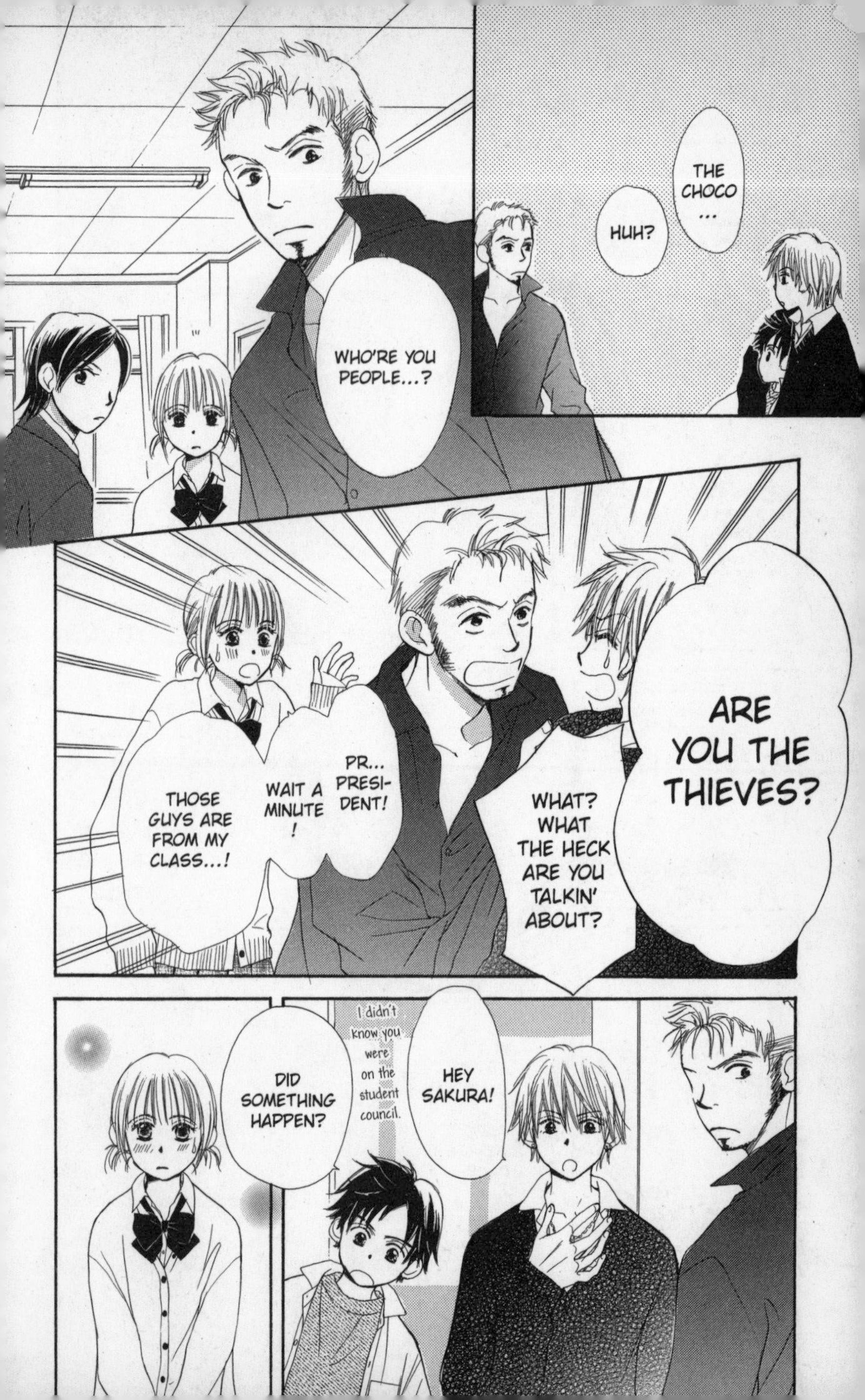
THE CHOCO...
HUH?
WHO'RE YOU PEOPLE...?
ARE YOU THE THIEVES?
WHAT? WHAT THE HECK ARE YOU TALKIN' ABOUT?
PR... PRESI-DENT!
WAIT A MINUTE!
THOSE GUYS ARE FROM MY CLASS...!
HEY SAKURA!
I didn't know you were on the student council.
DID SOMETHING HAPPEN?

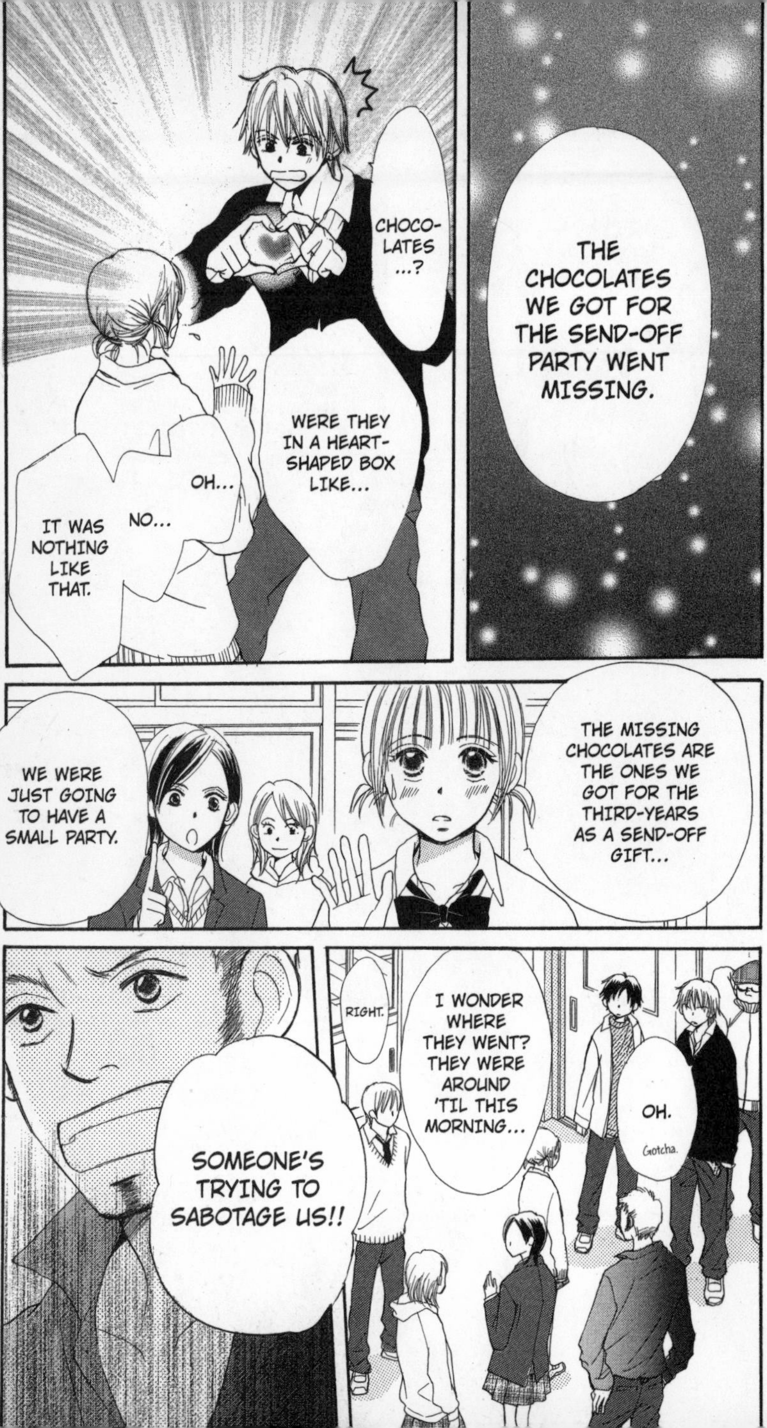
THE CHOCOLATES WE GOT FOR THE SEND-OFF PARTY WENT MISSING.
CHOCOLATES ...?
WERE THEY IN A HEART-SHAPED BOX LIKE...
OH...
NO...
IT WAS NOTHING LIKE THAT.
THE MISSING CHOCOLATES ARE THE ONES WE GOT FOR THE THIRD-YEARS AS A SEND-OFF GIFT...
WE WERE JUST GOING TO HAVE A SMALL PARTY.
I WONDER WHERE THEY WENT? THEY WERE AROUND 'TIL THIS MORNING...
RIGHT.
OH.
Gotcha.
SOMEONE'S TRYING TO SABOTAGE US!!

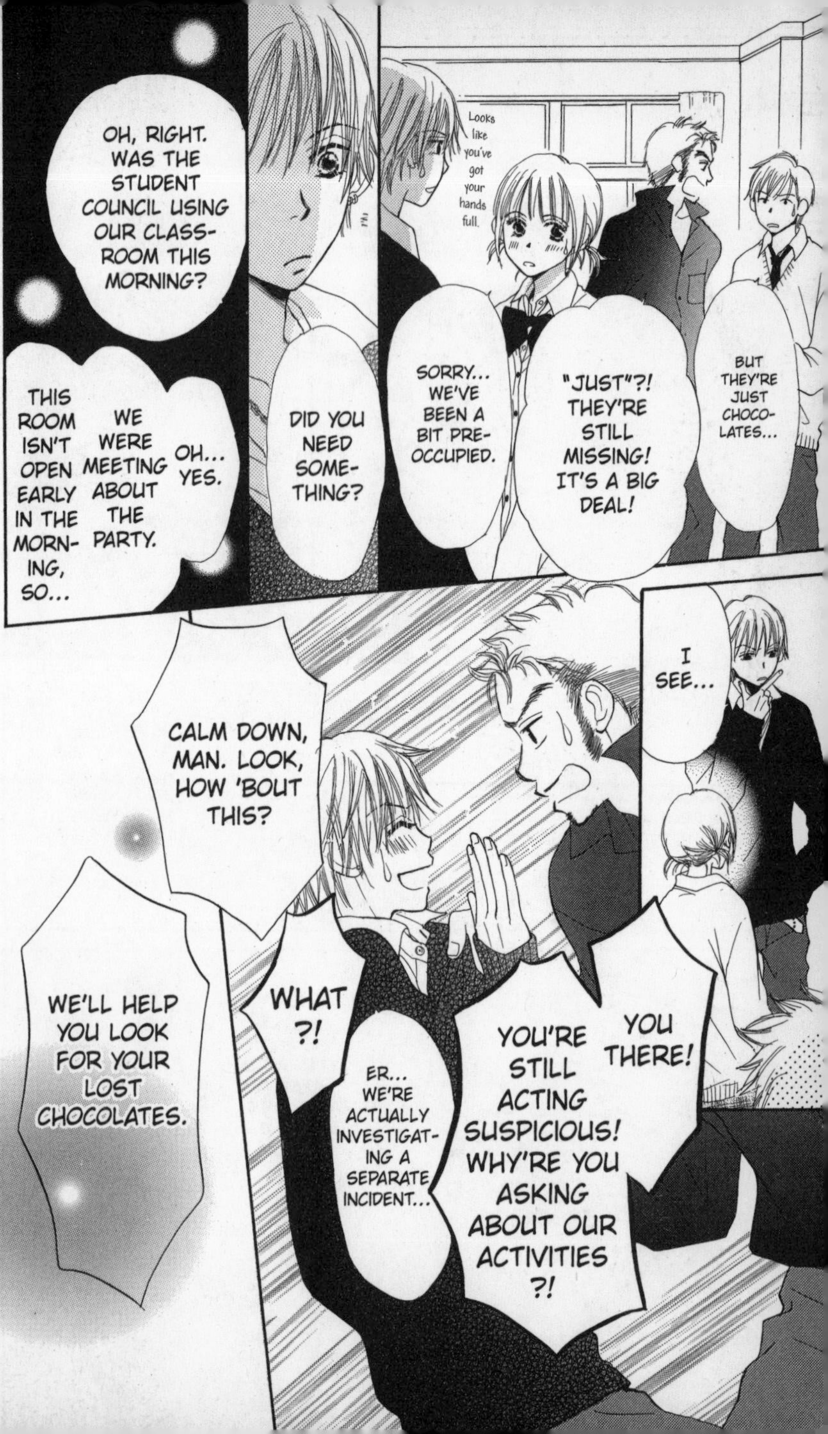
Looks like you've got your hands full.
BUT THEY'RE JUST CHOCOLATES...
"JUST"?! THEY'RE STILL MISSING! IT'S A BIG DEAL!
SORRY... WE'VE BEEN A BIT PRE-OCCUPIED.
DID YOU NEED SOME-THING?
OH, RIGHT. WAS THE STUDENT COUNCIL USING OUR CLASS-ROOM THIS MORNING?
OH... YES.
WE WERE MEETING ABOUT THE PARTY.
THIS ROOM ISN'T OPEN EARLY IN THE MORN-ING, SO...
I SEE...
YOU THERE!
YOU'RE STILL ACTING SUSPICIOUS! WHY'RE YOU ASKING ABOUT OUR ACTIVITIES?!
WHAT?!
ER... WE'RE ACTUALLY INVESTIGAT-ING A SEPARATE INCIDENT...
CALM DOWN, MAN. LOOK, HOW 'BOUT THIS?
WE'LL HELP YOU LOOK FOR YOUR LOST CHOCOLATES.

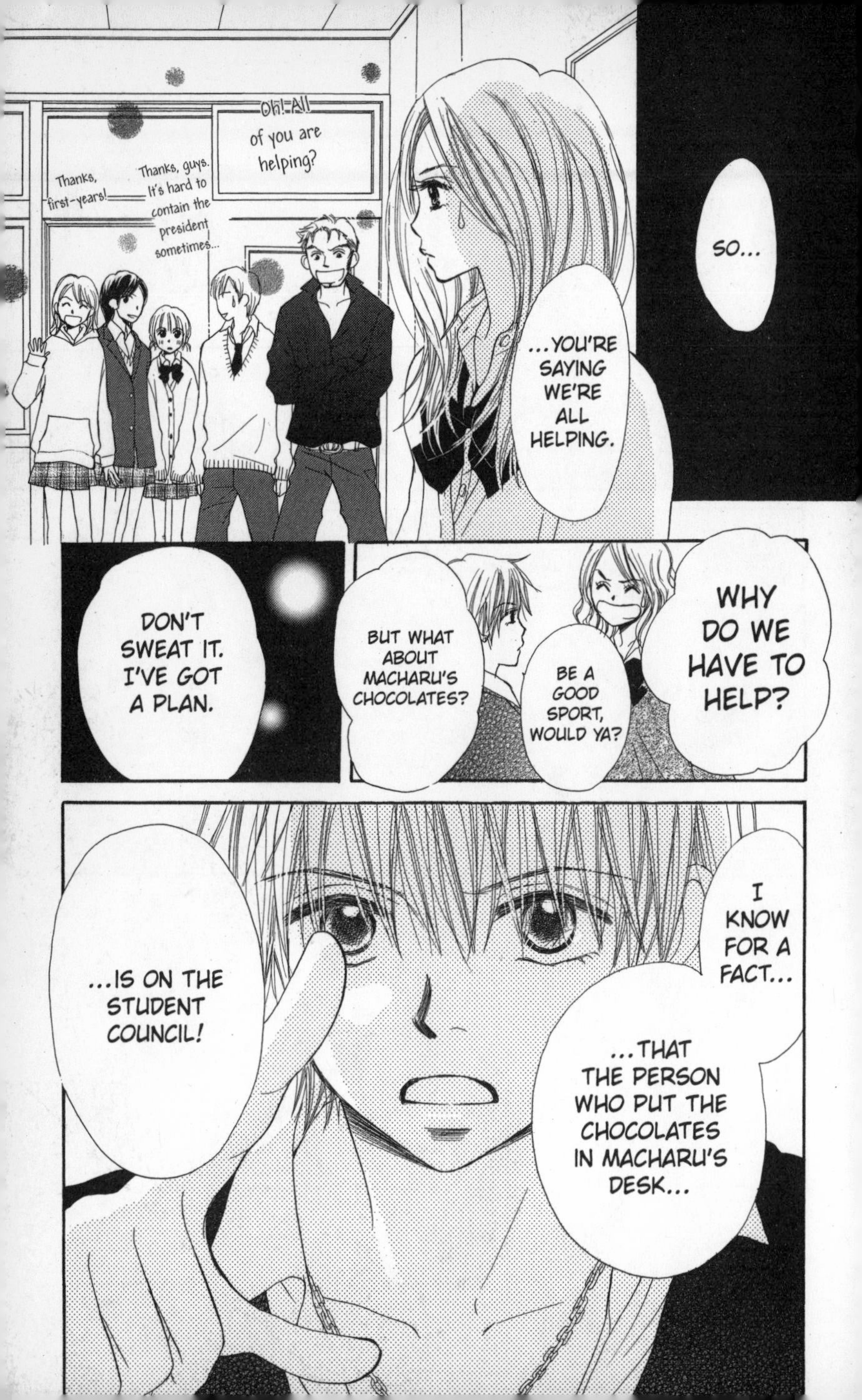
SO...
...YOU'RE SAYING WE'RE ALL HELPING.
Oh! All of you are helping?
Thanks, guys. It's hard to contain the president sometimes...
Thanks, first-years!
WHY DO WE HAVE TO HELP?
BE A GOOD SPORT, WOULD YA?
BUT WHAT ABOUT MACHARU'S CHOCOLATES?
DON'T SWEAT IT. I'VE GOT A PLAN.
I KNOW FOR A FACT...
...THAT THE PERSON WHO PUT THE CHOCOLATES IN MACHARU'S DESK...
...IS ON THE STUDENT COUNCIL!

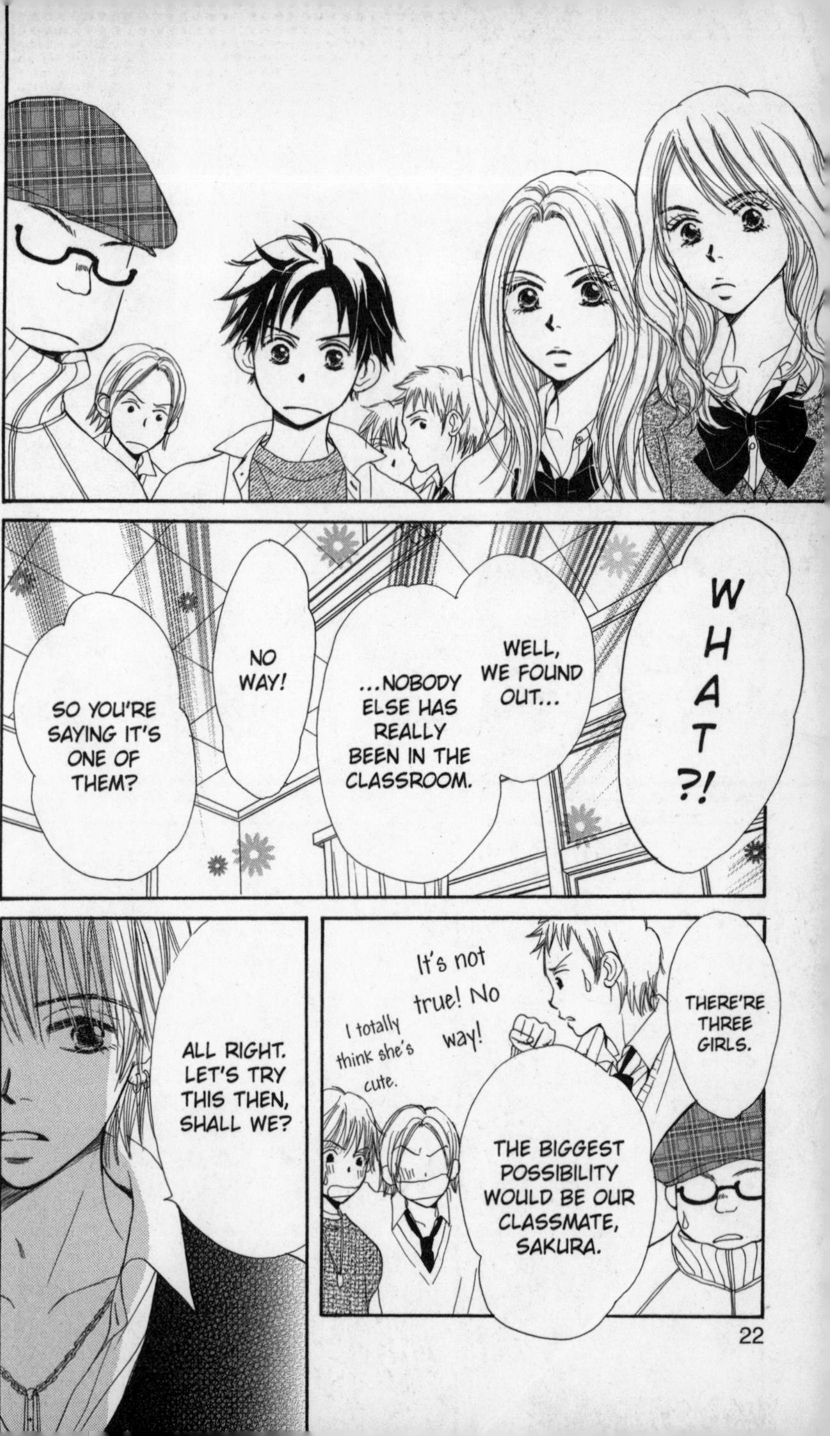
WHAT?!
WELL, WE FOUND OUT...
...NOBODY ELSE HAS REALLY BEEN IN THE CLASSROOM.
NO WAY!
SO YOU'RE SAYING IT'S ONE OF THEM?
THERE'RE THREE GIRLS.
THE BIGGEST POSSIBILITY WOULD BE OUR CLASSMATE, SAKURA.
It's not true! No way!
I totally think she's cute.
ALL RIGHT. LET'S TRY THIS THEN, SHALL WE?

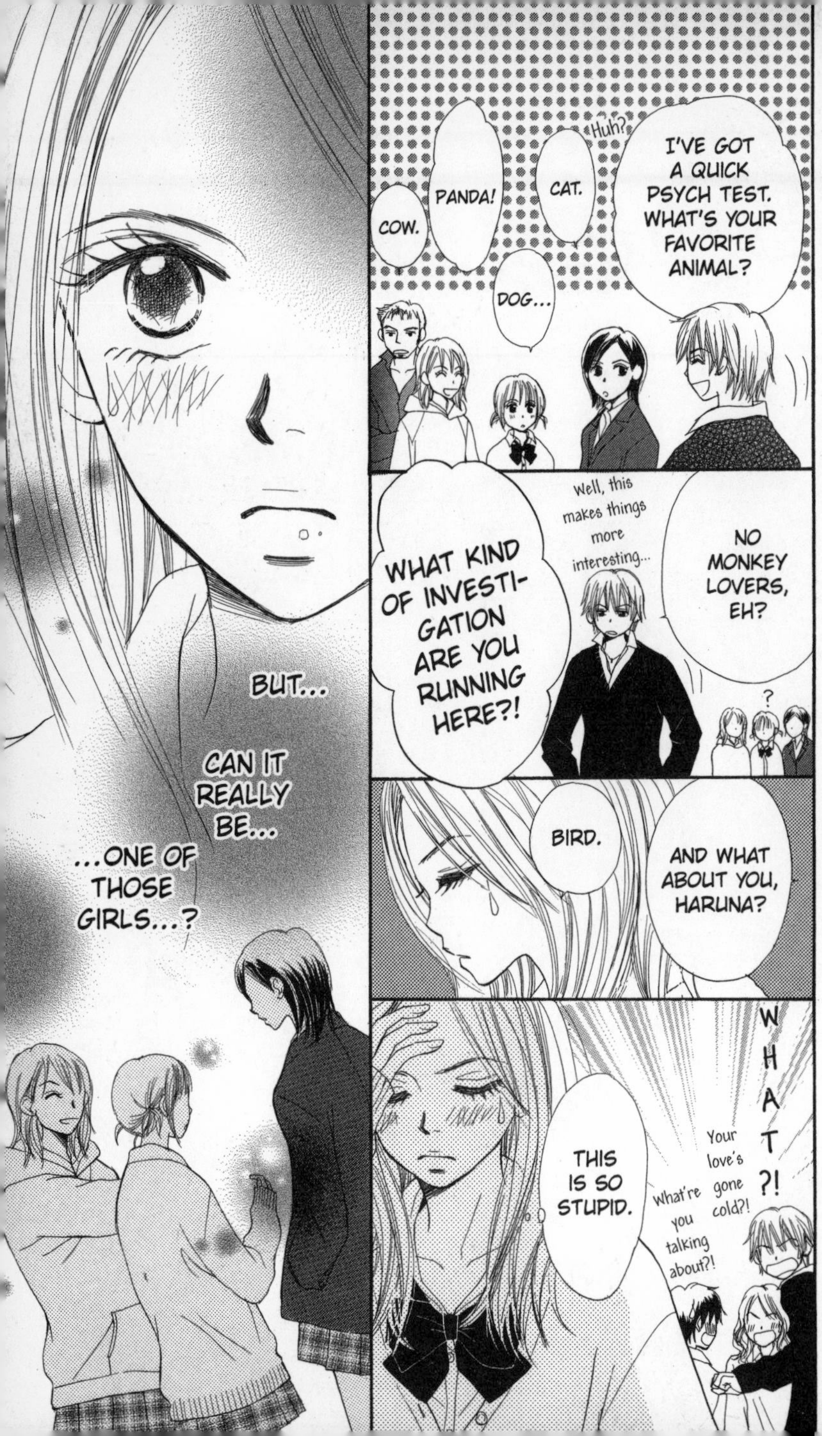

I'VE GOT A QUICK PSYCH TEST. WHAT'S YOUR FAVORITE ANIMAL?
Huh?
CAT.
PANDA!
DOG...
COW.
NO MONKEY LOVERS, EH?
Well, this makes things more interesting...
?
WHAT KIND OF INVESTIGATION ARE YOU RUNNING HERE?!
AND WHAT ABOUT YOU, HARUNA?
BIRD.
WHAT?!
Your love's gone cold?!
What're you talking about?!
THIS IS SO STUPID.
BUT...
CAN IT REALLY BE...
...ONE OF THOSE GIRLS...?

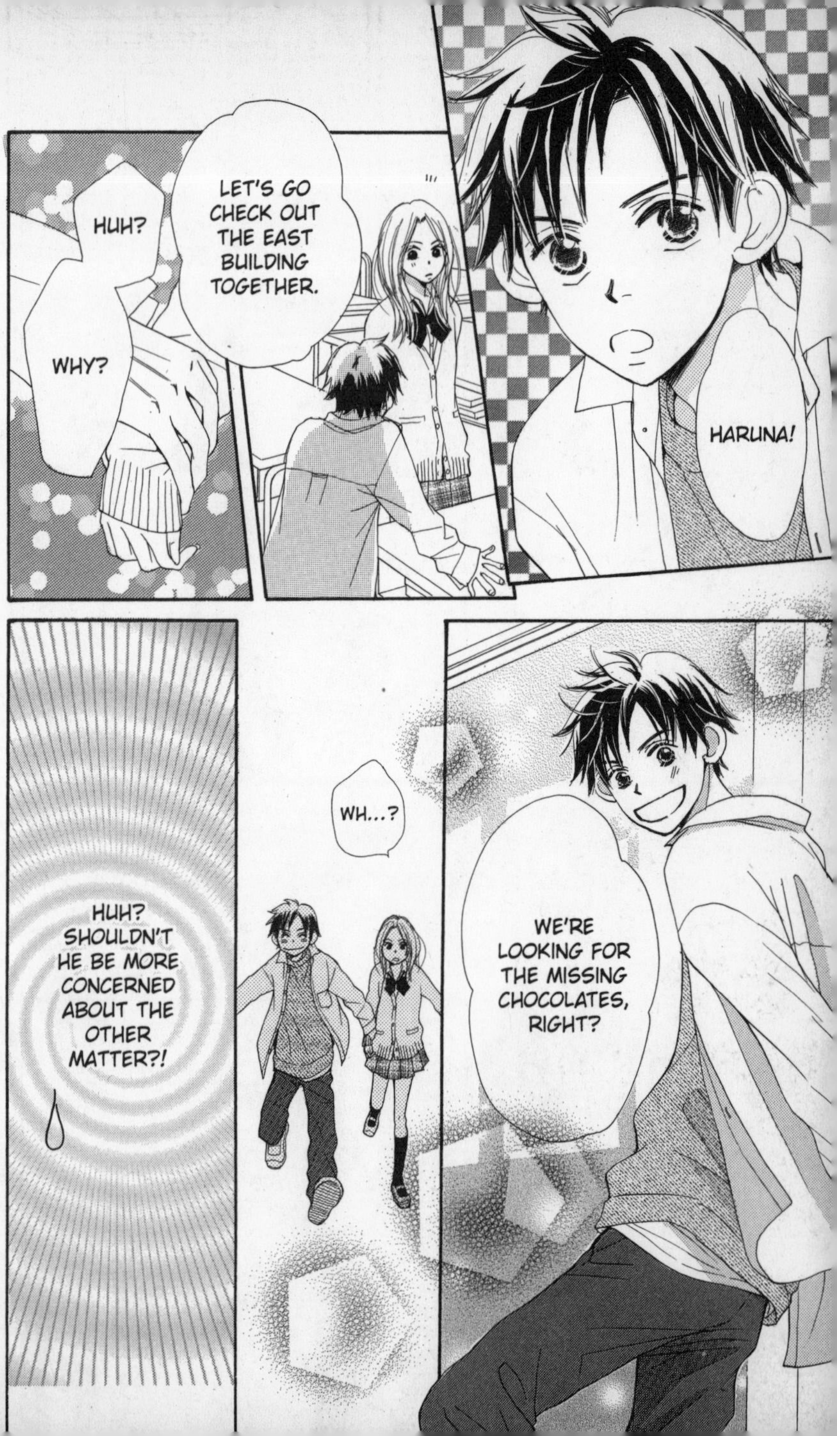
HARUNA!
LET'S GO CHECK OUT THE EAST BUILDING TOGETHER.
HUH?
WHY?
WE'RE LOOKING FOR THE MISSING CHOCOLATES, RIGHT?
WH...?
HUH? SHOULDN'T HE BE MORE CONCERNED ABOUT THE OTHER MATTER?!

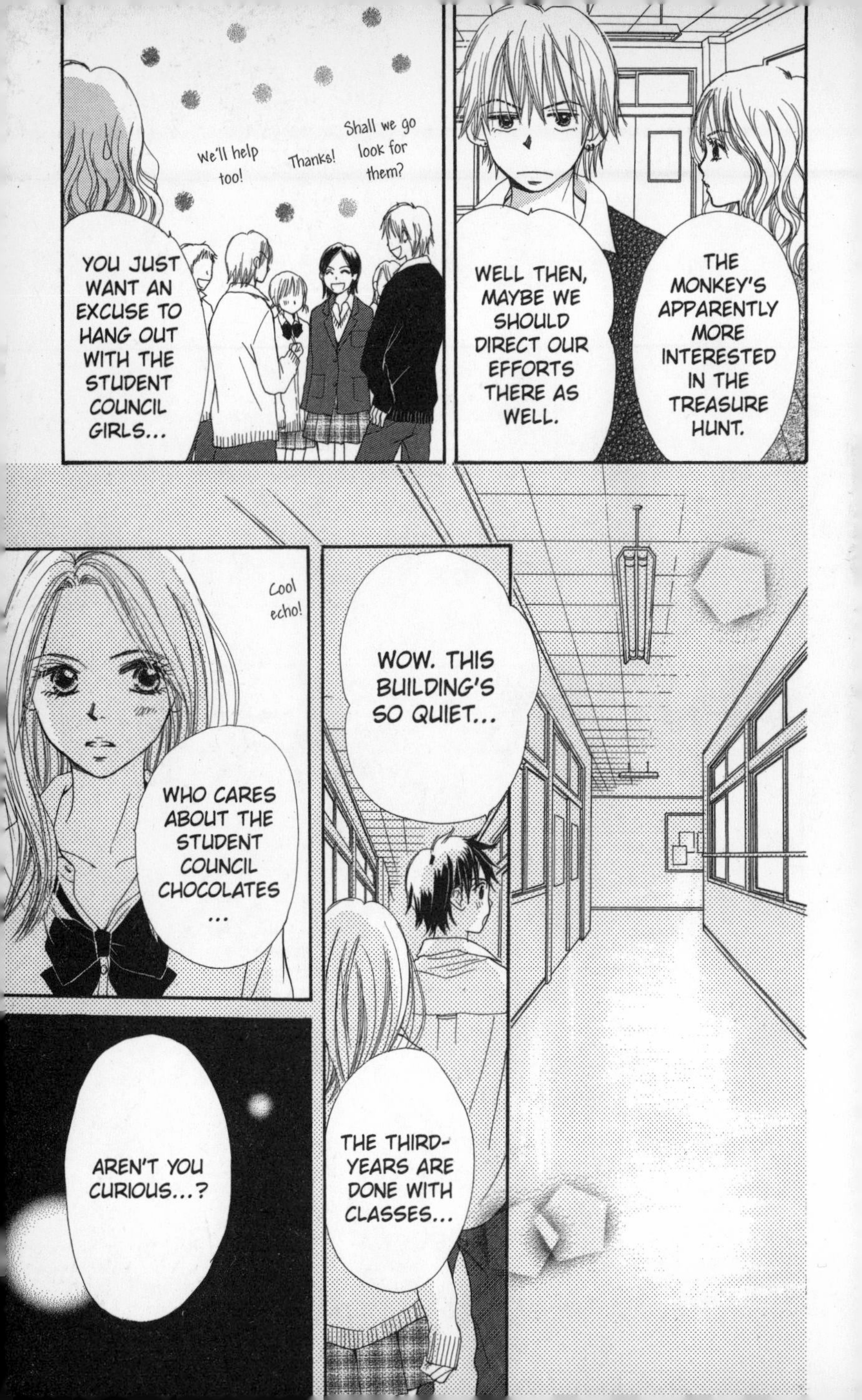
THE MONKEY'S APPARENTLY MORE INTERESTED IN THE TREASURE HUNT.
WELL THEN, MAYBE WE SHOULD DIRECT OUR EFFORTS THERE AS WELL.
Shall we go look for them?
Thanks!
We'll help too!
YOU JUST WANT AN EXCUSE TO HANG OUT WITH THE STUDENT COUNCIL GIRLS...
WOW. THIS BUILDING'S SO QUIET...
THE THIRD-YEARS ARE DONE WITH CLASSES...
Cool echo!
WHO CARES ABOUT THE STUDENT COUNCIL CHOCOLATES ...
AREN'T YOU CURIOUS...?

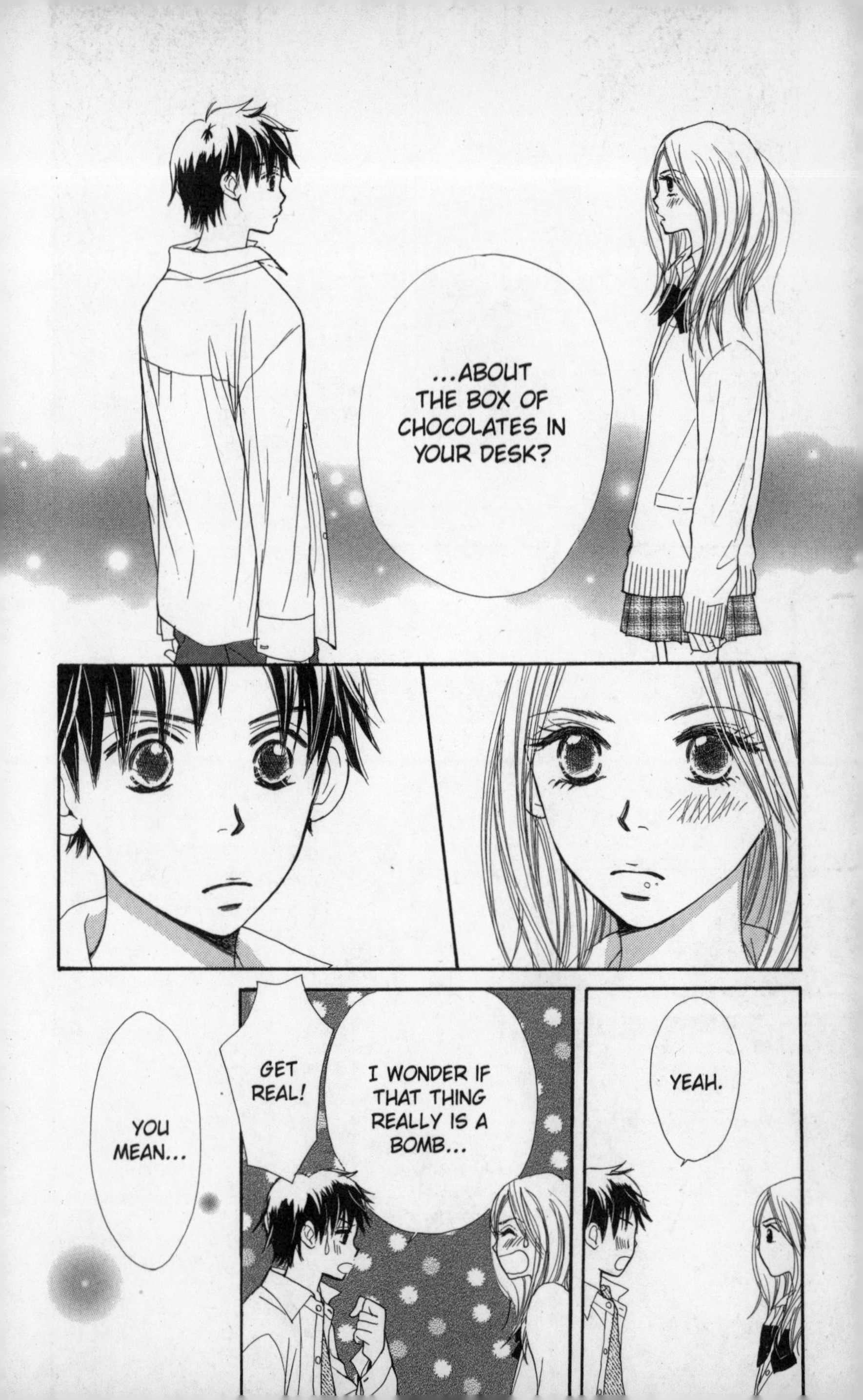
...ABOUT THE BOX OF CHOCOLATES IN YOUR DESK?
YEAH.
I WONDER IF THAT THING REALLY IS A BOMB...
GET REAL!
YOU MEAN...

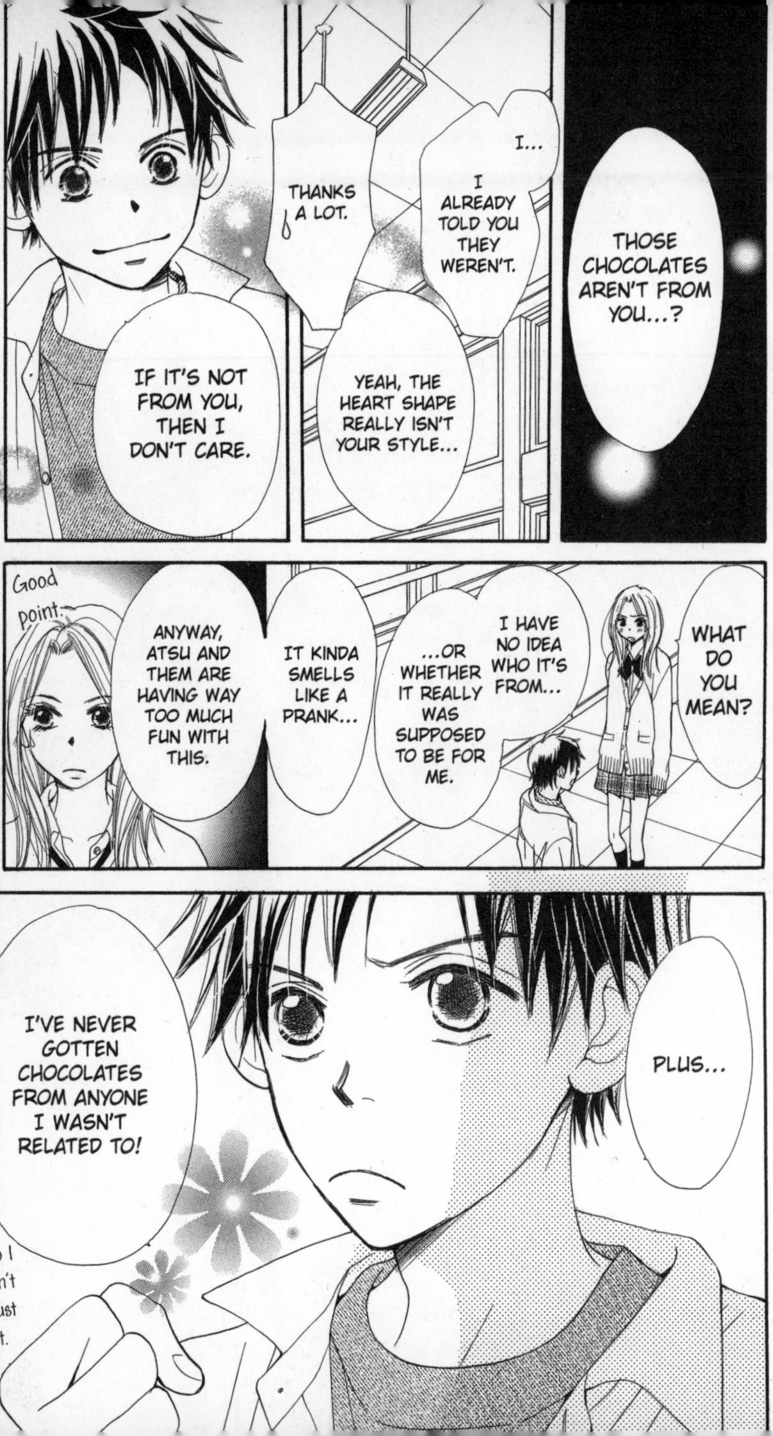
THOSE CHOCOLATES AREN'T FROM YOU...?
I...
I ALREADY TOLD YOU THEY WEREN'T.
YEAH, THE HEART SHAPE REALLY ISN'T YOUR STYLE...
THANKS A LOT.
IF IT'S NOT FROM YOU, THEN I DON'T CARE.
WHAT DO YOU MEAN?
I HAVE NO IDEA WHO IT'S FROM...
...OR WHETHER IT REALLY WAS SUPPOSED TO BE FOR ME.
IT KINDA SMELLS LIKE A PRANK...
ANYWAY, ATSU AND THEM ARE HAVING WAY TOO MUCH FUN WITH THIS.
Good point.
PLUS...
I'VE NEVER GOTTEN CHOCOLATES FROM ANYONE I WASN'T RELATED TO!
So I don't trust it.

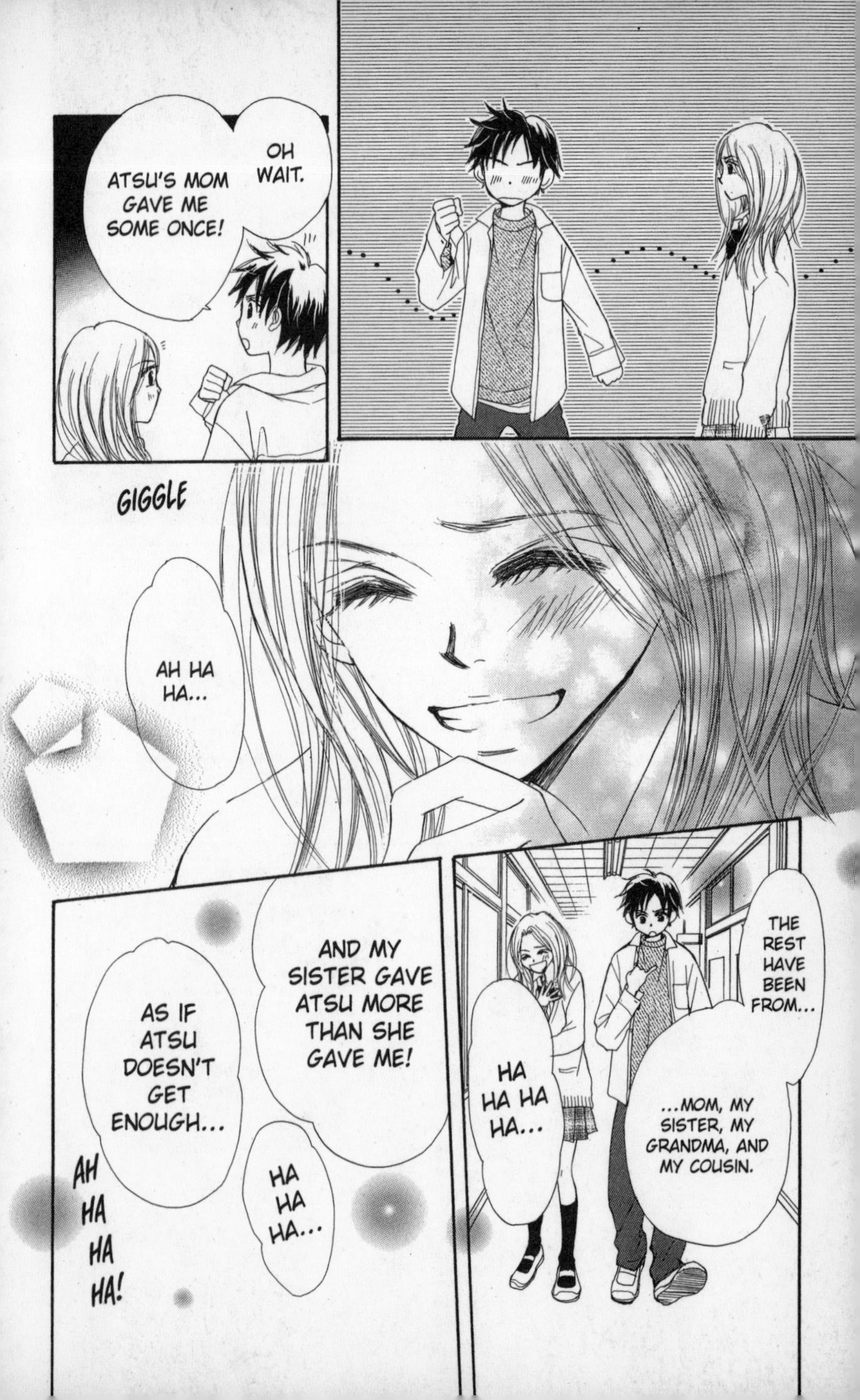
OH WAIT.
ATSU'S MOM GAVE ME SOME ONCE!
GIGGLE
AH HA HA...
THE REST HAVE BEEN FROM...
...MOM, MY SISTER, MY GRANDMA, AND MY COUSIN.
HA HA HA HA...
AND MY SISTER GAVE ATSU MORE THAN SHE GAVE ME!
HA HA HA...
AS IF ATSU DOESN'T GET ENOUGH...
AH HA HA HA!

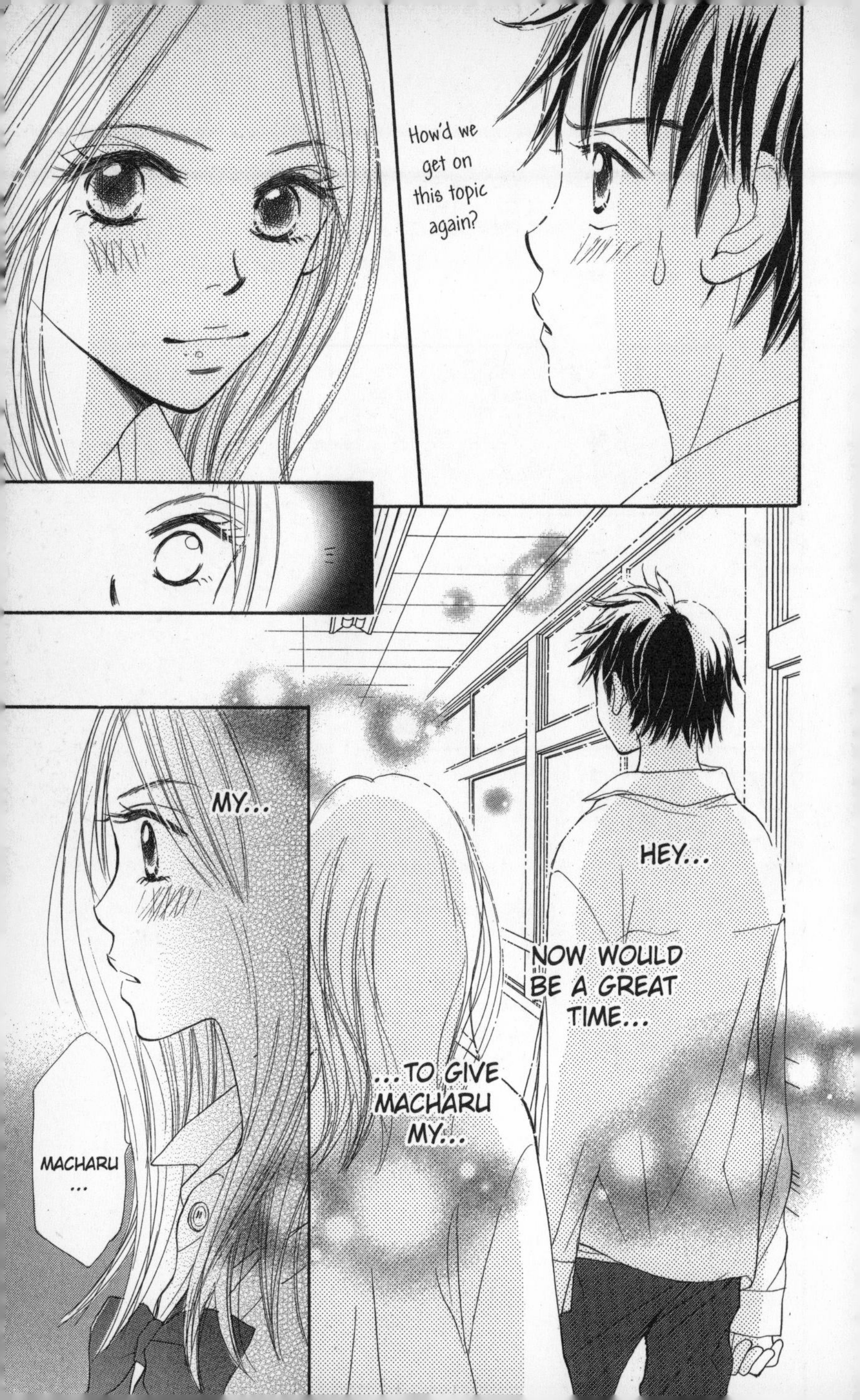
How'd we get on this topic again?
HEY...
NOW WOULD BE A GREAT TIME...
...TO GIVE MACHARU MY...
MY...
MACHARU ...

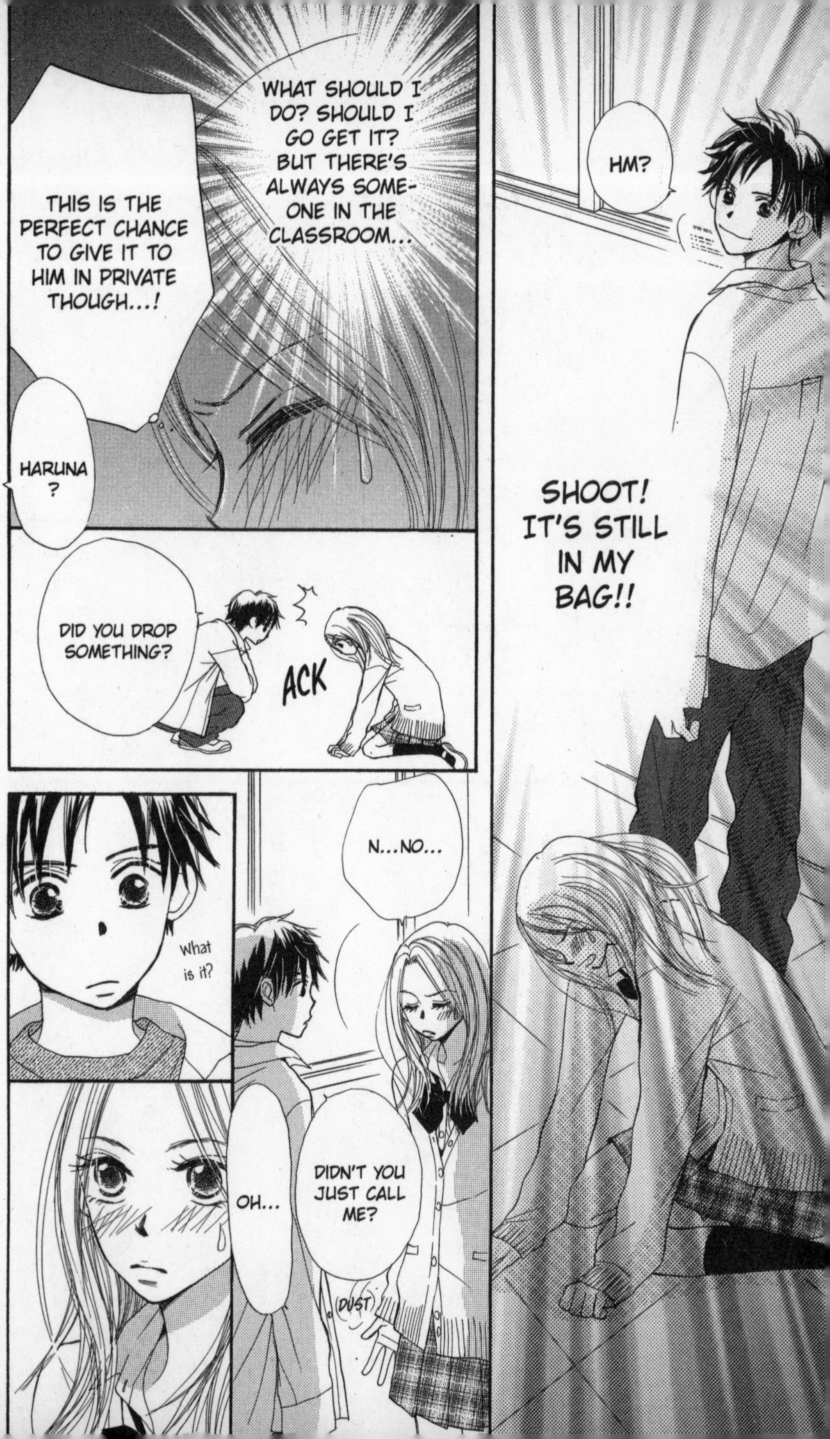
HM?
SHOOT! IT'S STILL IN MY BAG!!
WHAT SHOULD I DO? SHOULD I GO GET IT? BUT THERE'S ALWAYS SOME-ONE IN THE CLASSROOM...
THIS IS THE PERFECT CHANCE TO GIVE IT TO HIM IN PRIVATE THOUGH...!
HARUNA?
ACK
DID YOU DROP SOMETHING?
N...NO...
DIDN'T YOU JUST CALL ME?
OH...
DUST
What is it?

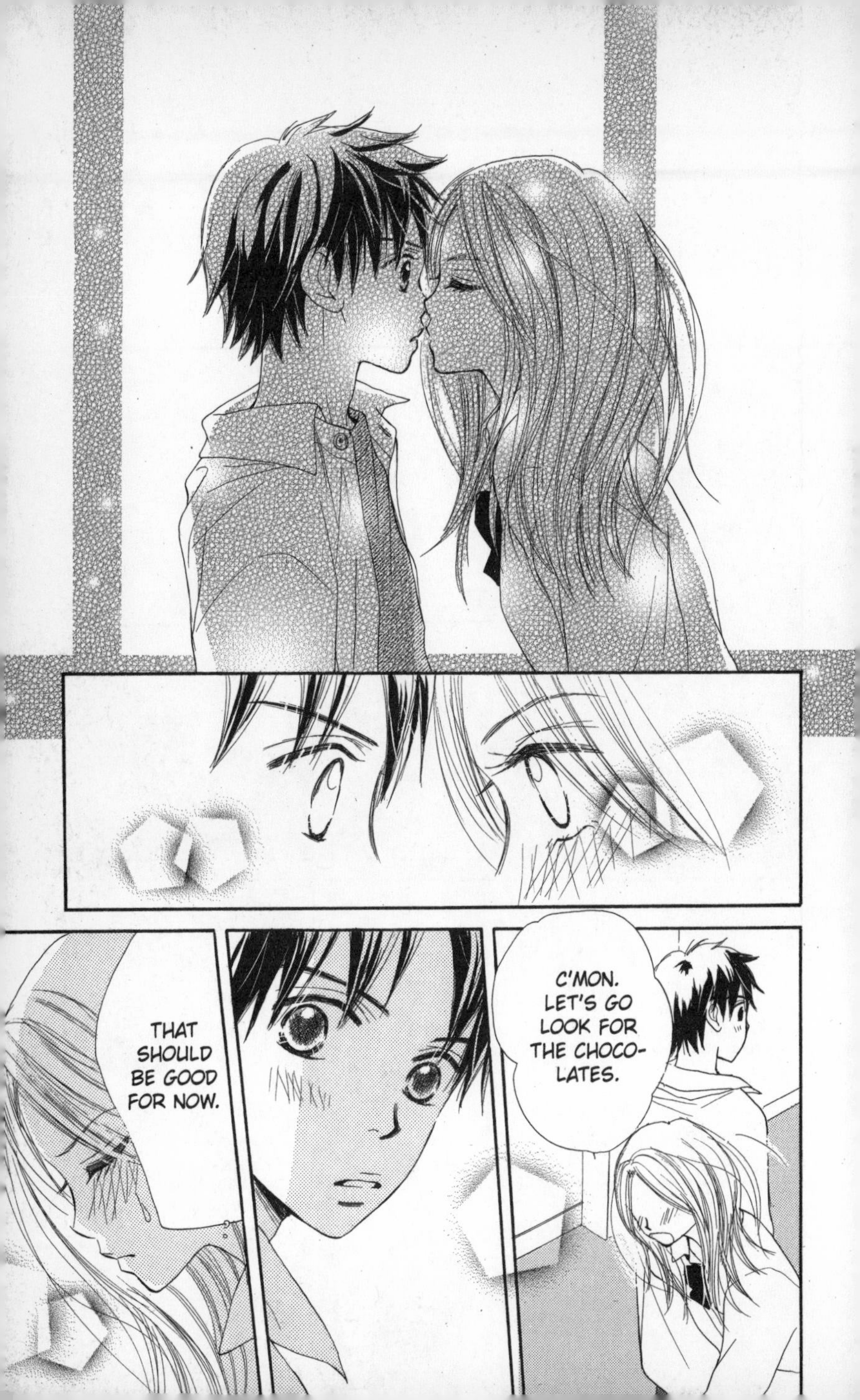
C'MON. LET'S GO LOOK FOR THE CHOCO-LATES.
THAT SHOULD BE GOOD FOR NOW.

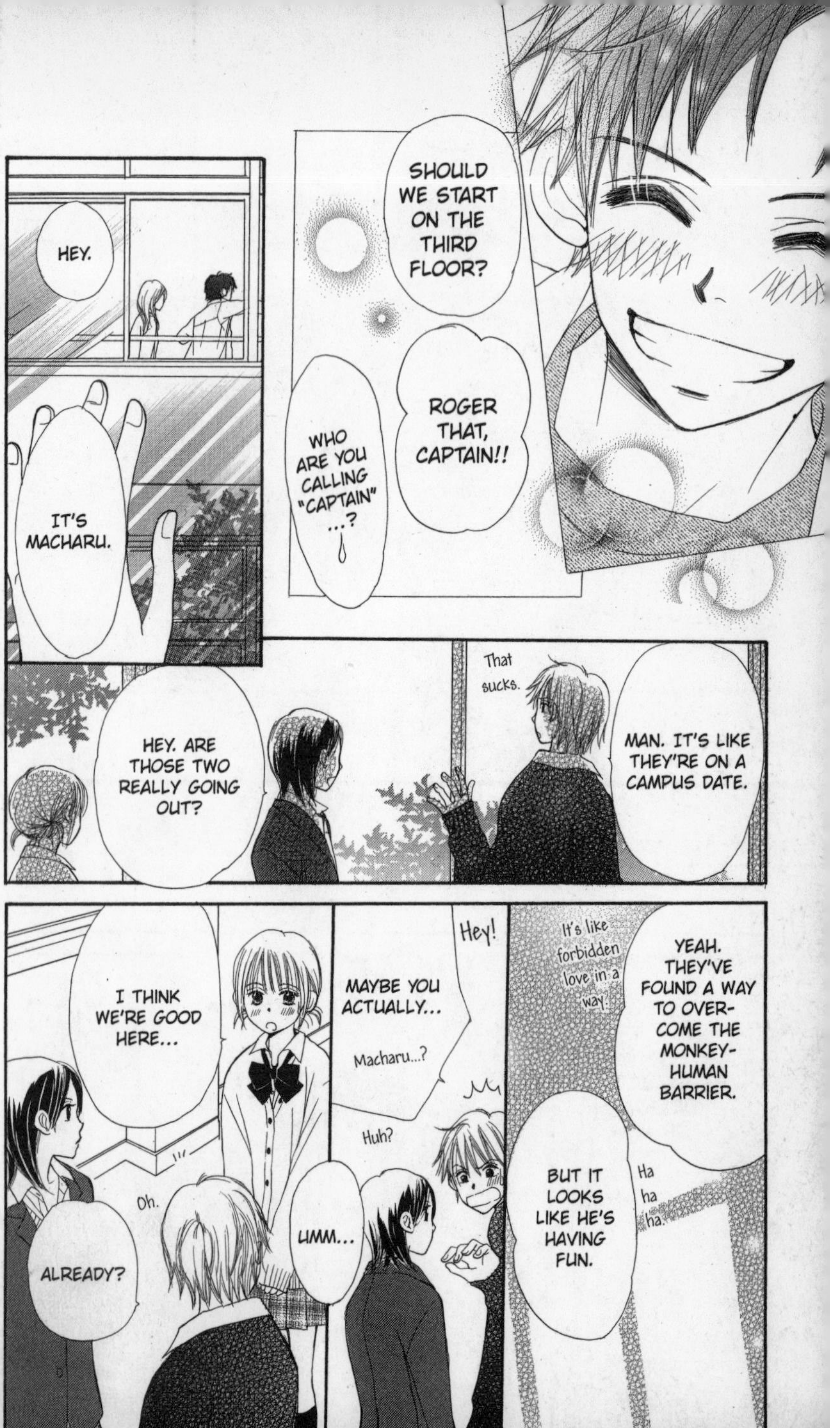
SHOULD WE START ON THE THIRD FLOOR?
ROGER THAT, CAPTAIN!!
WHO ARE YOU CALLING "CAPTAIN" ...?
HEY.
IT'S MACHARU.
MAN. IT'S LIKE THEY'RE ON A CAMPUS DATE.
That sucks.
HEY. ARE THOSE TWO REALLY GOING OUT?
YEAH. THEY'VE FOUND A WAY TO OVER-COME THE MONKEY-HUMAN BARRIER.
It's like forbidden love in a way.
BUT IT LOOKS LIKE HE'S HAVING FUN.
Ha ha ha.
Hey!
MAYBE YOU ACTUALLY...
Macharu...?
Huh?
UMM...
I THINK WE'RE GOOD HERE...
Oh.
ALREADY?

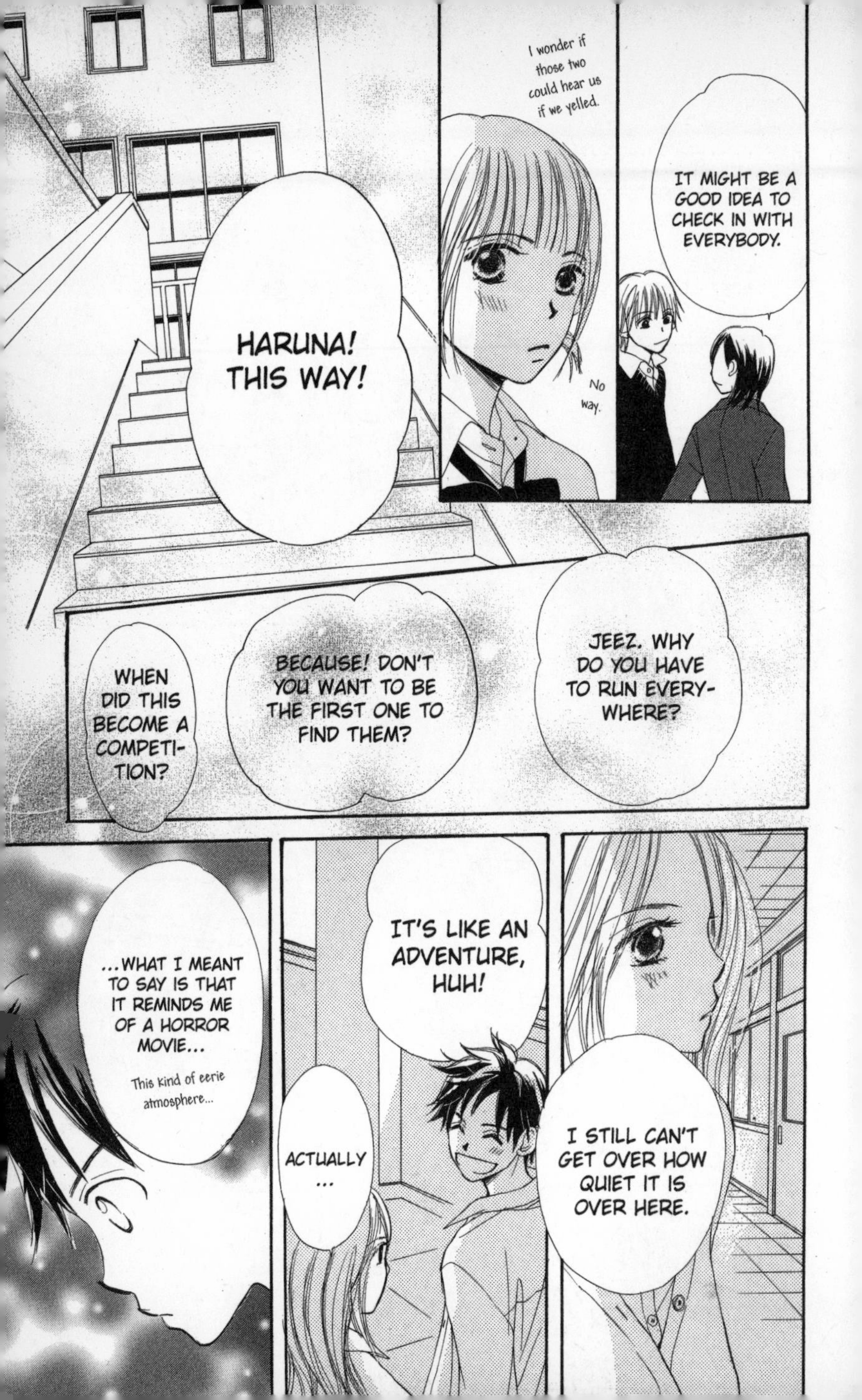
IT MIGHT BE A GOOD IDEA TO CHECK IN WITH EVERYBODY.
I wonder if those two could hear us if we yelled.
No way.
HARUNA! THIS WAY!
JEEZ. WHY DO YOU HAVE TO RUN EVERYWHERE?
BECAUSE! DON'T YOU WANT TO BE THE FIRST ONE TO FIND THEM?
WHEN DID THIS BECOME A COMPETITION?
I STILL CAN'T GET OVER HOW QUIET IT IS OVER HERE.
IT'S LIKE AN ADVENTURE, HUH!
ACTUALLY...
...WHAT I MEANT TO SAY IS THAT IT REMINDS ME OF A HORROR MOVIE...
This kind of eerie atmosphere...

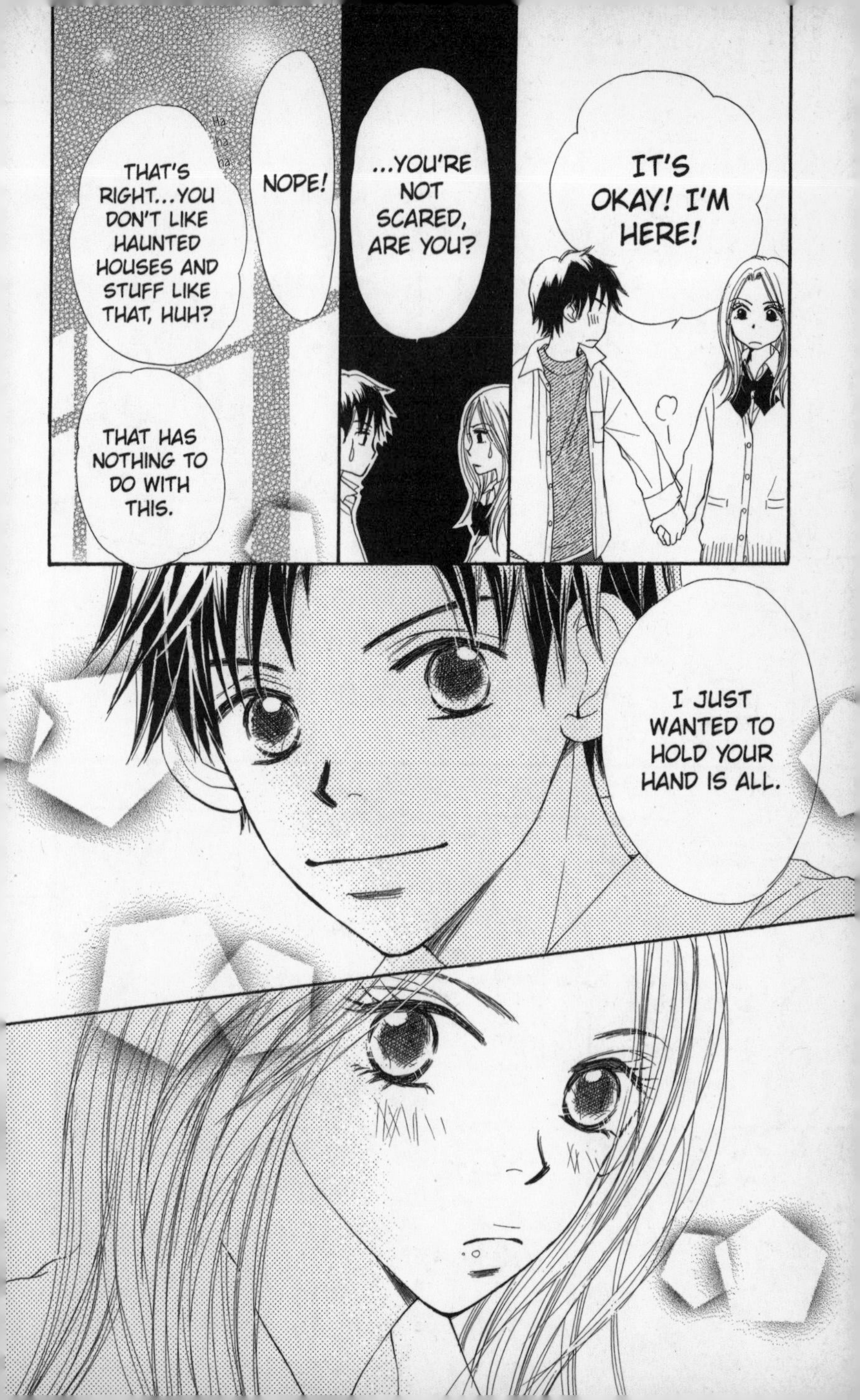
IT'S OKAY! I'M HERE!
...YOU'RE NOT SCARED, ARE YOU?
NOPE!
Ha ha ha
THAT'S RIGHT...YOU DON'T LIKE HAUNTED HOUSES AND STUFF LIKE THAT, HUH?
THAT HAS NOTHING TO DO WITH THIS.
I JUST WANTED TO HOLD YOUR HAND IS ALL.

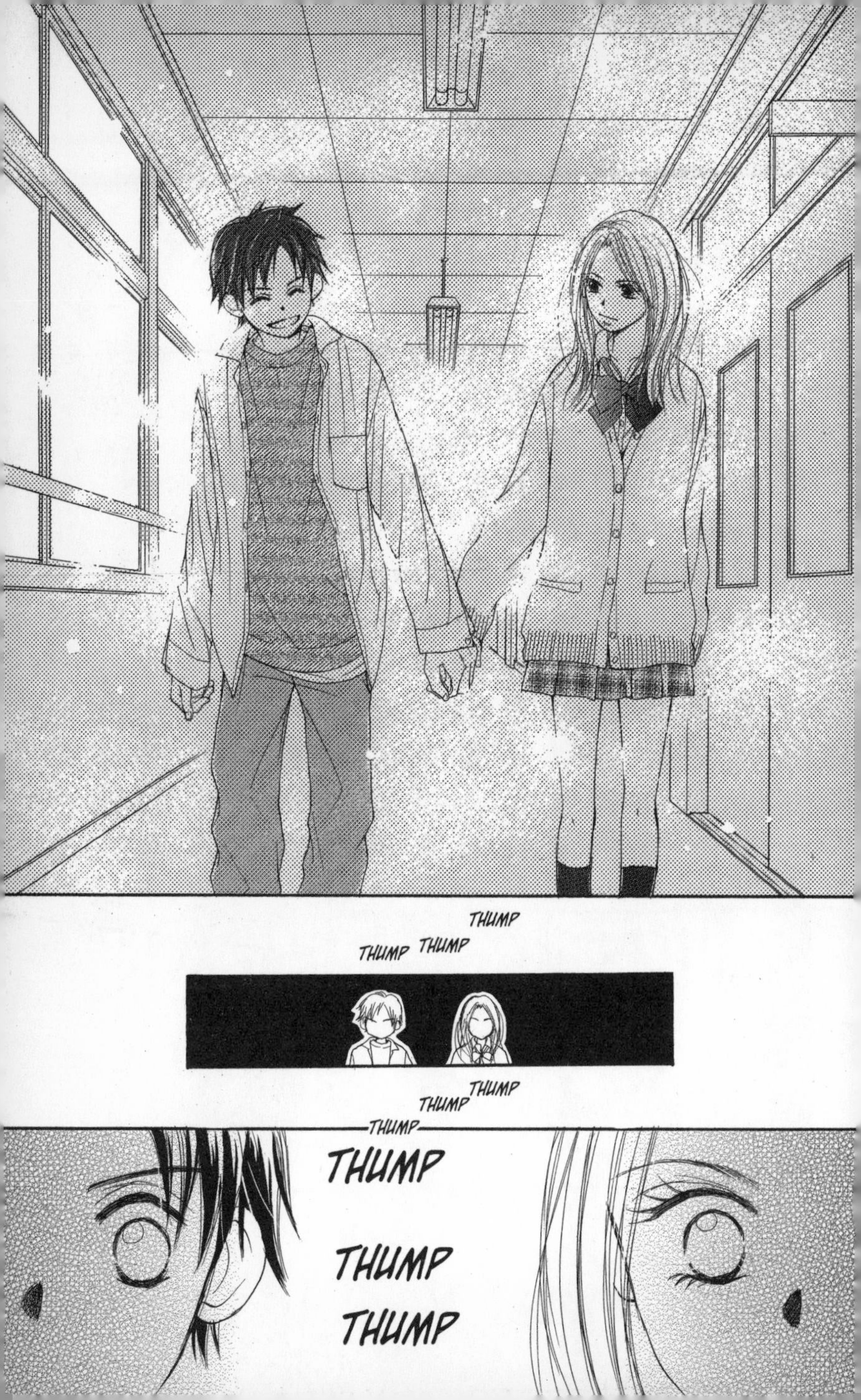
THUMP
THUMP THUMP
THUMP
THUMP
THUMP
THUMP
THUMP
THUMP

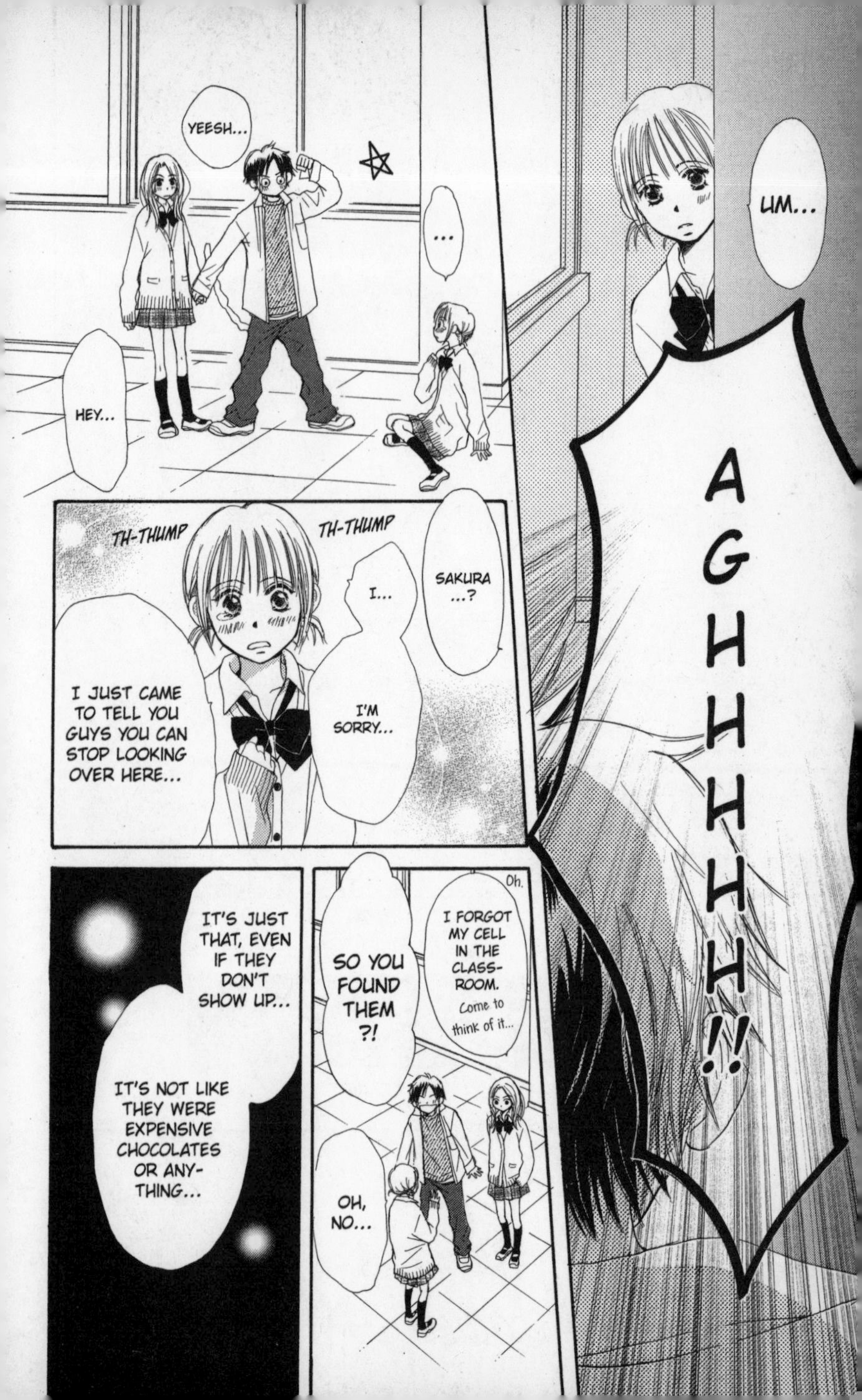
UM...
AGHHHHH!!
YEESH...
...
HEY...
SAKURA ...?
TH-THUMP
TH-THUMP
I...
I'M SORRY...
I JUST CAME TO TELL YOU GUYS YOU CAN STOP LOOKING OVER HERE...
Oh.
I FORGOT MY CELL IN THE CLASS-ROOM.
Come to think of it...
SO YOU FOUND THEM ?!
OH, NO...
IT'S JUST THAT, EVEN IF THEY DON'T SHOW UP...
IT'S NOT LIKE THEY WERE EXPENSIVE CHOCOLATES OR ANY-THING...

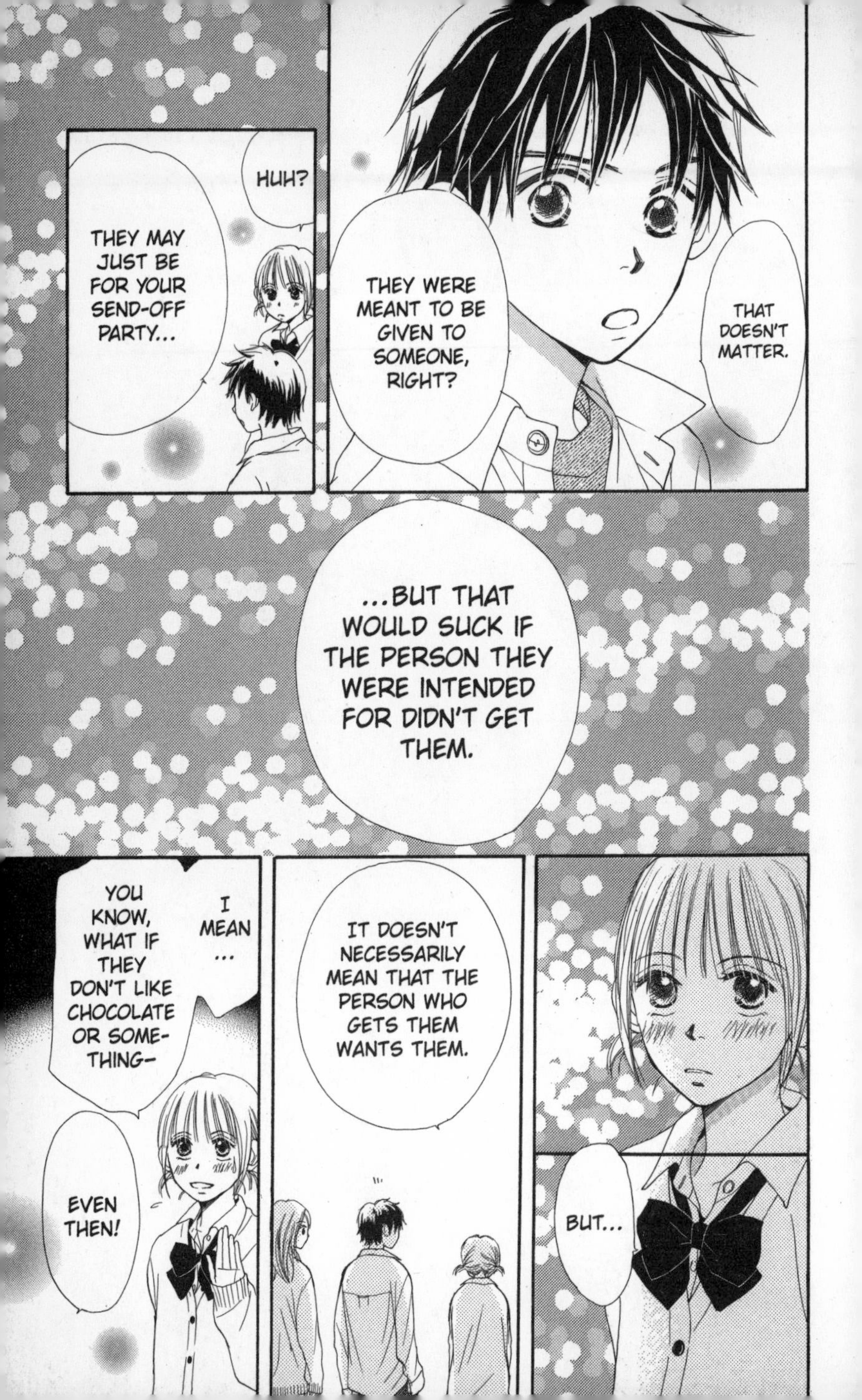

THAT DOESN'T MATTER.
THEY WERE MEANT TO BE GIVEN TO SOMEONE, RIGHT?
HUH?
THEY MAY JUST BE FOR YOUR SEND-OFF PARTY...
...BUT THAT WOULD SUCK IF THE PERSON THEY WERE INTENDED FOR DIDN'T GET THEM.
BUT...
IT DOESN'T NECESSARILY MEAN THAT THE PERSON WHO GETS THEM WANTS THEM.
I MEAN ...
YOU KNOW, WHAT IF THEY DON'T LIKE CHOCOLATE OR SOME-THING-
EVEN THEN!

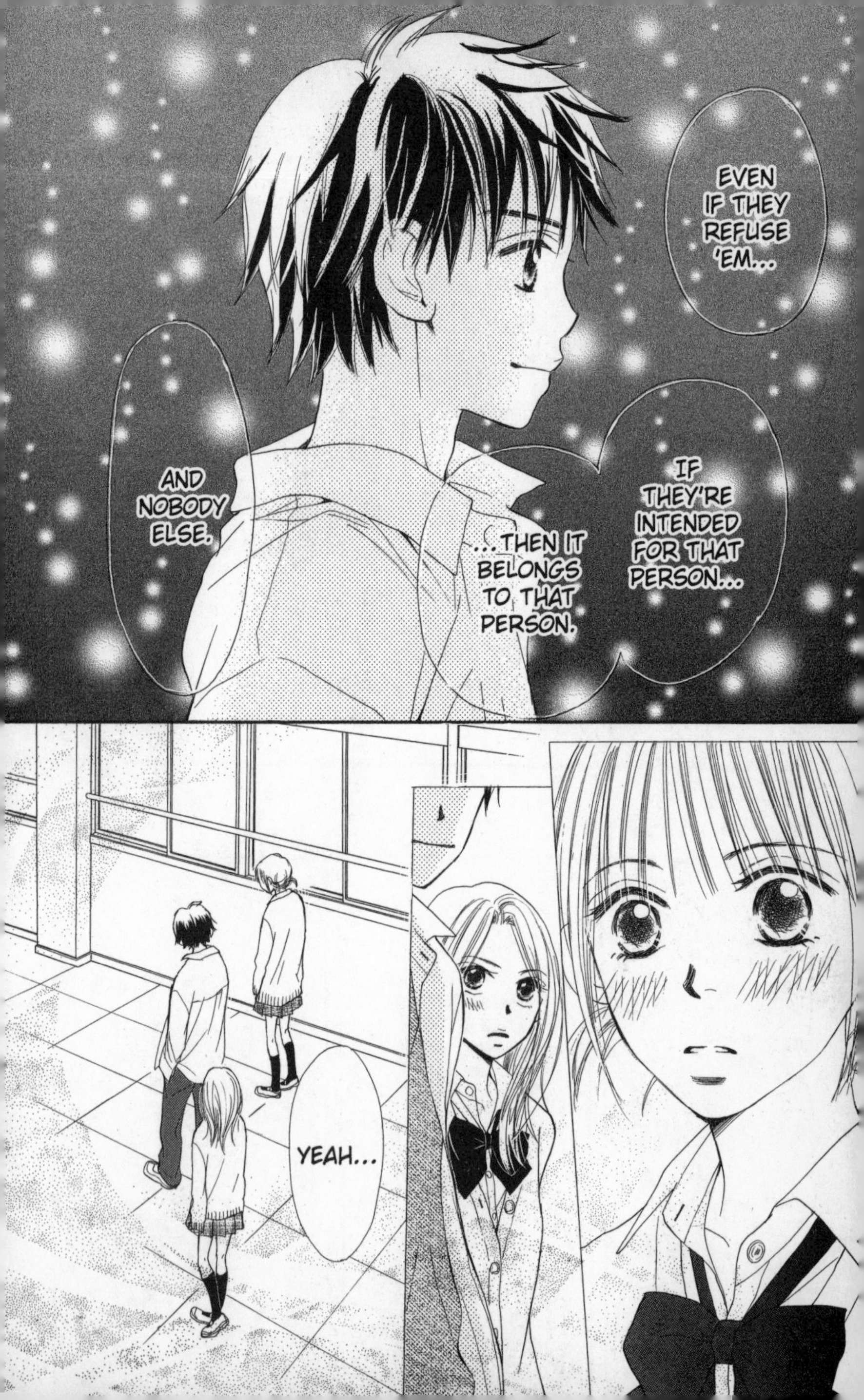
EVEN IF THEY REFUSE 'EM...
IF THEY'RE INTENDED FOR THAT PERSON...
...THEN IT BELONGS TO THAT PERSON.
AND NOBODY ELSE.
YEAH...

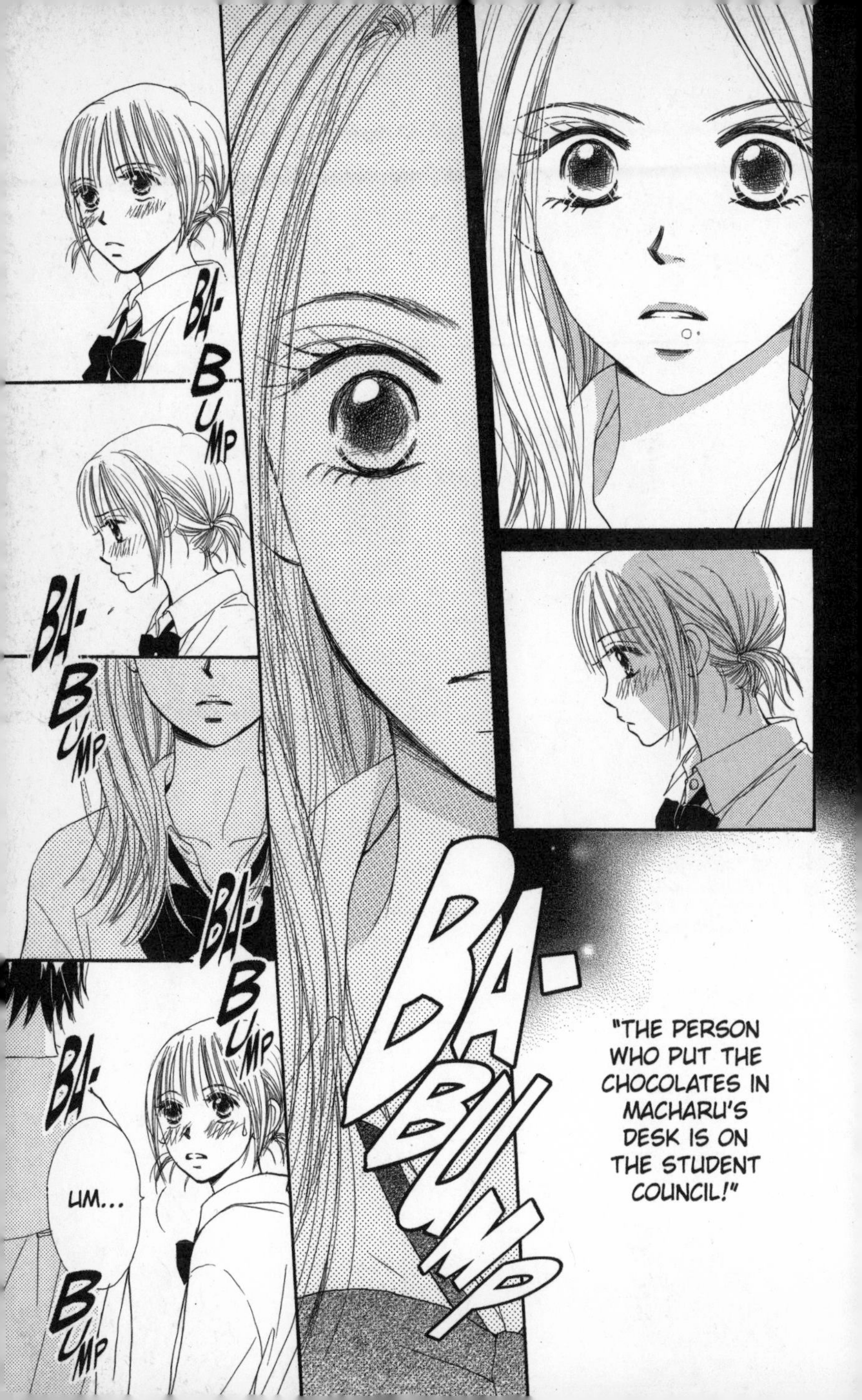
BA-BUMP!
"THE PERSON WHO PUT THE CHOCOLATES IN MACHARU'S DESK IS ON THE STUDENT COUNCIL!"
BA-BUMP
BA-BUMP
BA-BUMP
BA-BUMP
UM...
BA-BUMP

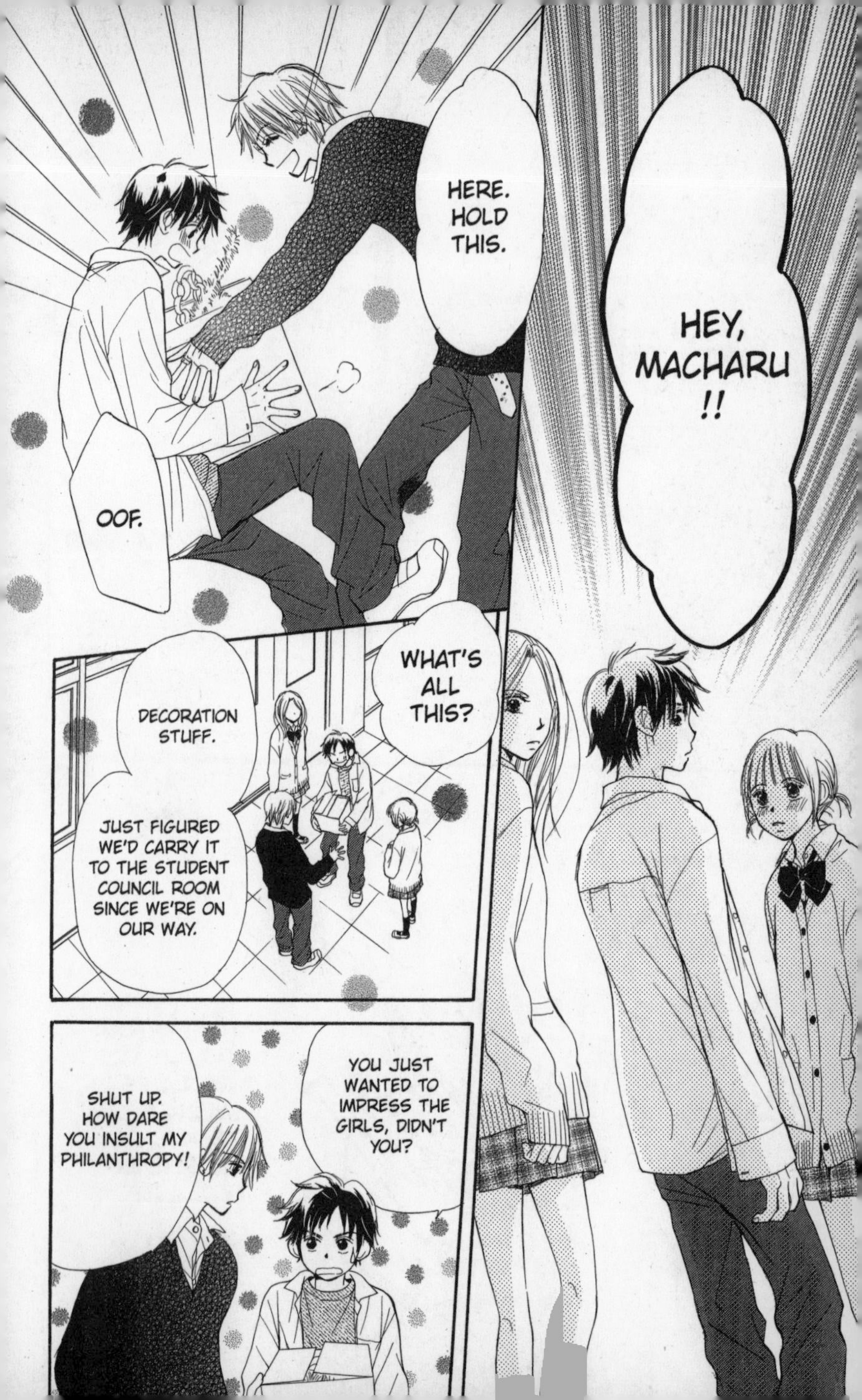
HEY, MACHARU!!
HERE. HOLD THIS.
OOF.
WHAT'S ALL THIS?
DECORATION STUFF.
JUST FIGURED WE'D CARRY IT TO THE STUDENT COUNCIL ROOM SINCE WE'RE ON OUR WAY.
YOU JUST WANTED TO IMPRESS THE GIRLS, DIDN'T YOU?
SHUT UP. HOW DARE YOU INSULT MY PHILANTHROPY!

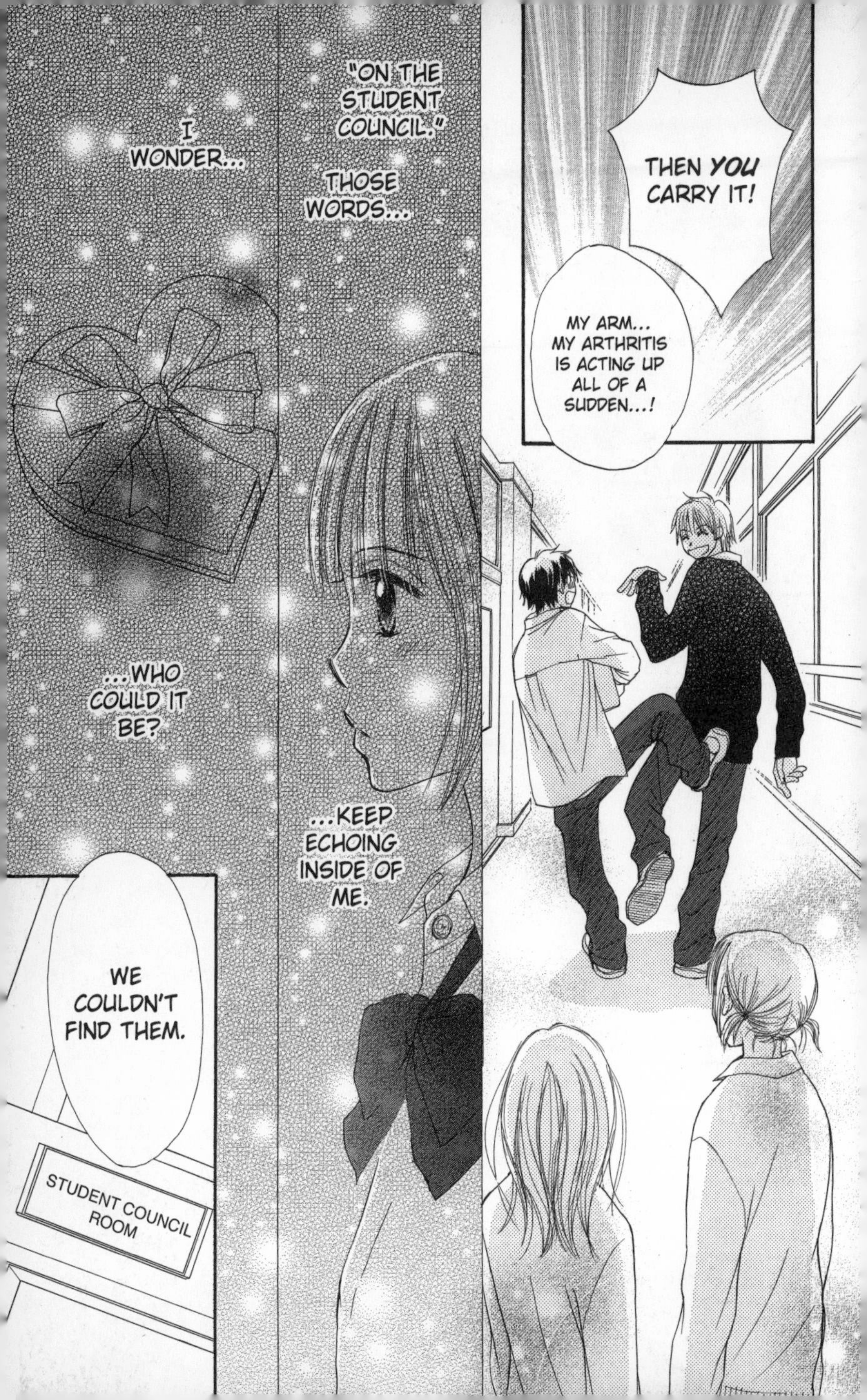
THEN *YOU* CARRY IT!
MY ARM... MY ARTHRITIS IS ACTING UP ALL OF A SUDDEN...!
"ON THE STUDENT COUNCIL."
THOSE WORDS...
...KEEP ECHOING INSIDE OF ME.
I WONDER...
...WHO COULD IT BE?
WE COULDN'T FIND THEM.
STUDENT COUNCIL ROOM

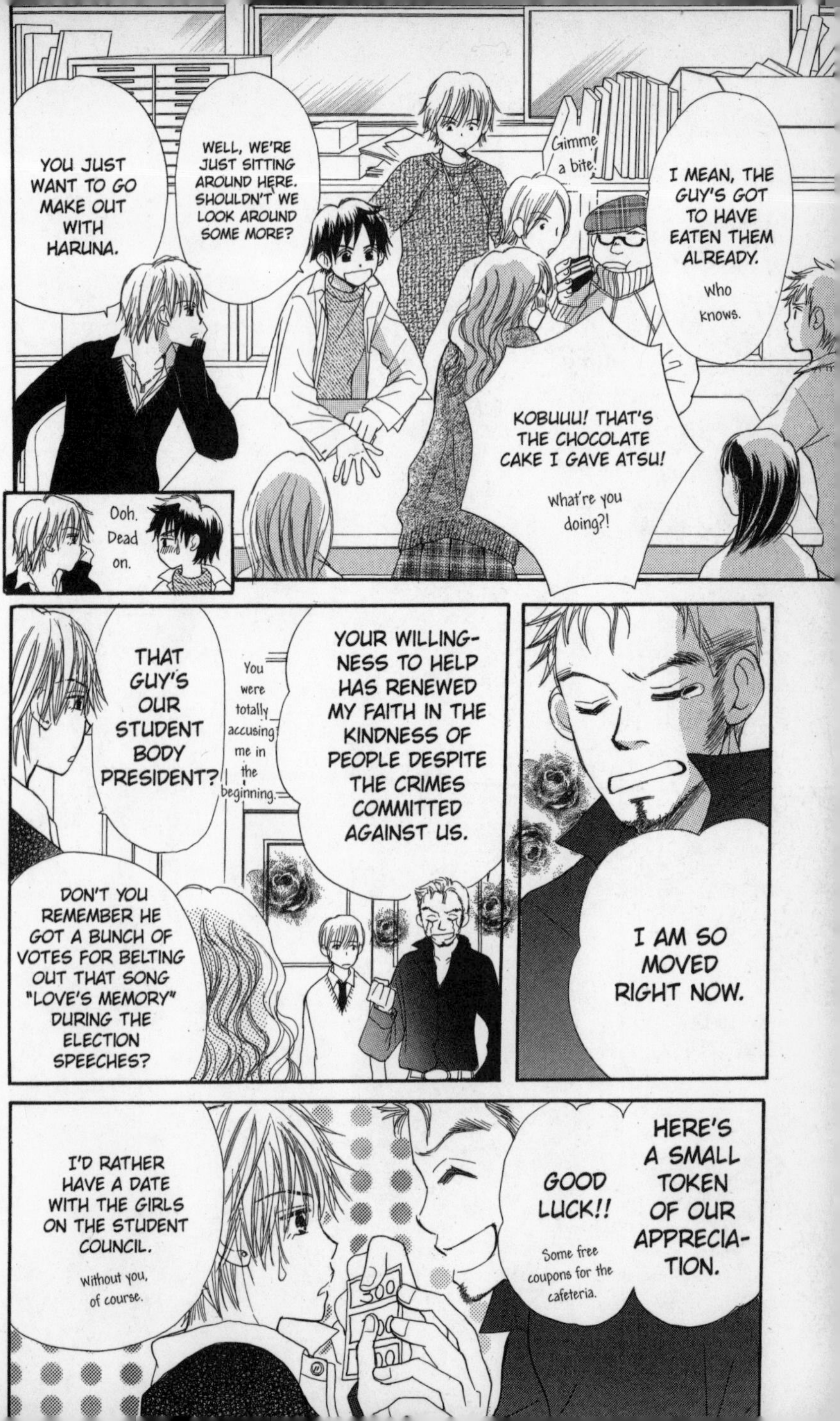
I MEAN, THE GUY'S GOT TO HAVE EATEN THEM ALREADY.
Who knows.
Gimme a bite!
WELL, WE'RE JUST SITTING AROUND HERE. SHOULDN'T WE LOOK AROUND SOME MORE?
YOU JUST WANT TO GO MAKE OUT WITH HARUNA.
KOBUUU! THAT'S THE CHOCOLATE CAKE I GAVE ATSU!
What're you doing?!
Ooh. Dead on.
I AM SO MOVED RIGHT NOW.
YOUR WILLING-NESS TO HELP HAS RENEWED MY FAITH IN THE KINDNESS OF PEOPLE DESPITE THE CRIMES COMMITTED AGAINST US.
You were totally accusing me in the beginning.
THAT GUY'S OUR STUDENT BODY PRESIDENT?
DON'T YOU REMEMBER HE GOT A BUNCH OF VOTES FOR BELTING OUT THAT SONG "LOVE'S MEMORY" DURING THE ELECTION SPEECHES?
HERE'S A SMALL TOKEN OF OUR APPRECIA-TION.
GOOD LUCK!!
Some free coupons for the cafeteria.
I'D RATHER HAVE A DATE WITH THE GIRLS ON THE STUDENT COUNCIL.
Without you, of course.

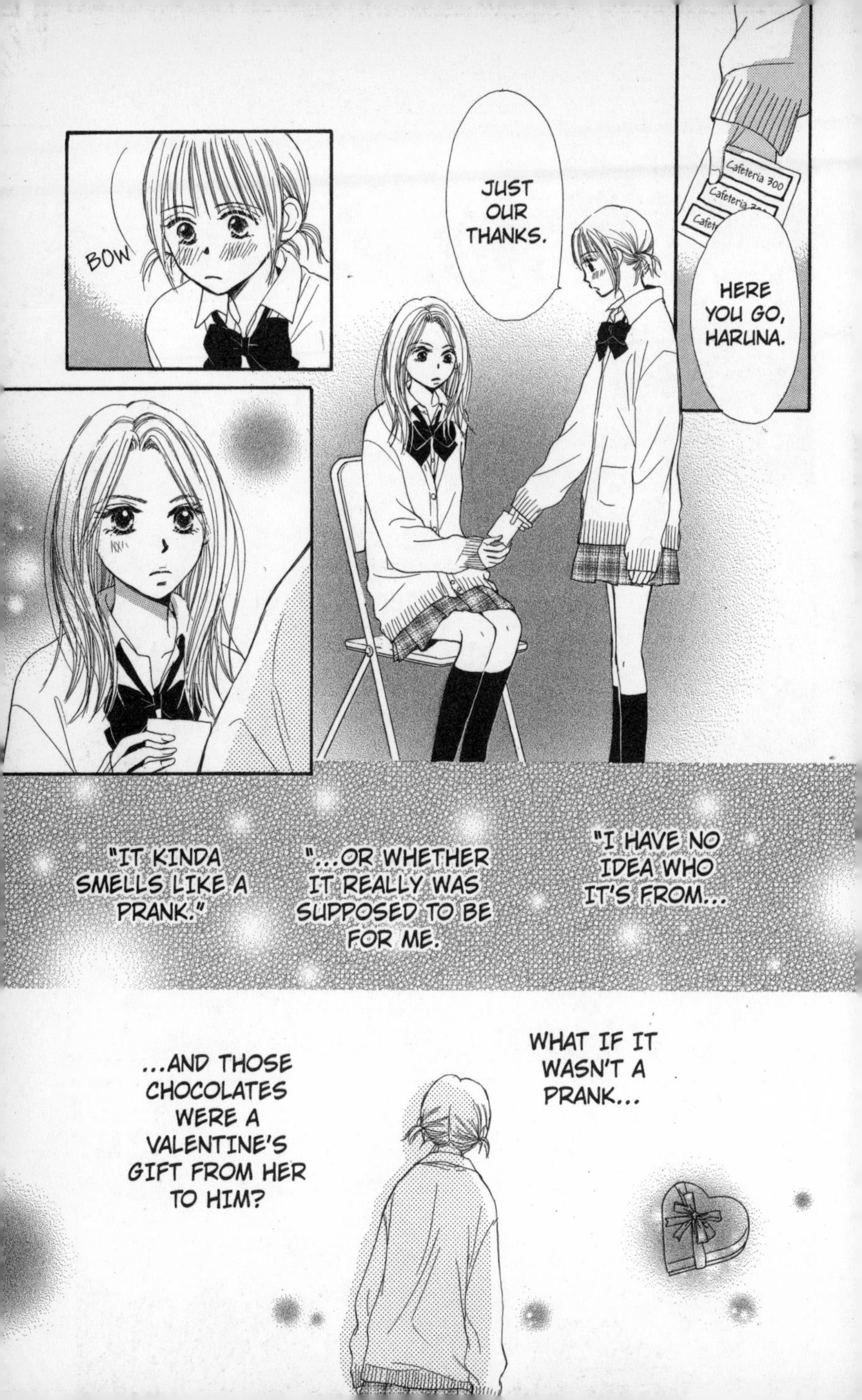
Cafeteria 300
HERE YOU GO, HARUNA.
JUST OUR THANKS.
BOW
"I HAVE NO IDEA WHO IT'S FROM...
"...OR WHETHER IT REALLY WAS SUPPOSED TO BE FOR ME.
"IT KINDA SMELLS LIKE A PRANK."
WHAT IF IT WASN'T A PRANK...
...AND THOSE CHOCOLATES WERE A VALENTINE'S GIFT FROM HER TO HIM?

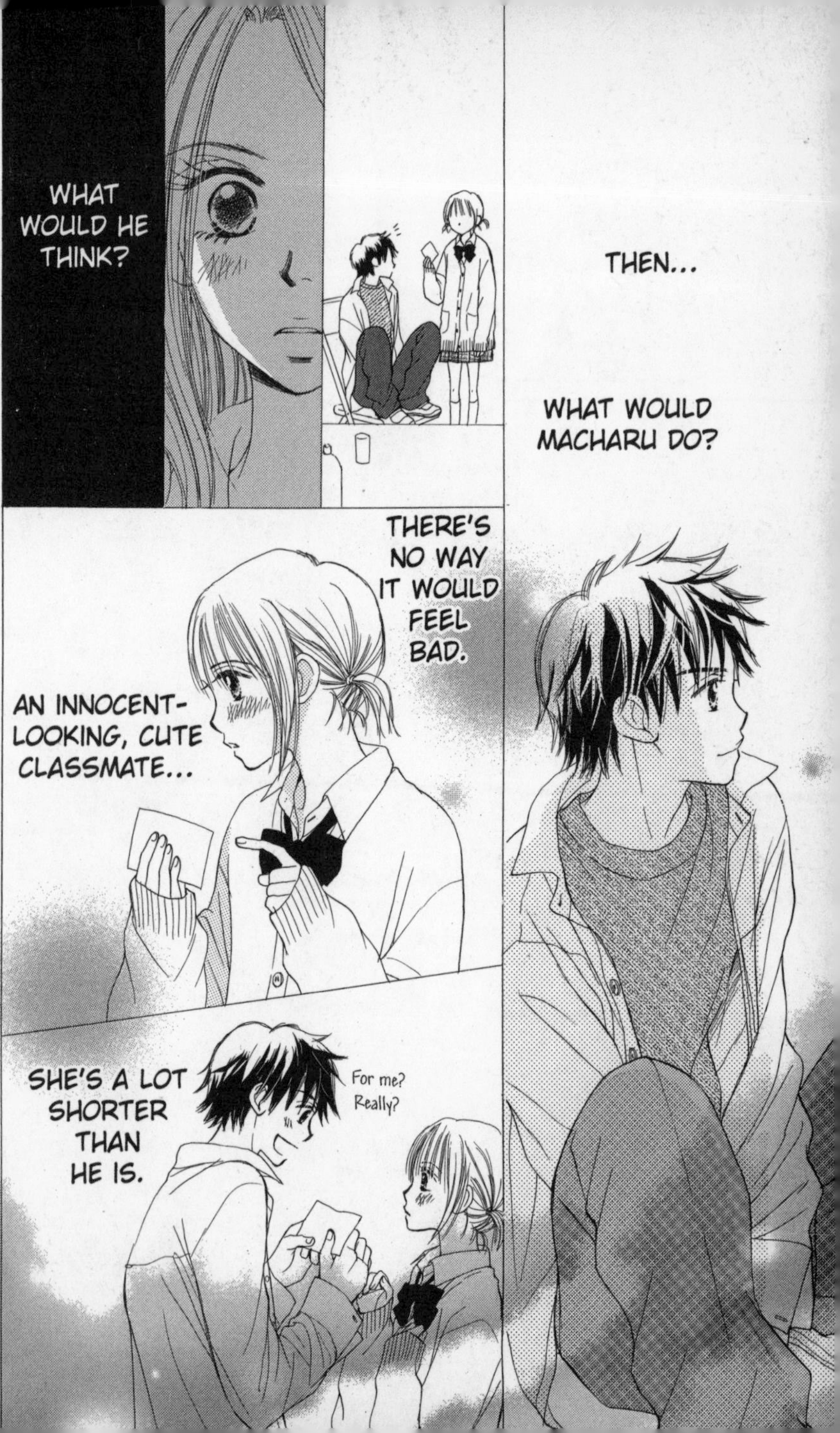
THEN...
WHAT WOULD MACHARU DO?
WHAT WOULD HE THINK?
THERE'S NO WAY IT WOULD FEEL BAD.
AN INNOCENT-LOOKING, CUTE CLASSMATE...
For me? Really?
SHE'S A LOT SHORTER THAN HE IS.

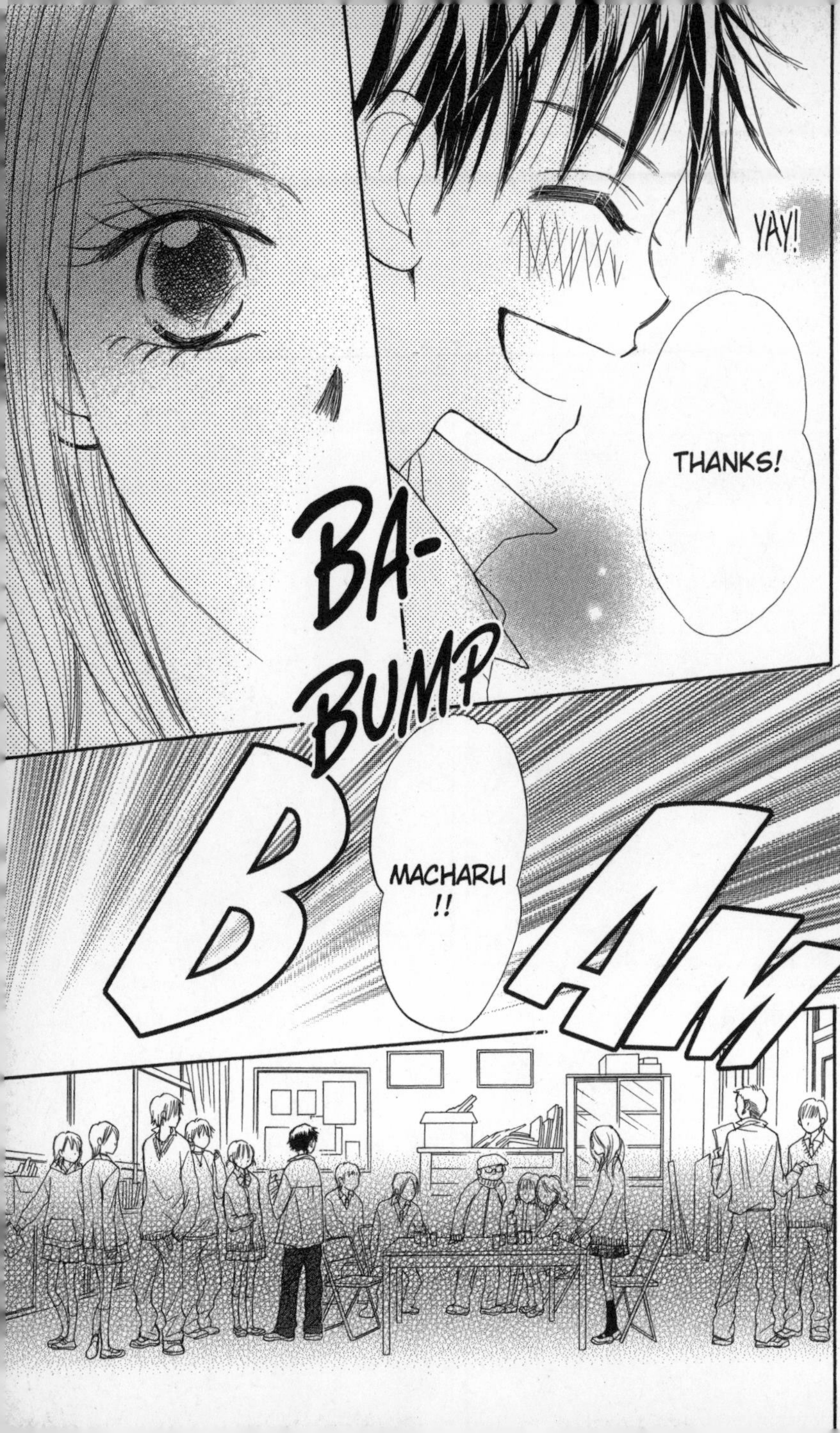
YAY!
THANKS!
BA-BUMP
MACHARU !!
BAM

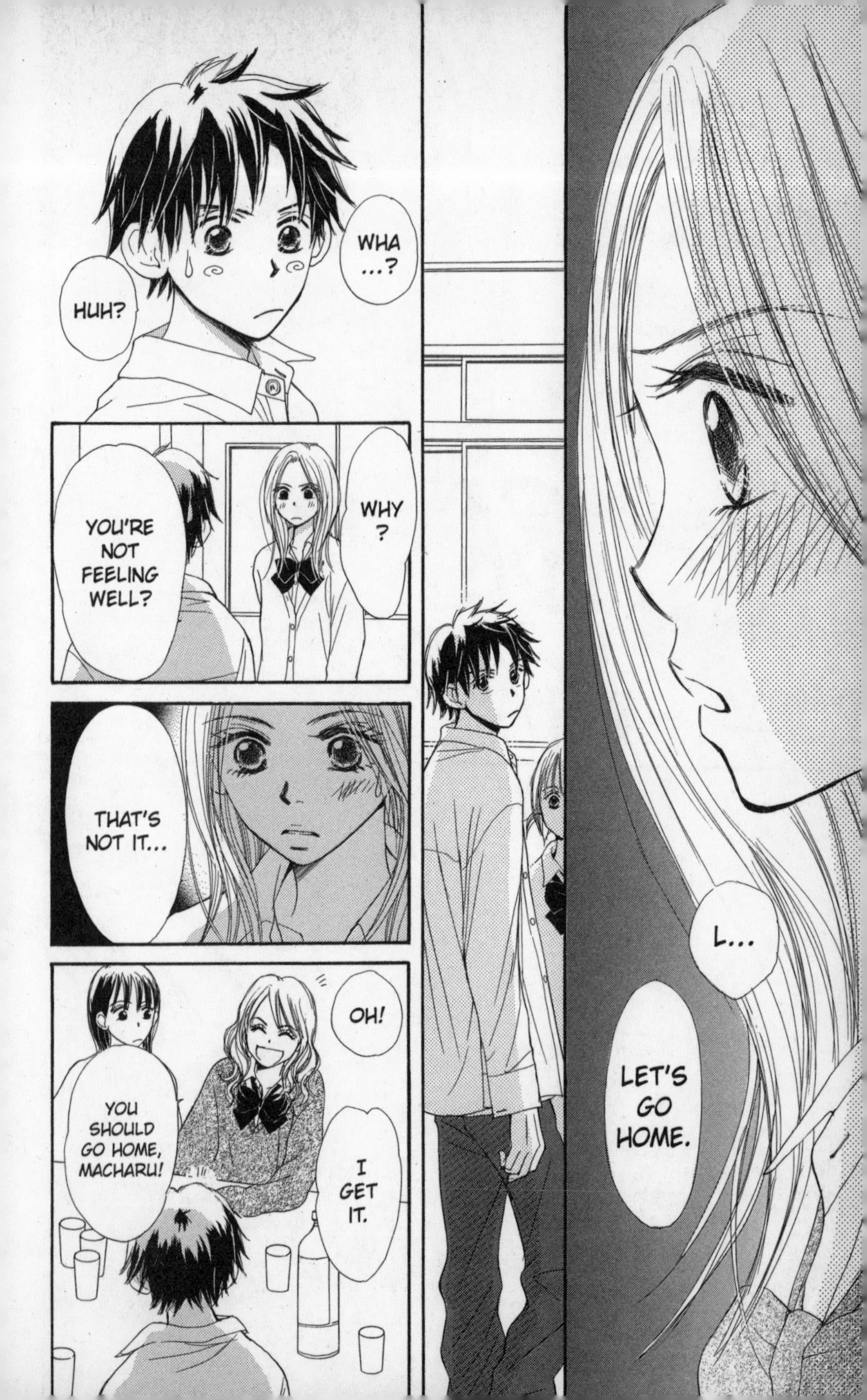
L...
LET'S GO HOME.
WHA ...?
HUH?
WHY?
YOU'RE NOT FEELING WELL?
THAT'S NOT IT...
OH!
I GET IT.
YOU SHOULD GO HOME, MACHARU!

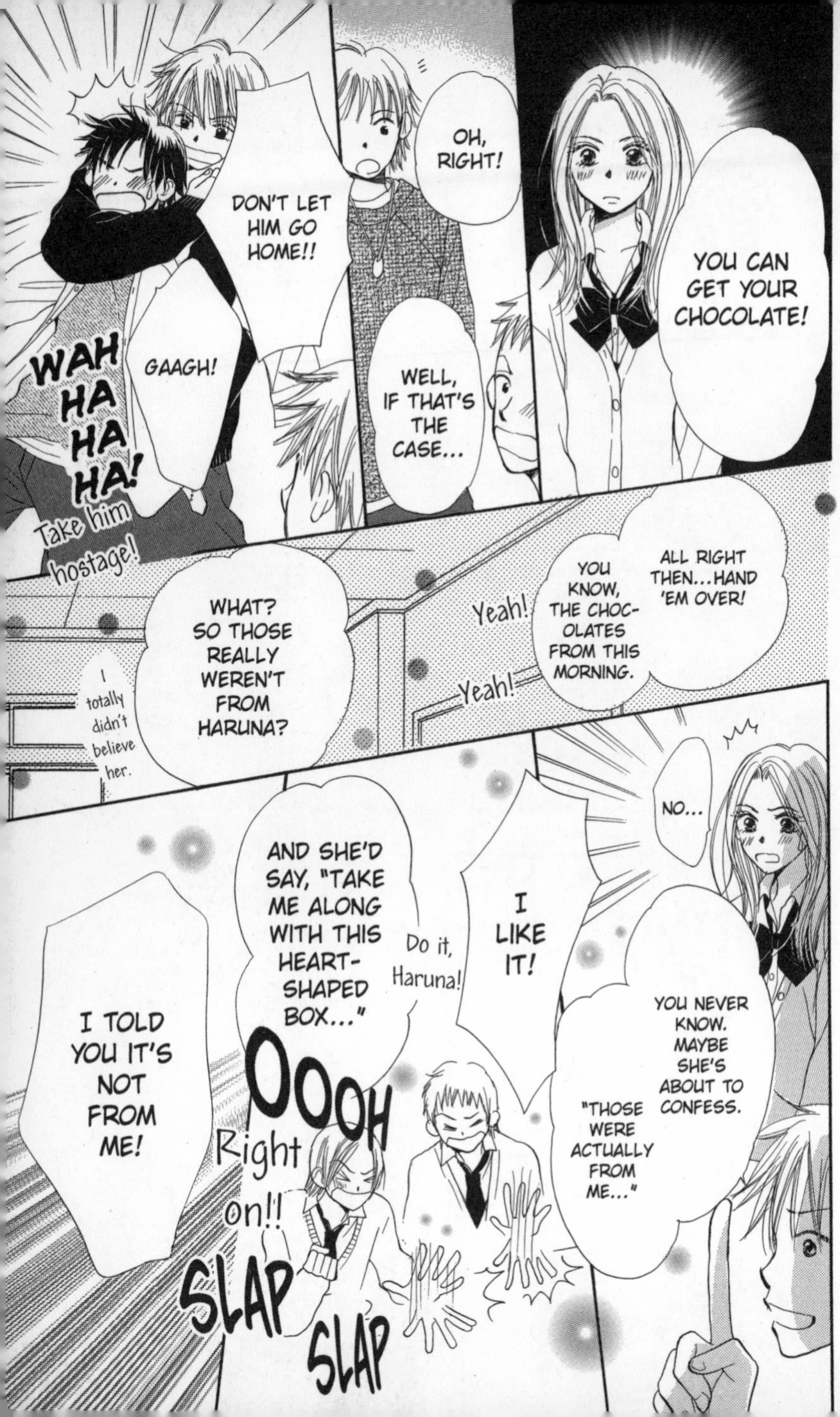
YOU CAN GET YOUR CHOCOLATE!
OH, RIGHT!
WELL, IF THAT'S THE CASE...
DON'T LET HIM GO HOME!!
GAAGH!
WAH HA HA HA!
Take him hostage!
ALL RIGHT THEN...HAND 'EM OVER!
YOU KNOW, THE CHOC-OLATES FROM THIS MORNING.
Yeah!
Yeah!
WHAT? SO THOSE REALLY WEREN'T FROM HARUNA?
I totally didn't believe her.
NO...
YOU NEVER KNOW. MAYBE SHE'S ABOUT TO CONFESS.
"THOSE WERE ACTUALLY FROM ME..."
I LIKE IT!
Do it, Haruna!
AND SHE'D SAY, "TAKE ME ALONG WITH THIS HEART-SHAPED BOX..."
OOOH
Right on!!
SLAP
SLAP
I TOLD YOU IT'S NOT FROM ME!

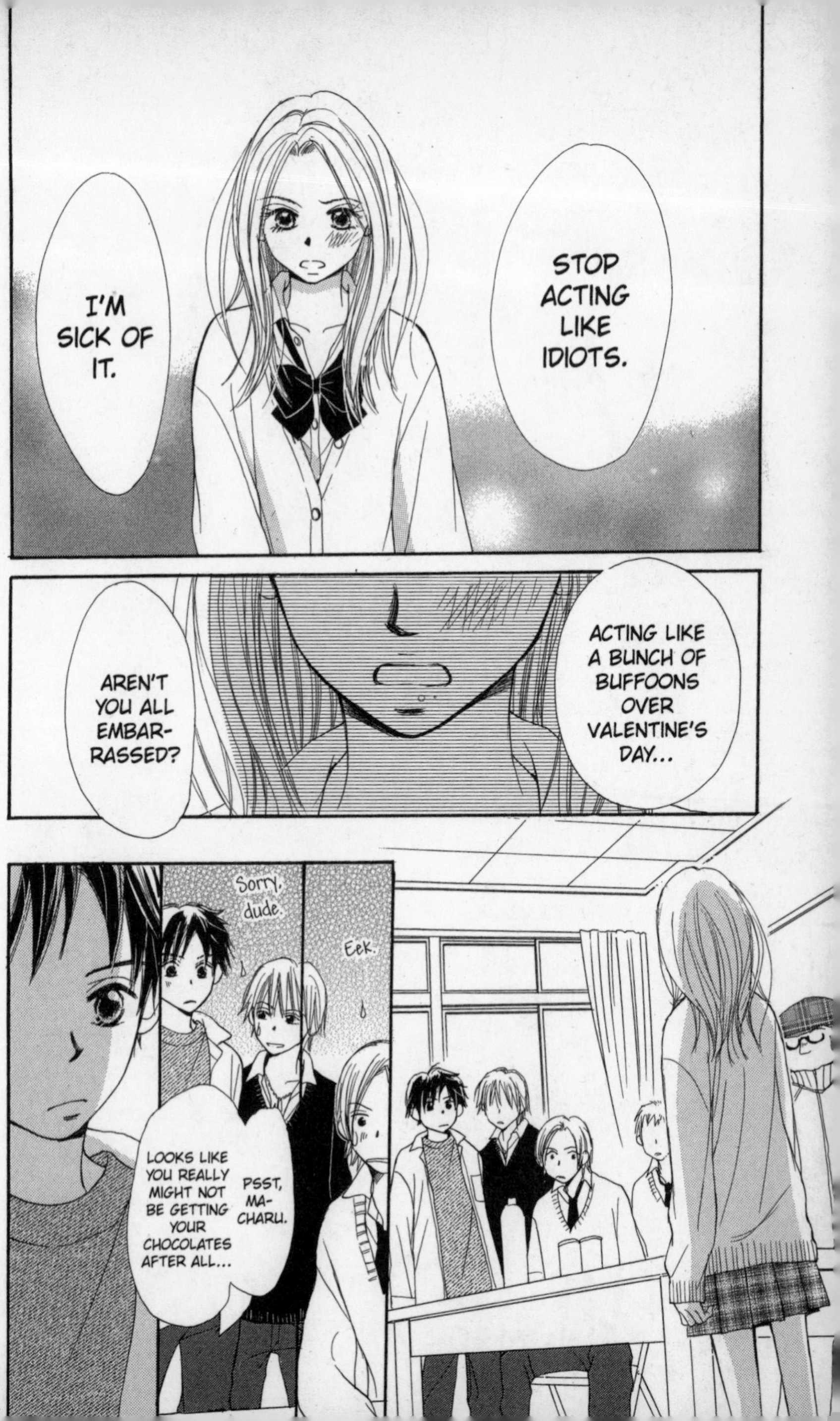
STOP ACTING LIKE IDIOTS.
I'M SICK OF IT.
ACTING LIKE A BUNCH OF BUFFOONS OVER VALENTINE'S DAY...
AREN'T YOU ALL EMBAR-RASSED?
Sorry, dude.
Eek.
PSST, MA-CHARU.
LOOKS LIKE YOU REALLY MIGHT NOT BE GETTING YOUR CHOCOLATES AFTER ALL...

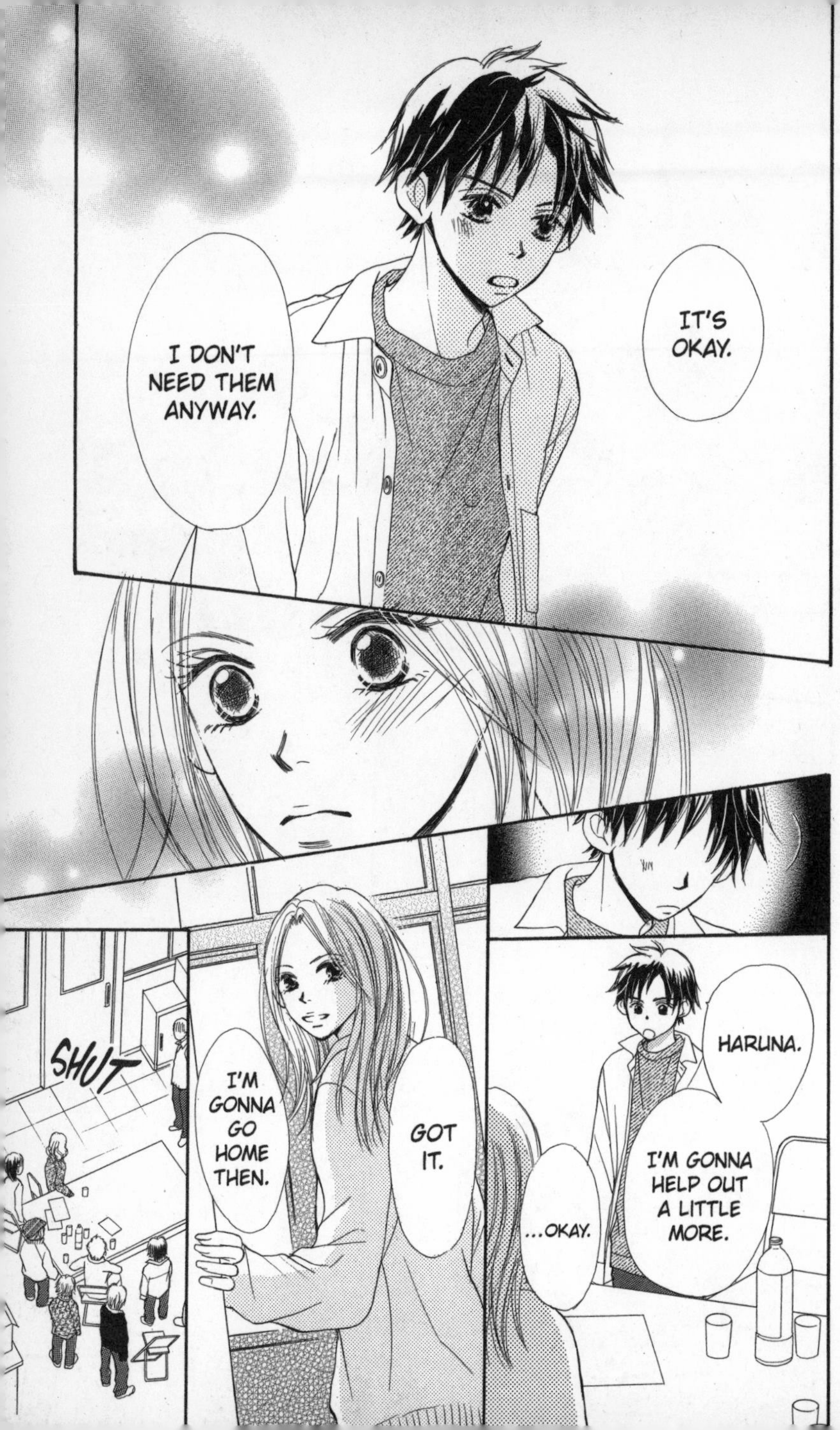
IT'S OKAY.
I DON'T NEED THEM ANYWAY.
HARUNA.
I'M GONNA HELP OUT A LITTLE MORE.
...OKAY.
GOT IT.
I'M GONNA GO HOME THEN.
SHUT

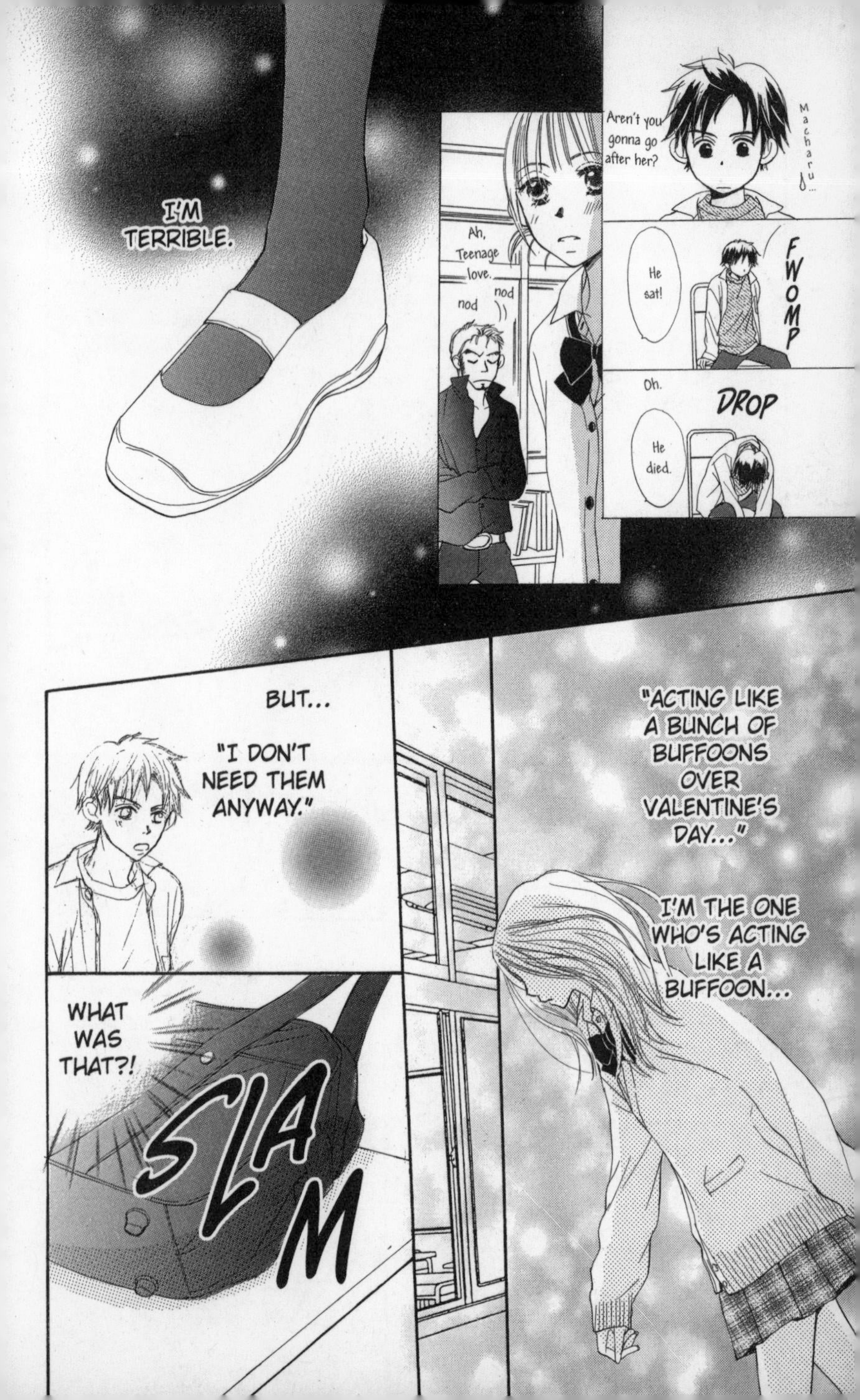
Aren't you gonna go after her?
Macharu...
He sat!
FWOMP
Oh.
DROP
He died.
Ah, Teenage love.
nod nod
I'M TERRIBLE.
"ACTING LIKE A BUNCH OF BUFFOONS OVER VALENTINE'S DAY..."
I'M THE ONE WHO'S ACTING LIKE A BUFFOON...
BUT...
"I DON'T NEED THEM ANYWAY."
WHAT WAS THAT?!
SLAM

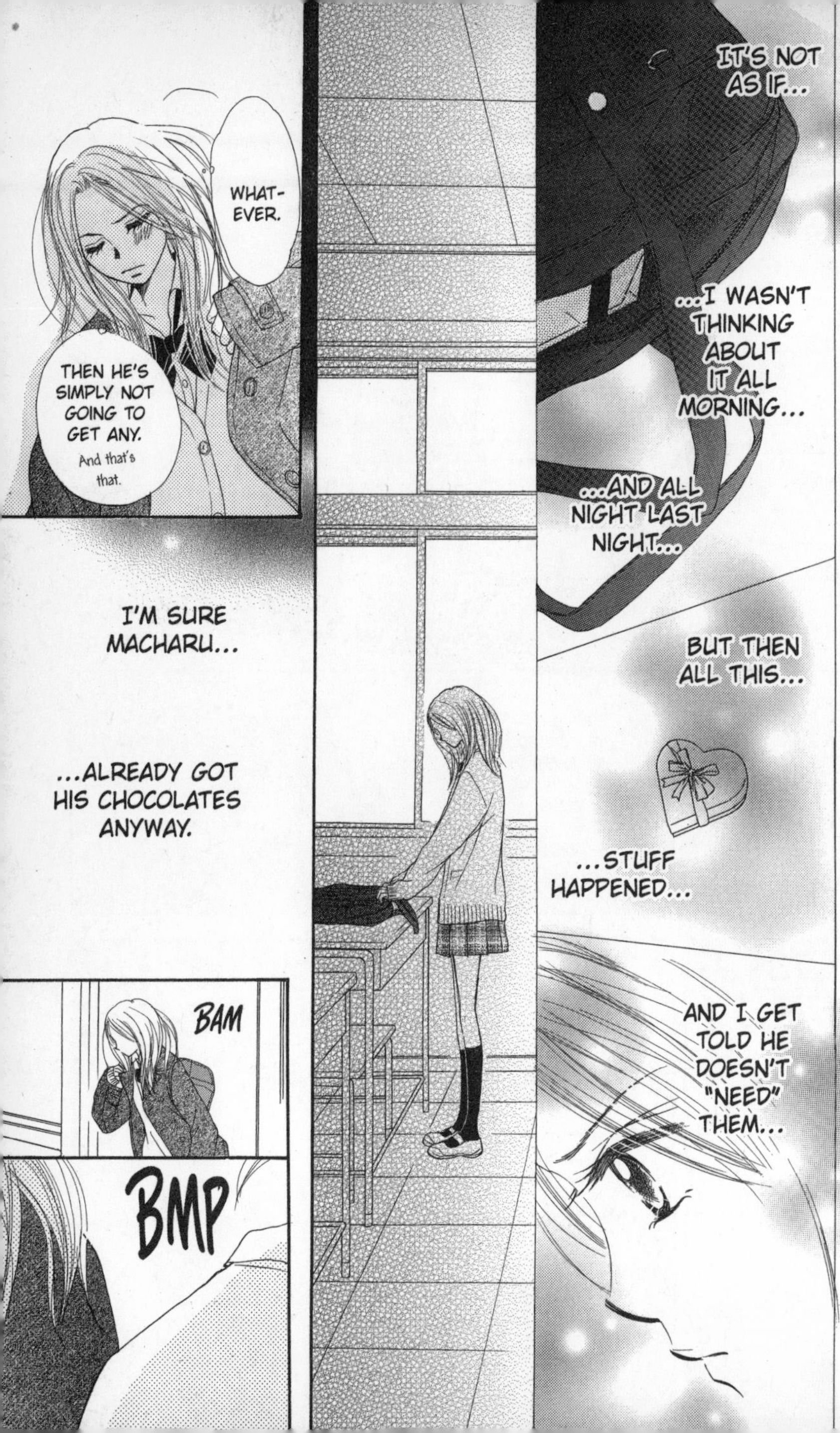
IT'S NOT AS IF...
...I WASN'T THINKING ABOUT IT ALL MORNING...
...AND ALL NIGHT LAST NIGHT...
BUT THEN ALL THIS...
...STUFF HAPPENED...
AND I GET TOLD HE DOESN'T "NEED" THEM...
WHAT-EVER.
THEN HE'S SIMPLY NOT GOING TO GET ANY. And that's that.
I'M SURE MACHARU...
...ALREADY GOT HIS CHOCOLATES ANYWAY.
BAM
BMP

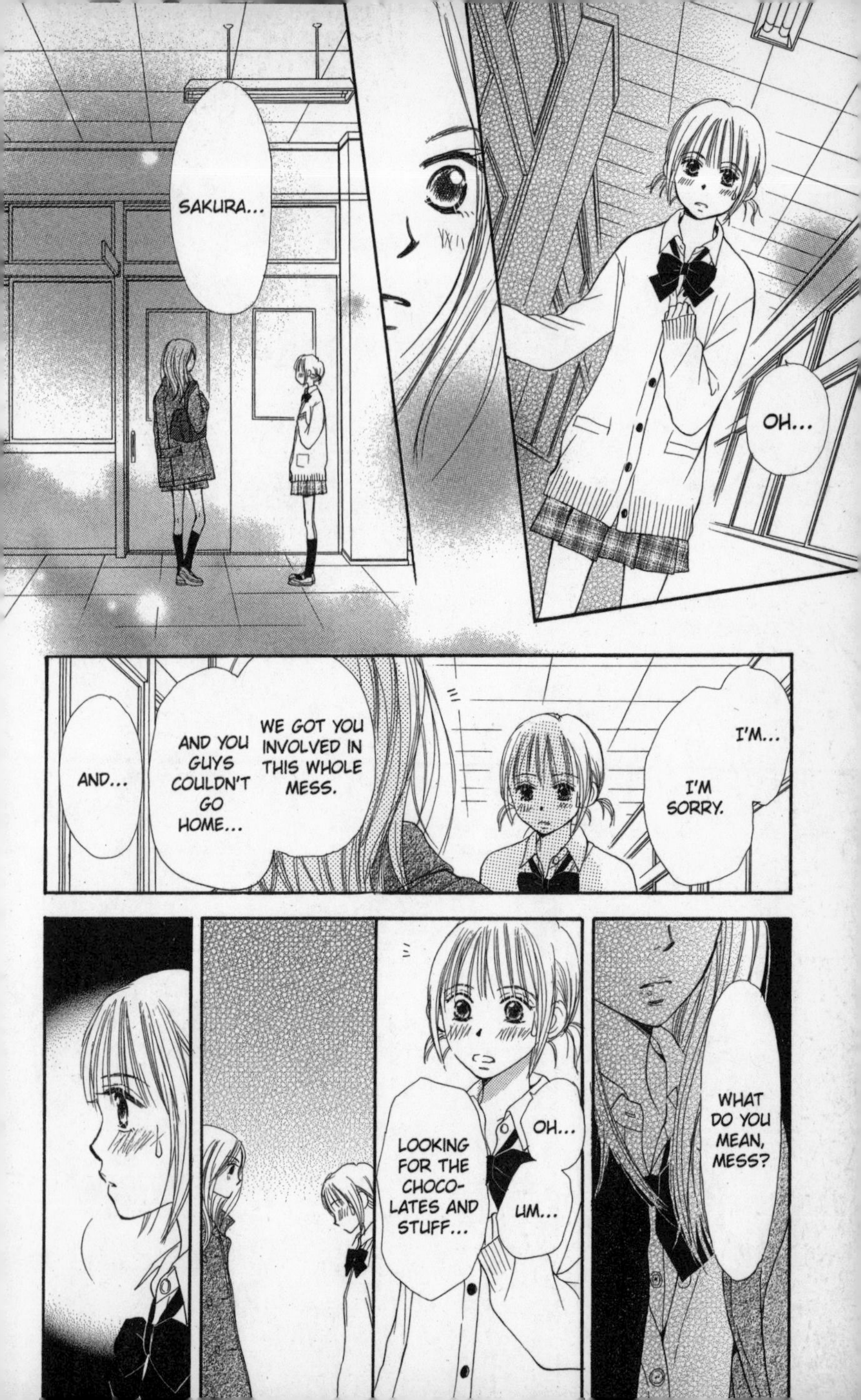
OH...
SAKURA...
I'M...
I'M SORRY.
WE GOT YOU INVOLVED IN THIS WHOLE MESS.
AND YOU GUYS COULDN'T GO HOME...
AND...
WHAT DO YOU MEAN, MESS?
OH...
UM...
LOOKING FOR THE CHOCO-LATES AND STUFF...

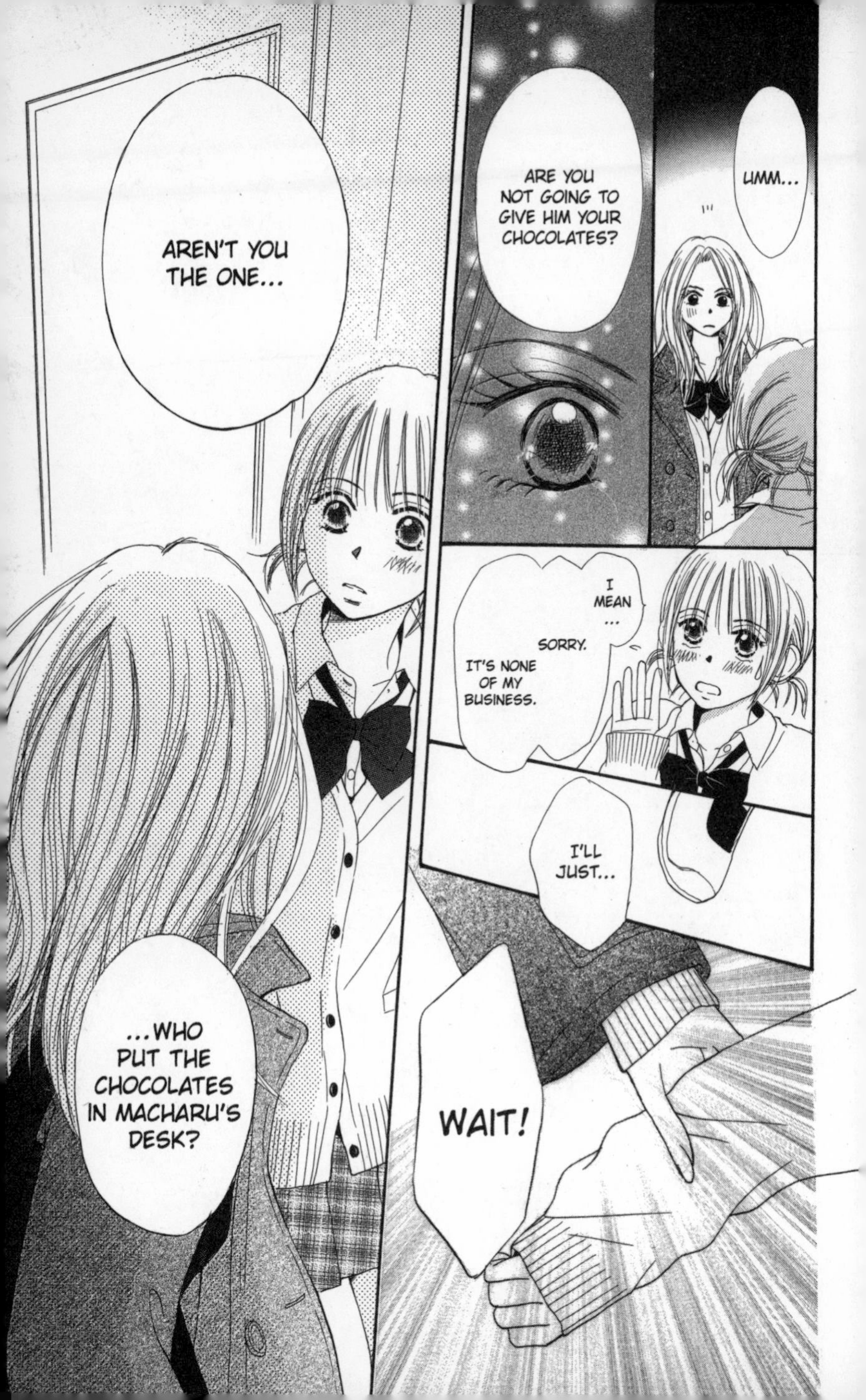
UMM...
ARE YOU NOT GOING TO GIVE HIM YOUR CHOCOLATES?
I MEAN...
SORRY.
IT'S NONE OF MY BUSINESS.
I'LL JUST...
WAIT!
AREN'T YOU THE ONE...
...WHO PUT THE CHOCOLATES IN MACHARU'S DESK?

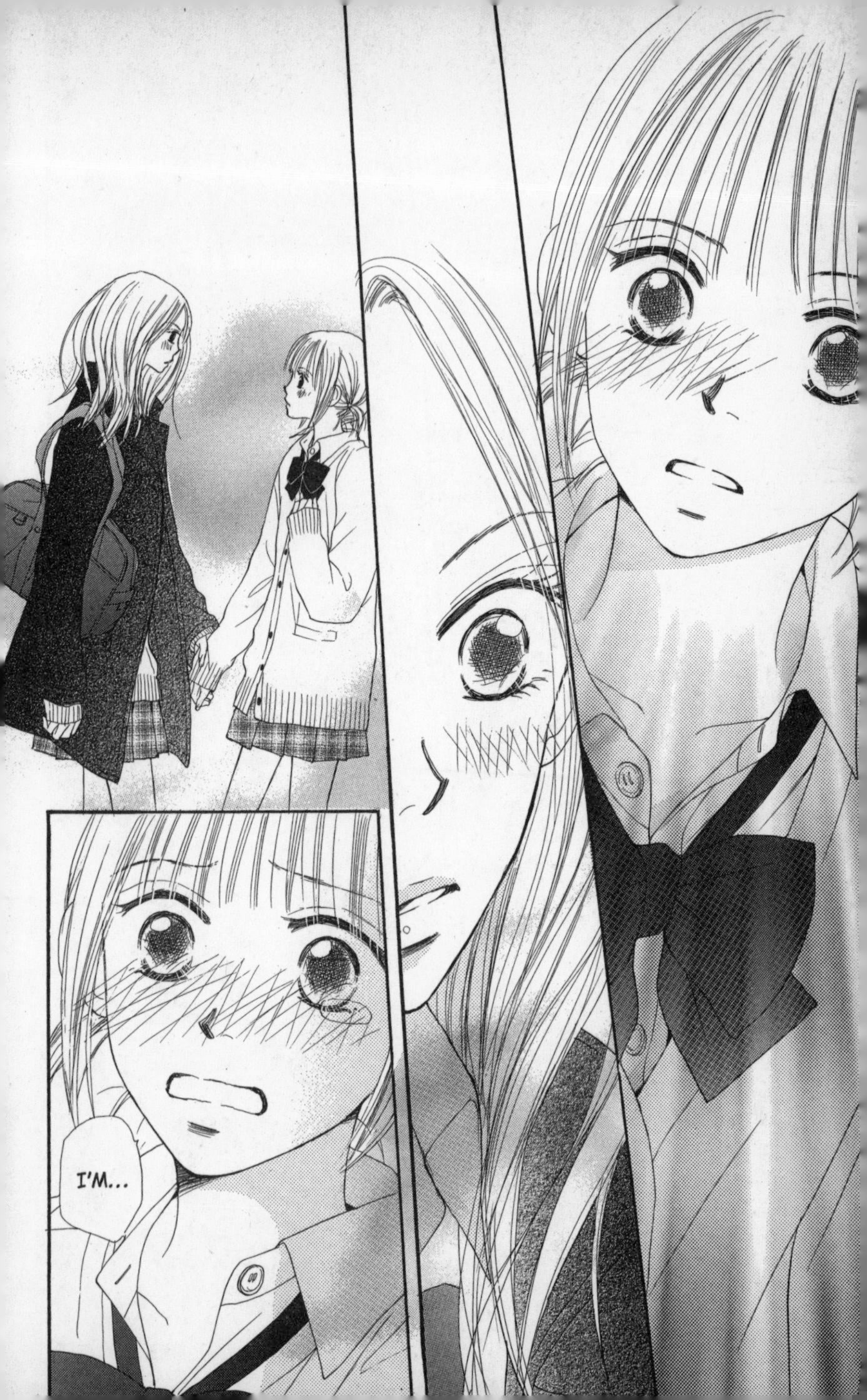
I'M...

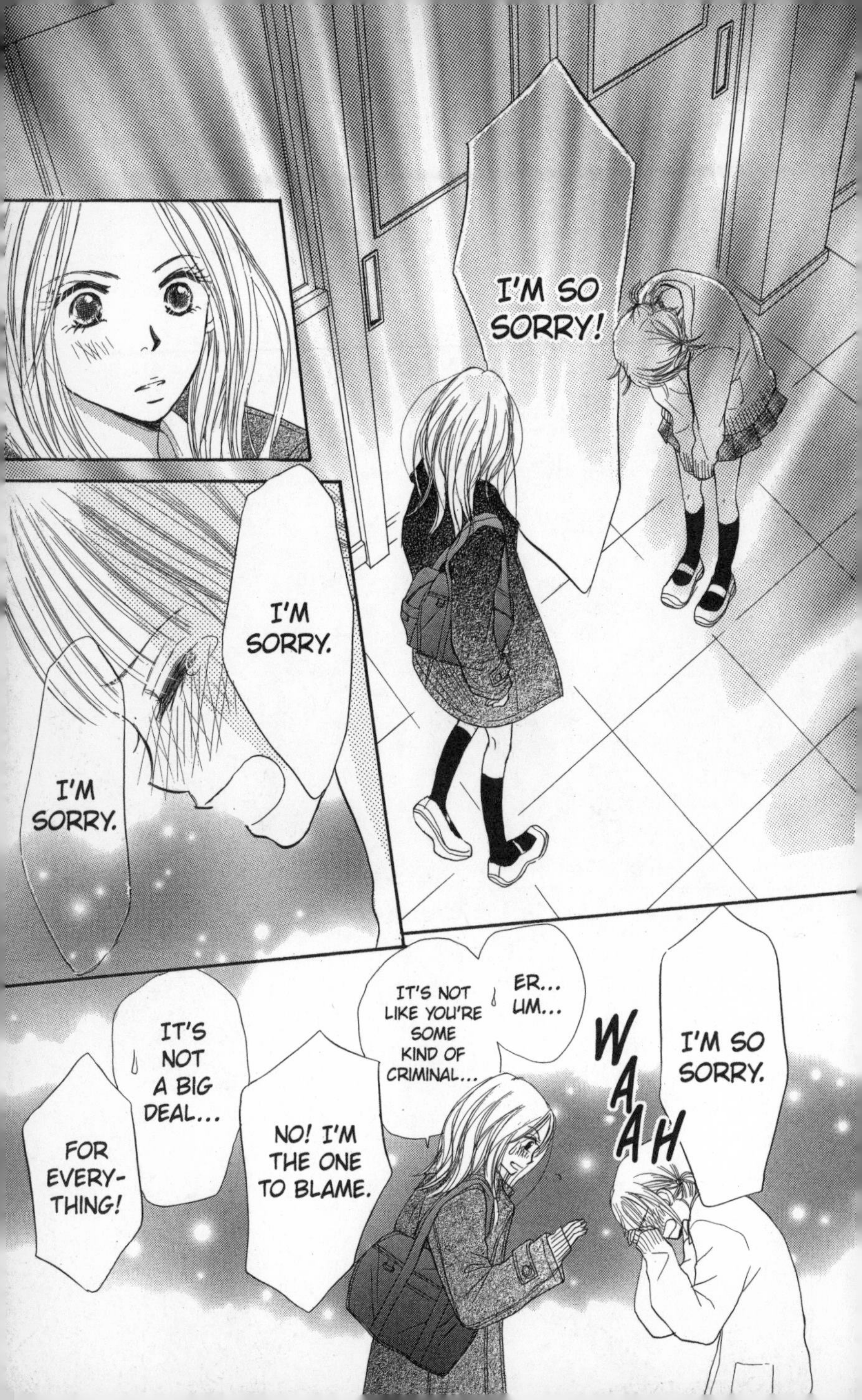

I'M SO SORRY!
I'M SORRY.
I'M SORRY.
I'M SO SORRY.
WAAH
ER... UM...
IT'S NOT LIKE YOU'RE SOME KIND OF CRIMINAL...
IT'S NOT A BIG DEAL...
NO! I'M THE ONE TO BLAME.
FOR EVERY-THING!

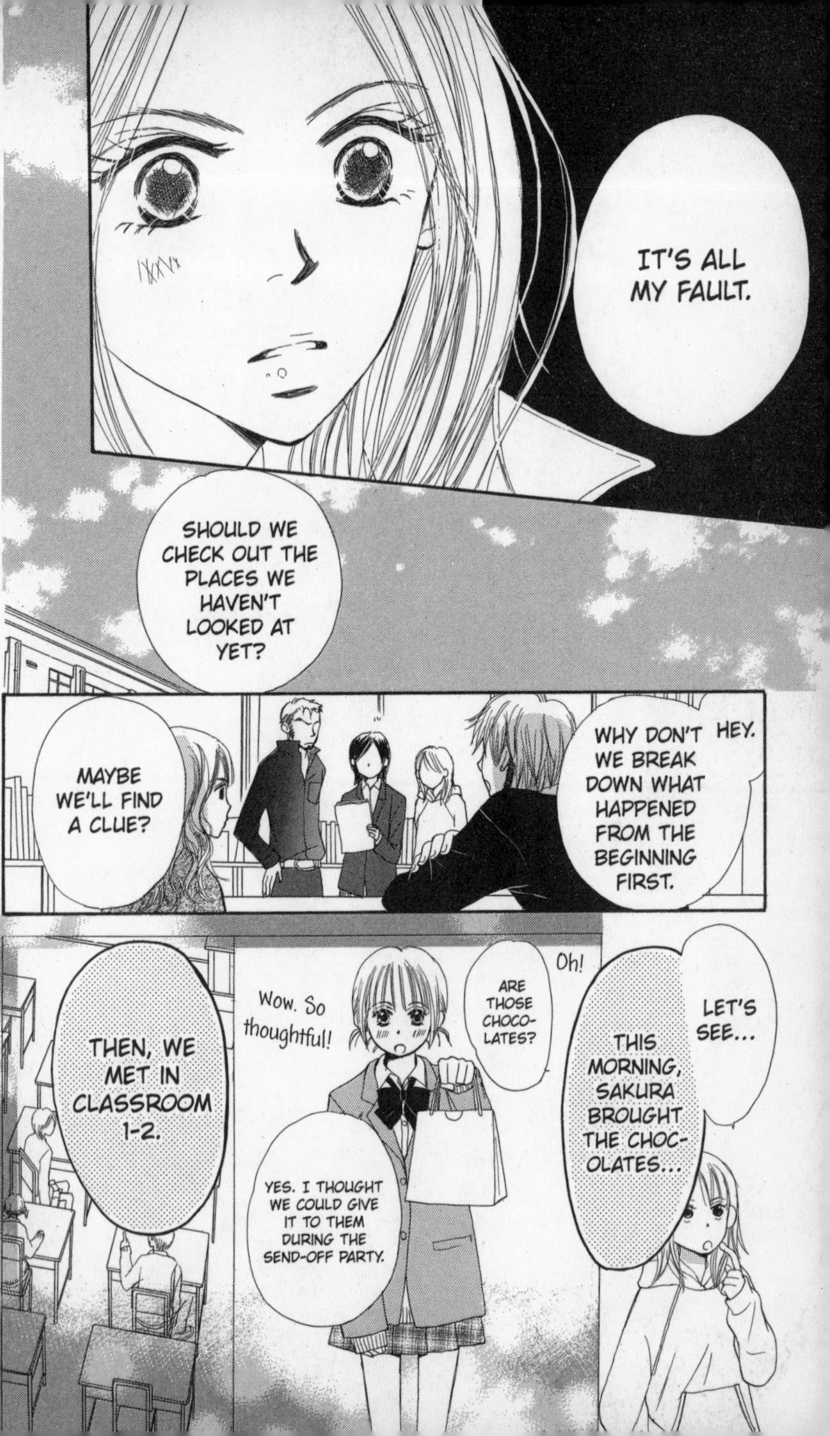
IT'S ALL MY FAULT.
SHOULD WE CHECK OUT THE PLACES WE HAVEN'T LOOKED AT YET?
HEY.
WHY DON'T WE BREAK DOWN WHAT HAPPENED FROM THE BEGINNING FIRST.
MAYBE WE'LL FIND A CLUE?
LET'S SEE...
THIS MORNING, SAKURA BROUGHT THE CHOCOLATES...
Oh!
ARE THOSE CHOCOLATES?
Wow. So thoughtful!
YES. I THOUGHT WE COULD GIVE IT TO THEM DURING THE SEND-OFF PARTY.
THEN, WE MET IN CLASSROOM 1-2.

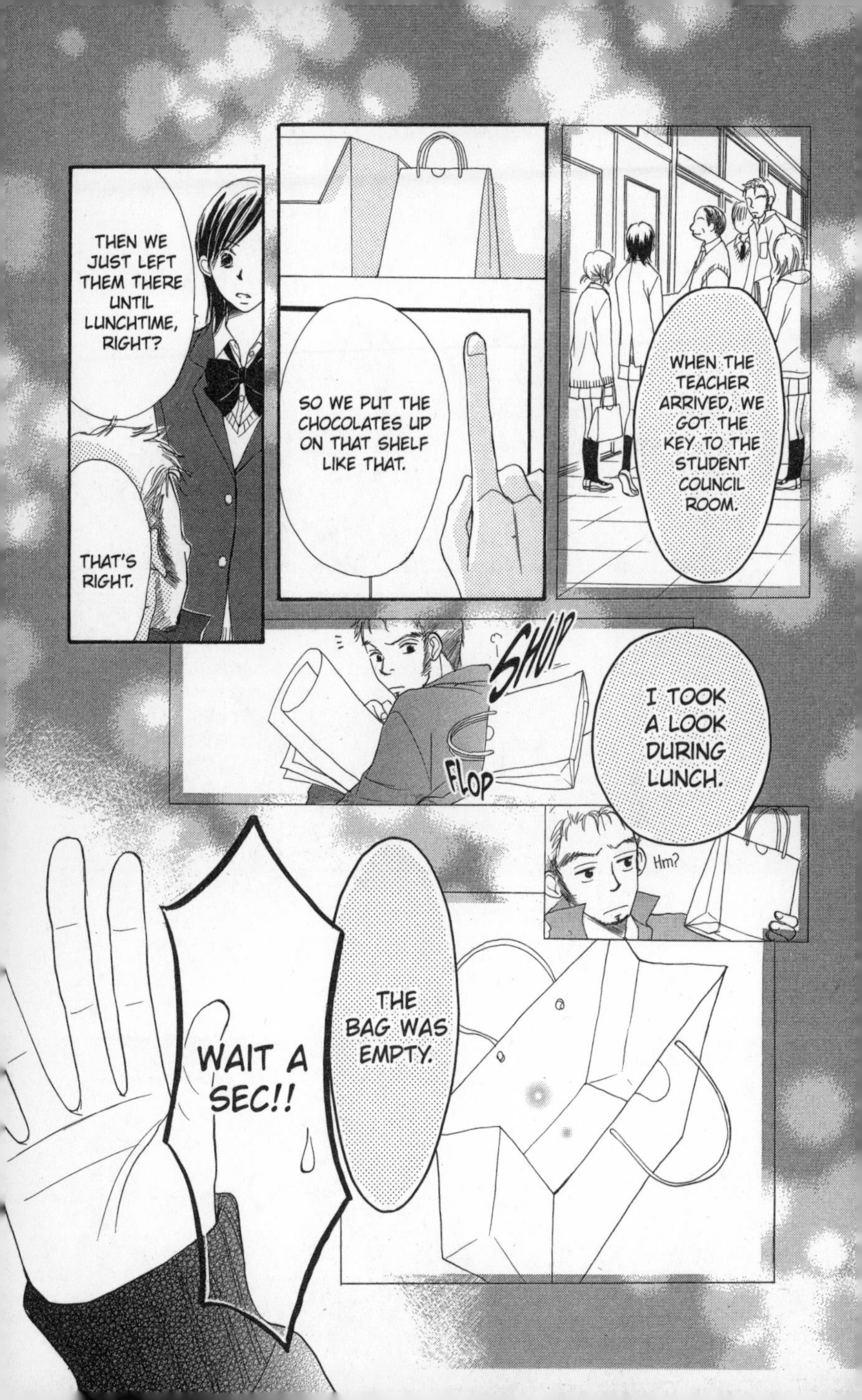
WHEN THE TEACHER ARRIVED, WE GOT THE KEY TO THE STUDENT COUNCIL ROOM.
SO WE PUT THE CHOCOLATES UP ON THAT SHELF LIKE THAT.
THEN WE JUST LEFT THEM THERE UNTIL LUNCHTIME, RIGHT?
THAT'S RIGHT.
I TOOK A LOOK DURING LUNCH.
SHUP
FLOP
Hm?
THE BAG WAS EMPTY.
WAIT A SEC!!

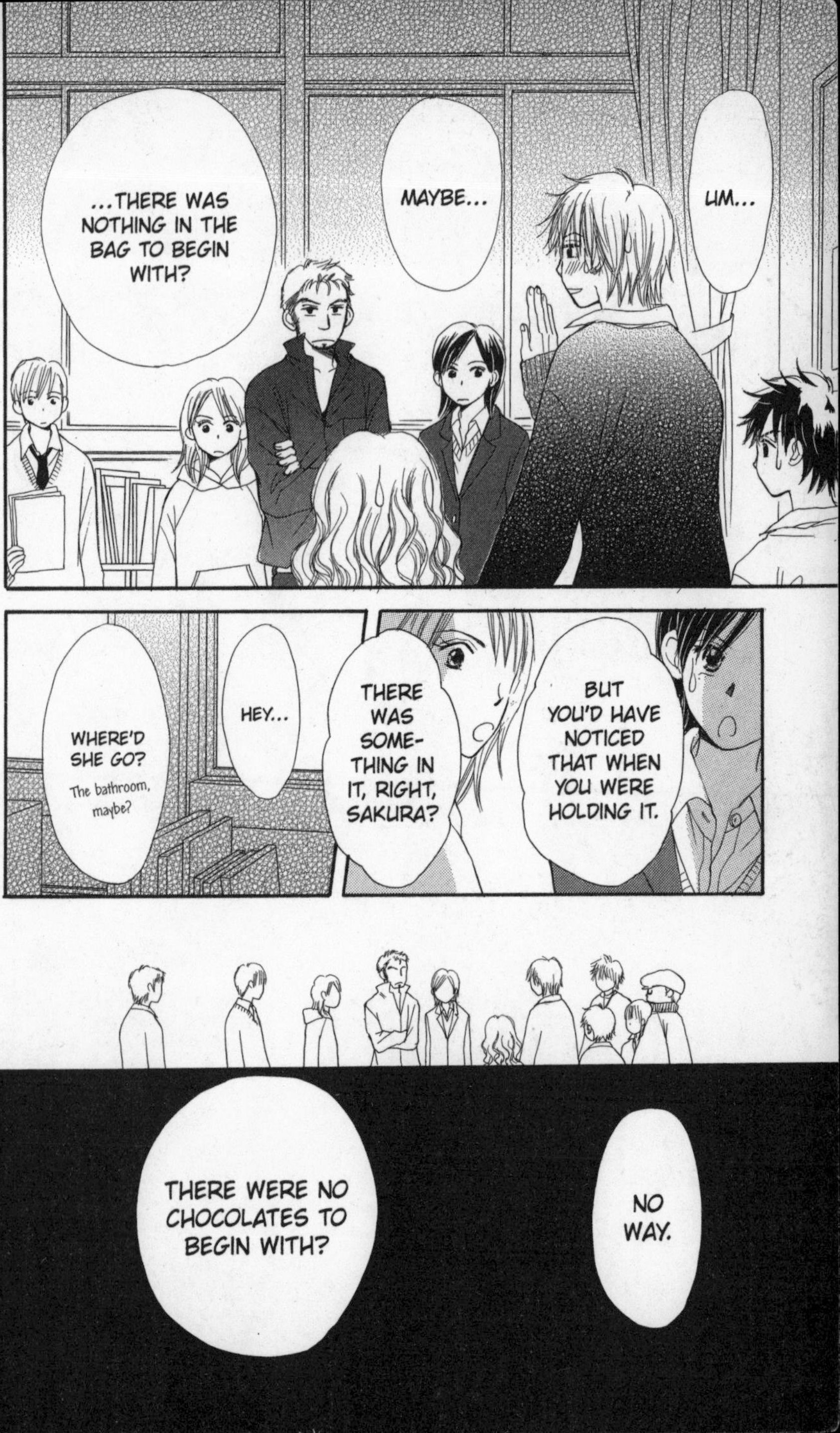
UM...
MAYBE...
...THERE WAS NOTHING IN THE BAG TO BEGIN WITH?
BUT YOU'D HAVE NOTICED THAT WHEN YOU WERE HOLDING IT.
THERE WAS SOME-THING IN IT, RIGHT, SAKURA?
HEY...
WHERE'D SHE GO?
The bathroom, maybe?
NO WAY.
THERE WERE NO CHOCOLATES TO BEGIN WITH?

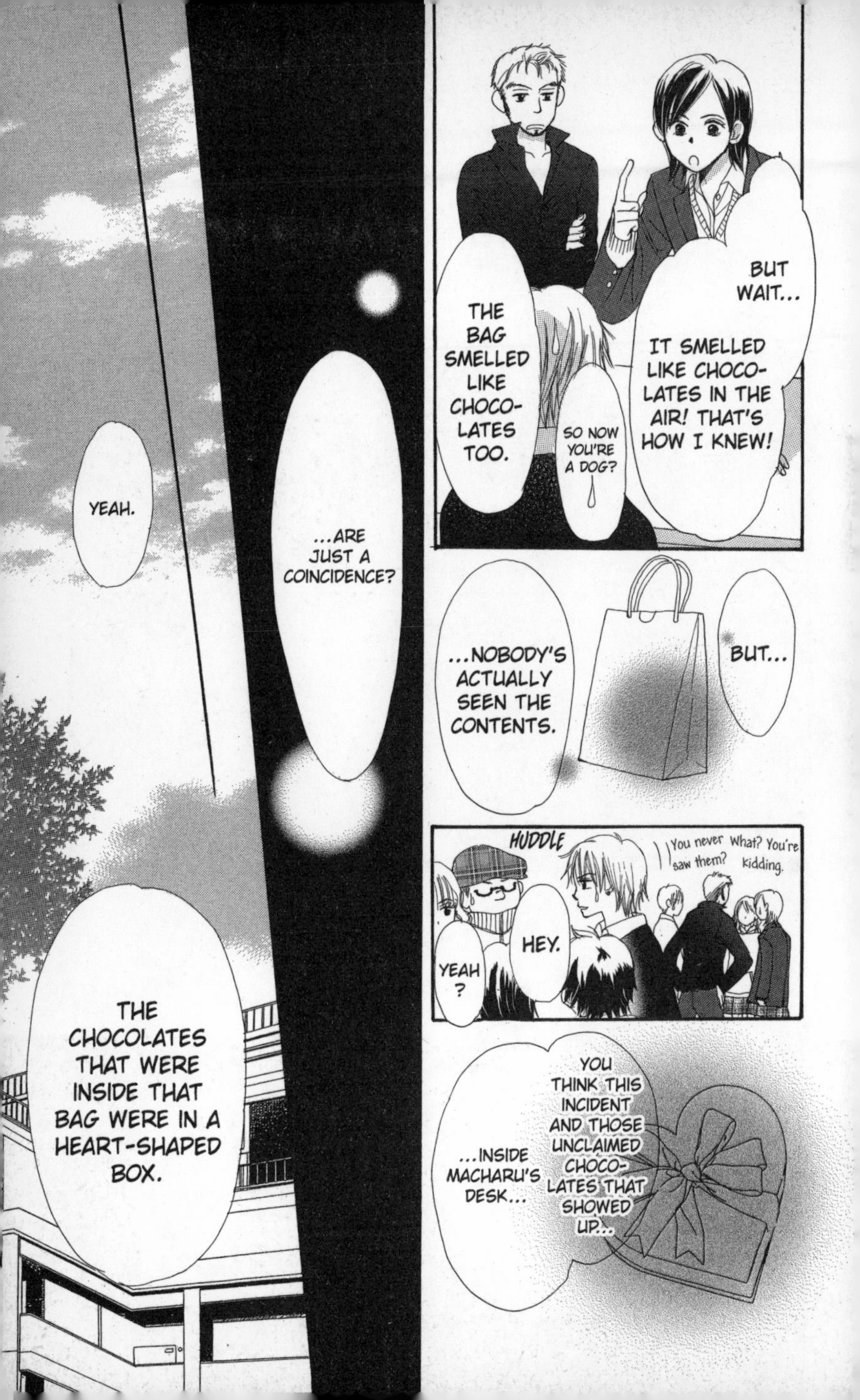
BUT WAIT...
IT SMELLED LIKE CHOCOLATES IN THE AIR! THAT'S HOW I KNEW!
SO NOW YOU'RE A DOG?
THE BAG SMELLED LIKE CHOCOLATES TOO.
BUT...
...NOBODY'S ACTUALLY SEEN THE CONTENTS.
HUDDLE
What? You're kidding.
You never saw them?
HEY.
YEAH?
YOU THINK THIS INCIDENT AND THOSE UNCLAIMED CHOCOLATES THAT SHOWED UP...
...INSIDE MACHARU'S DESK...
...ARE JUST A COINCIDENCE?
YEAH.
THE CHOCOLATES THAT WERE INSIDE THAT BAG WERE IN A HEART-SHAPED BOX.

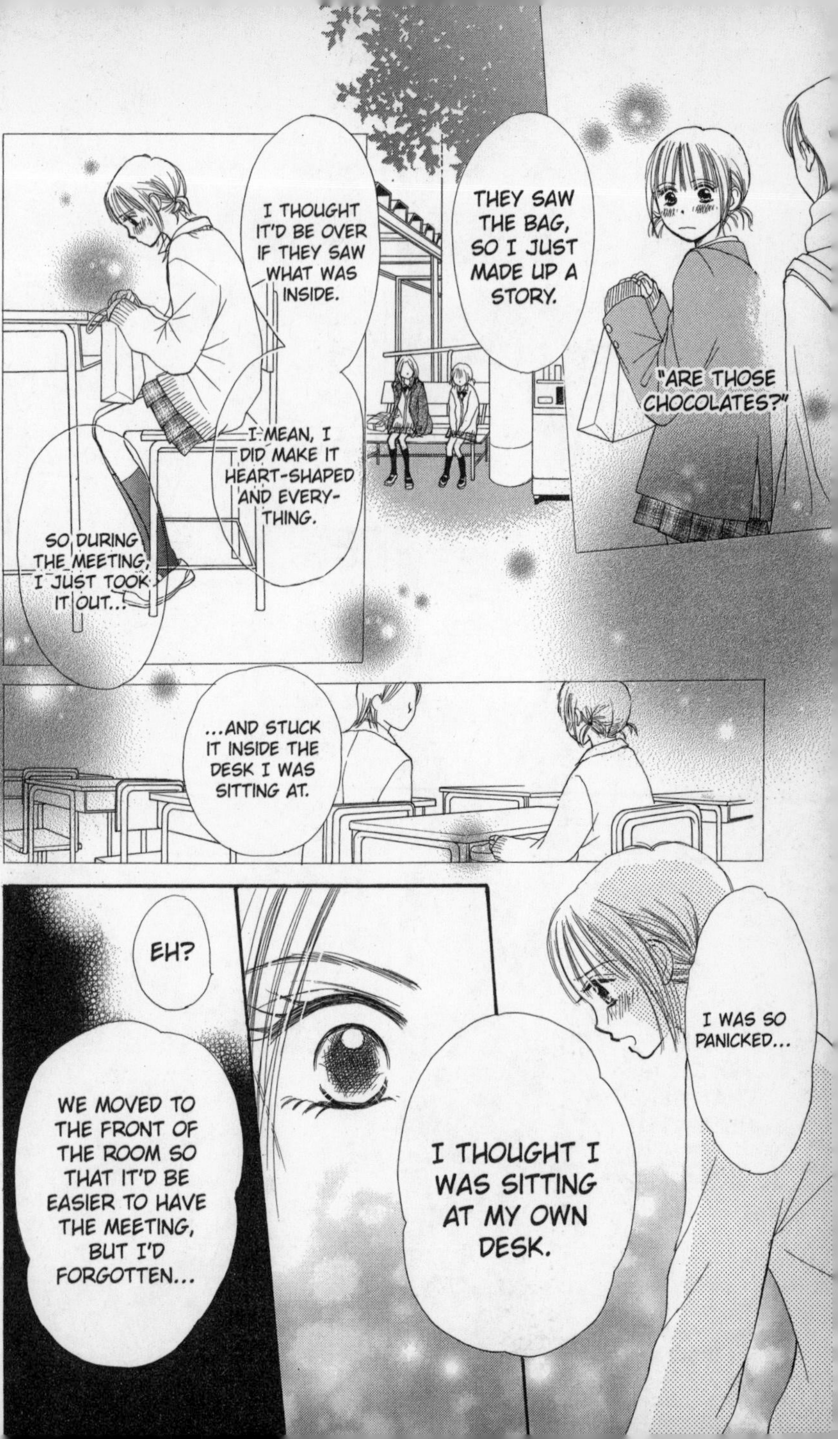
"ARE THOSE CHOCOLATES?"
THEY SAW THE BAG, SO I JUST MADE UP A STORY.
I THOUGHT IT'D BE OVER IF THEY SAW WHAT WAS INSIDE.
I MEAN, I DID MAKE IT HEART-SHAPED AND EVERY-THING.
SO DURING THE MEETING, I JUST TOOK IT OUT...
...AND STUCK IT INSIDE THE DESK I WAS SITTING AT.
I WAS SO PANICKED...
I THOUGHT I WAS SITTING AT MY OWN DESK.
EH?
WE MOVED TO THE FRONT OF THE ROOM SO THAT IT'D BE EASIER TO HAVE THE MEETING, BUT I'D FORGOTTEN...

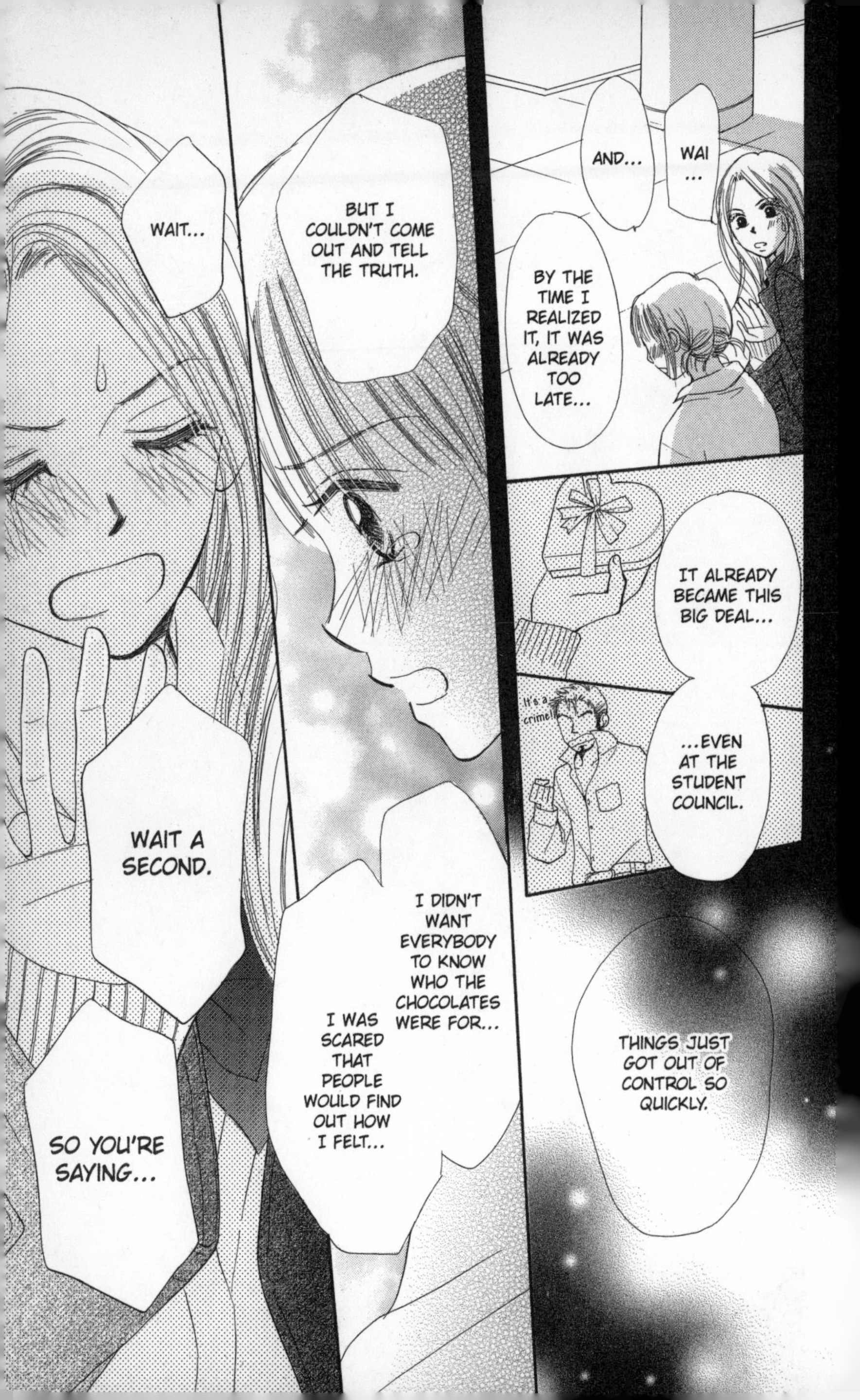
WAI...
AND...
BY THE TIME I REALIZED IT, IT WAS ALREADY TOO LATE...
IT ALREADY BECAME THIS BIG DEAL...
...EVEN AT THE STUDENT COUNCIL.
It's a crime!
THINGS JUST GOT OUT OF CONTROL SO QUICKLY.
BUT I COULDN'T COME OUT AND TELL THE TRUTH.
I DIDN'T WANT EVERYBODY TO KNOW WHO THE CHOCOLATES WERE FOR...
I WAS SCARED THAT PEOPLE WOULD FIND OUT HOW I FELT...
WAIT...
WAIT A SECOND.
SO YOU'RE SAYING...

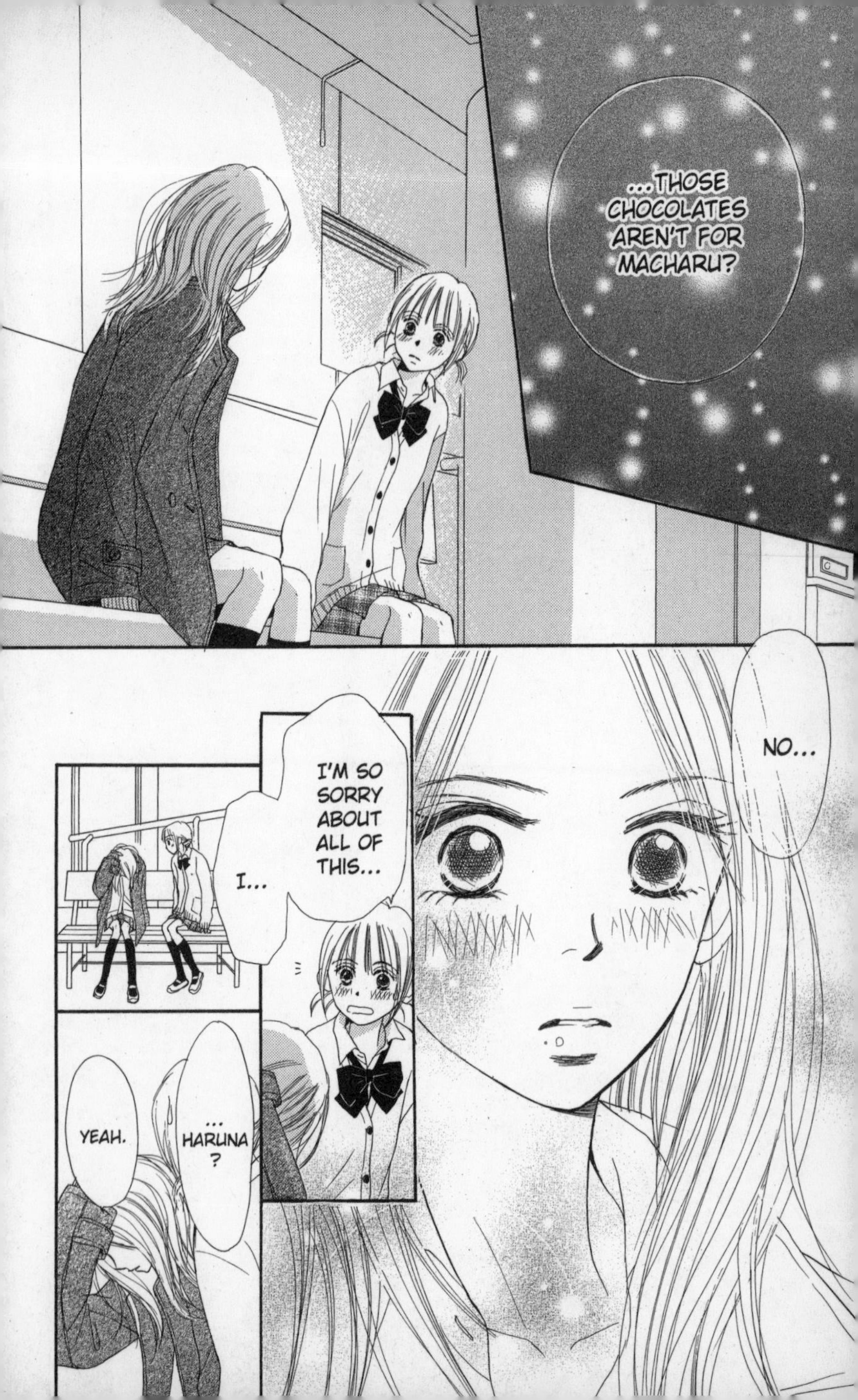
...THOSE CHOCOLATES AREN'T FOR MACHARU?
NO...
I'M SO SORRY ABOUT ALL OF THIS...
I...
...HARUNA?
YEAH.

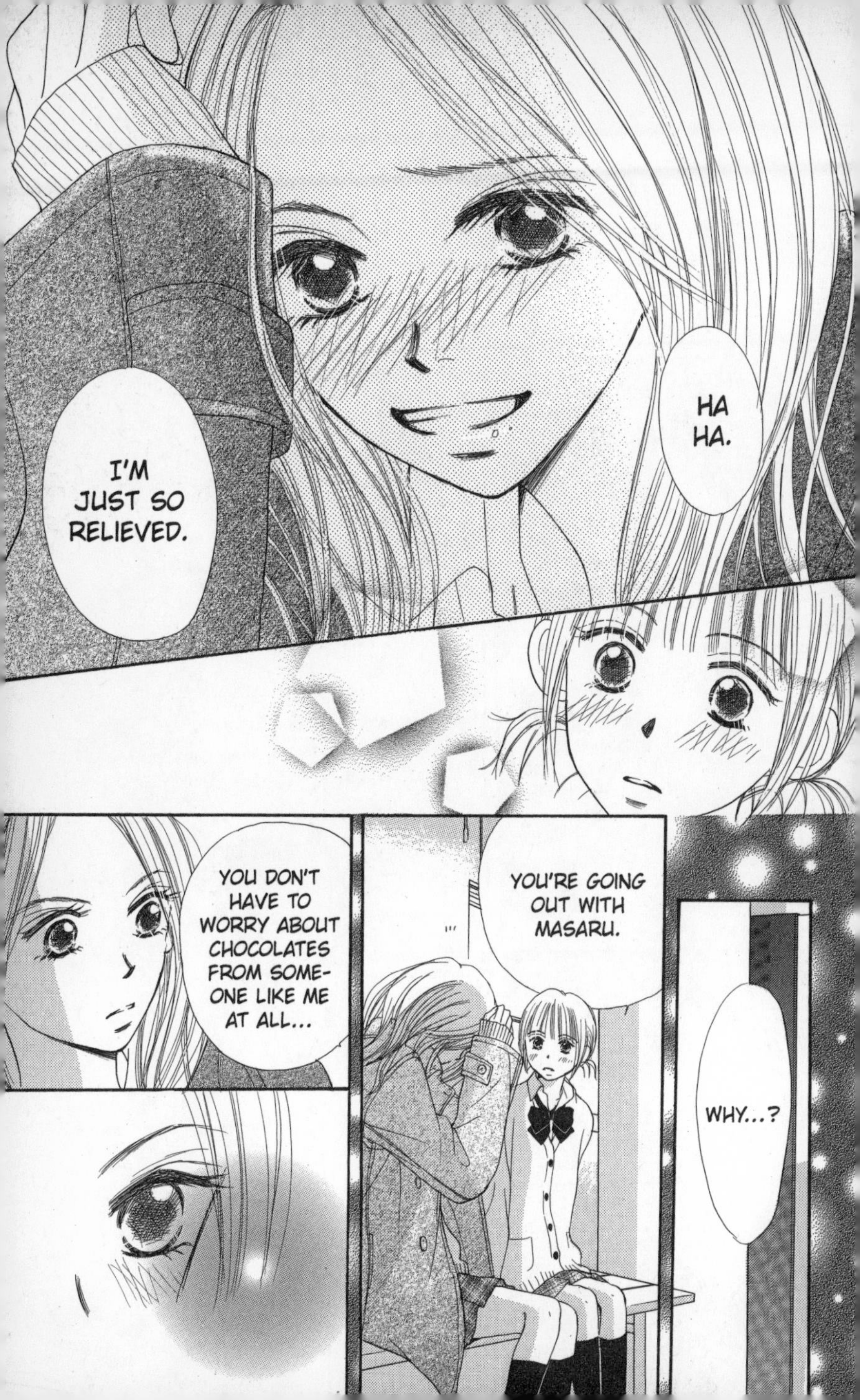
HA HA.
I'M JUST SO RELIEVED.
WHY...?
YOU'RE GOING OUT WITH MASARU.
YOU DON'T HAVE TO WORRY ABOUT CHOCOLATES FROM SOME- ONE LIKE ME AT ALL...

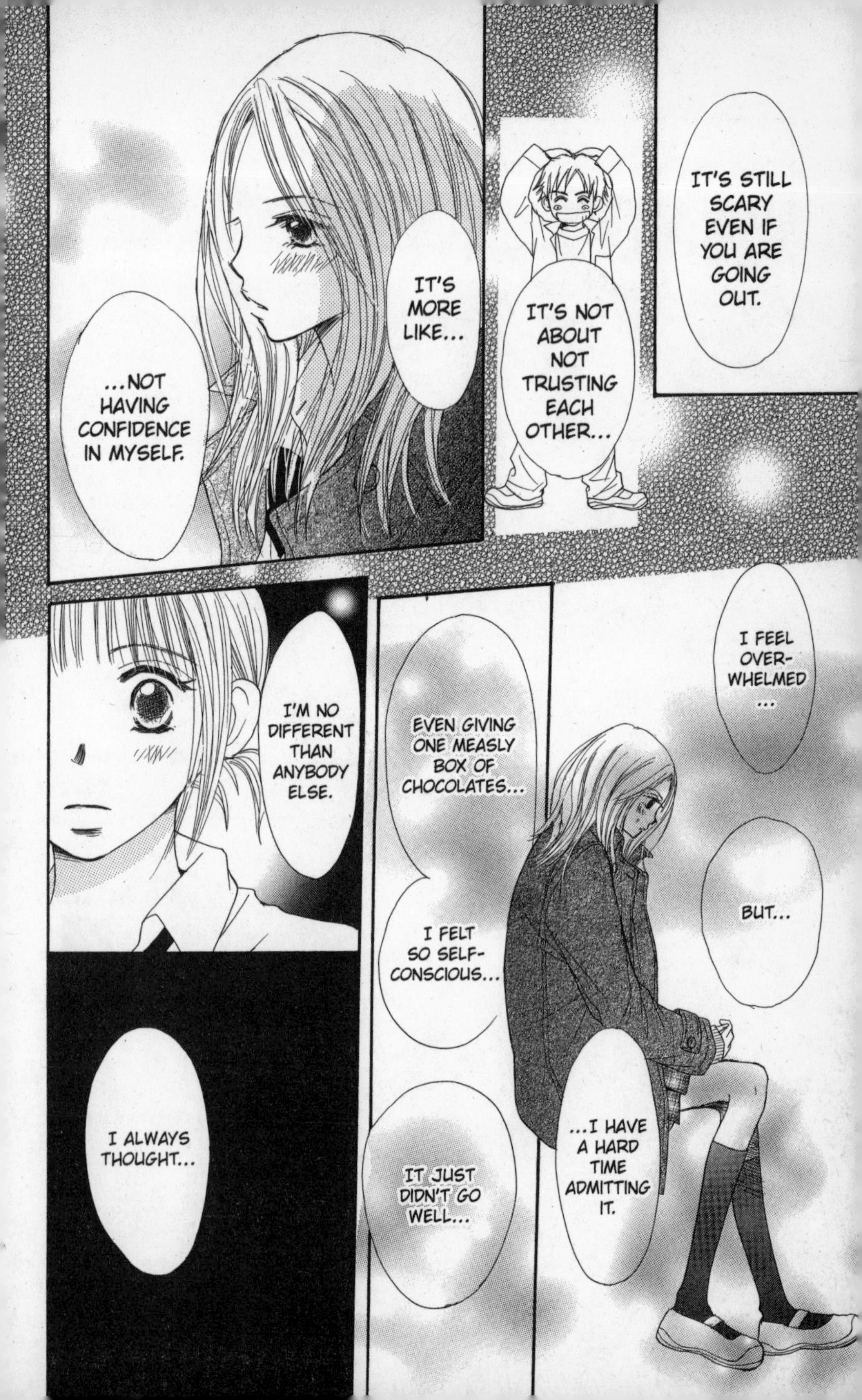
IT'S STILL SCARY EVEN IF YOU ARE GOING OUT.
IT'S NOT ABOUT NOT TRUSTING EACH OTHER...
IT'S MORE LIKE...
...NOT HAVING CONFIDENCE IN MYSELF.
I FEEL OVER-WHELMED...
EVEN GIVING ONE MEASLY BOX OF CHOCOLATES...
BUT...
I FELT SO SELF-CONSCIOUS...
...I HAVE A HARD TIME ADMITTING IT.
IT JUST DIDN'T GO WELL...
I'M NO DIFFERENT THAN ANYBODY ELSE.
I ALWAYS THOUGHT...

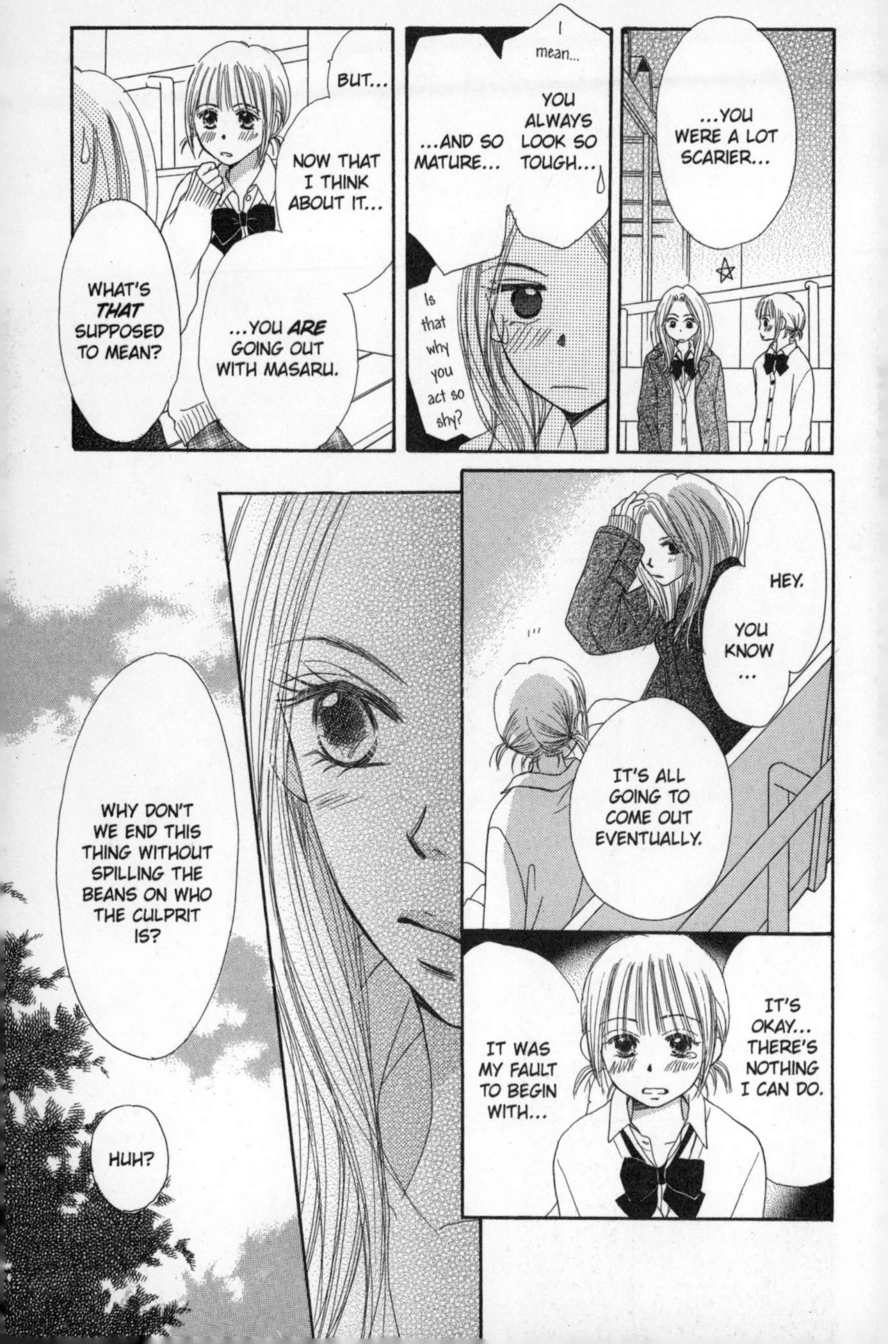
...YOU WERE A LOT SCARIER...
I mean...
YOU ALWAYS LOOK SO TOUGH...
...AND SO MATURE...
Is that why you act so shy?
BUT...
NOW THAT I THINK ABOUT IT...
...YOU *ARE* GOING OUT WITH MASARU.
WHAT'S *THAT* SUPPOSED TO MEAN?
HEY.
YOU KNOW ...
IT'S ALL GOING TO COME OUT EVENTUALLY.
IT'S OKAY... THERE'S NOTHING I CAN DO.
IT WAS MY FAULT TO BEGIN WITH...
WHY DON'T WE END THIS THING WITHOUT SPILLING THE BEANS ON WHO THE CULPRIT IS?
HUH?

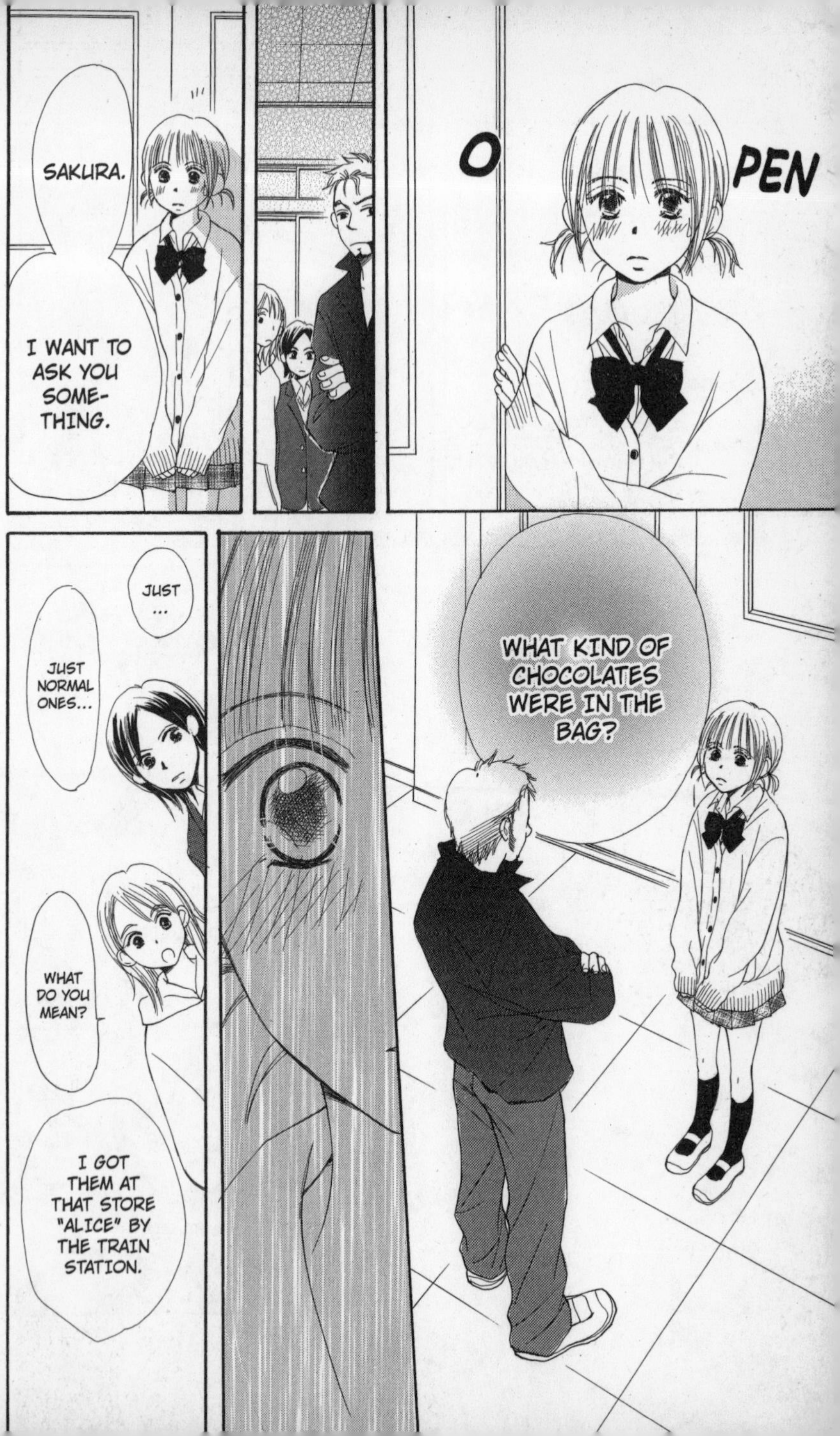
O
PEN
SAKURA.
I WANT TO ASK YOU SOME-THING.
WHAT KIND OF CHOCOLATES WERE IN THE BAG?
JUST ...
JUST NORMAL ONES...
WHAT DO YOU MEAN?
I GOT THEM AT THAT STORE "ALICE" BY THE TRAIN STATION.

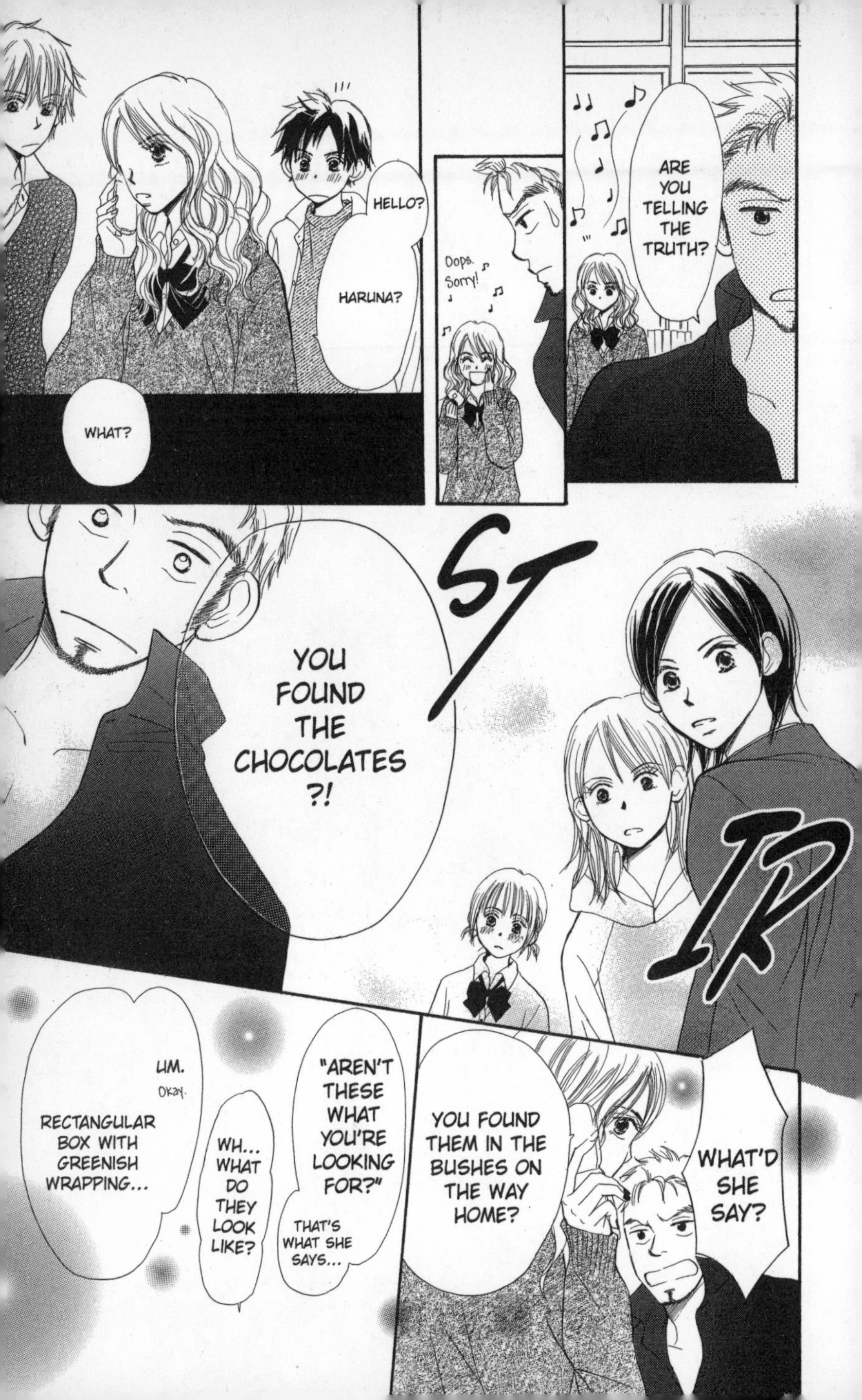
ARE YOU TELLING THE TRUTH?
Oops. Sorry!
HELLO?
HARUNA?
WHAT?
ST
IR
YOU FOUND THE CHOCOLATES?!
WHAT'D SHE SAY?
YOU FOUND THEM IN THE BUSHES ON THE WAY HOME?
"AREN'T THESE WHAT YOU'RE LOOKING FOR?"
THAT'S WHAT SHE SAYS...
WH... WHAT DO THEY LOOK LIKE?
UM.
Okay.
RECTANGULAR BOX WITH GREENISH WRAPPING...

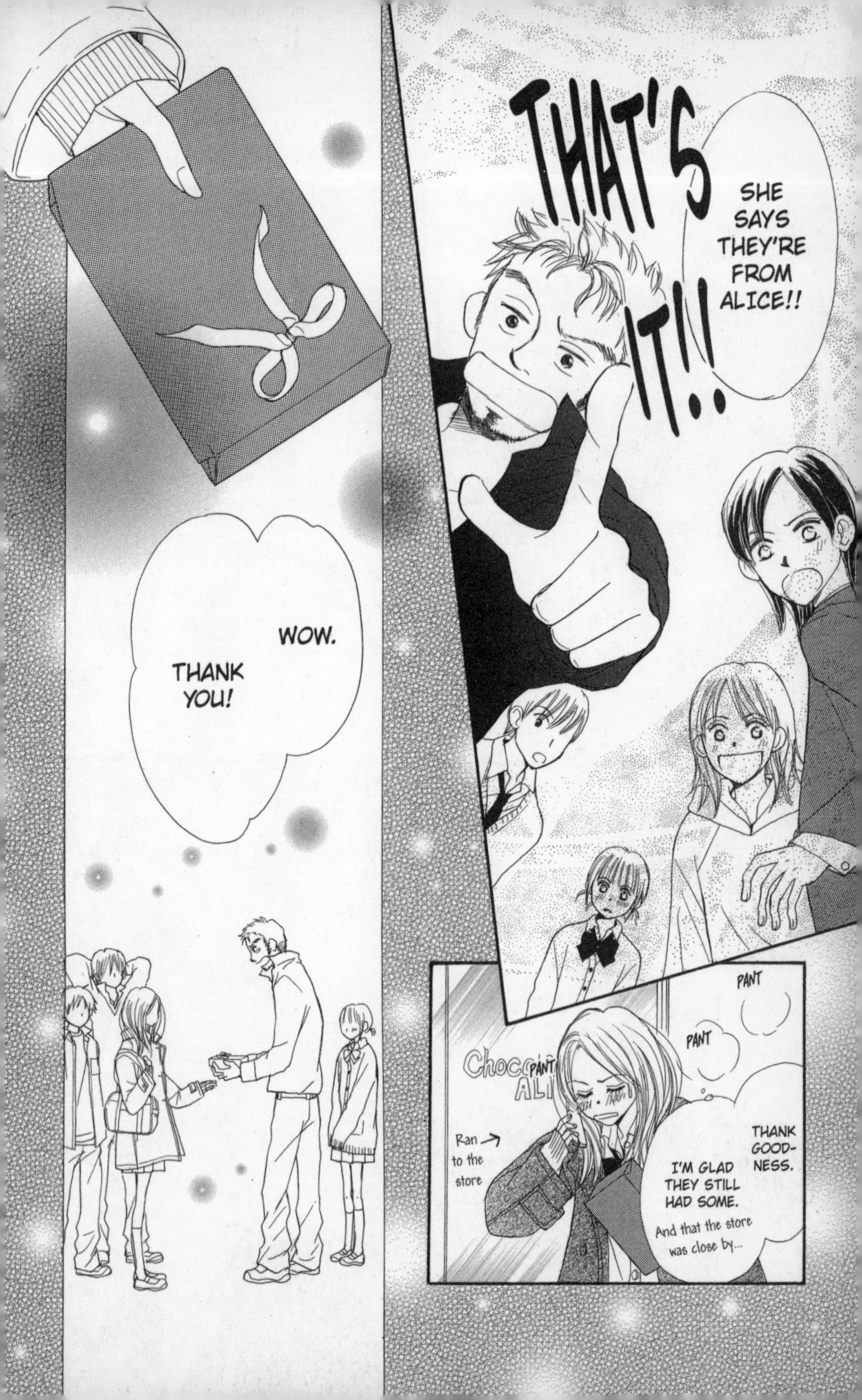
SHE SAYS THEY'RE FROM ALICE!!
THAT'S IT!!
PANT
PANT
PANT
Choc
ALI
THANK GOODNESS.
I'M GLAD THEY STILL HAD SOME.
And that the store was close by...
Ran → to the store
WOW.
THANK YOU!

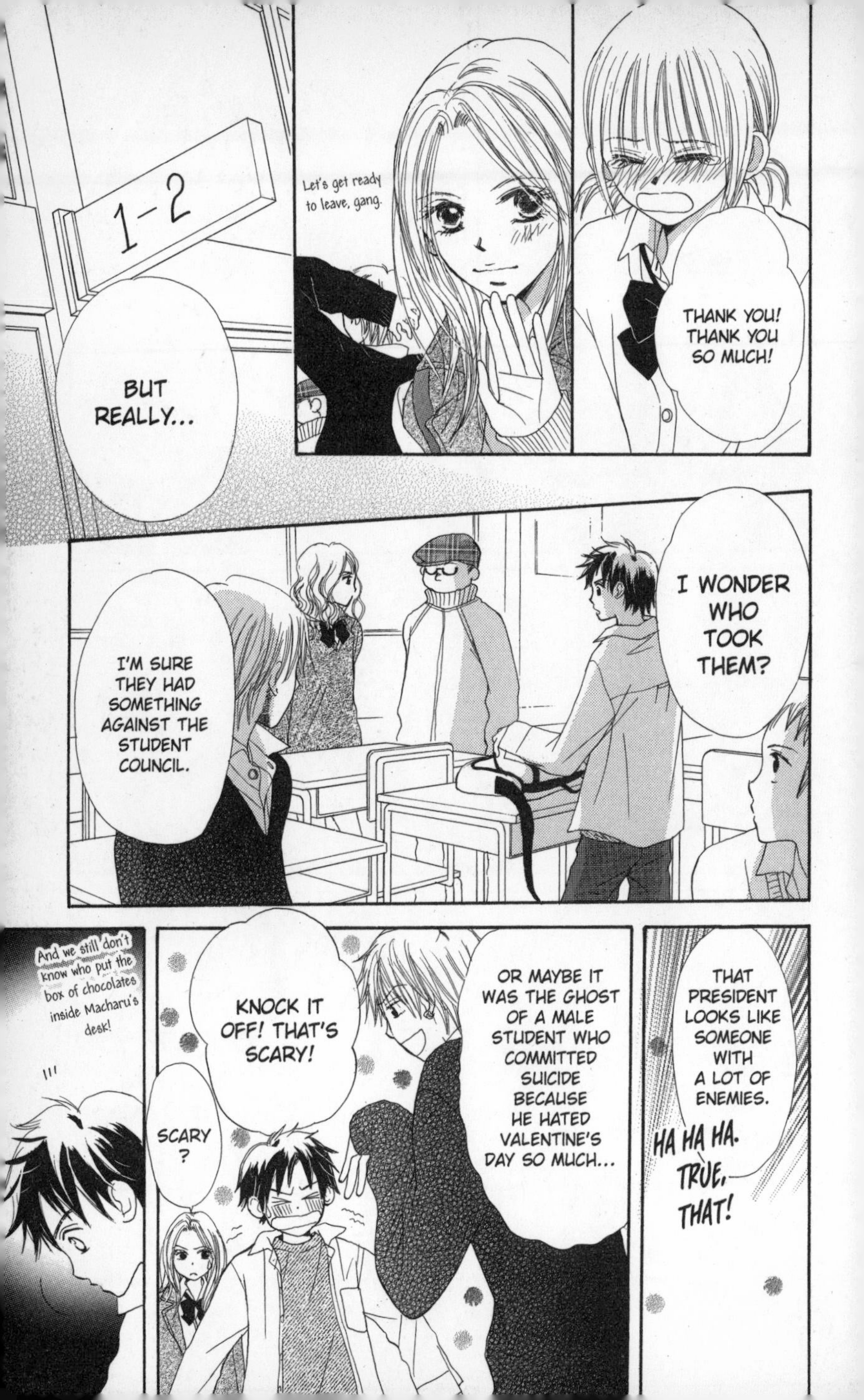
THANK YOU! THANK YOU SO MUCH!
Let's get ready to leave, gang.
1-2
BUT REALLY...
I WONDER WHO TOOK THEM?
I'M SURE THEY HAD SOMETHING AGAINST THE STUDENT COUNCIL.
THAT PRESIDENT LOOKS LIKE SOMEONE WITH A LOT OF ENEMIES.
HA HA HA. TRUE, THAT!
OR MAYBE IT WAS THE GHOST OF A MALE STUDENT WHO COMMITTED SUICIDE BECAUSE HE HATED VALENTINE'S DAY SO MUCH...
KNOCK IT OFF! THAT'S SCARY!
SCARY?
And we still don't know who put the box of chocolates inside Macharu's desk!

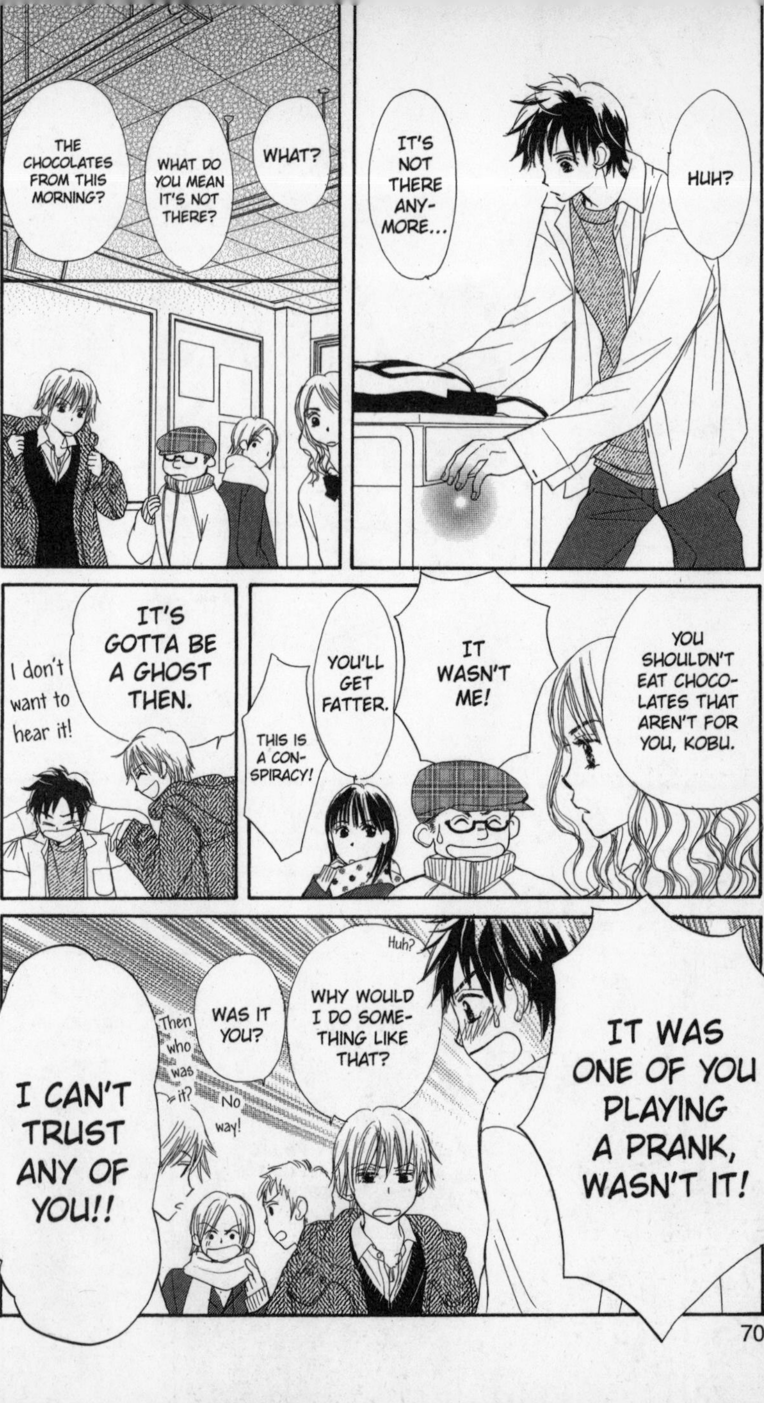
HUH?
IT'S NOT THERE ANYMORE...
WHAT?
WHAT DO YOU MEAN IT'S NOT THERE?
THE CHOCOLATES FROM THIS MORNING?
YOU SHOULDN'T EAT CHOCOLATES THAT AREN'T FOR YOU, KOBU.
IT WASN'T ME!
YOU'LL GET FATTER.
THIS IS A CONSPIRACY!
IT'S GOTTA BE A GHOST THEN.
I don't want to hear it!
IT WAS ONE OF YOU PLAYING A PRANK, WASN'T IT!
Huh?
WHY WOULD I DO SOMETHING LIKE THAT?
WAS IT YOU?
Then who was it?
No way!
I CAN'T TRUST ANY OF YOU!!

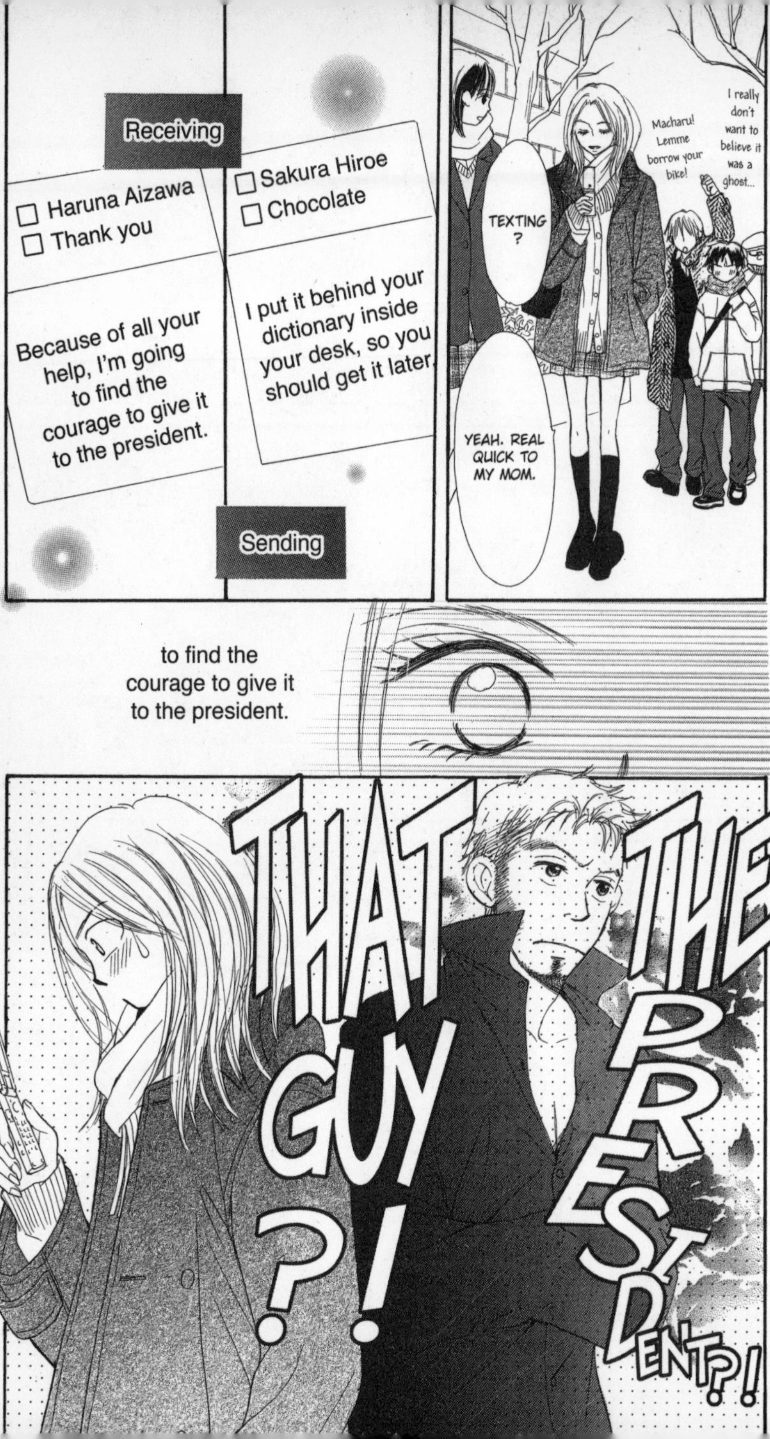

I really don't want to believe it was a ghost...
Macharu! Lemme borrow your bike!
TEXTING?
YEAH. REAL QUICK TO MY MOM.
Sakura Hiroe
Chocolate
I put it behind your dictionary inside your desk, so you should get it later.
Sending
Receiving
Haruna Aizawa
Thank you
Because of all your help, I'm going to find the courage to give it to the president.
to find the courage to give it to the president.
THE PRESIDENT?!
THAT GUY?!

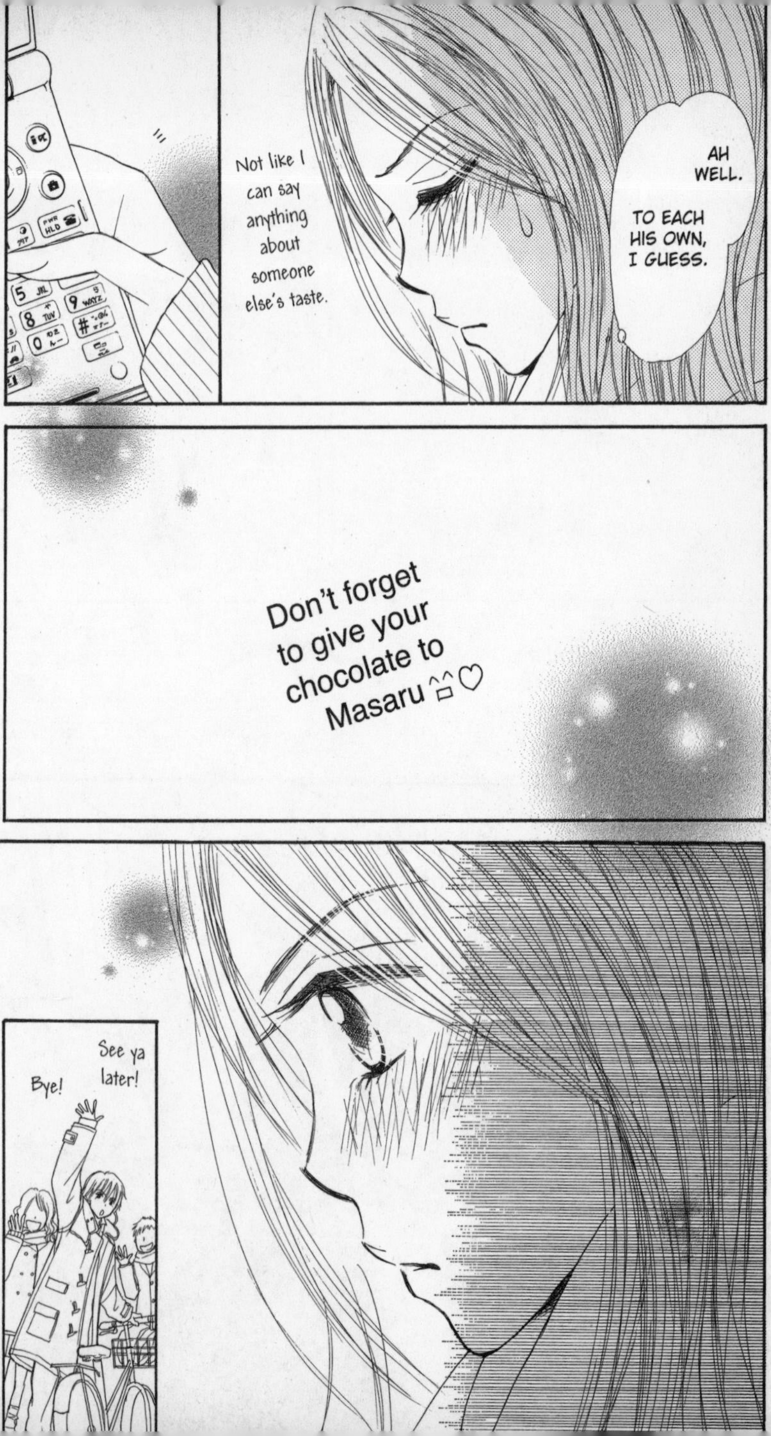
AH WELL.
TO EACH HIS OWN, I GUESS.
Not like I can say anything about someone else's taste.
Don't forget to give your chocolate to Masaru ^^♡
See ya later!
Bye!

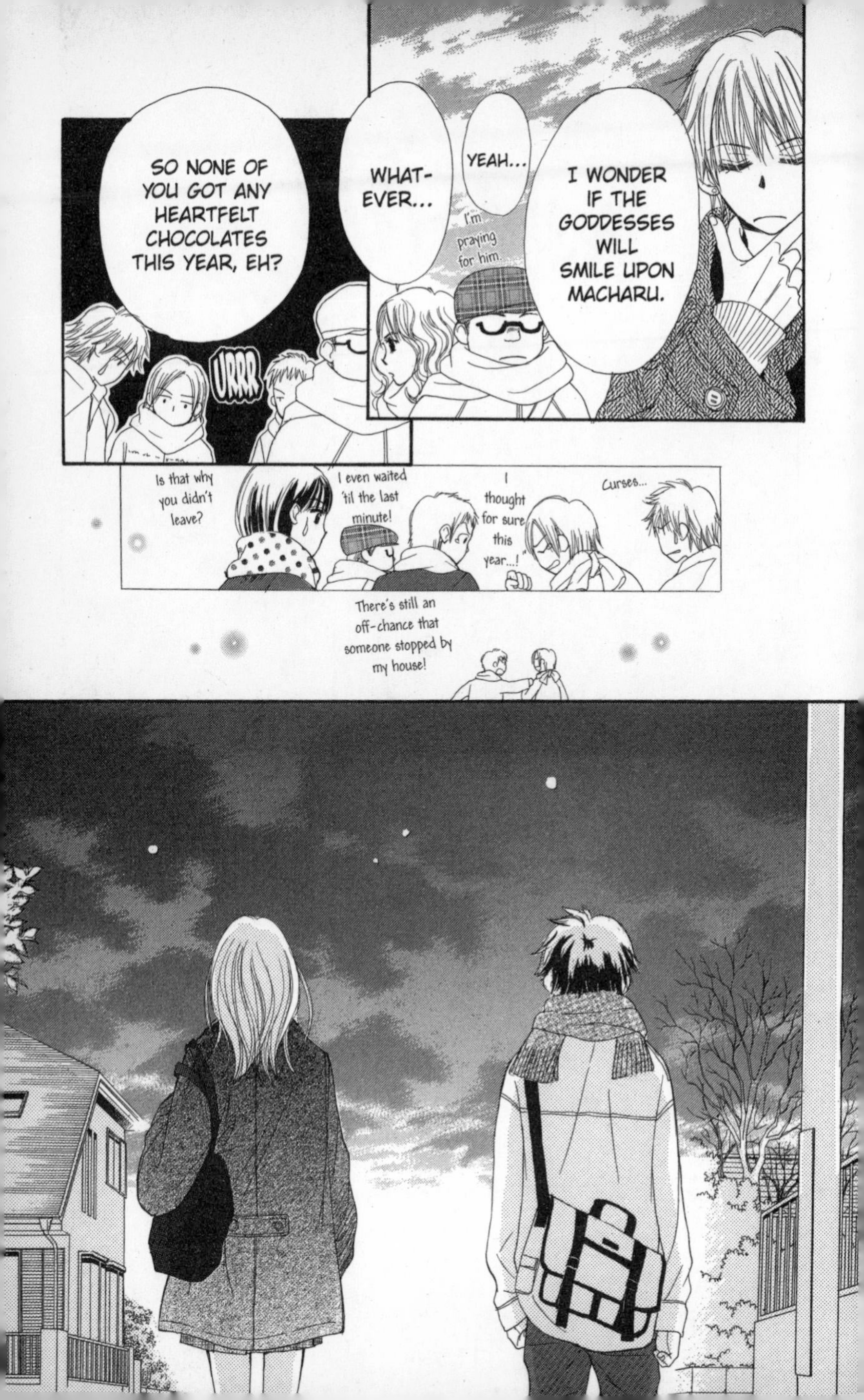
I WONDER IF THE GODDESSES WILL SMILE UPON MACHARU.
YEAH...
I'm praying for him.
WHAT-EVER...
SO NONE OF YOU GOT ANY HEARTFELT CHOCOLATES THIS YEAR, EH?
URRR
Curses...
I thought for sure this year...!
I even waited 'til the last minute!
Is that why you didn't leave?
There's still an off-chance that someone stopped by my house!

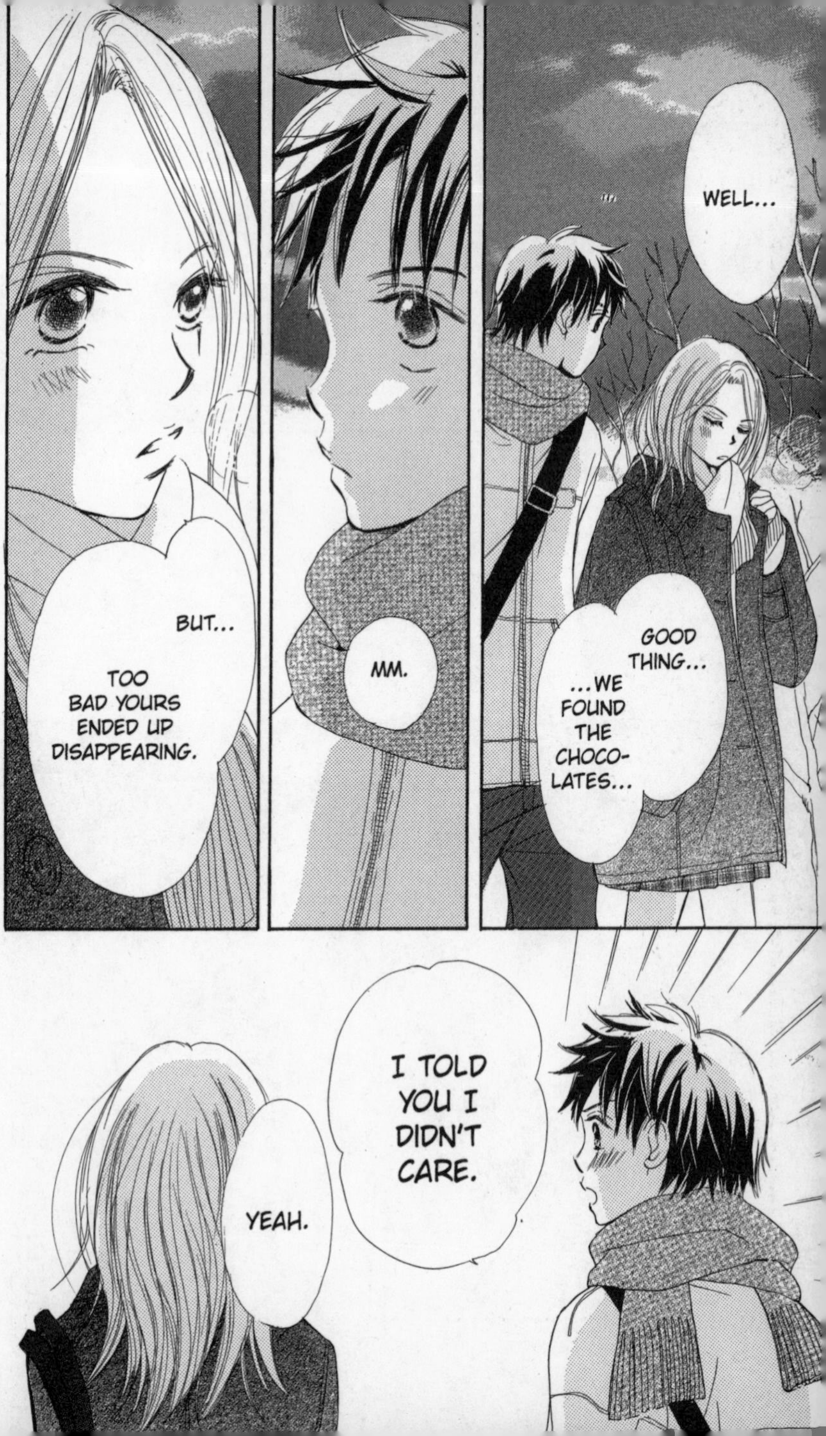
WELL...
GOOD THING...
...WE FOUND THE CHOCOLATES...
MM.
BUT...
TOO BAD YOURS ENDED UP DISAPPEARING.
I TOLD YOU I DIDN'T CARE.
YEAH.

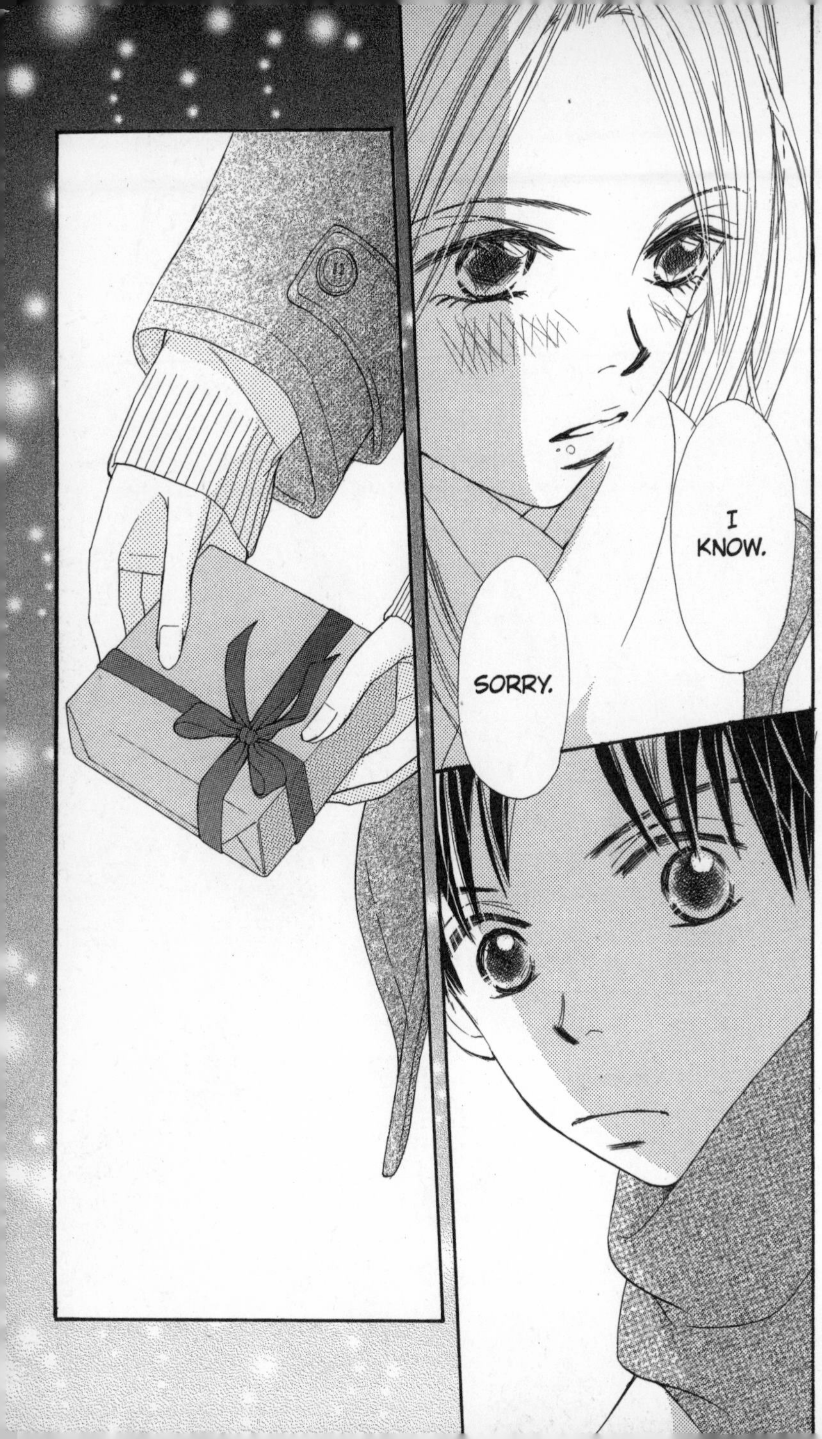
I KNOW.
SORRY.

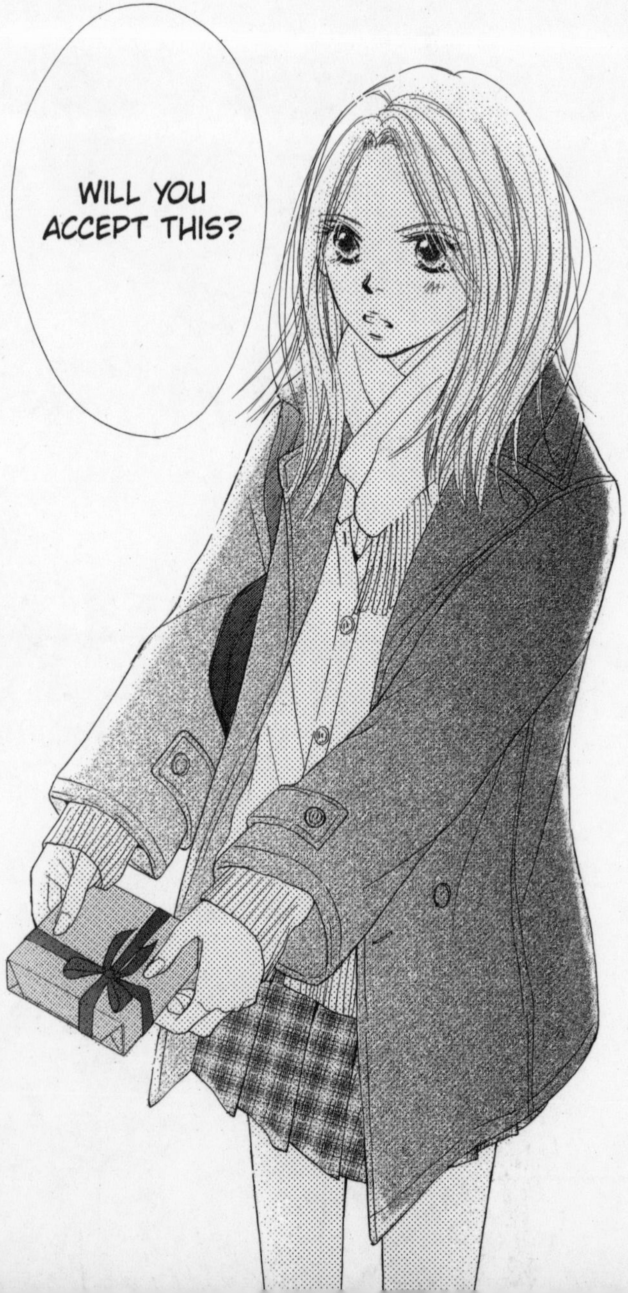
WILL YOU ACCEPT THIS?

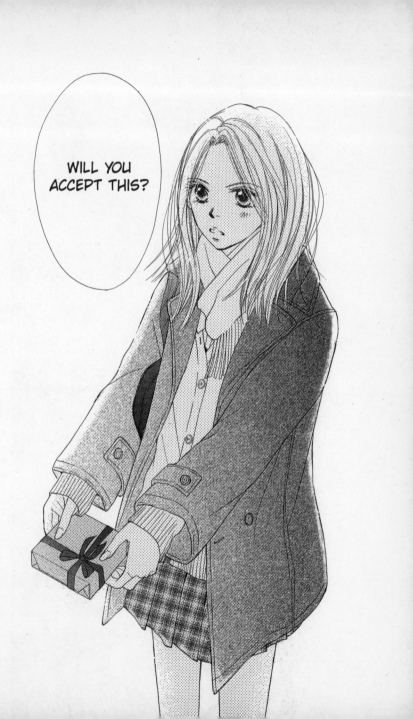

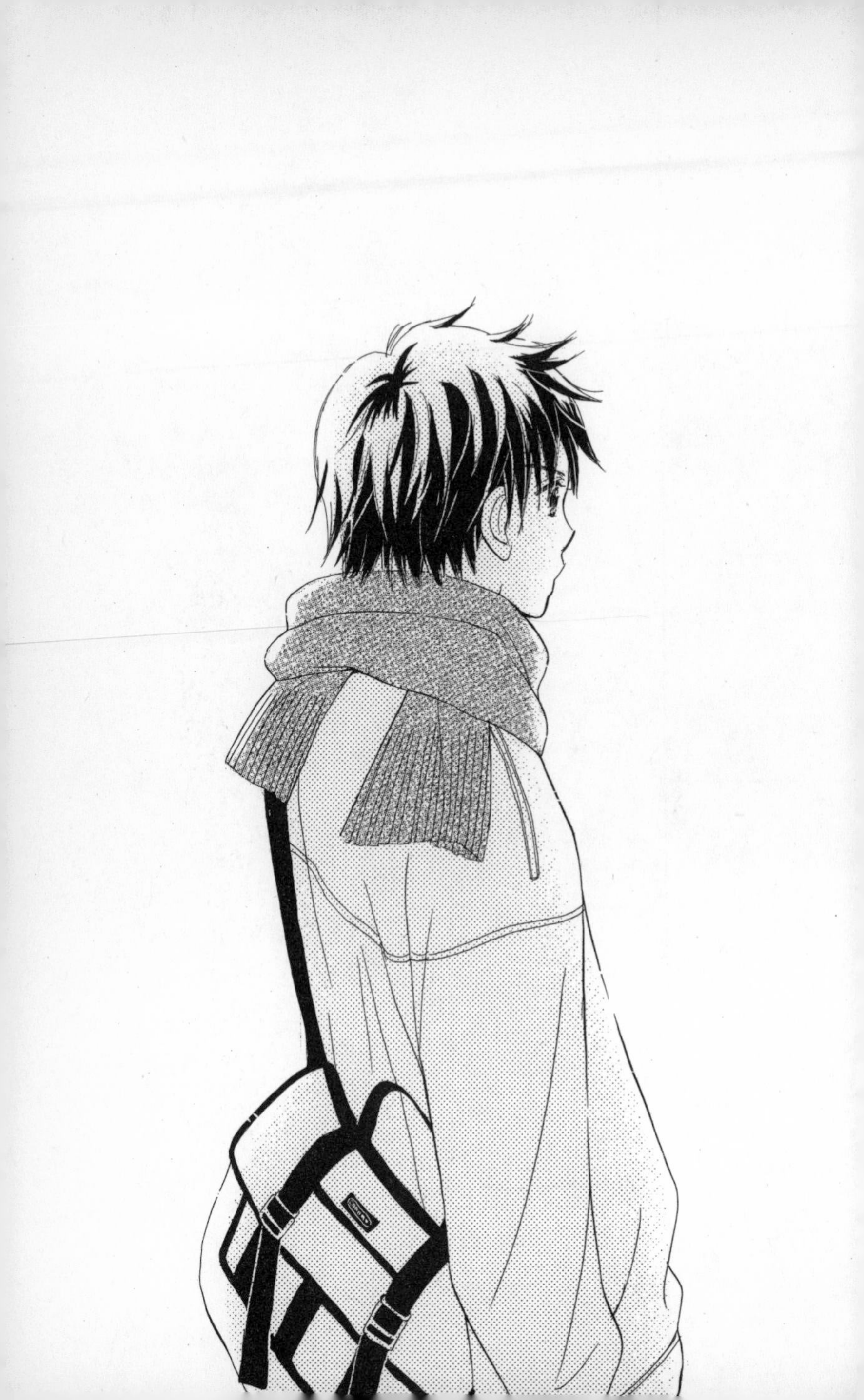

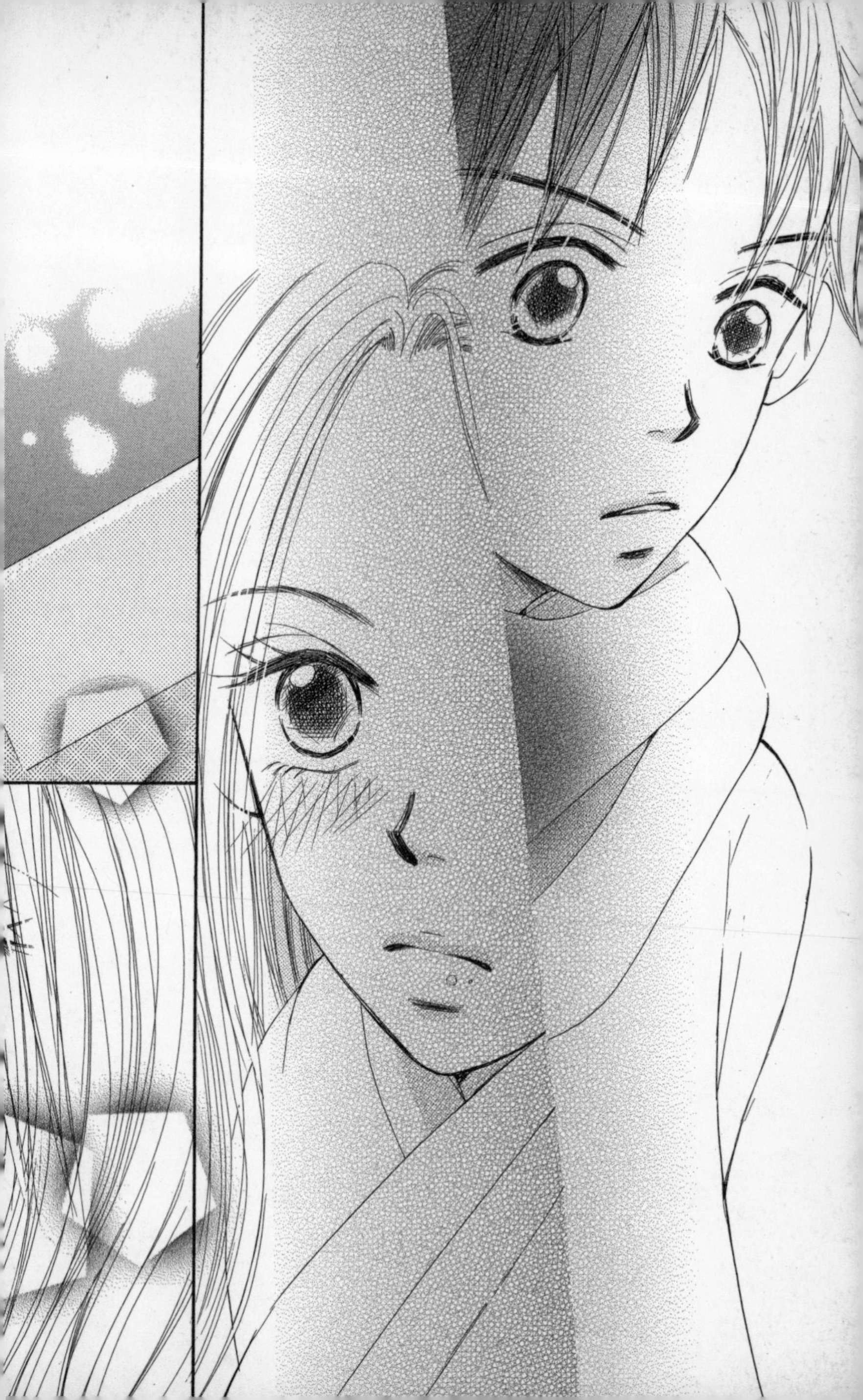

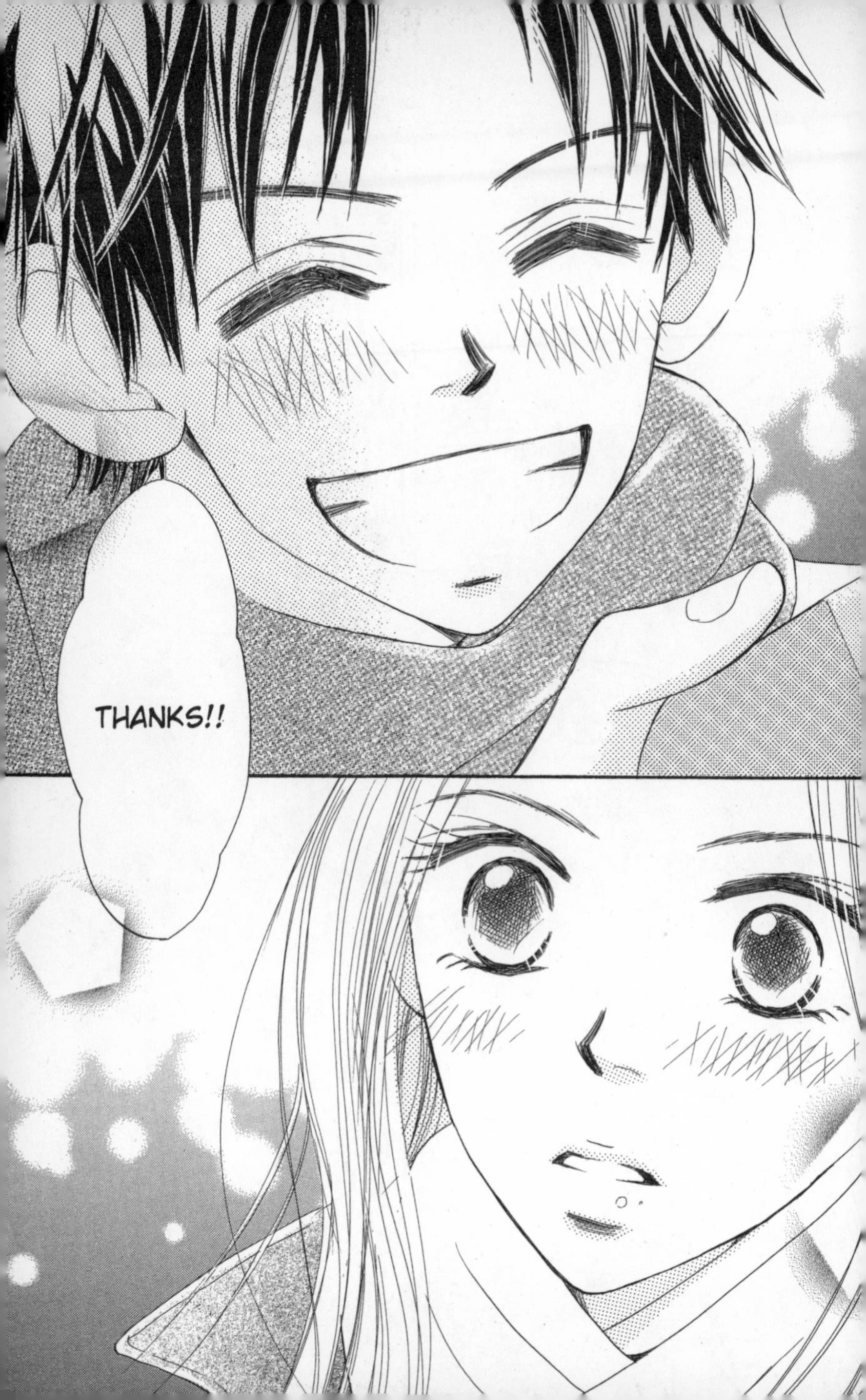
THANKS!!

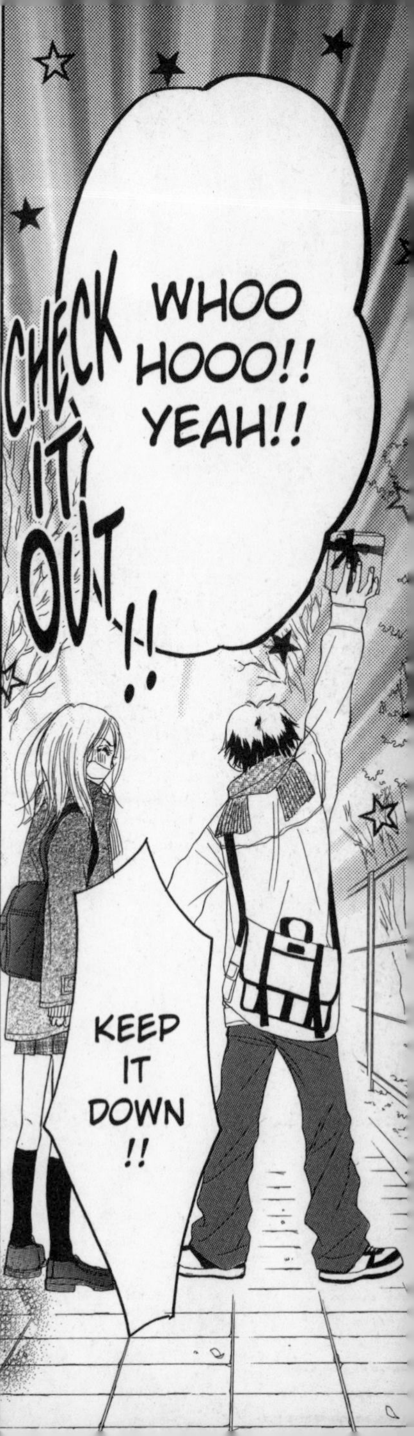
WHOO HOOO!! YEAH!!
CHECK IT OUT!!
KEEP IT DOWN!!

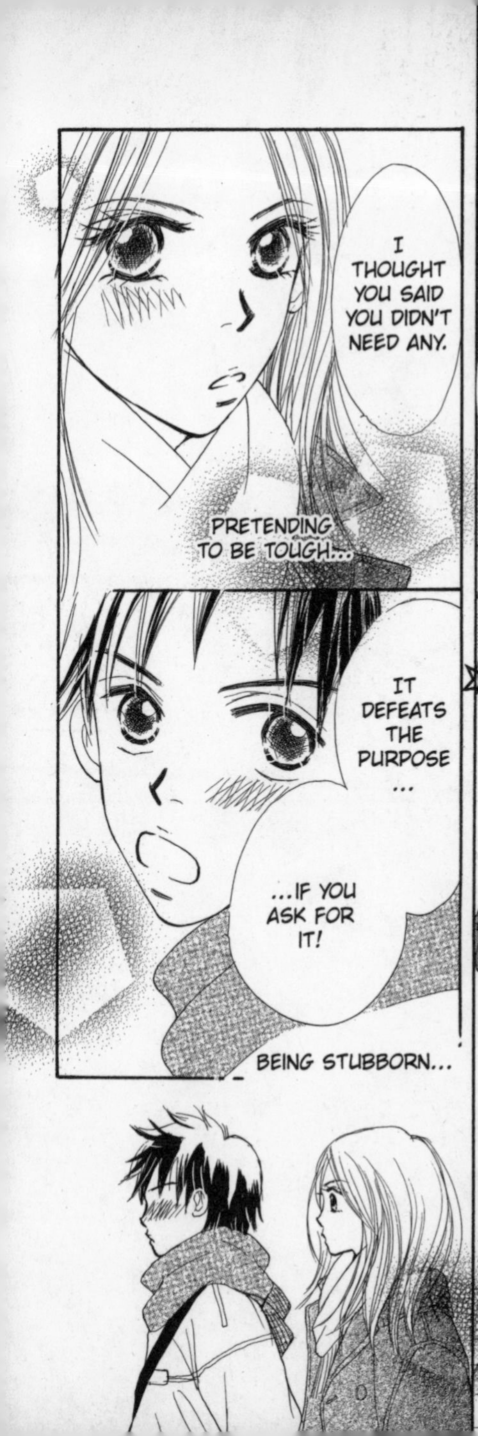
I THOUGHT YOU SAID YOU DIDN'T NEED ANY.
PRETENDING TO BE TOUGH...
IT DEFEATS THE PURPOSE...
...IF YOU ASK FOR IT!
BEING STUBBORN...

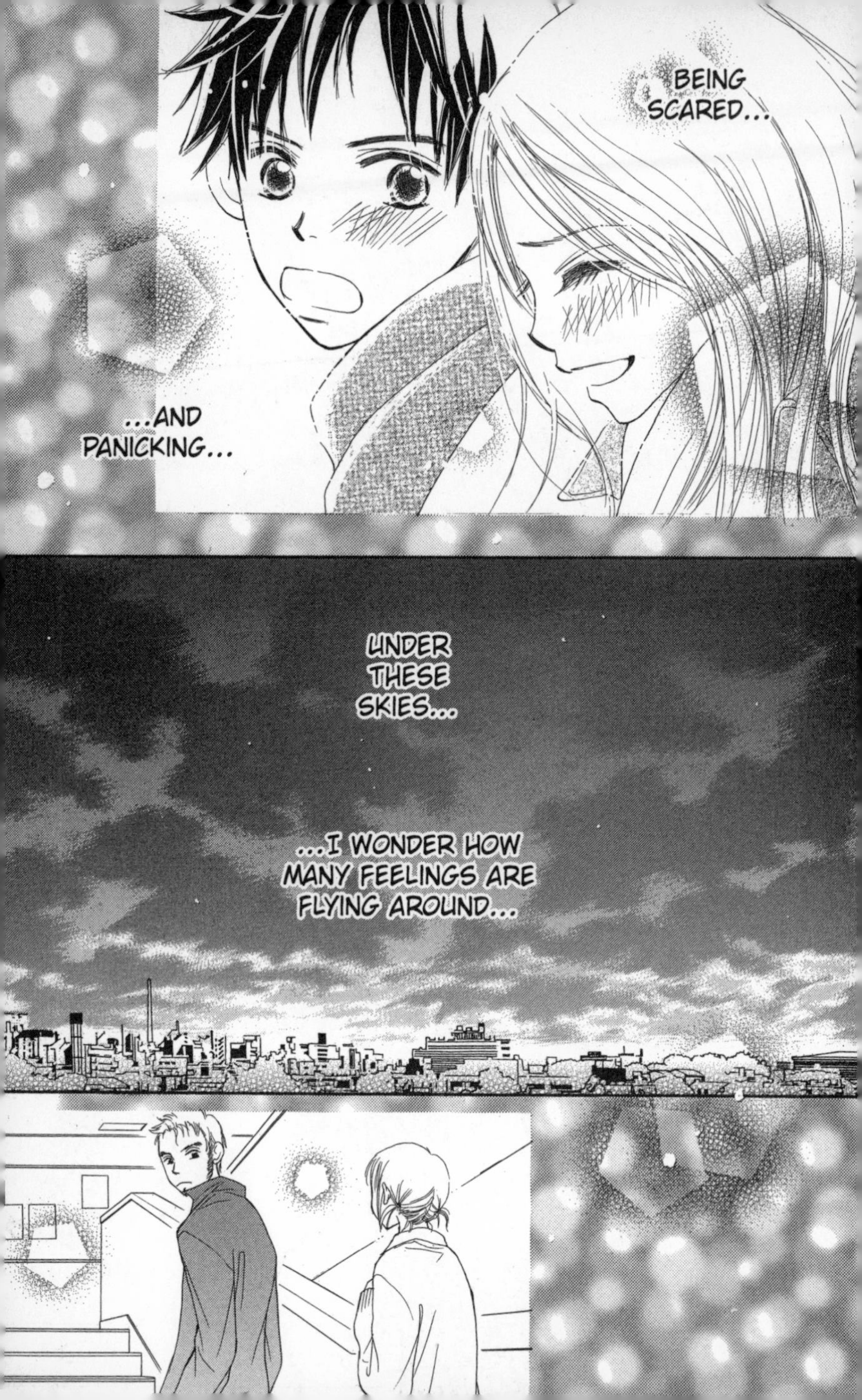
BEING SCARED...
...AND PANICKING...
UNDER THESE SKIES...
...I WONDER HOW MANY FEELINGS ARE FLYING AROUND...

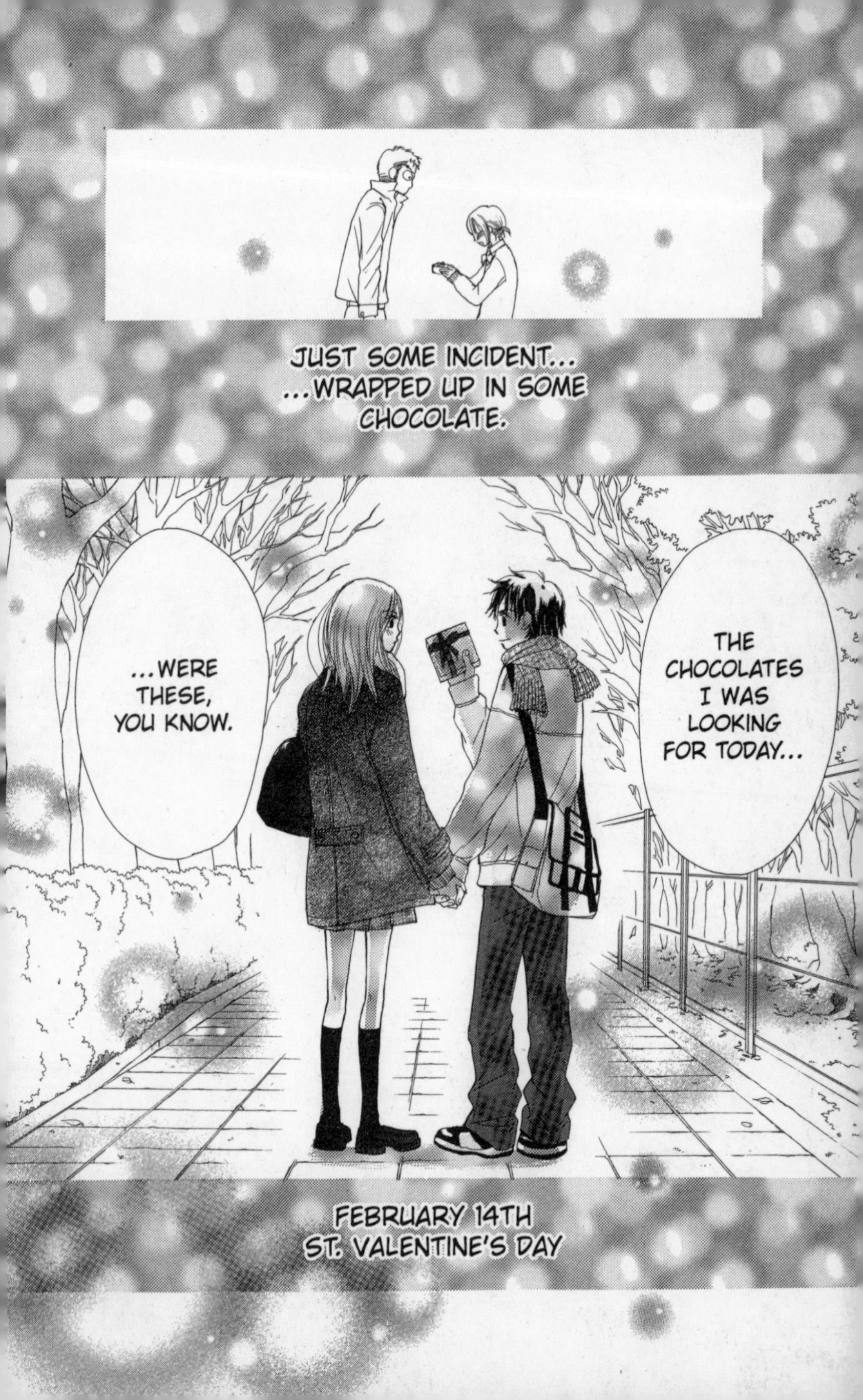
JUST SOME INCIDENT...
...WRAPPED UP IN SOME CHOCOLATE.
THE CHOCOLATES I WAS LOOKING FOR TODAY...
...WERE THESE, YOU KNOW.
FEBRUARY 14TH
ST. VALENTINE'S DAY

HAPPY BIRTHDAY

IN THIS WORLD THAT RESEMBLES A MONKEY MOUNTAIN, COUNTLESS FEELINGS COME TO LIGHT...

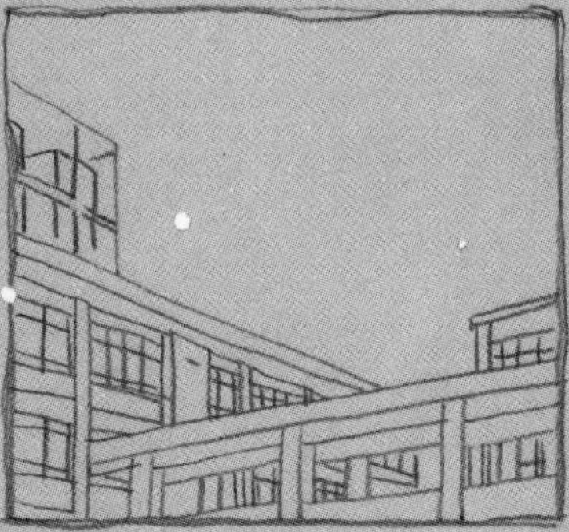

EVERY SINGLE DAY...

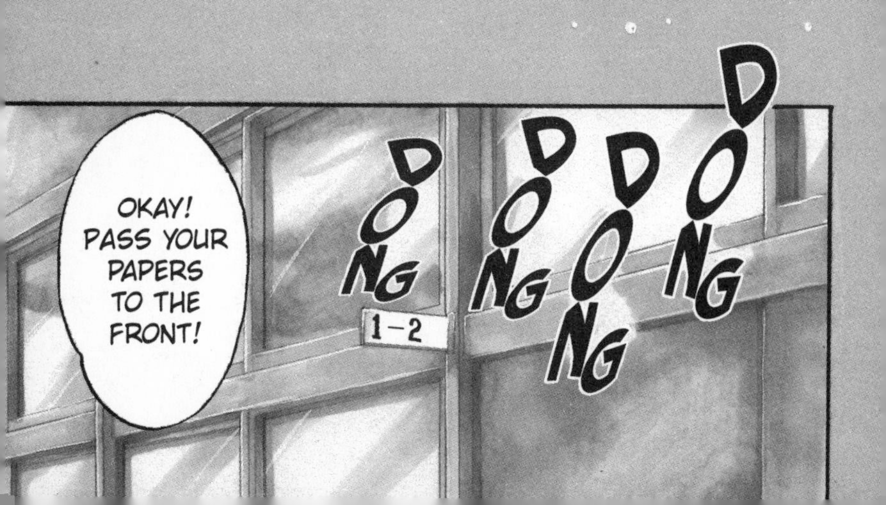
DONG DONG DONG DONG
1-2
OKAY! PASS YOUR PAPERS TO THE FRONT!

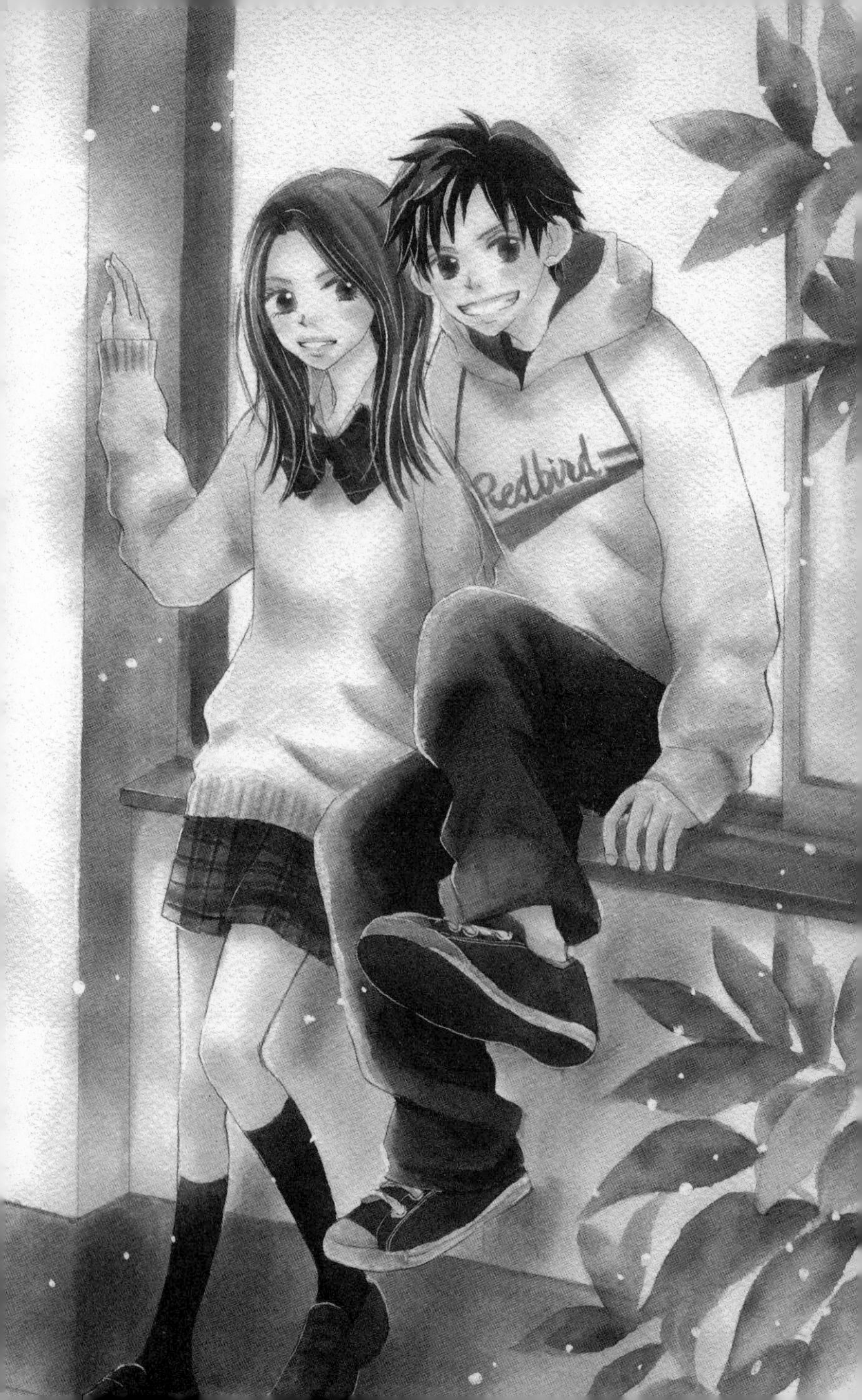
Redbird

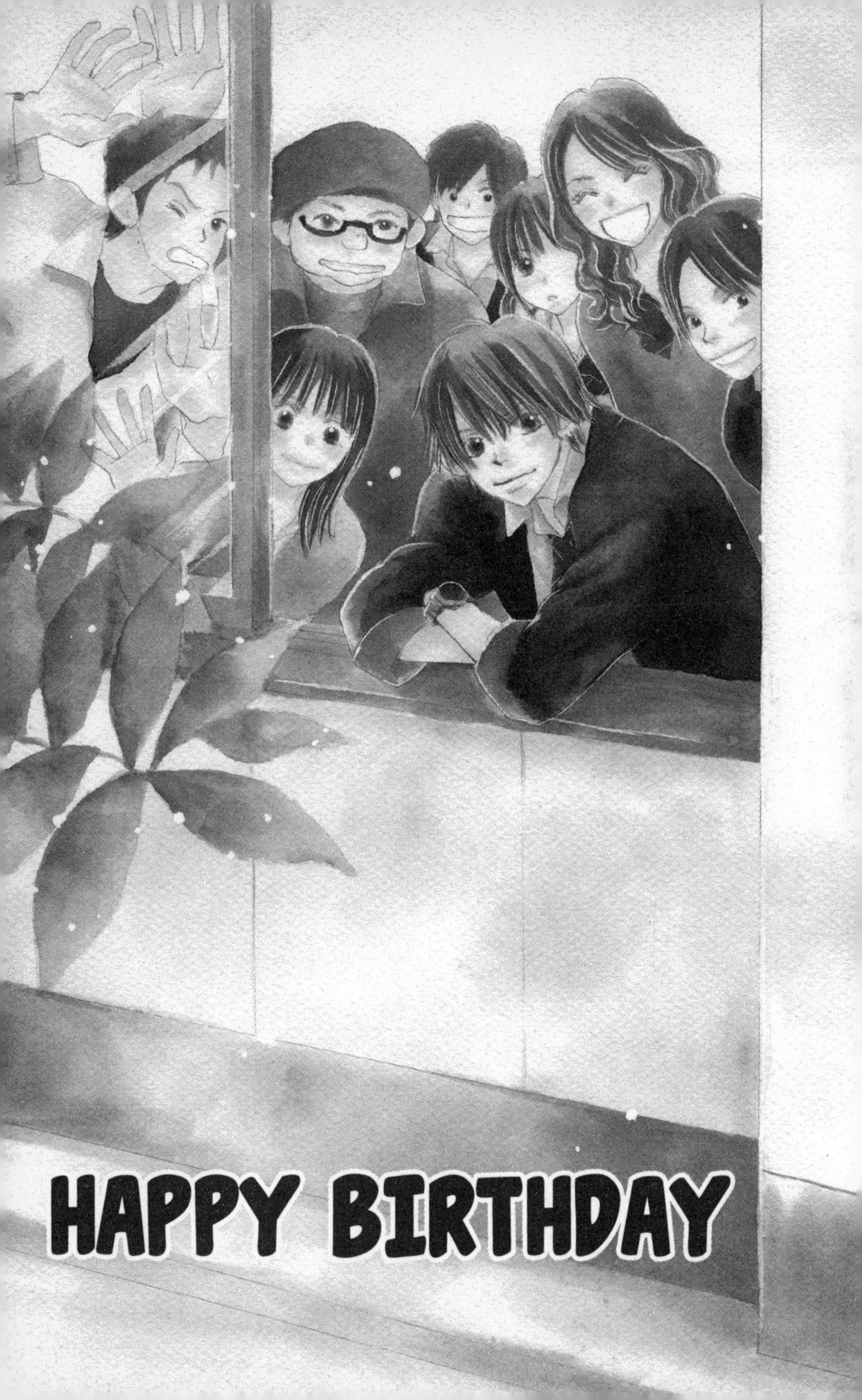
HAPPY BIRTHDAY

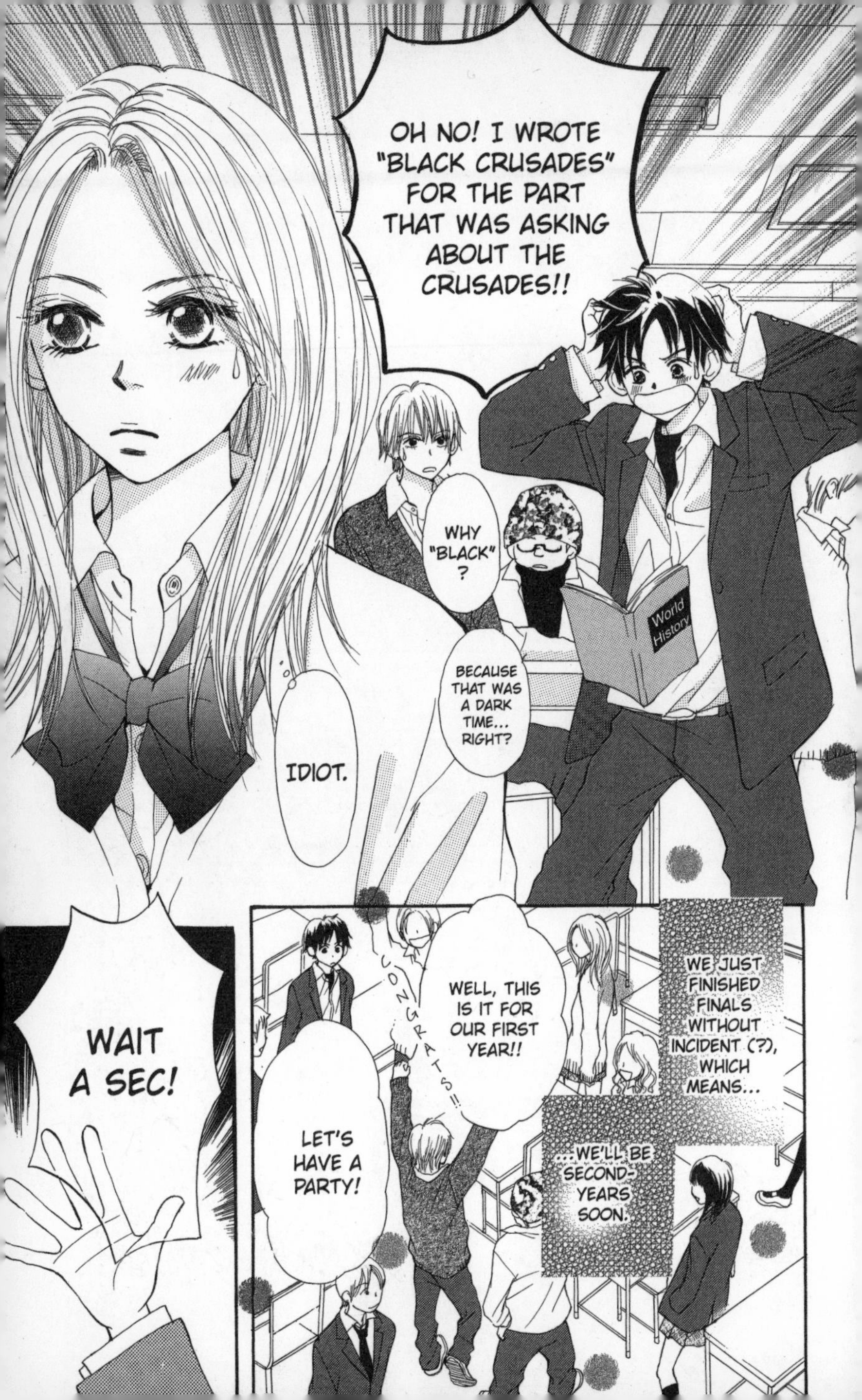
OH NO! I WROTE "BLACK CRUSADES" FOR THE PART THAT WAS ASKING ABOUT THE CRUSADES!!
WHY "BLACK"?
BECAUSE THAT WAS A DARK TIME... RIGHT?
IDIOT.
WE JUST FINISHED FINALS WITHOUT INCIDENT (?), WHICH MEANS...
...WE'LL BE SECOND-YEARS SOON.
WELL, THIS IS IT FOR OUR FIRST YEAR!!
CONGRATS!!
LET'S HAVE A PARTY!
WAIT A SEC!

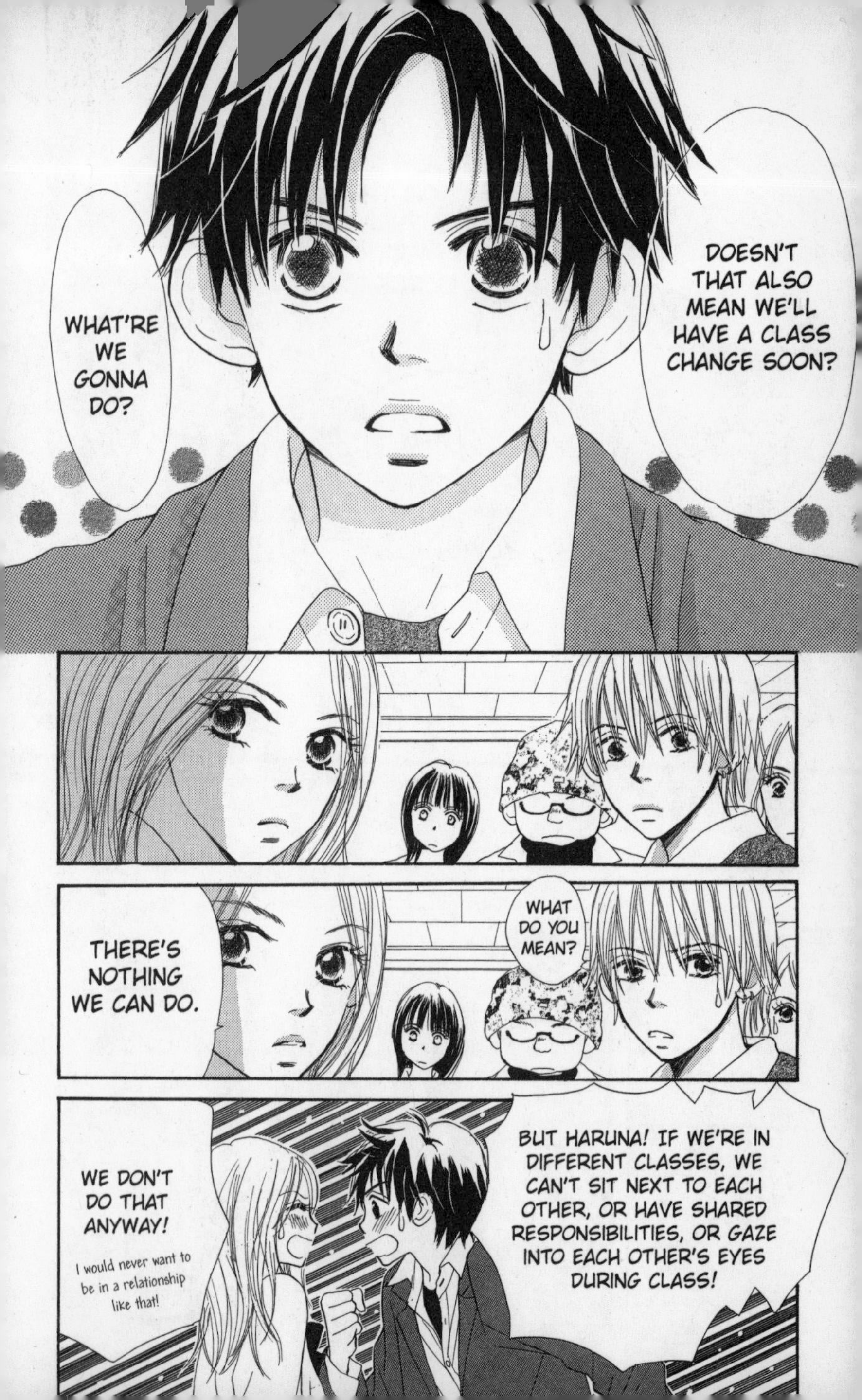
DOESN'T THAT ALSO MEAN WE'LL HAVE A CLASS CHANGE SOON?
WHAT'RE WE GONNA DO?
WHAT DO YOU MEAN?
THERE'S NOTHING WE CAN DO.
BUT HARUNA! IF WE'RE IN DIFFERENT CLASSES, WE CAN'T SIT NEXT TO EACH OTHER, OR HAVE SHARED RESPONSIBILITIES, OR GAZE INTO EACH OTHER'S EYES DURING CLASS!
WE DON'T DO THAT ANYWAY!
I would never want to be in a relationship like that!

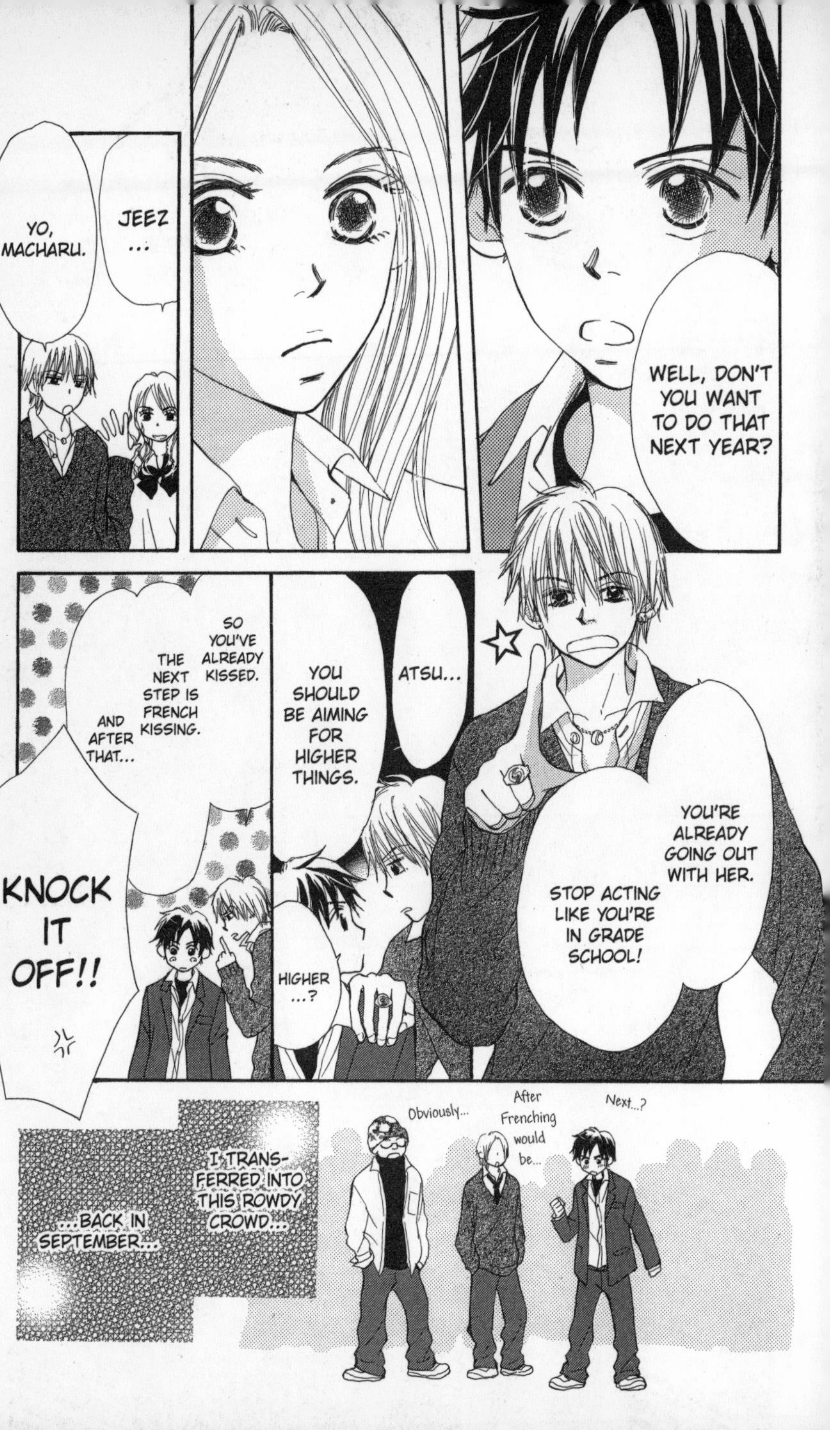

WELL, DON'T YOU WANT TO DO THAT NEXT YEAR?
JEEZ ...
YO, MACHARU.
YOU'RE ALREADY GOING OUT WITH HER.
STOP ACTING LIKE YOU'RE IN GRADE SCHOOL!
ATSU...
YOU SHOULD BE AIMING FOR HIGHER THINGS.
HIGHER ...?
SO YOU'VE ALREADY KISSED.
THE NEXT STEP IS FRENCH KISSING.
AND AFTER THAT...
KNOCK IT OFF!!
Next...?
After Frenching would be...
Obviously...
I TRANS-FERRED INTO THIS ROWDY CROWD...
...BACK IN SEPTEMBER...

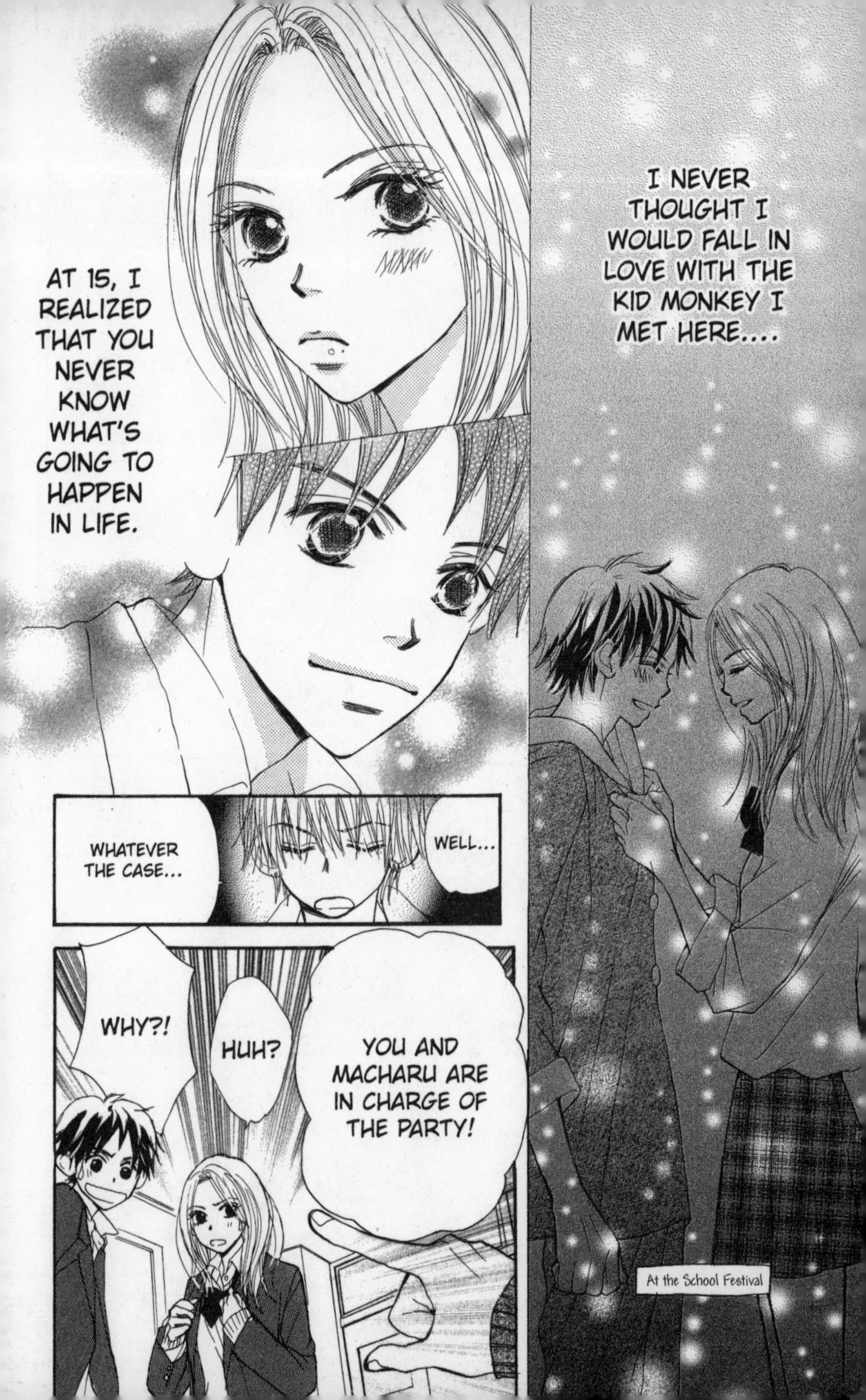
I NEVER THOUGHT I WOULD FALL IN LOVE WITH THE KID MONKEY I MET HERE....
At the School Festival
AT 15, I REALIZED THAT YOU NEVER KNOW WHAT'S GOING TO HAPPEN IN LIFE.
WELL...
WHATEVER THE CASE...
YOU AND MACHARU ARE IN CHARGE OF THE PARTY!
HUH?
WHY?!

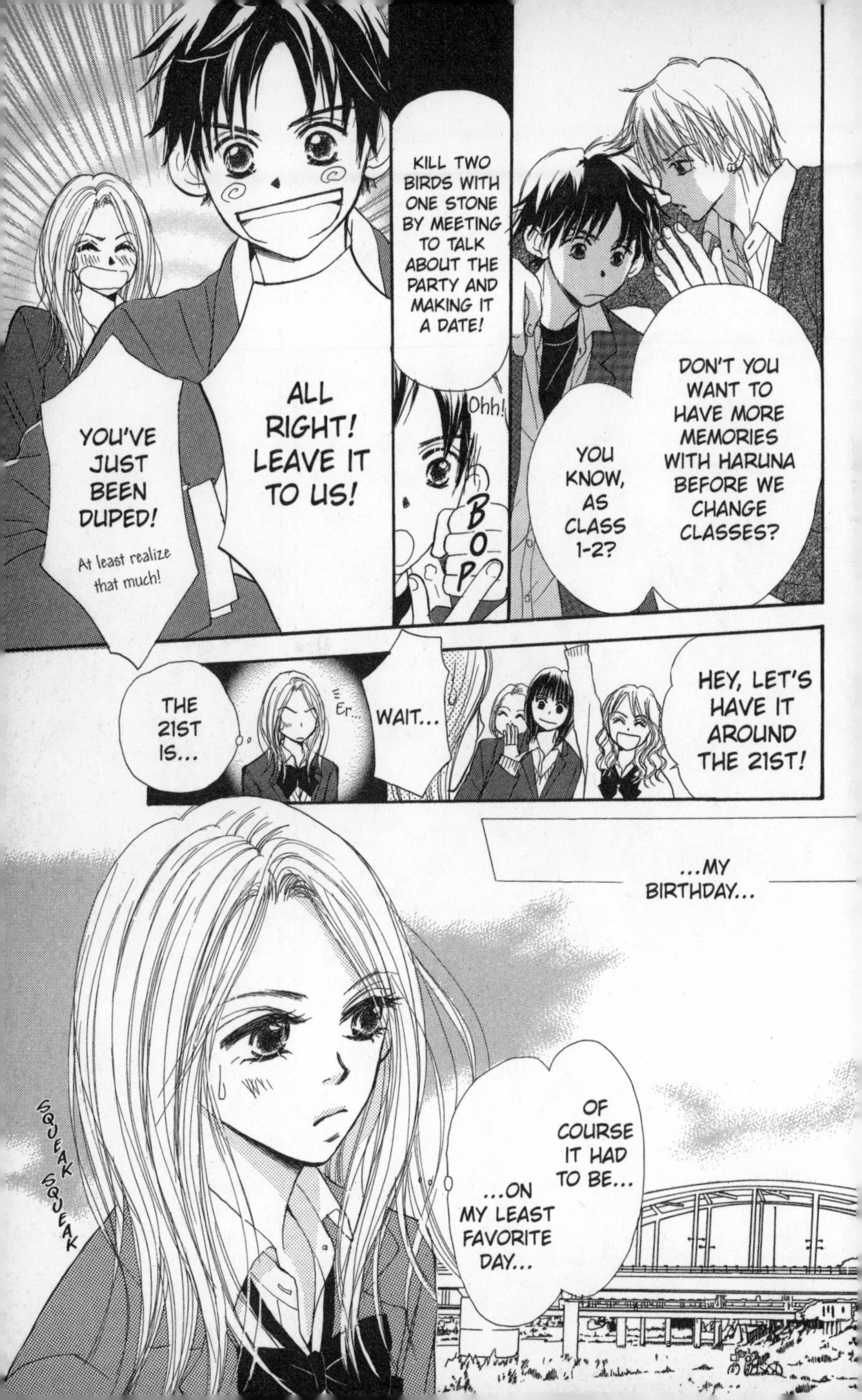
DON'T YOU WANT TO HAVE MORE MEMORIES WITH HARUNA BEFORE WE CHANGE CLASSES?
YOU KNOW, AS CLASS 1-2?
KILL TWO BIRDS WITH ONE STONE BY MEETING TO TALK ABOUT THE PARTY AND MAKING IT A DATE!
Ohh!
BOP
ALL RIGHT! LEAVE IT TO US!
YOU'VE JUST BEEN DUPED!
At least realize that much!
HEY, LET'S HAVE IT AROUND THE 21ST!
WAIT...
Er...
THE 21ST IS...
...MY BIRTHDAY...
OF COURSE IT HAD TO BE...
...ON MY LEAST FAVORITE DAY...
SQUEAK SQUEAK

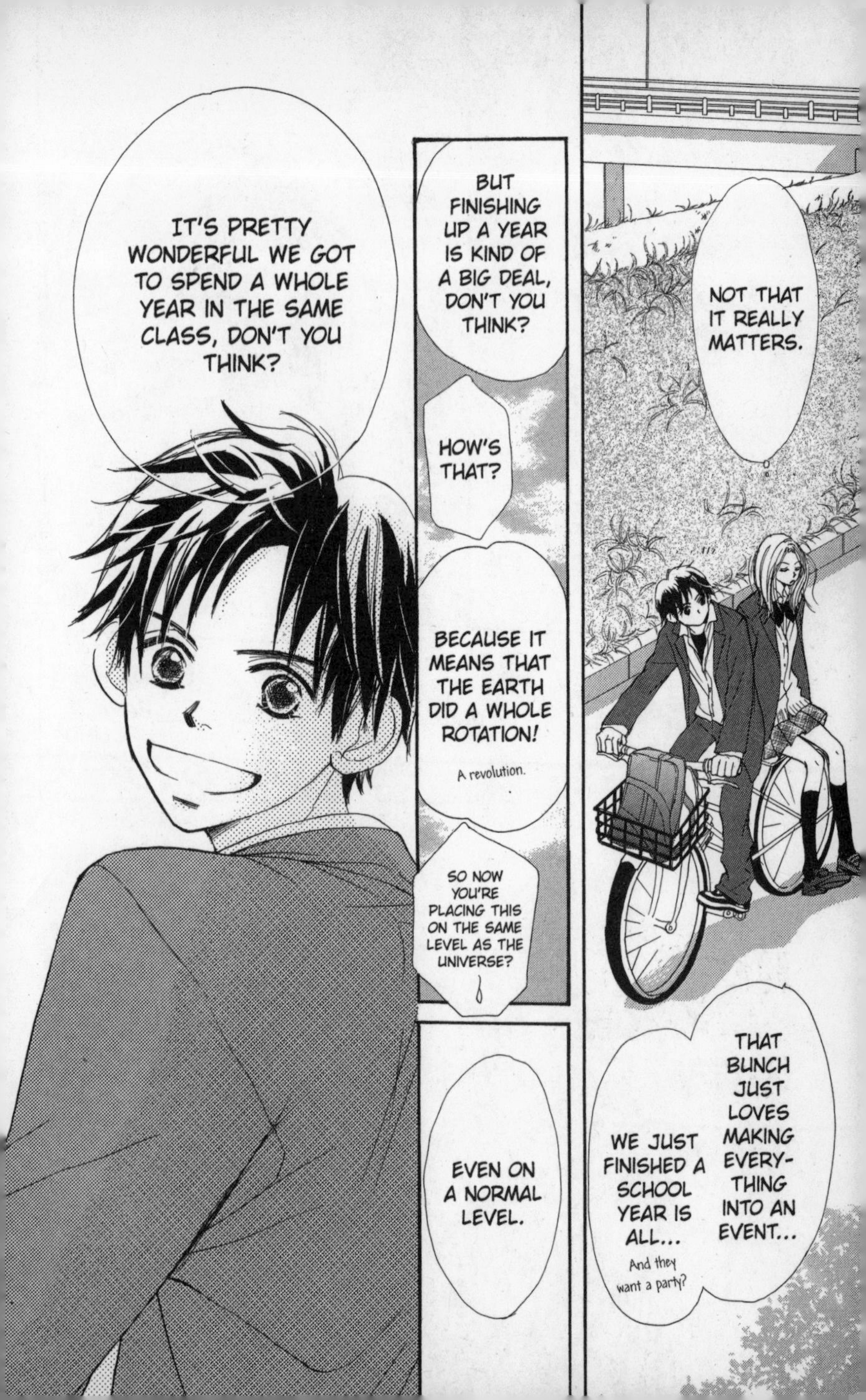
NOT THAT IT REALLY MATTERS.
THAT BUNCH JUST LOVES MAKING EVERY-THING INTO AN EVENT...
WE JUST FINISHED A SCHOOL YEAR IS ALL...
And they want a party?
BUT FINISHING UP A YEAR IS KIND OF A BIG DEAL, DON'T YOU THINK?
HOW'S THAT?
BECAUSE IT MEANS THAT THE EARTH DID A WHOLE ROTATION!
A revolution.
SO NOW YOU'RE PLACING THIS ON THE SAME LEVEL AS THE UNIVERSE?
EVEN ON A NORMAL LEVEL.
IT'S PRETTY WONDERFUL WE GOT TO SPEND A WHOLE YEAR IN THE SAME CLASS, DON'T YOU THINK?

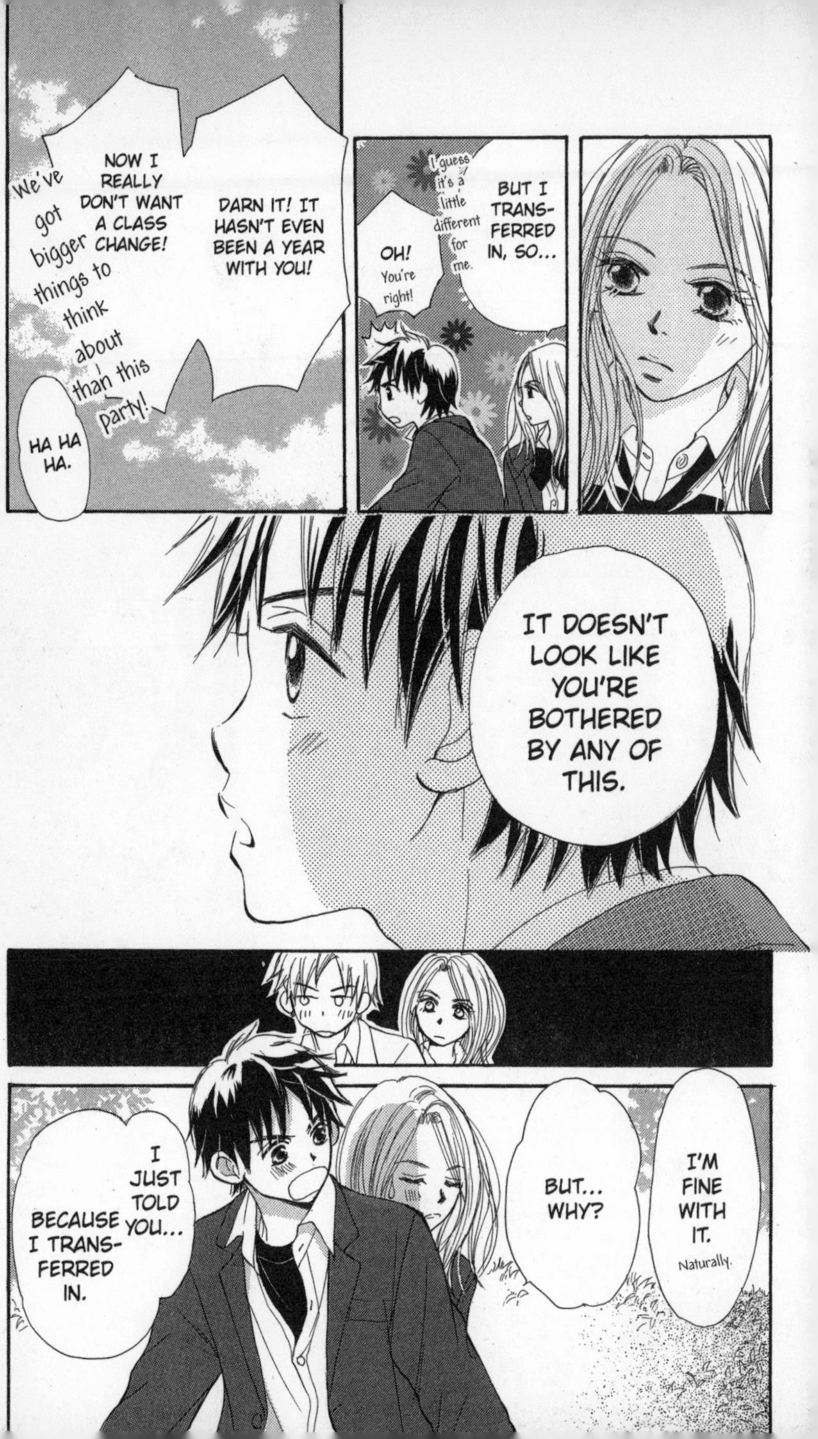
BUT I TRANSFERRED IN, SO...
I guess it's a little different for me.
OH! You're right!
DARN IT! IT HASN'T EVEN BEEN A YEAR WITH YOU!
NOW I REALLY DON'T WANT A CLASS CHANGE!
We've got bigger things to think about than this party!
HA HA HA.
IT DOESN'T LOOK LIKE YOU'RE BOTHERED BY ANY OF THIS.
I'M FINE WITH IT.
Naturally.
BUT... WHY?
I JUST TOLD YOU...
BECAUSE I TRANSFERRED IN.

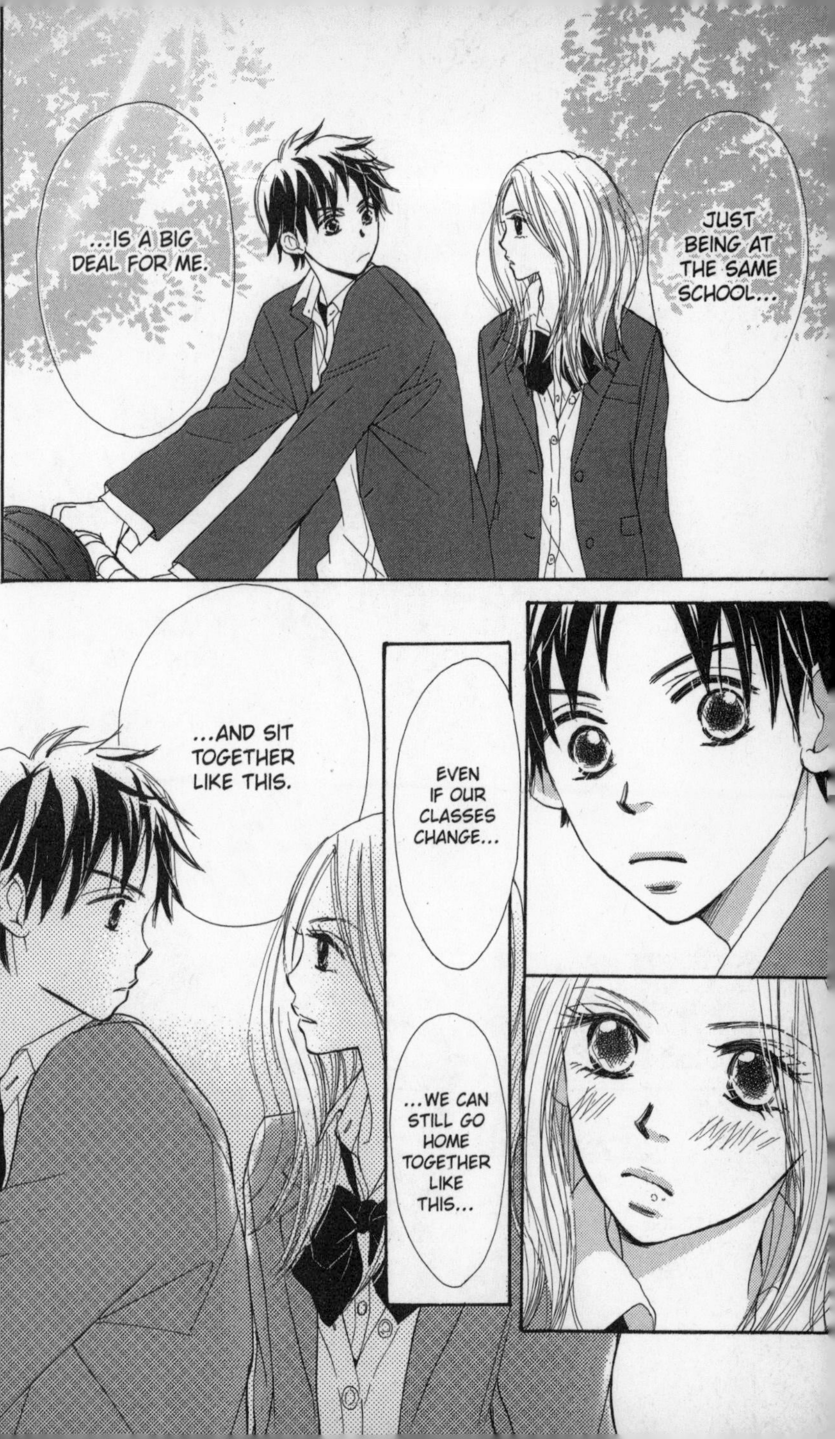
JUST BEING AT THE SAME SCHOOL...
...IS A BIG DEAL FOR ME.
EVEN IF OUR CLASSES CHANGE...
...WE CAN STILL GO HOME TOGETHER LIKE THIS...
...AND SIT TOGETHER LIKE THIS.

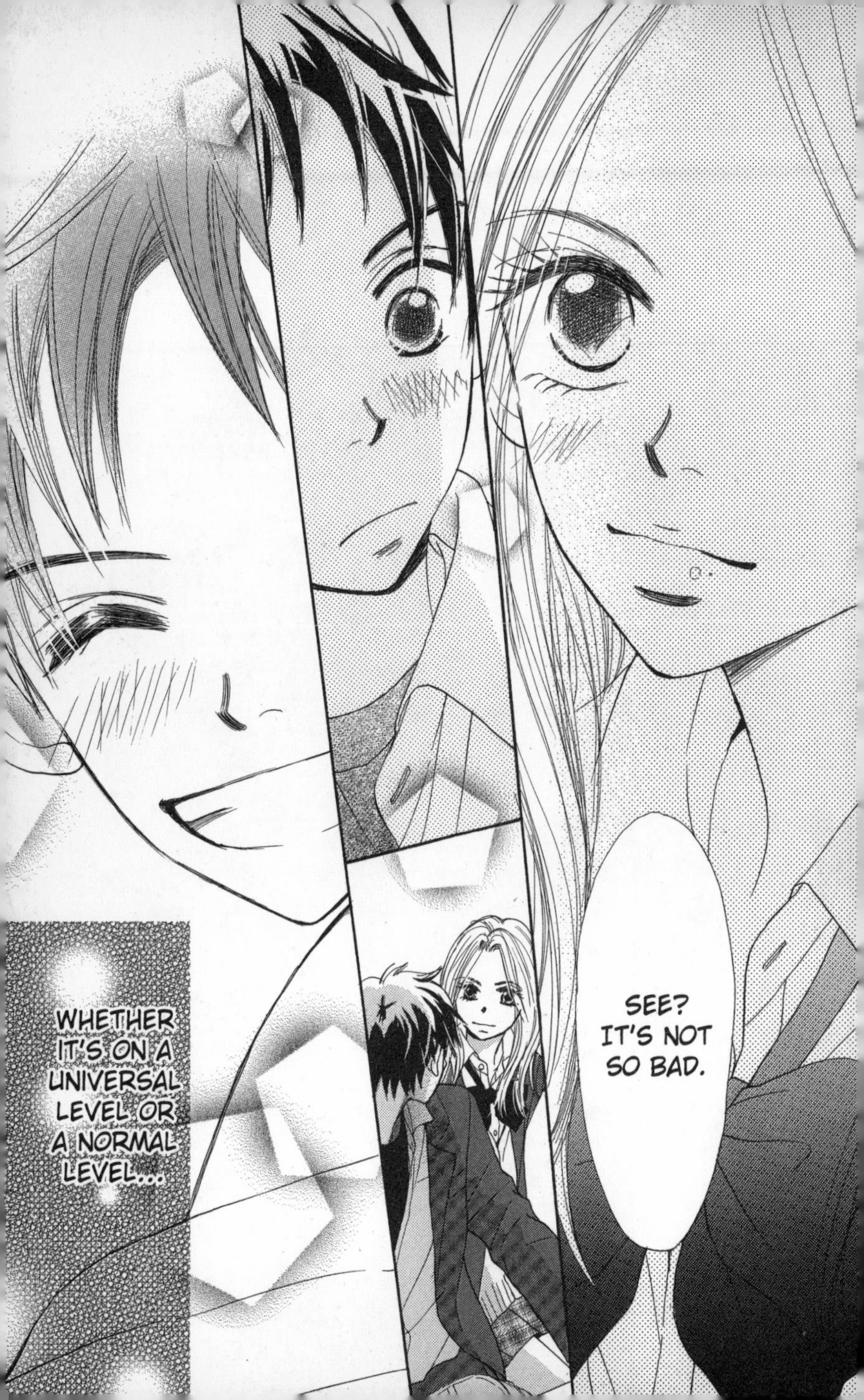
SEE? IT'S NOT SO BAD.
WHETHER IT'S ON A UNIVERSAL LEVEL OR A NORMAL LEVEL...

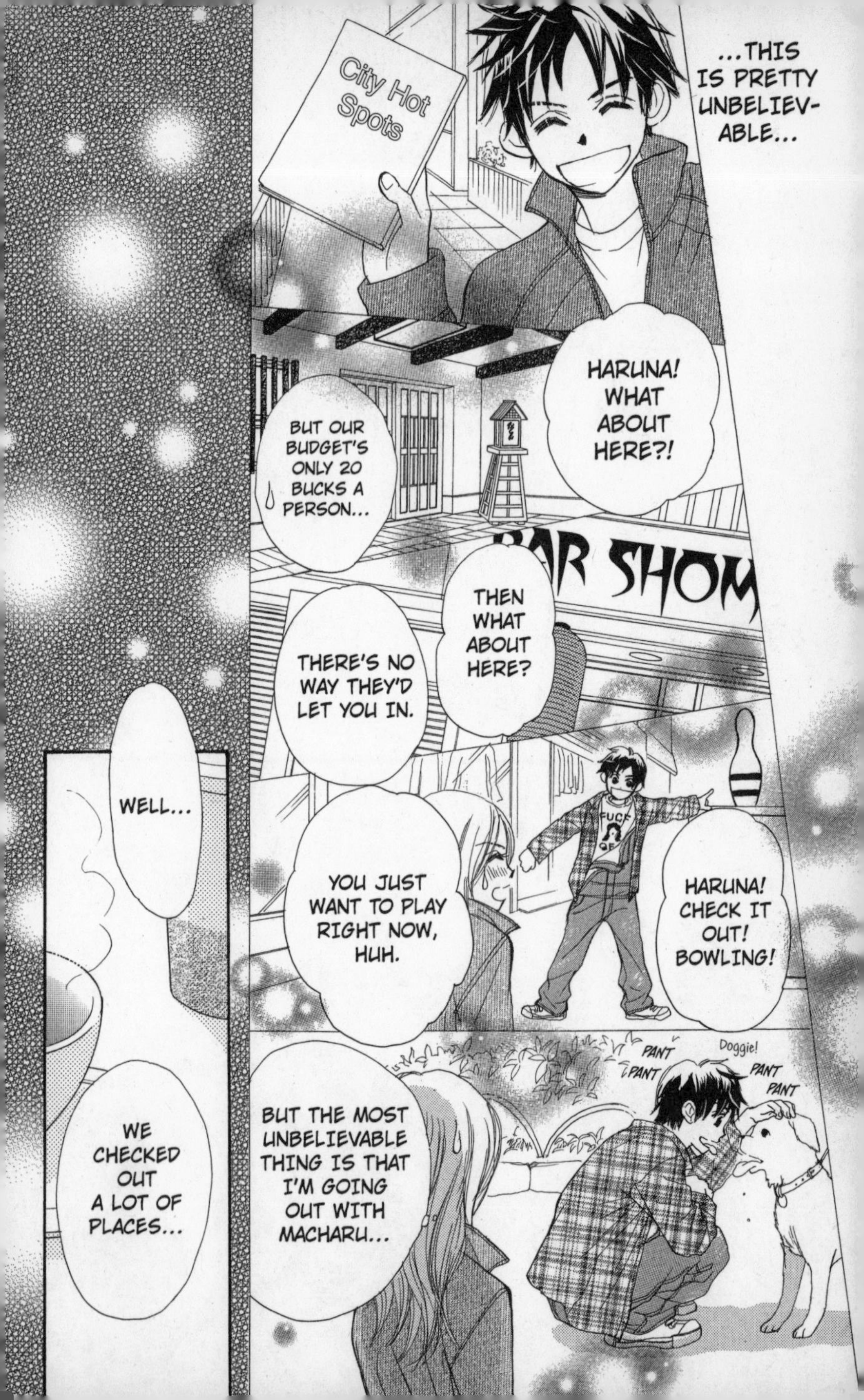
...THIS IS PRETTY UNBELIEV-ABLE...
City Hot Spots
HARUNA! WHAT ABOUT HERE?!
BUT OUR BUDGET'S ONLY 20 BUCKS A PERSON...
BAR SHOM
THEN WHAT ABOUT HERE?
THERE'S NO WAY THEY'D LET YOU IN.
HARUNA! CHECK IT OUT! BOWLING!
YOU JUST WANT TO PLAY RIGHT NOW, HUH.
PANT PANT
Doggie!
PANT PANT
BUT THE MOST UNBELIEVABLE THING IS THAT I'M GOING OUT WITH MACHARU...
WELL...
WE CHECKED OUT A LOT OF PLACES...

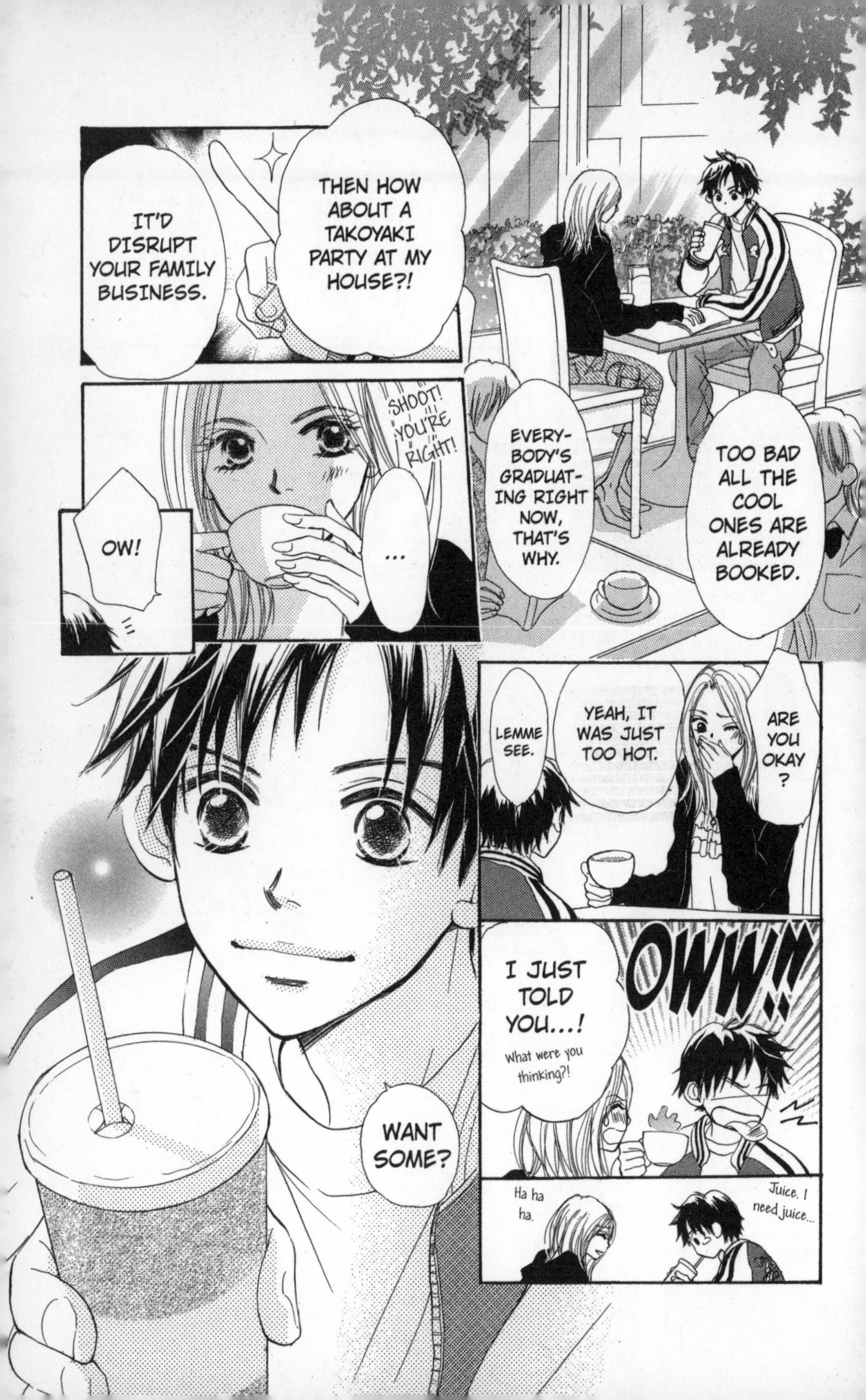
TOO BAD ALL THE COOL ONES ARE ALREADY BOOKED.
EVERYBODY'S GRADUATING RIGHT NOW, THAT'S WHY.
THEN HOW ABOUT A TAKOYAKI PARTY AT MY HOUSE?!
IT'D DISRUPT YOUR FAMILY BUSINESS.
SHOOT! YOU'RE RIGHT!
...
OW!
ARE YOU OKAY?
YEAH, IT WAS JUST TOO HOT.
LEMME SEE.
OWW!!
I JUST TOLD YOU...!
What were you thinking?!
Juice. I need juice...
Ha ha ha.
WANT SOME?

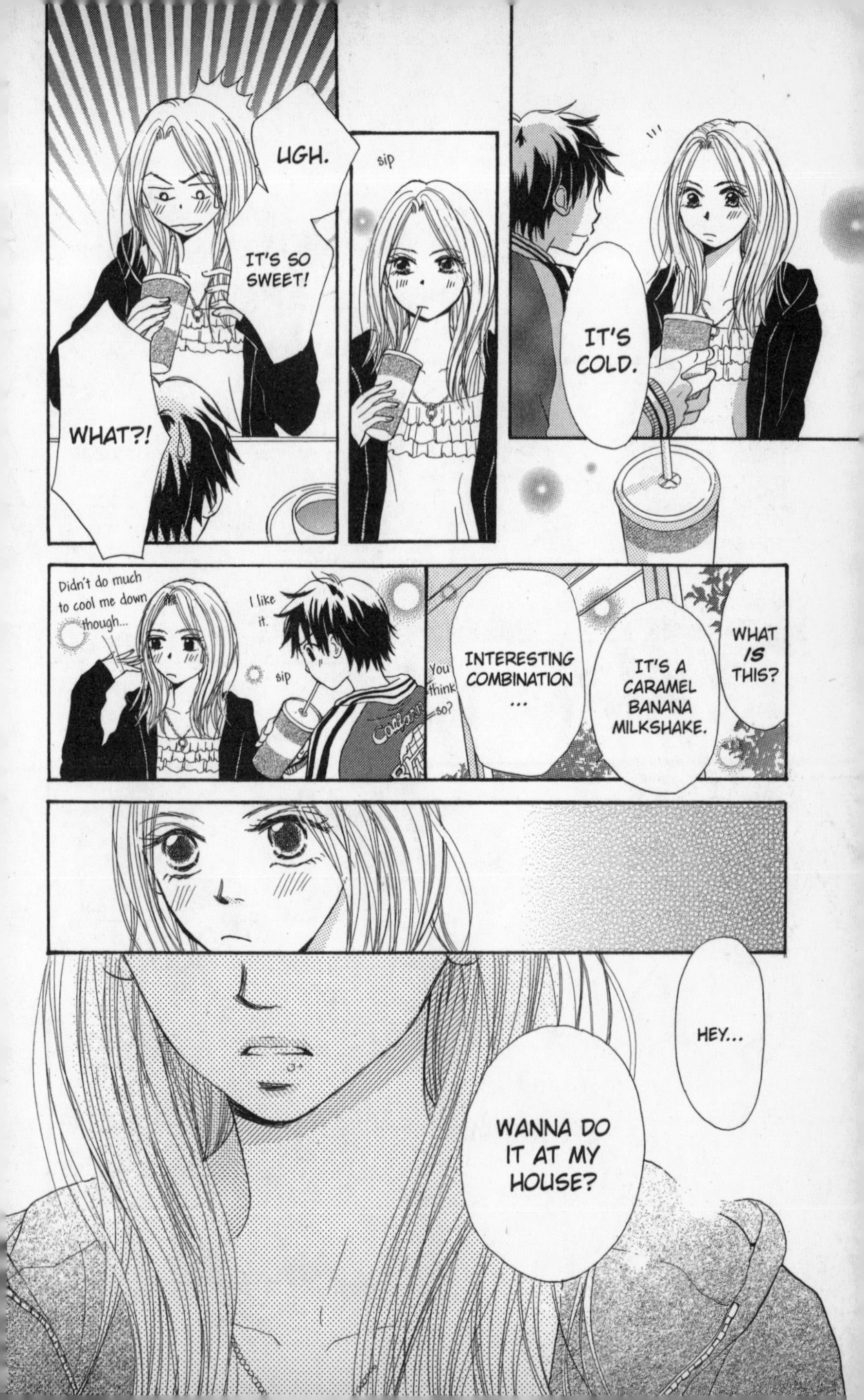
IT'S COLD.
sip
UGH.
IT'S SO SWEET!
WHAT?!
WHAT IS THIS?
IT'S A CARAMEL BANANA MILKSHAKE.
INTERESTING COMBINATION ...
You think so?
I like it.
sip
Didn't do much to cool me down though...
HEY...
WANNA DO IT AT MY HOUSE?

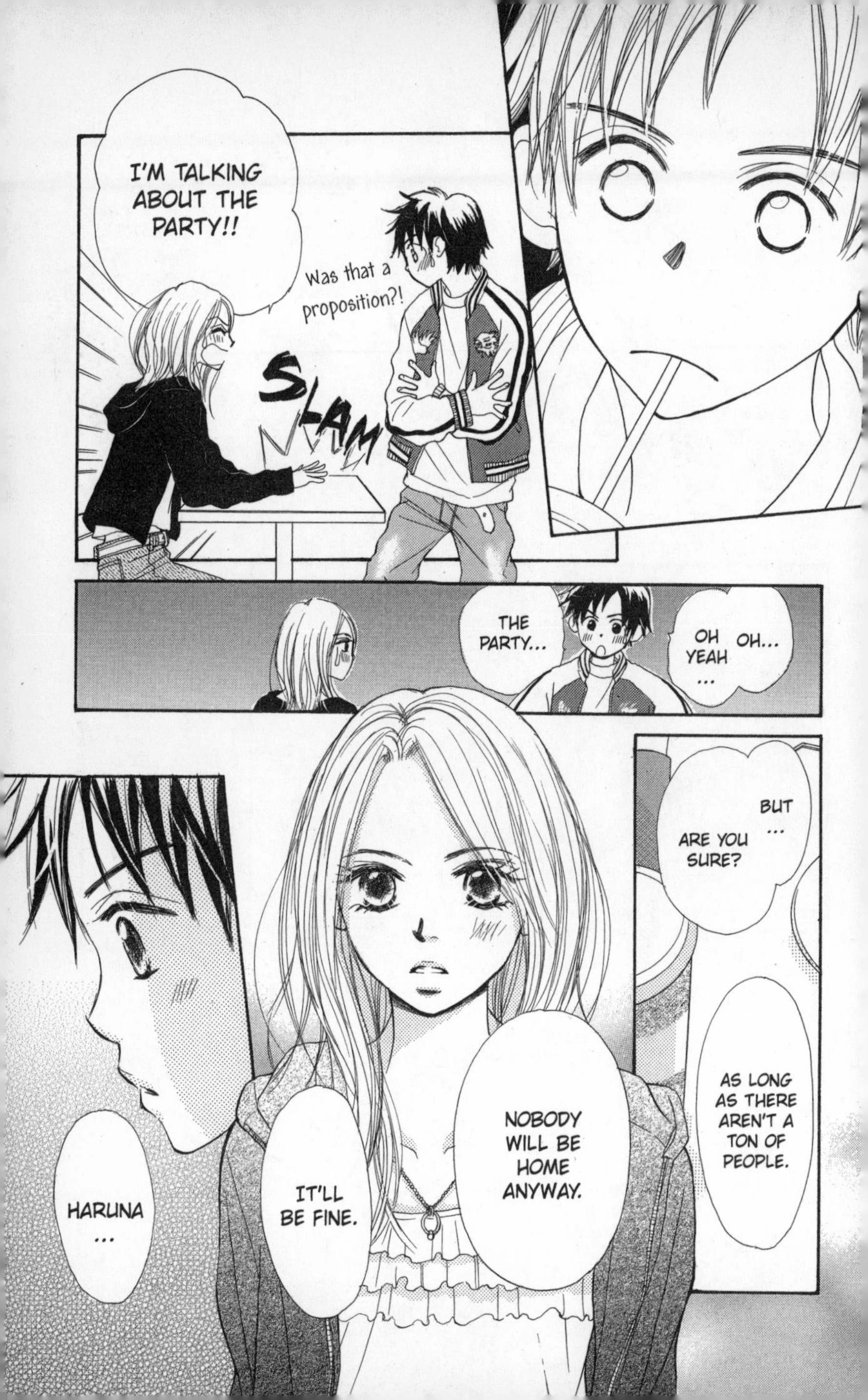
Was that a proposition?!
I'M TALKING ABOUT THE PARTY!!
SLAM
OH...
OH YEAH...
THE PARTY...
BUT...
ARE YOU SURE?
AS LONG AS THERE AREN'T A TON OF PEOPLE.
NOBODY WILL BE HOME ANYWAY.
IT'LL BE FINE.
HARUNA...

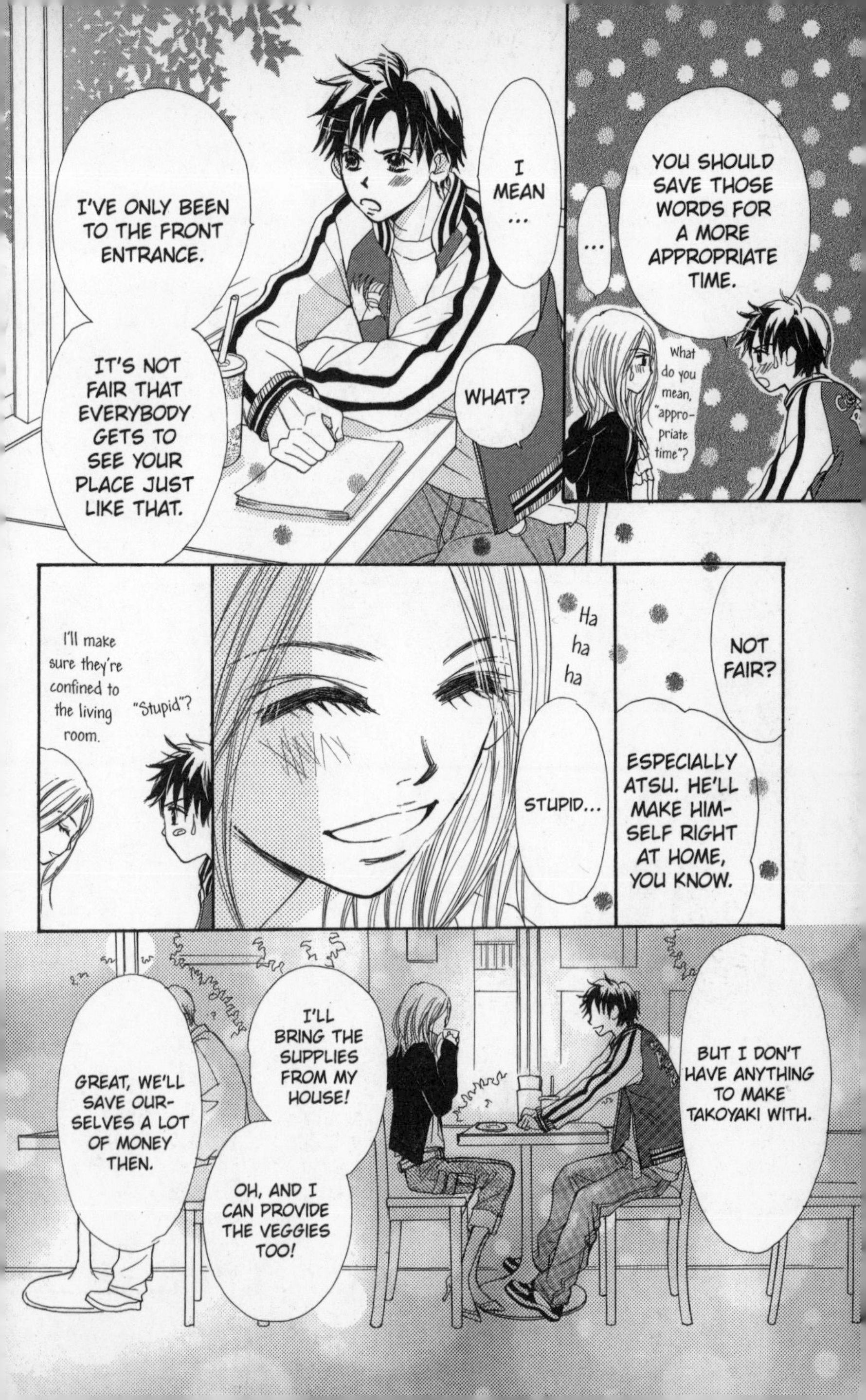
YOU SHOULD SAVE THOSE WORDS FOR A MORE APPROPRIATE TIME.
...
What do you mean, "appropriate time"?
I MEAN...
I'VE ONLY BEEN TO THE FRONT ENTRANCE.
WHAT?
IT'S NOT FAIR THAT EVERYBODY GETS TO SEE YOUR PLACE JUST LIKE THAT.
NOT FAIR?
ESPECIALLY ATSU. HE'LL MAKE HIMSELF RIGHT AT HOME, YOU KNOW.
Ha ha ha
STUPID...
"Stupid"?
I'll make sure they're confined to the living room.
BUT I DON'T HAVE ANYTHING TO MAKE TAKOYAKI WITH.
I'LL BRING THE SUPPLIES FROM MY HOUSE!
OH, AND I CAN PROVIDE THE VEGGIES TOO!
GREAT, WE'LL SAVE OURSELVES A LOT OF MONEY THEN.

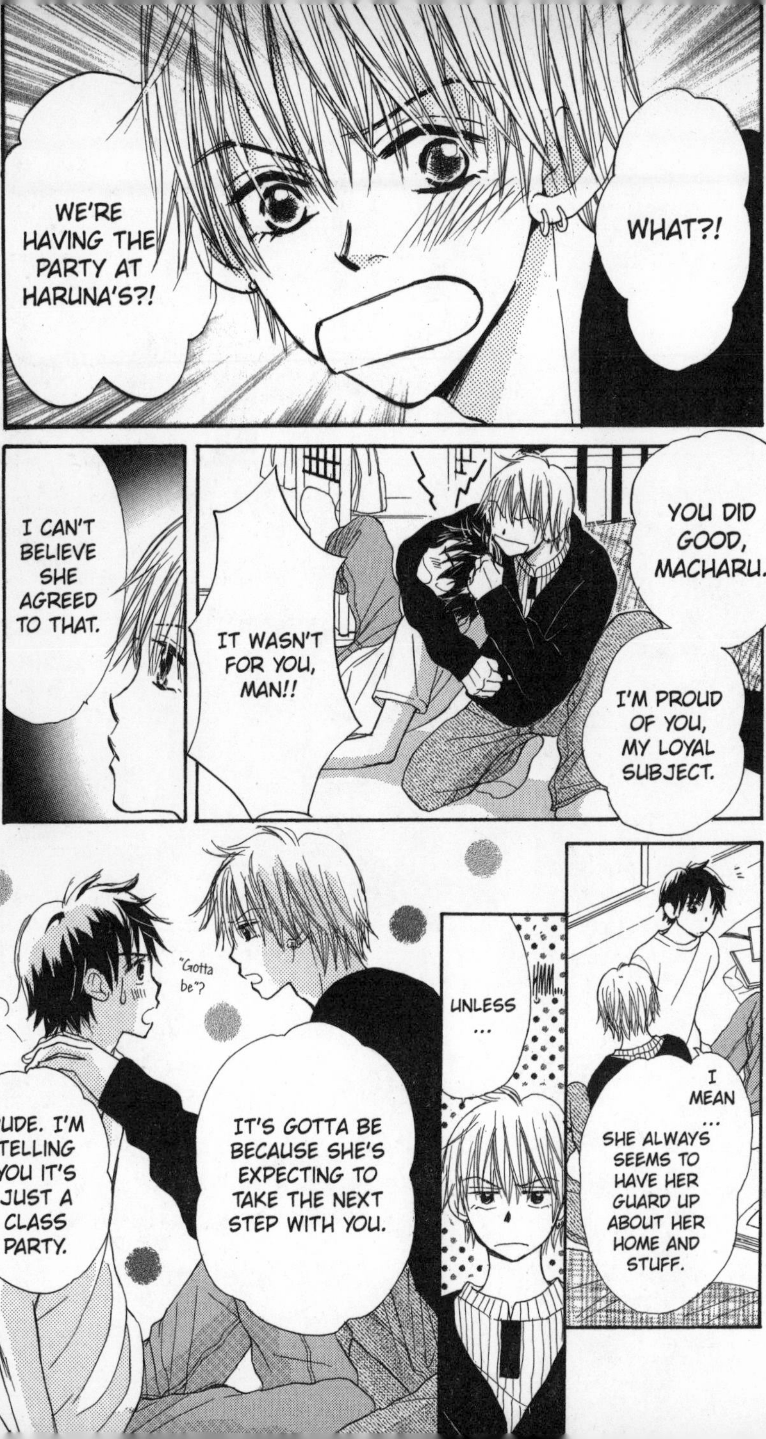
WHAT?!
WE'RE HAVING THE PARTY AT HARUNA'S?!
YOU DID GOOD, MACHARU.
I'M PROUD OF YOU, MY LOYAL SUBJECT.
IT WASN'T FOR YOU, MAN!!
I CAN'T BELIEVE SHE AGREED TO THAT.
I MEAN ...
SHE ALWAYS SEEMS TO HAVE HER GUARD UP ABOUT HER HOME AND STUFF.
HMM..
UNLESS ...
IT'S GOTTA BE BECAUSE SHE'S EXPECTING TO TAKE THE NEXT STEP WITH YOU.
"Gotta be"?
DUDE. I'M TELLING YOU IT'S JUST A CLASS PARTY.

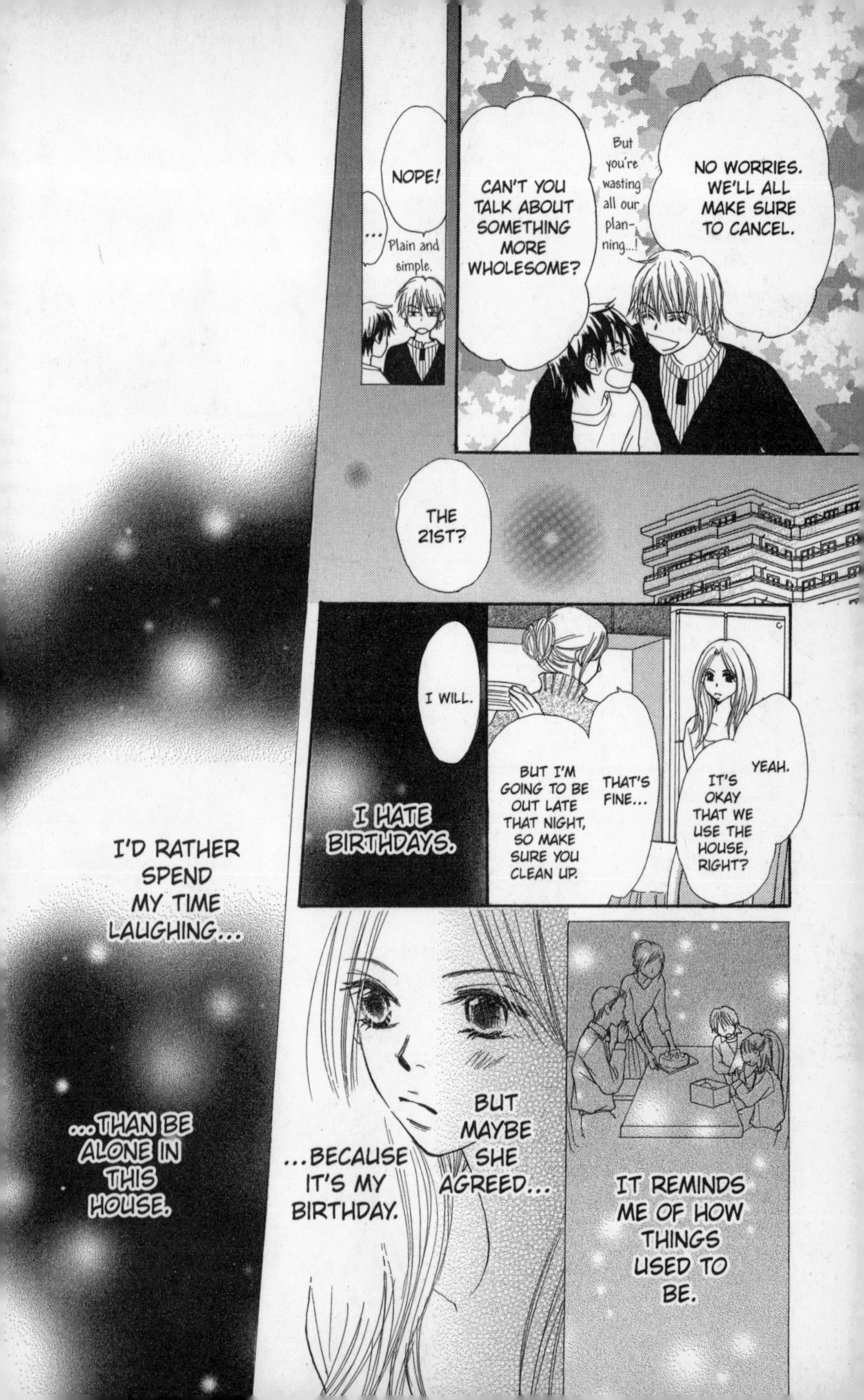
NO WORRIES. WE'LL ALL MAKE SURE TO CANCEL.
But you're wasting all our plan-ning...!
CAN'T YOU TALK ABOUT SOMETHING MORE WHOLESOME?
NOPE!
Plain and simple.
...
THE 21ST?
YEAH.
IT'S OKAY THAT WE USE THE HOUSE, RIGHT?
THAT'S FINE...
BUT I'M GOING TO BE OUT LATE THAT NIGHT, SO MAKE SURE YOU CLEAN UP.
I WILL.
I HATE BIRTHDAYS.
IT REMINDS ME OF HOW THINGS USED TO BE.
BUT MAYBE SHE AGREED...
...BECAUSE IT'S MY BIRTHDAY.
I'D RATHER SPEND MY TIME LAUGHING...
...THAN BE ALONE IN THIS HOUSE.

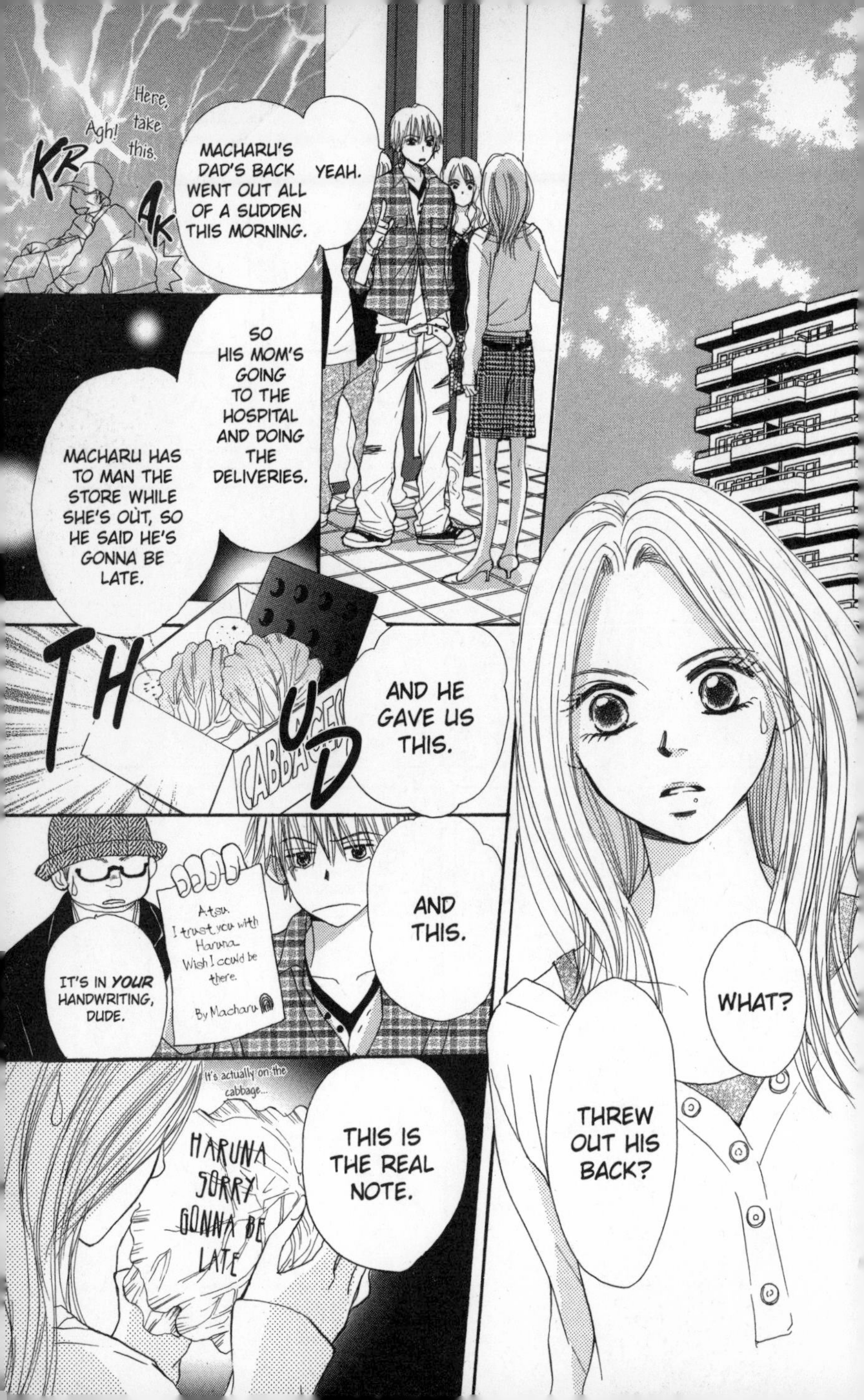
WHAT?
THREW OUT HIS BACK?
YEAH.
MACHARU'S DAD'S BACK WENT OUT ALL OF A SUDDEN THIS MORNING.
Here, take this.
Agh!
KRAK
SO HIS MOM'S GOING TO THE HOSPITAL AND DOING THE DELIVERIES.
MACHARU HAS TO MAN THE STORE WHILE SHE'S OUT, SO HE SAID HE'S GONNA BE LATE.
AND HE GAVE US THIS.
CABBAGES
THUD
AND THIS.
Atsu. I trust you with Haruna. Wish I could be there. By Macharu
IT'S IN *YOUR* HANDWRITING, DUDE.
THIS IS THE REAL NOTE.
It's actually on the cabbage...
HARUNA SORRY GONNA BE LATE

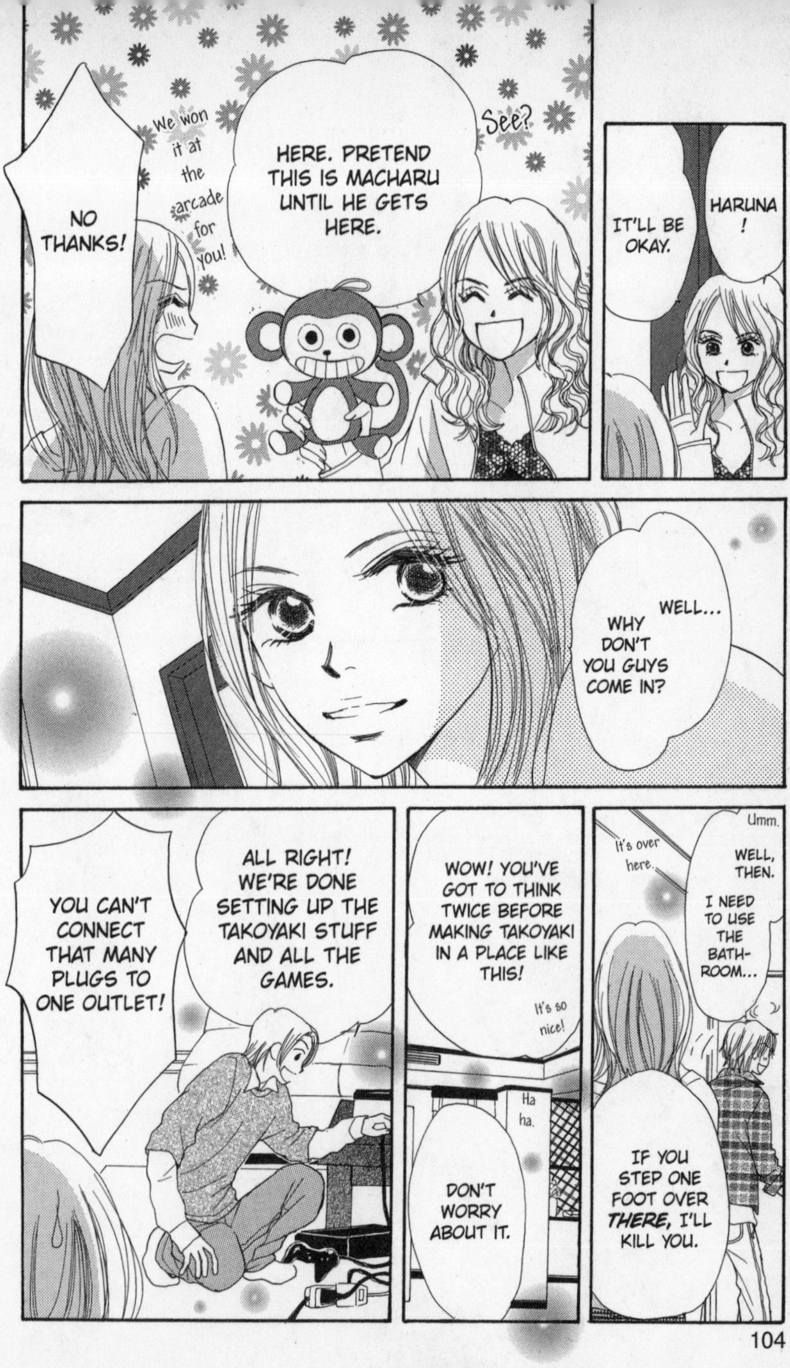

HARUNA!
IT'LL BE OKAY.
See?
HERE. PRETEND THIS IS MACHARU UNTIL HE GETS HERE.
We won it at the arcade for you!
NO THANKS!
WELL... WHY DON'T YOU GUYS COME IN?
Umm.
WELL, THEN. I NEED TO USE THE BATH-ROOM...
It's over here.
IF YOU STEP ONE FOOT OVER *THERE*, I'LL KILL YOU.
WOW! YOU'VE GOT TO THINK TWICE BEFORE MAKING TAKOYAKI IN A PLACE LIKE THIS!
It's so nice!
Ha ha.
DON'T WORRY ABOUT IT.
ALL RIGHT! WE'RE DONE SETTING UP THE TAKOYAKI STUFF AND ALL THE GAMES.
YOU CAN'T CONNECT THAT MANY PLUGS TO ONE OUTLET!

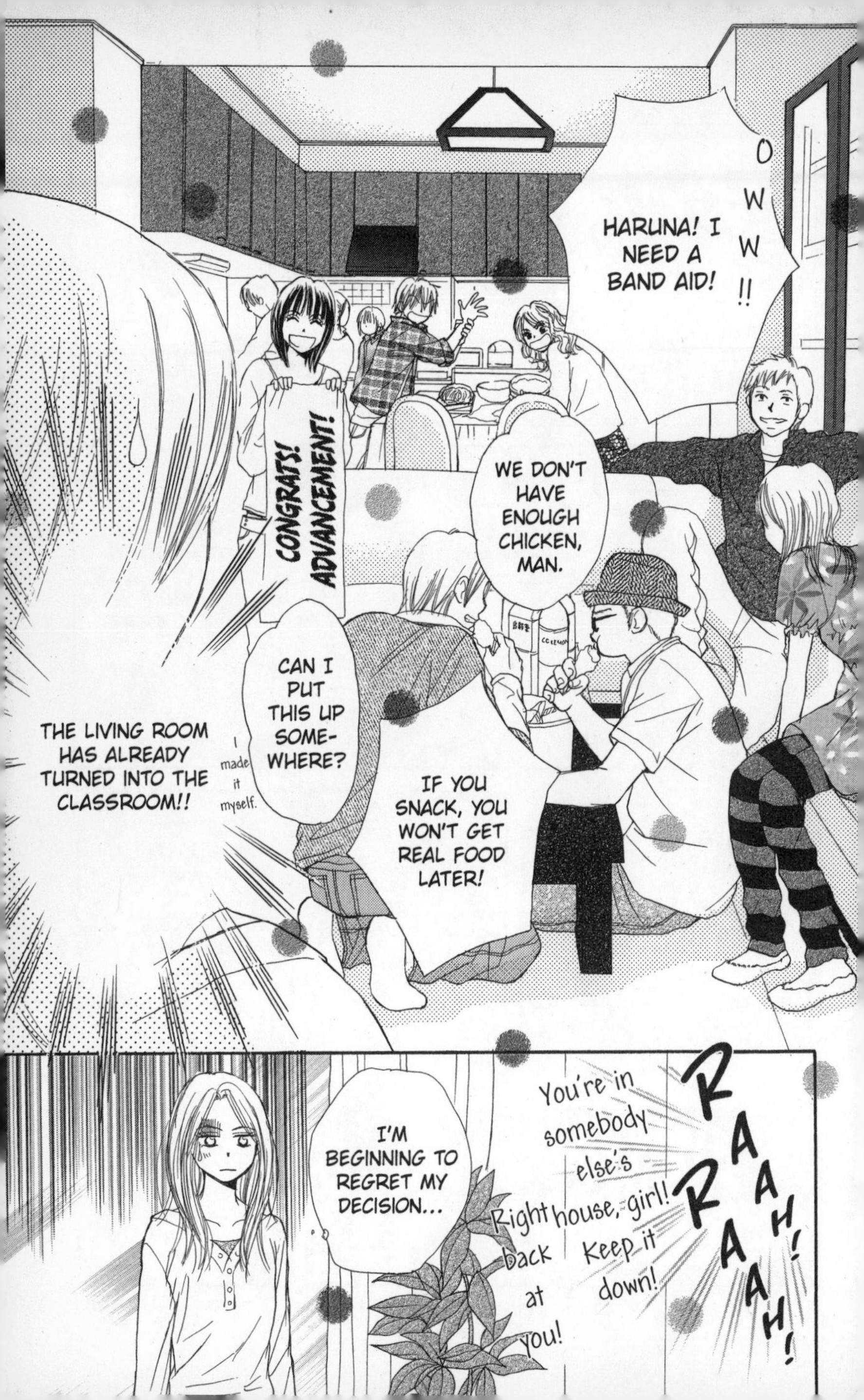
OWW!!
HARUNA! I NEED A BAND AID!
WE DON'T HAVE ENOUGH CHICKEN, MAN.
CONGRATS! ADVANCEMENT!
CAN I PUT THIS UP SOMEWHERE?
I made it myself.
IF YOU SNACK, YOU WON'T GET REAL FOOD LATER!
THE LIVING ROOM HAS ALREADY TURNED INTO THE CLASSROOM!!
RAAH! RAAH!
You're in somebody else's house, girl! Keep it down!
Right back at you!
I'M BEGINNING TO REGRET MY DECISION...

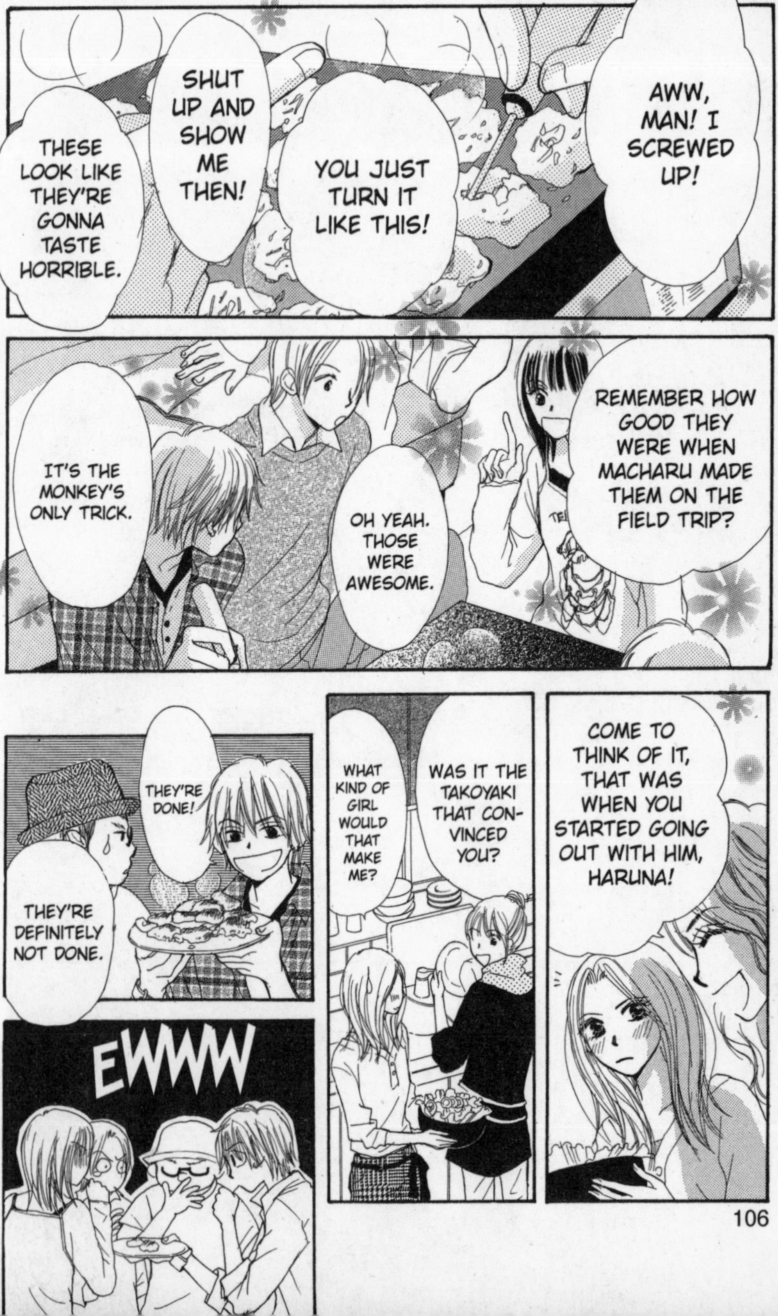
AWW, MAN! I SCREWED UP!
YOU JUST TURN IT LIKE THIS!
SHUT UP AND SHOW ME THEN!
THESE LOOK LIKE THEY'RE GONNA TASTE HORRIBLE.
REMEMBER HOW GOOD THEY WERE WHEN MACHARU MADE THEM ON THE FIELD TRIP?
OH YEAH. THOSE WERE AWESOME.
IT'S THE MONKEY'S ONLY TRICK.
COME TO THINK OF IT, THAT WAS WHEN YOU STARTED GOING OUT WITH HIM, HARUNA!
WAS IT THE TAKOYAKI THAT CON-VINCED YOU?
WHAT KIND OF GIRL WOULD THAT MAKE ME?
THEY'RE DONE!
THEY'RE DEFINITELY NOT DONE.
EWWW

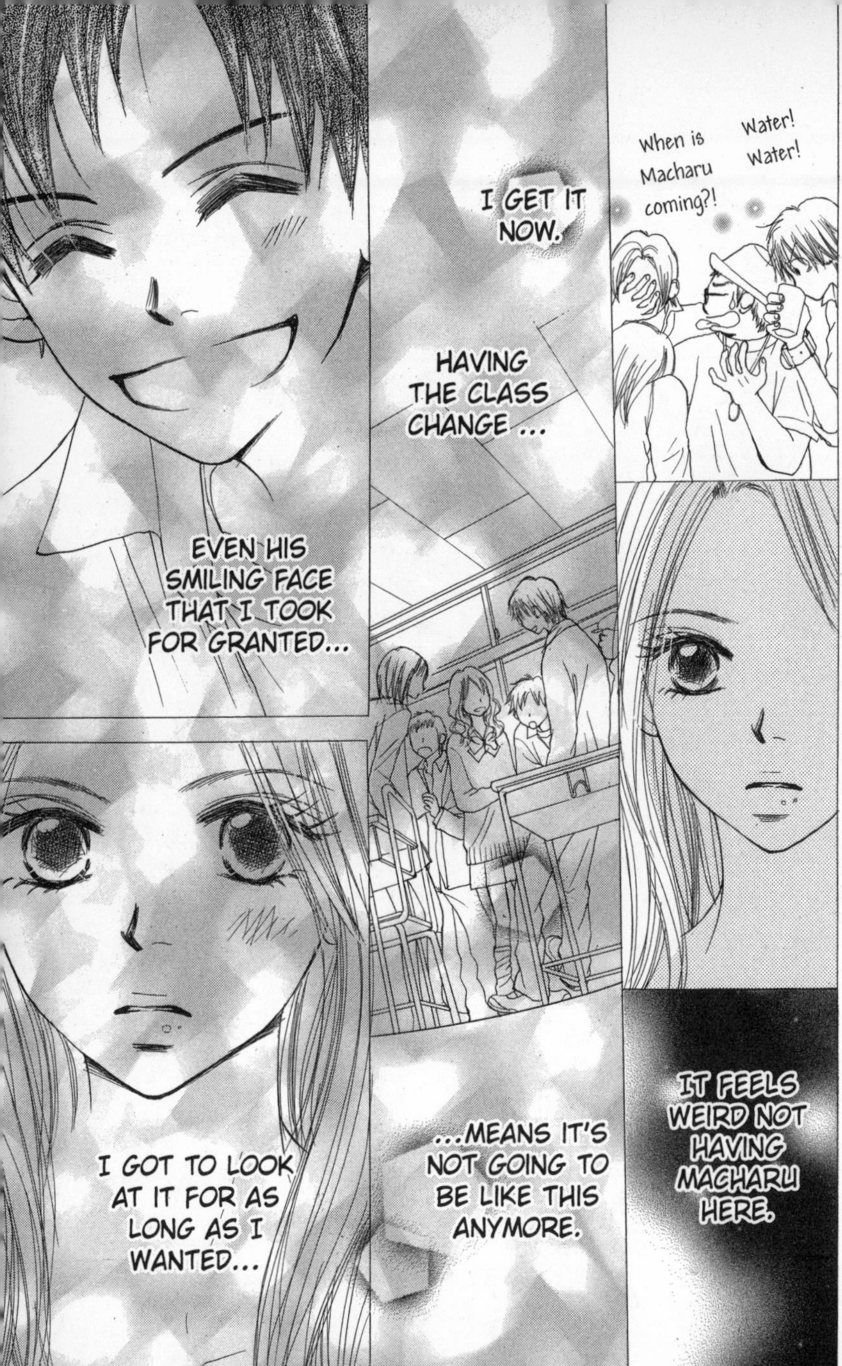
Water! Water!
When is Macharu coming?!
IT FEELS WEIRD NOT HAVING MACHARU HERE.
I GET IT NOW.
HAVING THE CLASS CHANGE ...
...MEANS IT'S NOT GOING TO BE LIKE THIS ANYMORE.
EVEN HIS SMILING FACE THAT I TOOK FOR GRANTED...
I GOT TO LOOK AT IT FOR AS LONG AS I WANTED...

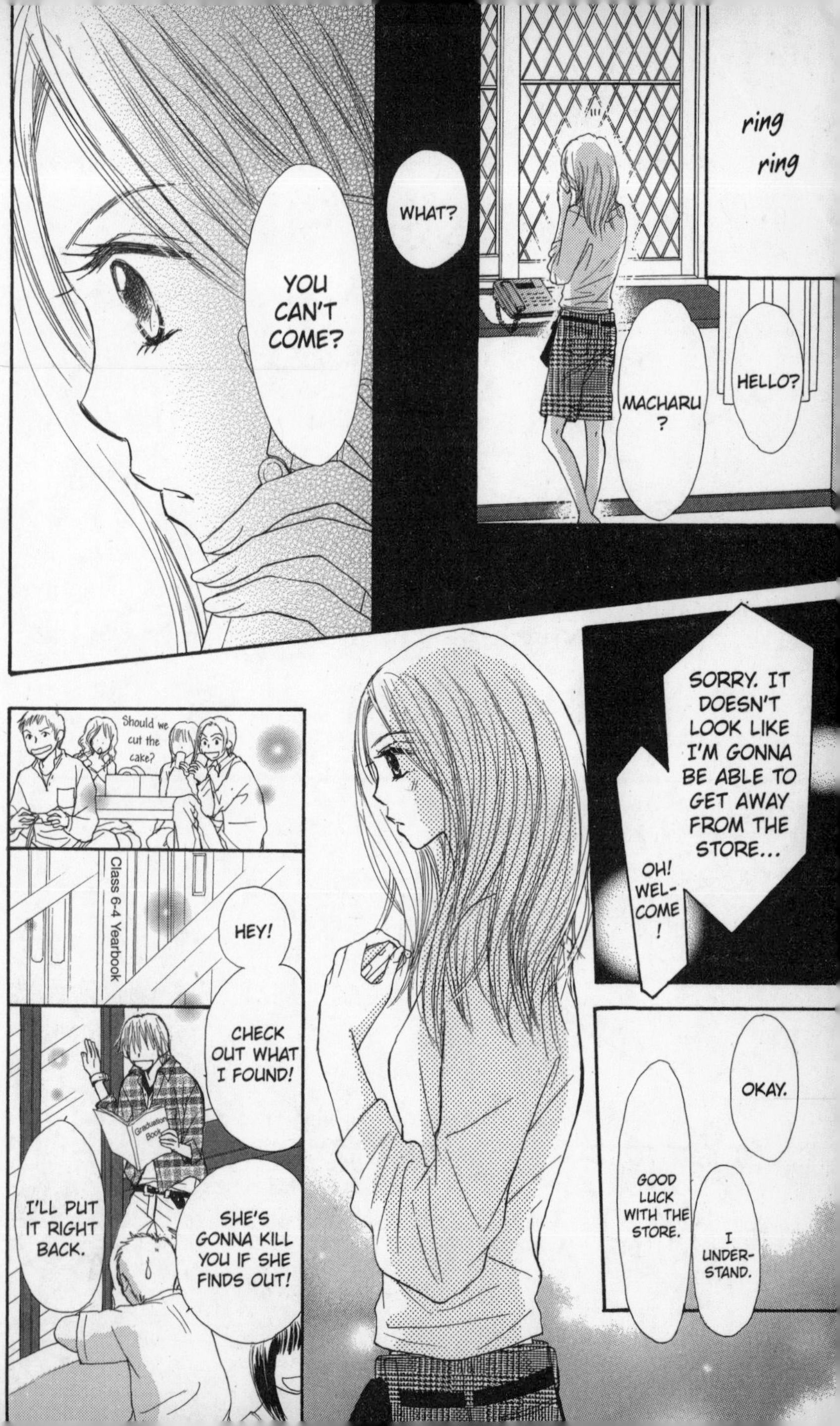
ring
ring
HELLO?
MACHARU?
WHAT?
YOU CAN'T COME?
SORRY. IT DOESN'T LOOK LIKE I'M GONNA BE ABLE TO GET AWAY FROM THE STORE...
OH! WELCOME!
OKAY.
I UNDERSTAND.
GOOD LUCK WITH THE STORE.
Should we cut the cake?
Class 6-4 Yearbook
HEY!
CHECK OUT WHAT I FOUND!
Graduation Book
SHE'S GONNA KILL YOU IF SHE FINDS OUT!
I'LL PUT IT RIGHT BACK.

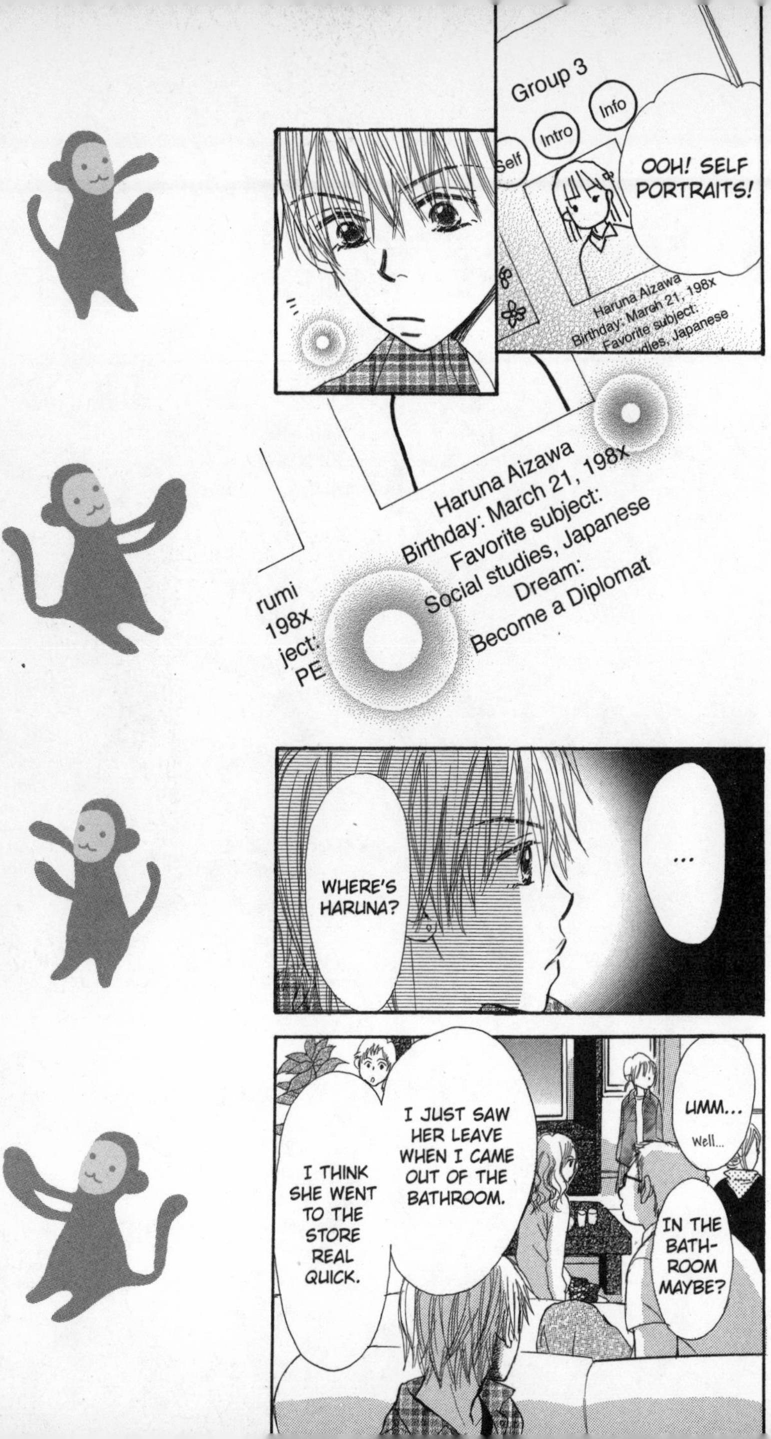
Group 3
Self
Intro
Info
OOH! SELF PORTRAITS!
Haruna Aizawa
Birthday: March 21, 198x
Favorite subject:
Haruna Aizawa
Birthday: March 21, 198x
Favorite subject:
Social studies, Japanese
Dream:
Become a Diplomat
rumi
198x
ject:
PE
...
WHERE'S HARUNA?
UMM...
Well...
IN THE BATH-ROOM MAYBE?
I JUST SAW HER LEAVE WHEN I CAME OUT OF THE BATHROOM.
I THINK SHE WENT TO THE STORE REAL QUICK.

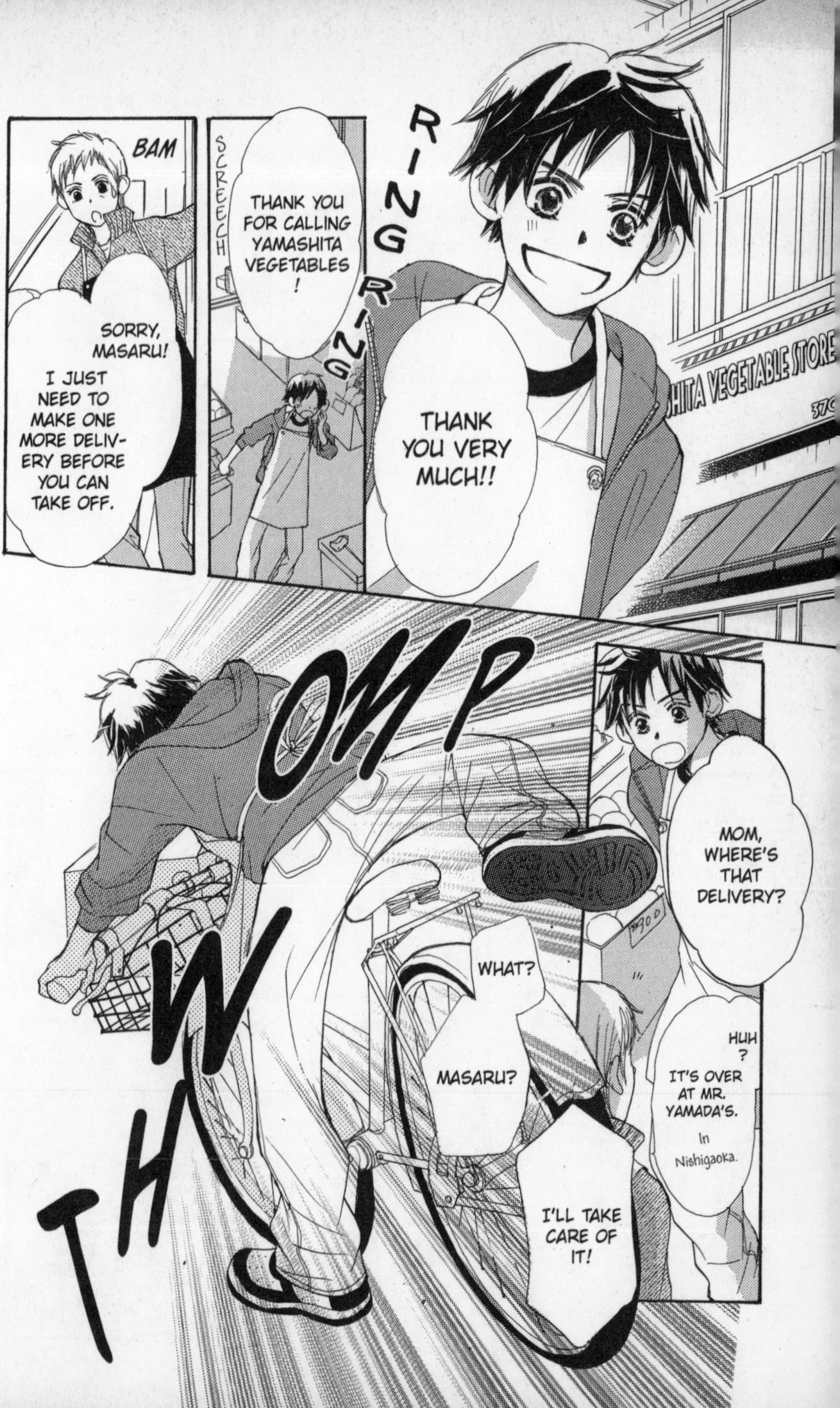
RING RING RING
SHITA VEGETABLE STORE
THANK YOU VERY MUCH!!
SCREECH
THANK YOU FOR CALLING YAMASHITA VEGETABLES!
BAM
SORRY, MASARU!
I JUST NEED TO MAKE ONE MORE DELIVERY BEFORE YOU CAN TAKE OFF.
MOM, WHERE'S THAT DELIVERY?
HUH?
IT'S OVER AT MR. YAMADA'S.
In Nishigaoka.
WHAT?
MASARU?
I'LL TAKE CARE OF IT!
THWOMP

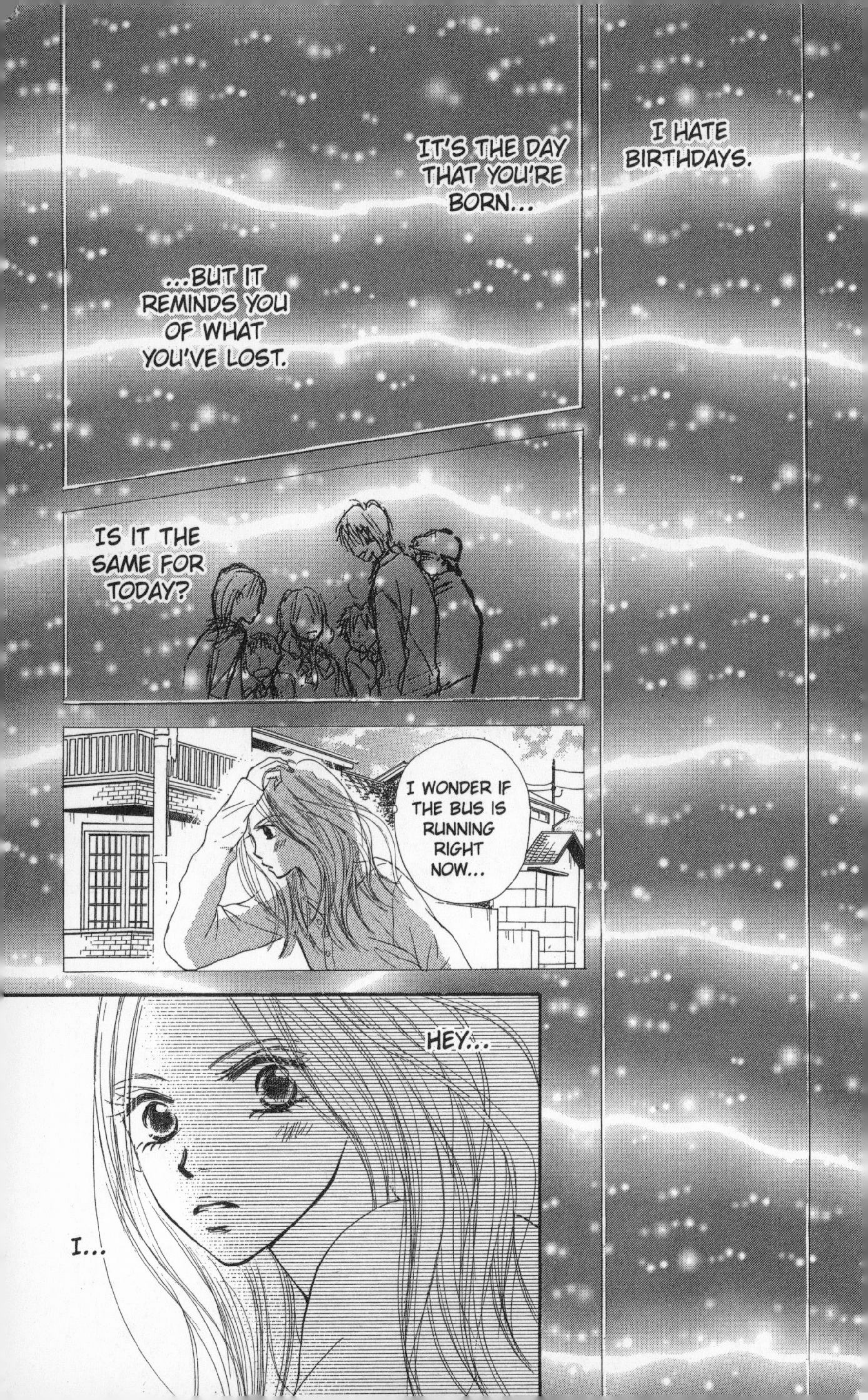
I HATE BIRTHDAYS.
IT'S THE DAY THAT YOU'RE BORN...
...BUT IT REMINDS YOU OF WHAT YOU'VE LOST.
IS IT THE SAME FOR TODAY?
I WONDER IF THE BUS IS RUNNING RIGHT NOW...
HEY...
I...

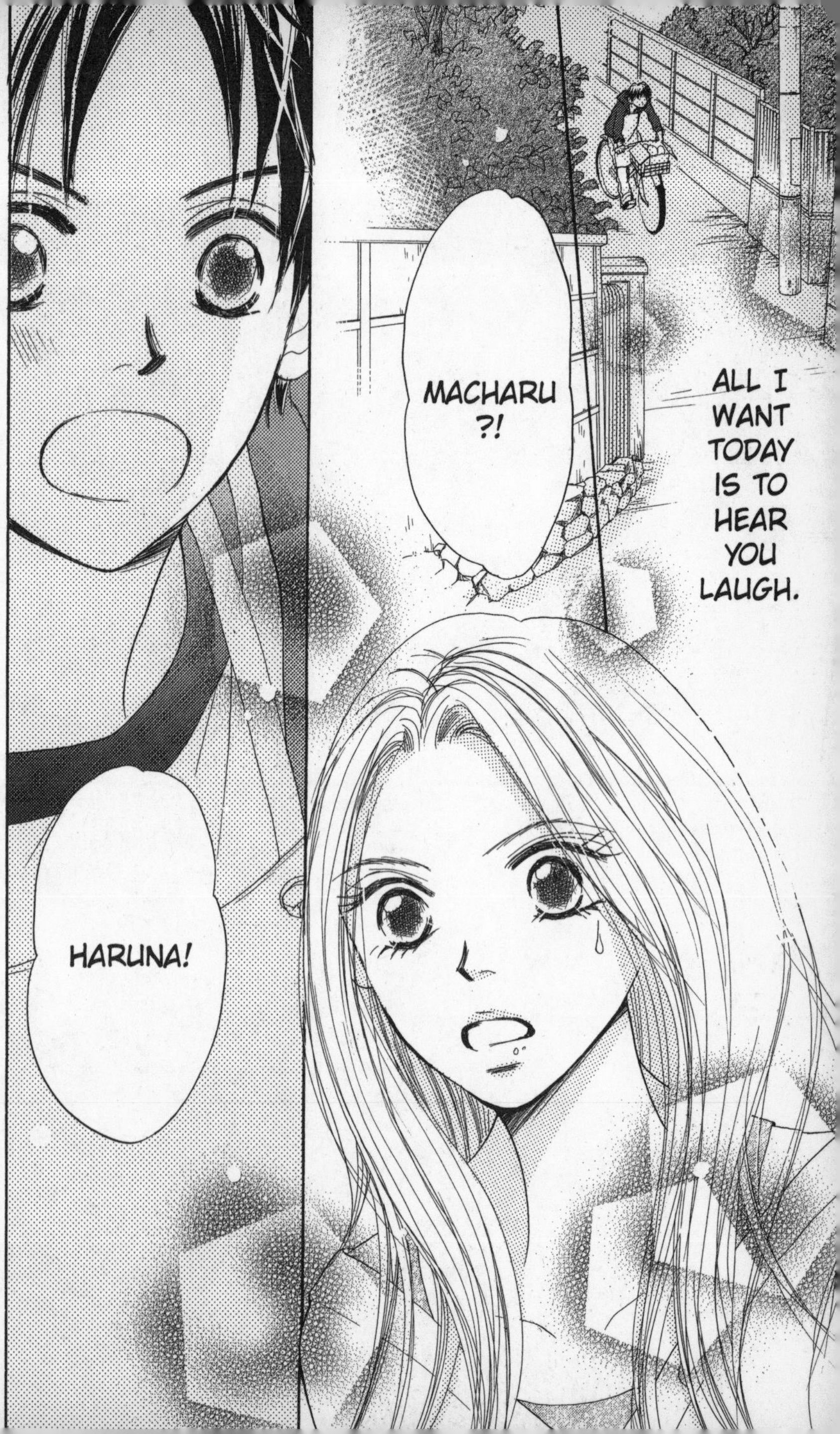
ALL I WANT TODAY IS TO HEAR YOU LAUGH.
MACHARU ?!
HARUNA!

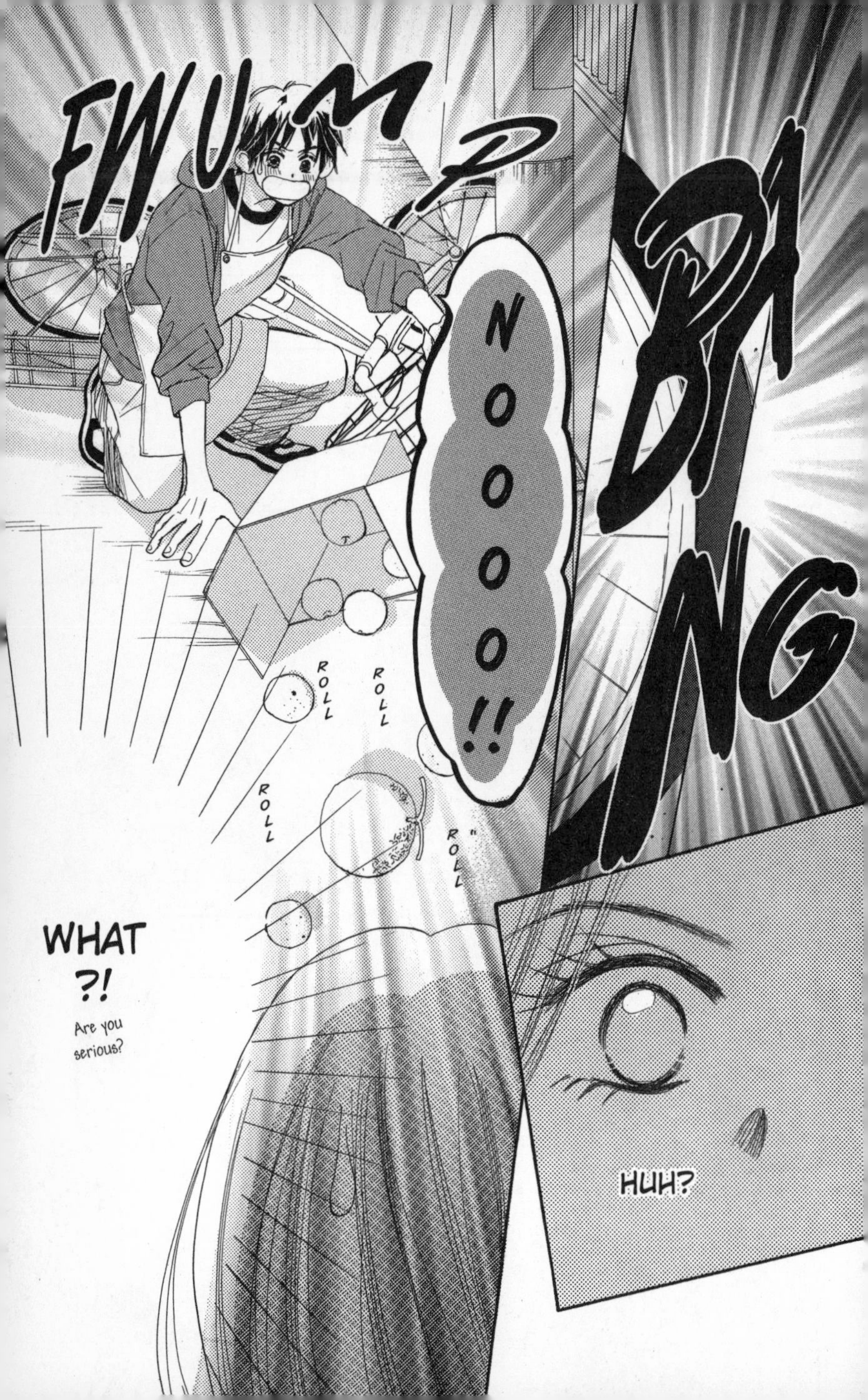
DING
FWUMP
NOOOOO!!
ROLL
ROLL
ROLL
ROLL
HUH?
WHAT ?!
Are you serious?

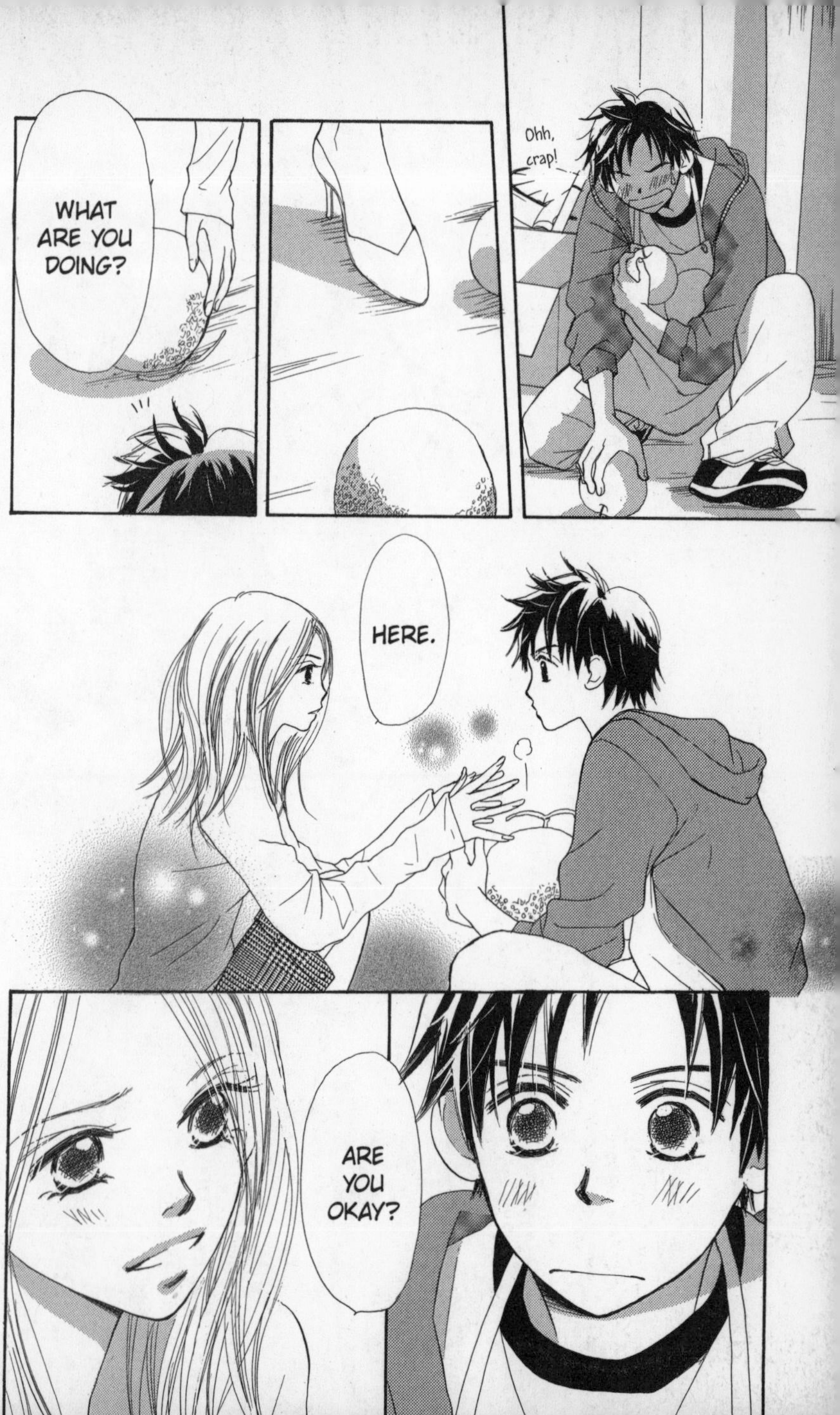
Ohh, crap!
WHAT ARE YOU DOING?
HERE.
ARE YOU OKAY?

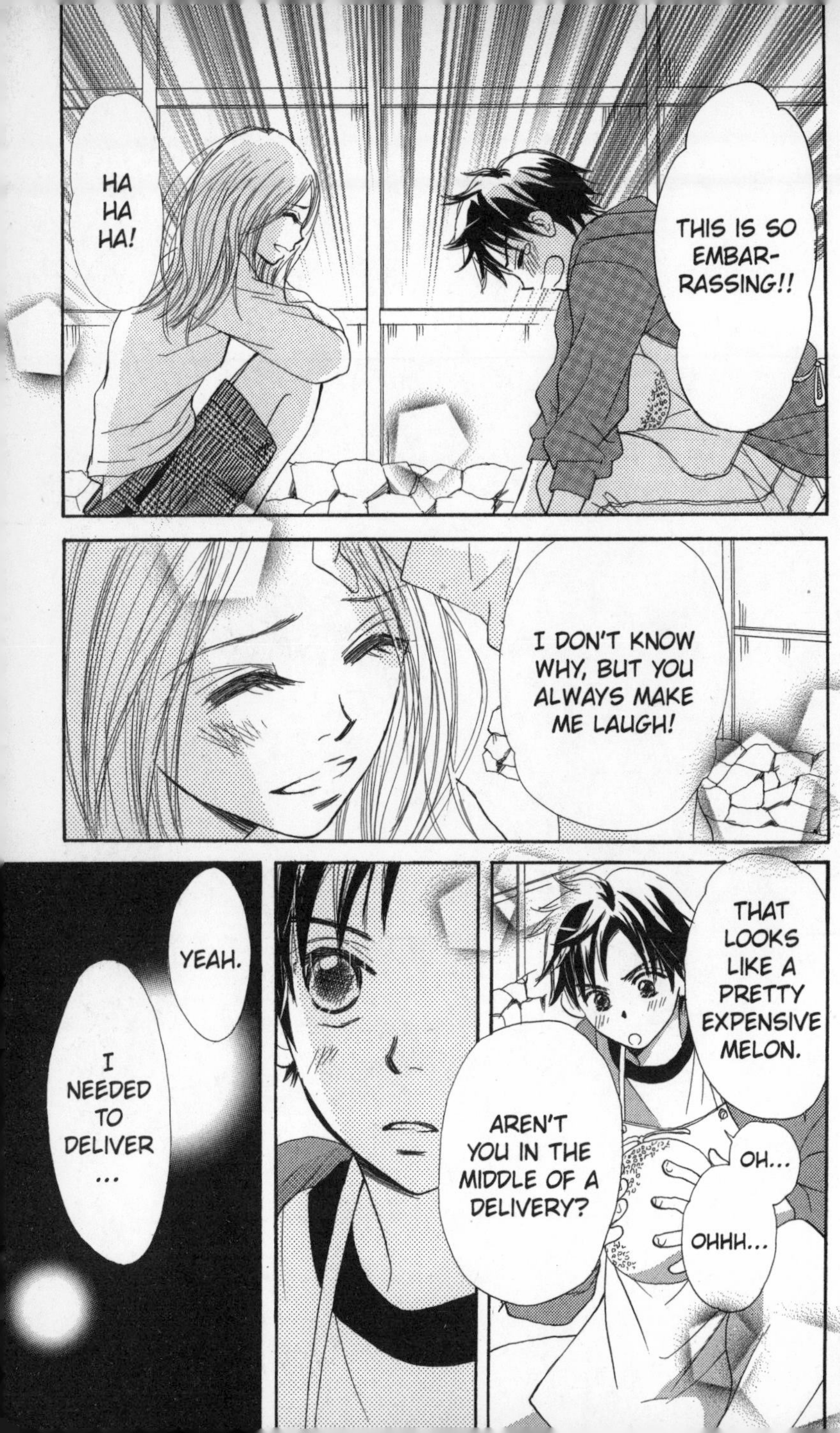
THIS IS SO EMBAR-RASSING!!
HA HA HA!
I DON'T KNOW WHY, BUT YOU ALWAYS MAKE ME LAUGH!
THAT LOOKS LIKE A PRETTY EXPENSIVE MELON.
OH...
OHHH...
AREN'T YOU IN THE MIDDLE OF A DELIVERY?
YEAH.
I NEEDED TO DELIVER...

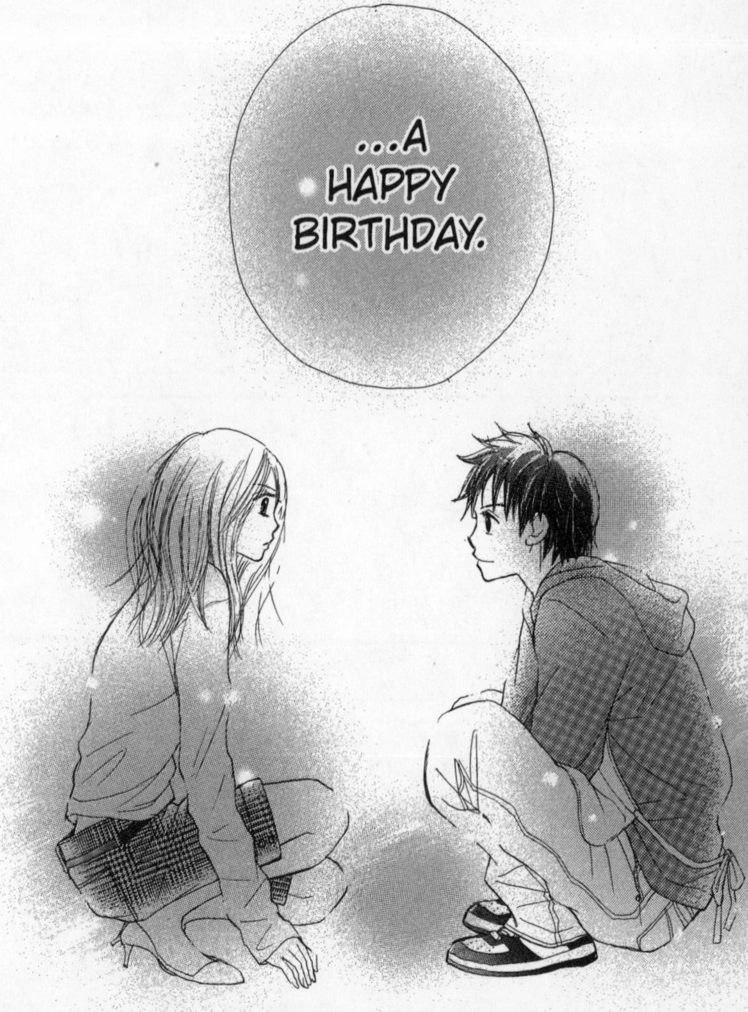
...A HAPPY BIRTHDAY.

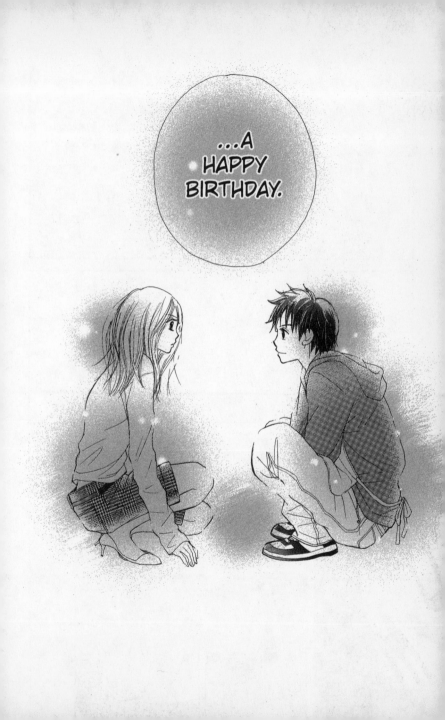

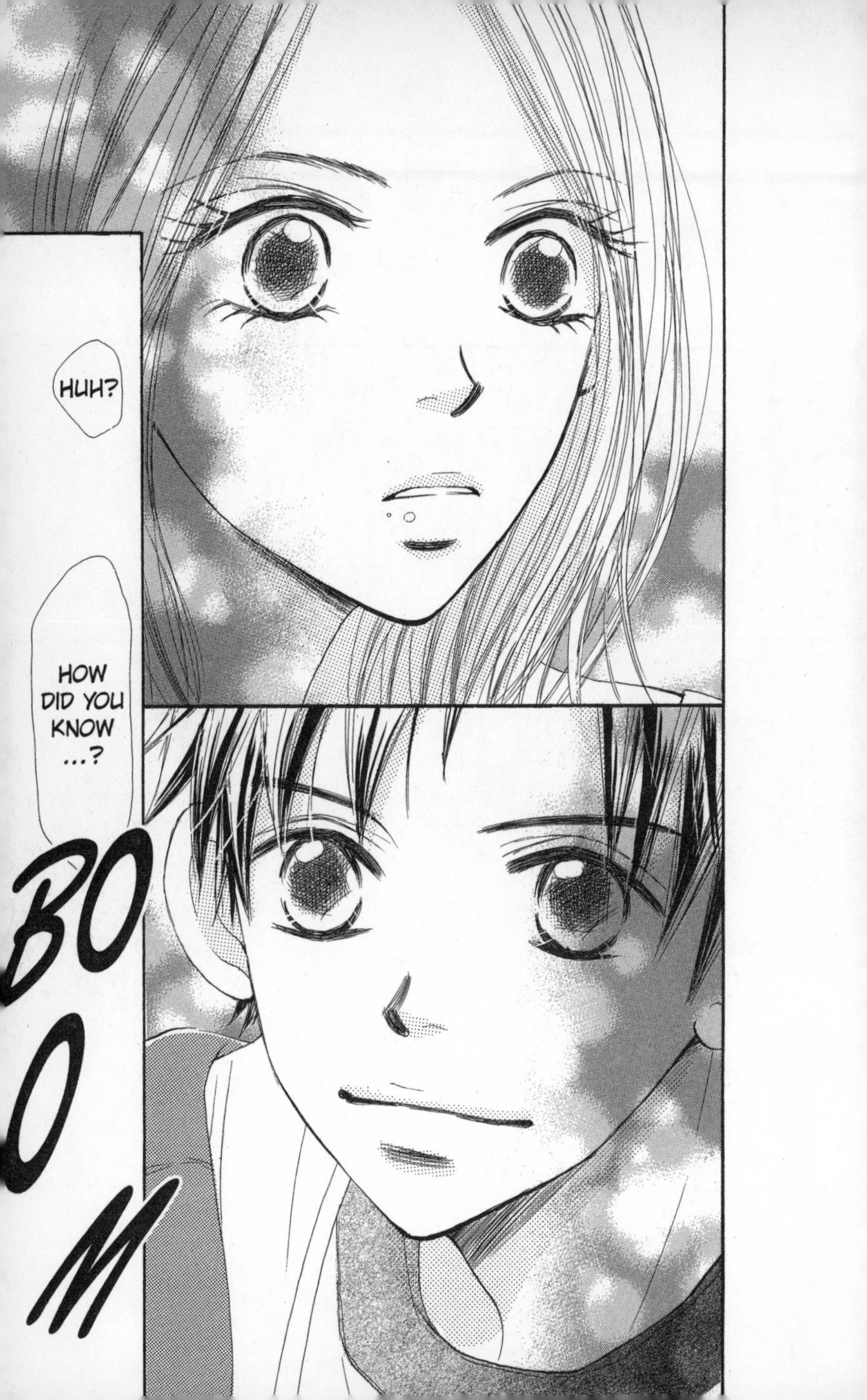
HUH?
HOW DID YOU KNOW ...?
BOOM

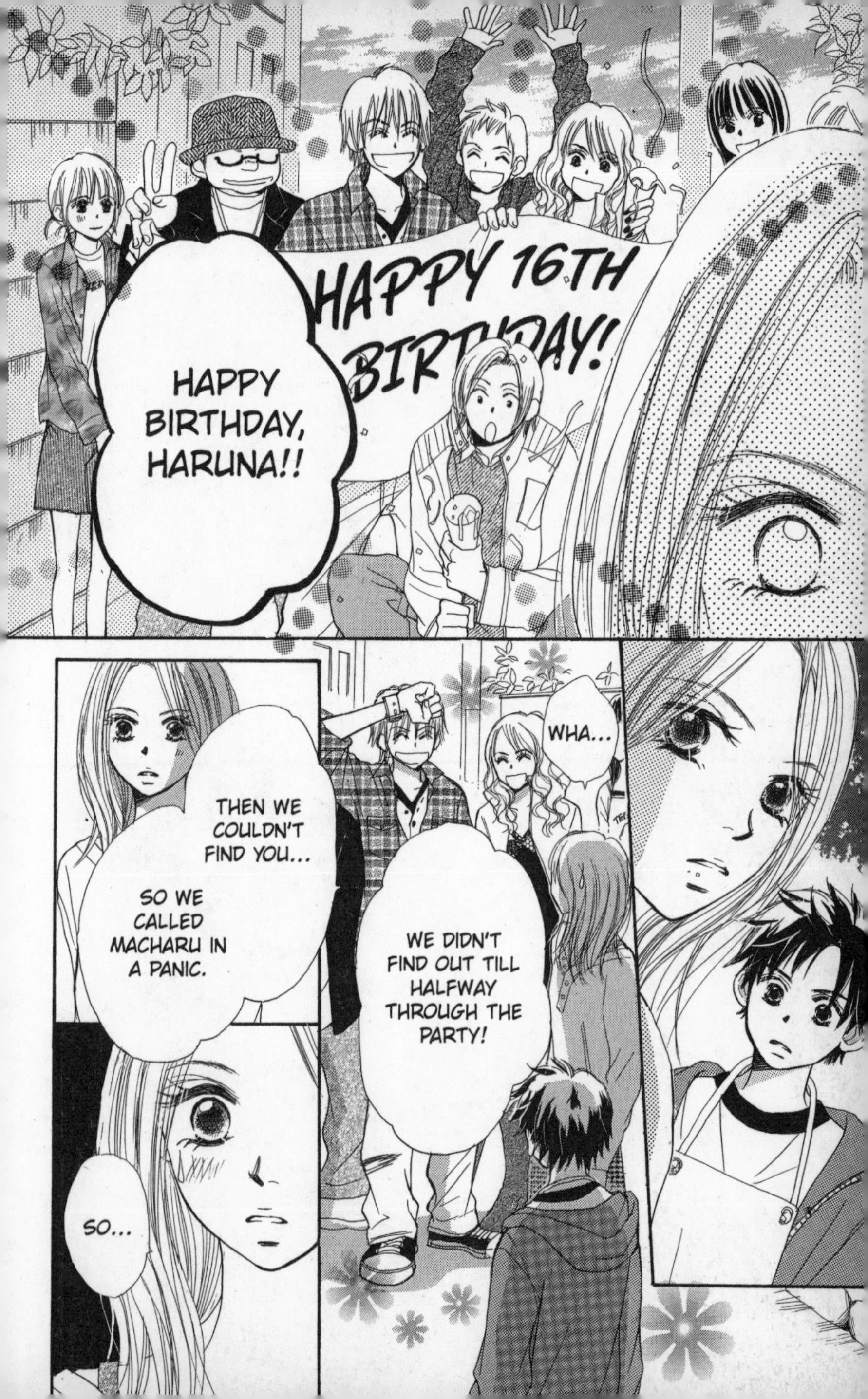
HAPPY 16TH BIRTHDAY!
HAPPY BIRTHDAY, HARUNA!!
WHA...
WE DIDN'T FIND OUT TILL HALFWAY THROUGH THE PARTY!
THEN WE COULDN'T FIND YOU...
SO WE CALLED MACHARU IN A PANIC.
SO...

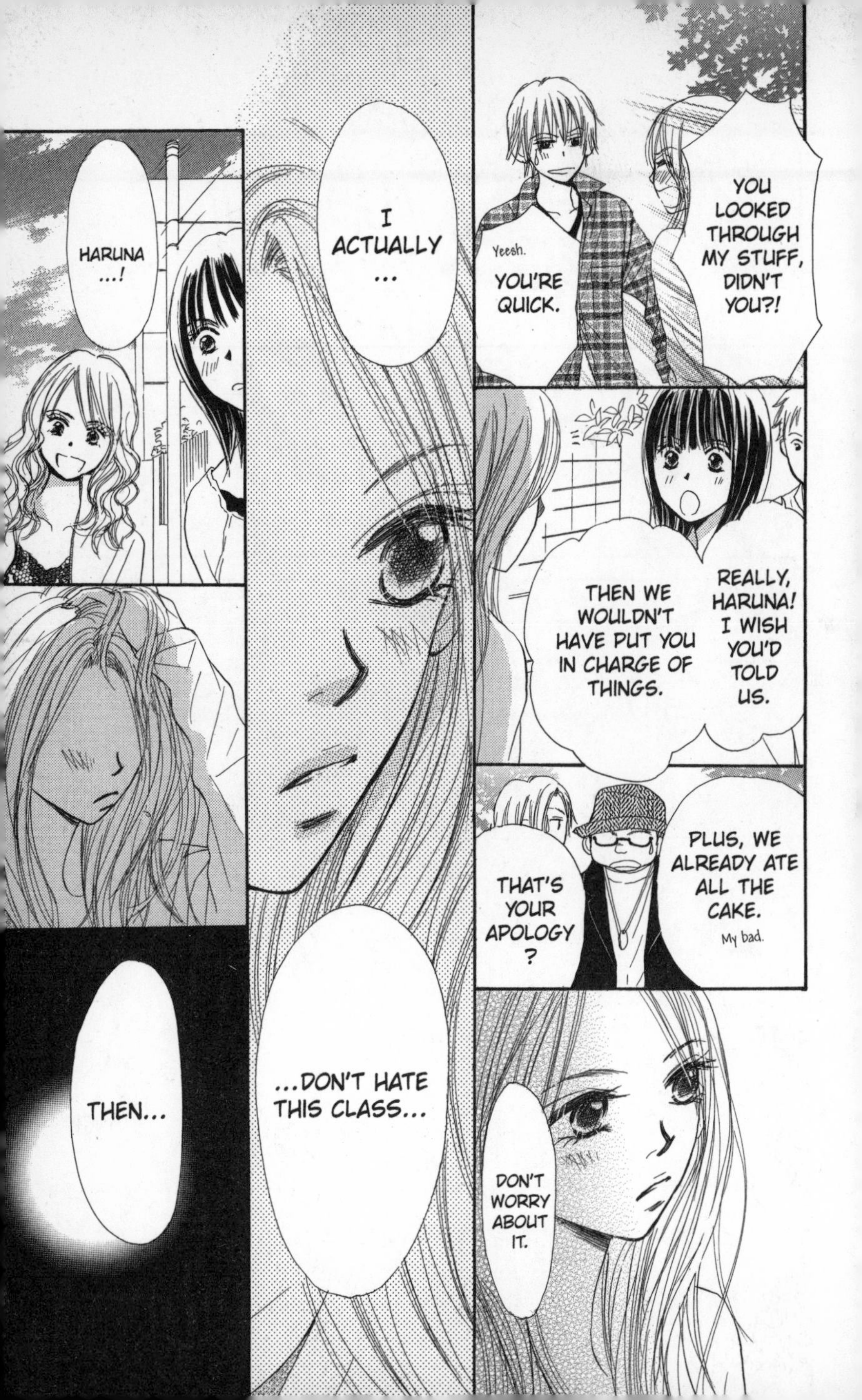
YOU LOOKED THROUGH MY STUFF, DIDN'T YOU?!
Yeesh.
YOU'RE QUICK.
REALLY, HARUNA! I WISH YOU'D TOLD US.
THEN WE WOULDN'T HAVE PUT YOU IN CHARGE OF THINGS.
PLUS, WE ALREADY ATE ALL THE CAKE.
My bad.
THAT'S YOUR APOLOGY?
DON'T WORRY ABOUT IT.
I ACTUALLY...
...DON'T HATE THIS CLASS...
HARUNA...!
THEN...

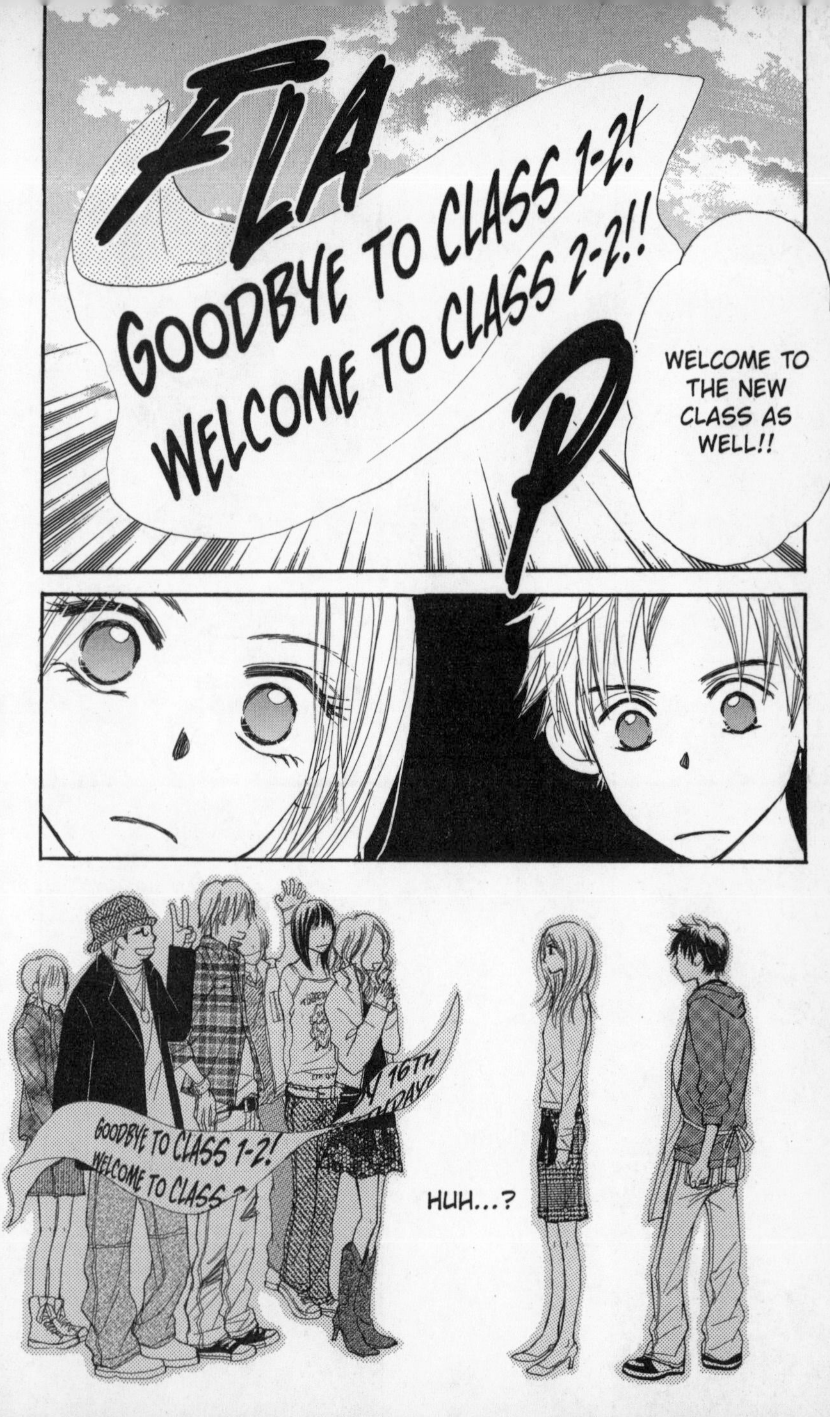
FLAP
GOODBYE TO CLASS 1-2! WELCOME TO CLASS 2-2!!
WELCOME TO THE NEW CLASS AS WELL!!
HUH...?
GOODBYE TO CLASS 1-2! WELCOME TO CLASS

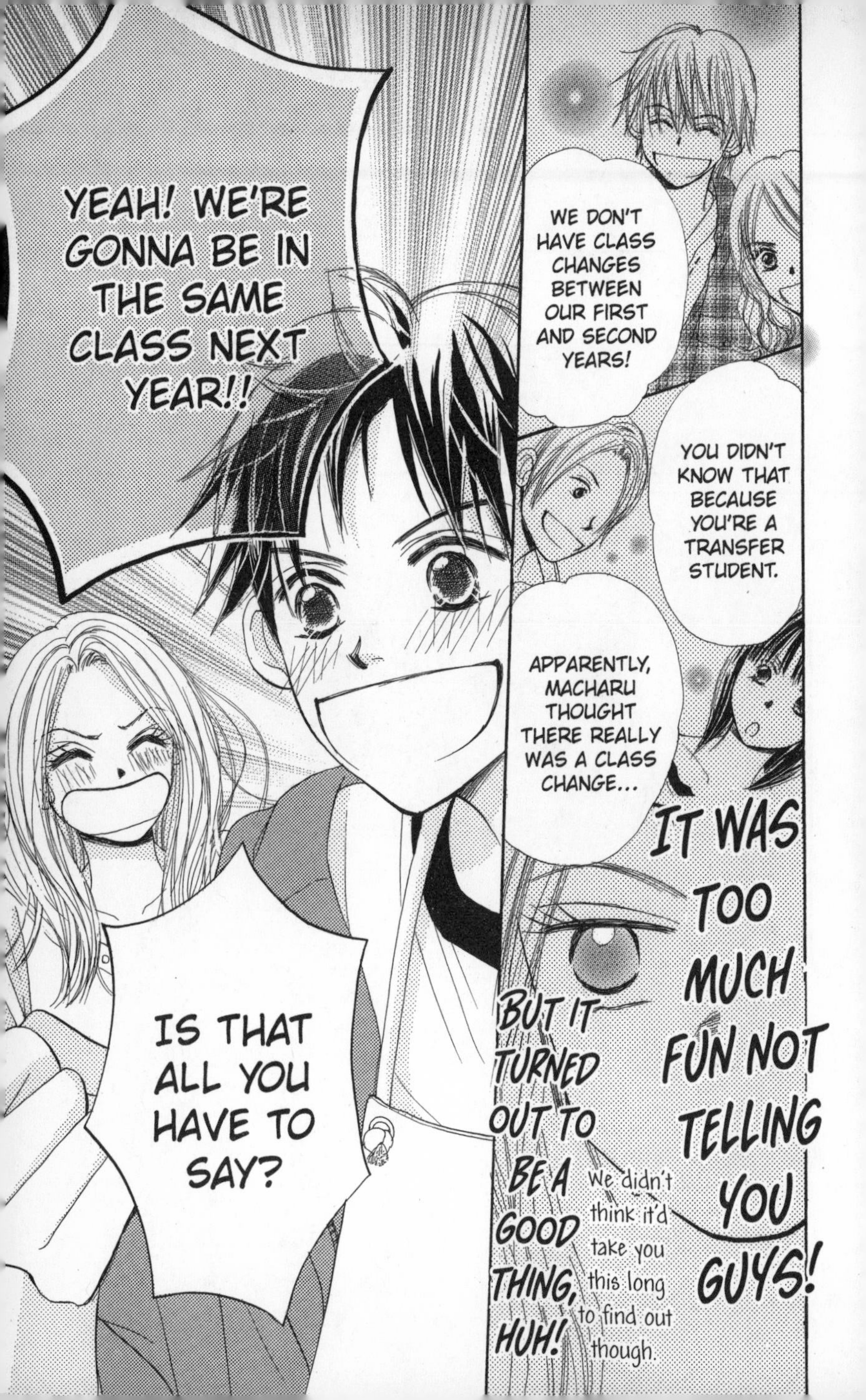
WE DON'T HAVE CLASS CHANGES BETWEEN OUR FIRST AND SECOND YEARS!
YOU DIDN'T KNOW THAT BECAUSE YOU'RE A TRANSFER STUDENT.
APPARENTLY, MACHARU THOUGHT THERE REALLY WAS A CLASS CHANGE...
IT WAS TOO MUCH FUN NOT TELLING YOU GUYS!
BUT IT TURNED OUT TO BE A GOOD THING, HUH!
We didn't think it'd take you this long to find out though.
YEAH! WE'RE GONNA BE IN THE SAME CLASS NEXT YEAR!!
IS THAT ALL YOU HAVE TO SAY?

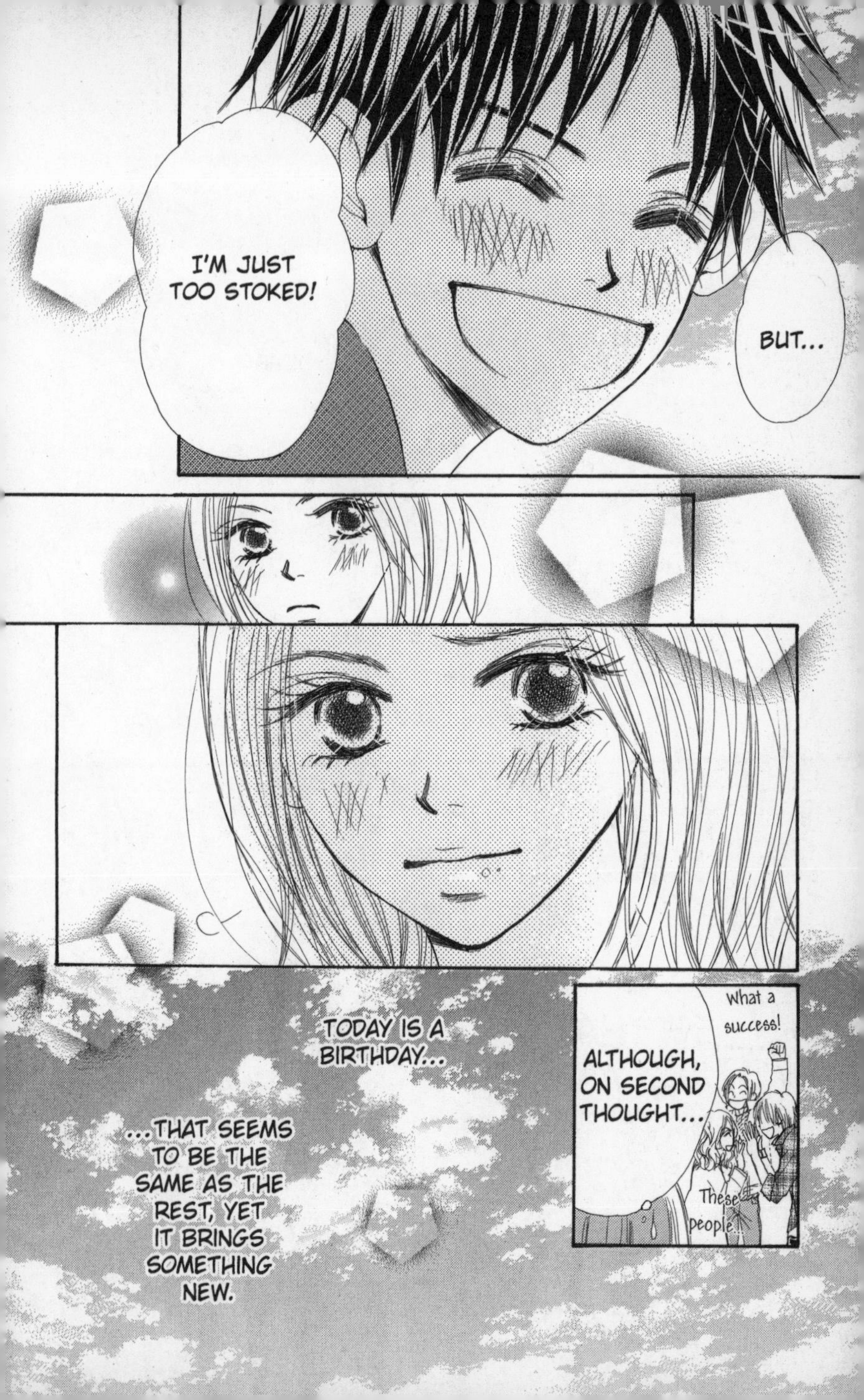
BUT...
I'M JUST TOO STOKED!
What a success!
ALTHOUGH, ON SECOND THOUGHT...
These people...
TODAY IS A BIRTHDAY...
...THAT SEEMS TO BE THE SAME AS THE REST, YET IT BRINGS SOMETHING NEW.

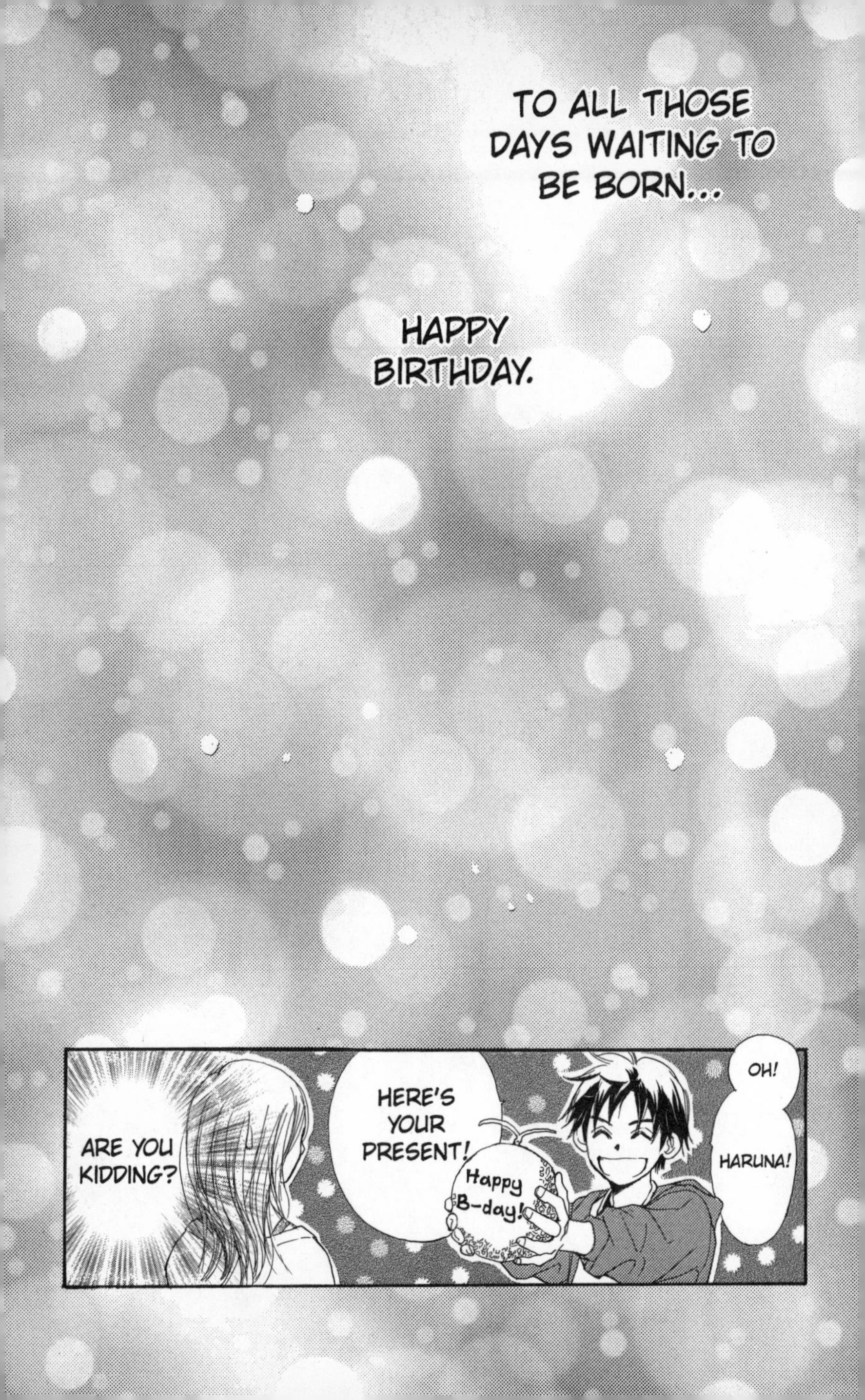
TO ALL THOSE DAYS WAITING TO BE BORN...
HAPPY BIRTHDAY.
OH!
HARUNA!
HERE'S YOUR PRESENT!
Happy B-day!
ARE YOU KIDDING?

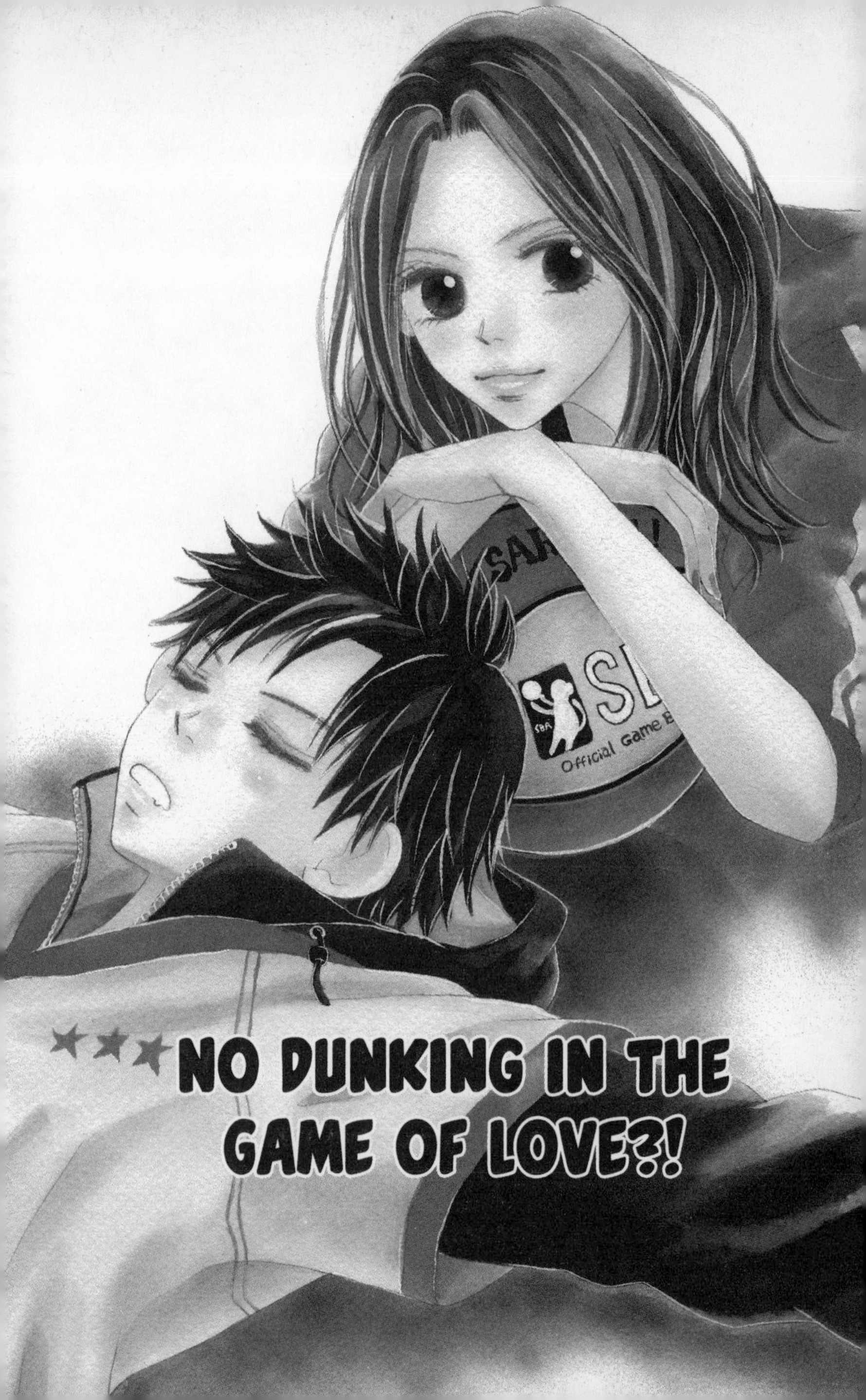
NO DUNKING IN THE GAME OF LOVE?!

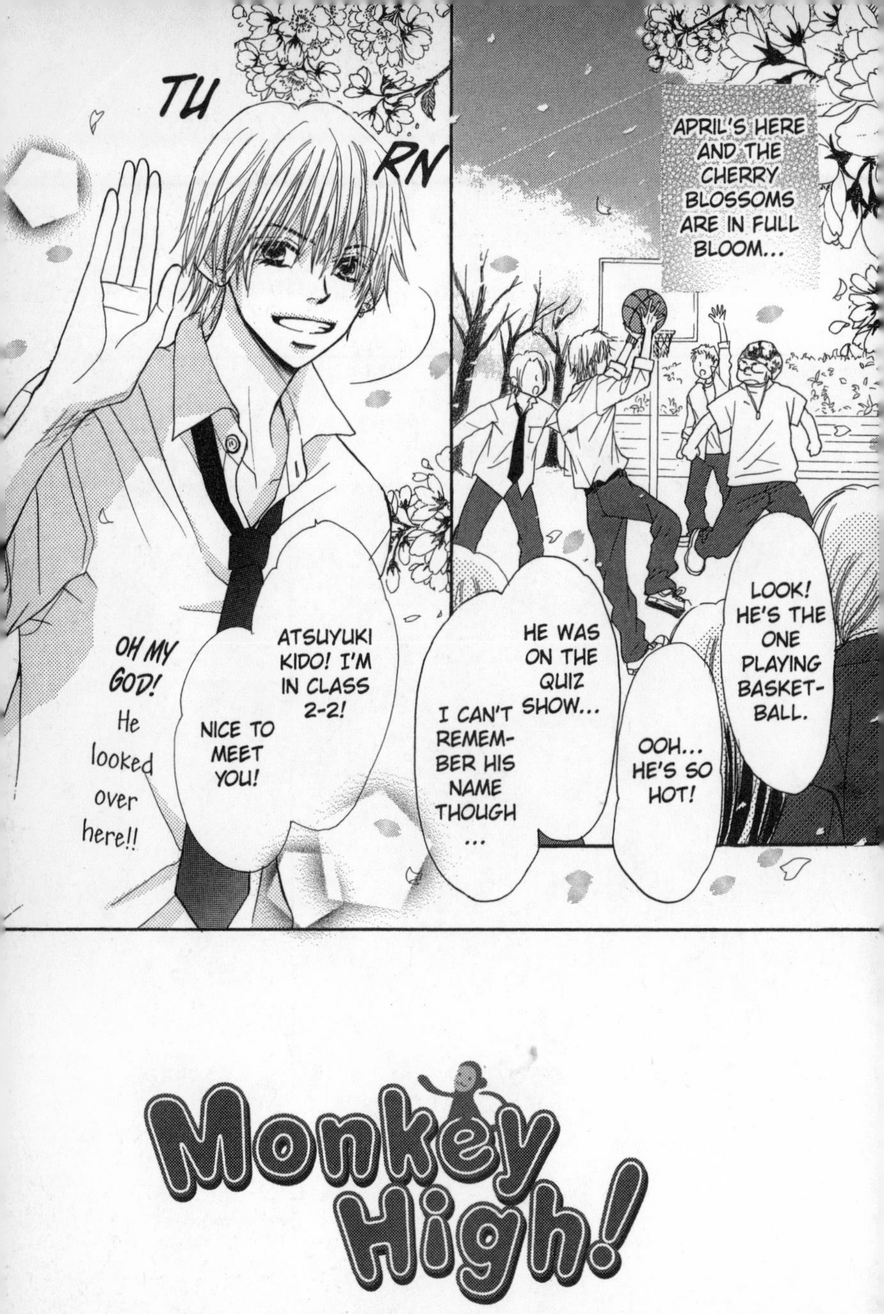
APRIL'S HERE AND THE CHERRY BLOSSOMS ARE IN FULL BLOOM...
LOOK! HE'S THE ONE PLAYING BASKETBALL.
OOH... HE'S SO HOT!
HE WAS ON THE QUIZ SHOW...
I CAN'T REMEMBER HIS NAME THOUGH...
TURN
ATSUYUKI KIDO! I'M IN CLASS 2-2!
NICE TO MEET YOU!
OH MY GOD! He looked over here!!

Monkey High!

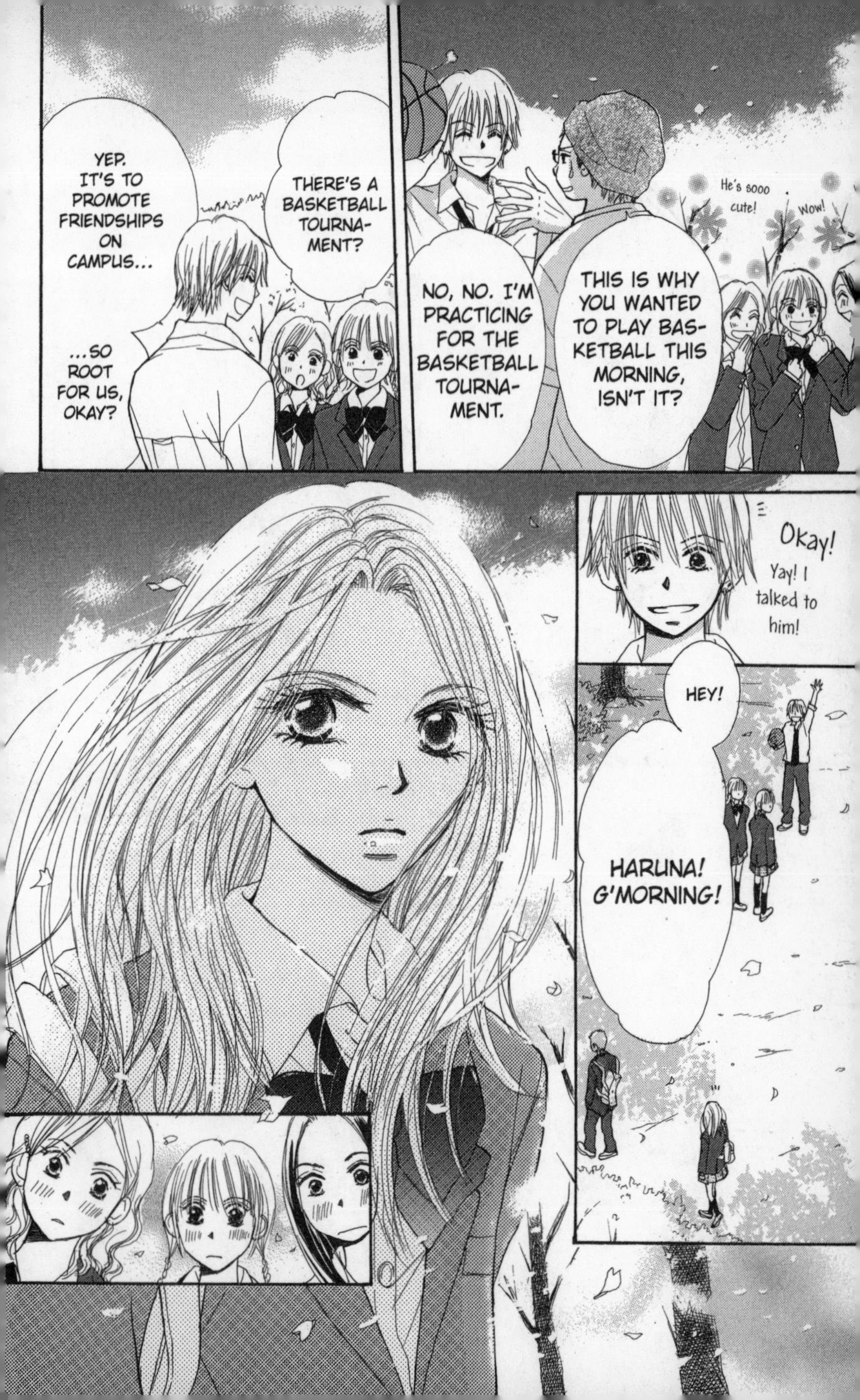
Wow!
He's sooo cute!
THIS IS WHY YOU WANTED TO PLAY BASKETBALL THIS MORNING, ISN'T IT?
NO, NO. I'M PRACTICING FOR THE BASKETBALL TOURNAMENT.
THERE'S A BASKETBALL TOURNAMENT?
YEP. IT'S TO PROMOTE FRIENDSHIPS ON CAMPUS...
...SO ROOT FOR US, OKAY?
Okay!
Yay! I talked to him!
HEY!
HARUNA! G'MORNING!

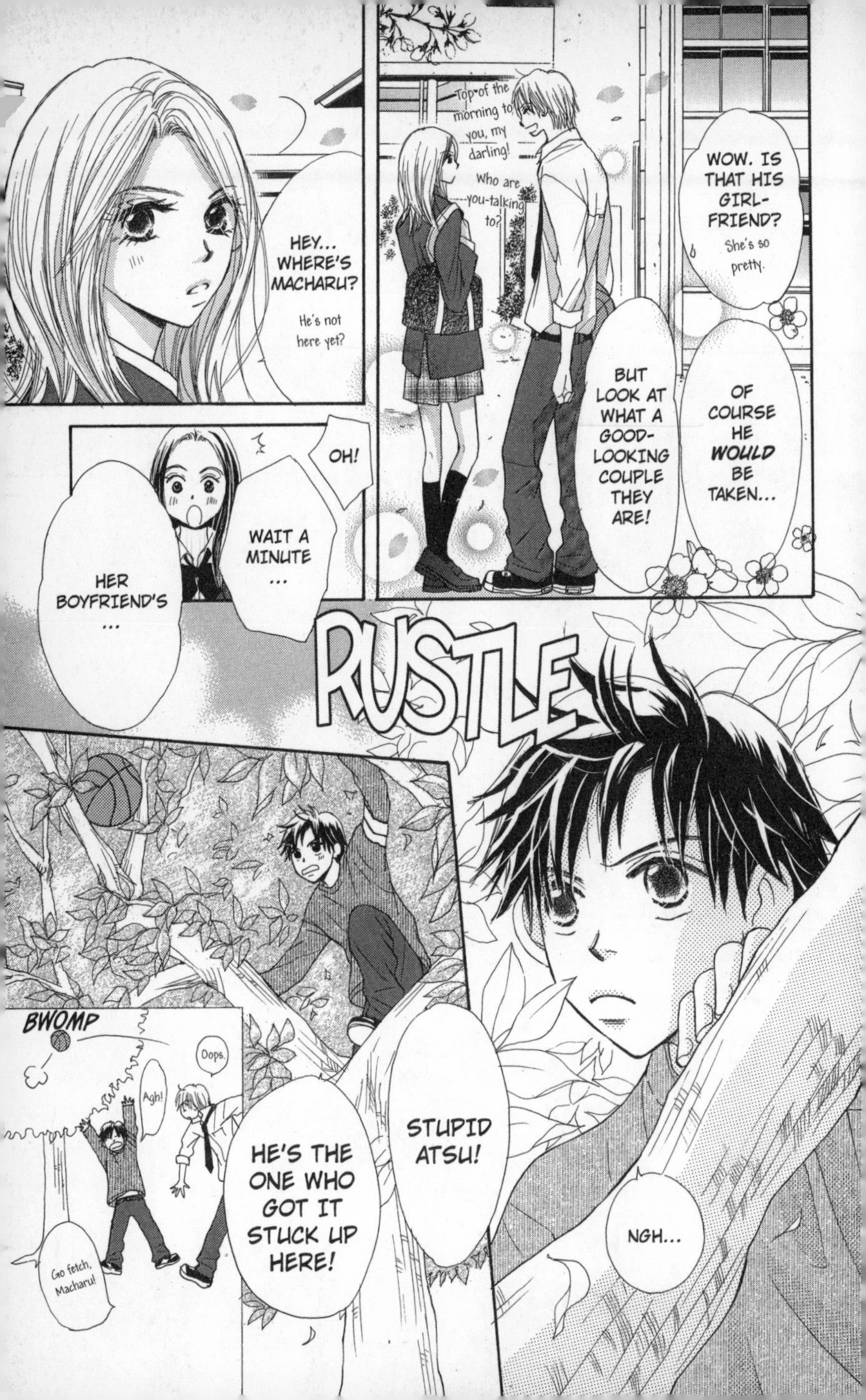
Top of the morning to you, my darling!
Who are you-talking to?
WOW. IS THAT HIS GIRL-FRIEND?
She's so pretty.
OF COURSE HE WOULD BE TAKEN...
BUT LOOK AT WHAT A GOOD-LOOKING COUPLE THEY ARE!
HEY... WHERE'S MACHARU?
He's not here yet?
OH!
WAIT A MINUTE...
HER BOYFRIEND'S...
RUSTLE
NGH...
STUPID ATSU!
HE'S THE ONE WHO GOT IT STUCK UP HERE!
BWOMP
Oops.
Agh!
Go fetch, Macharu!

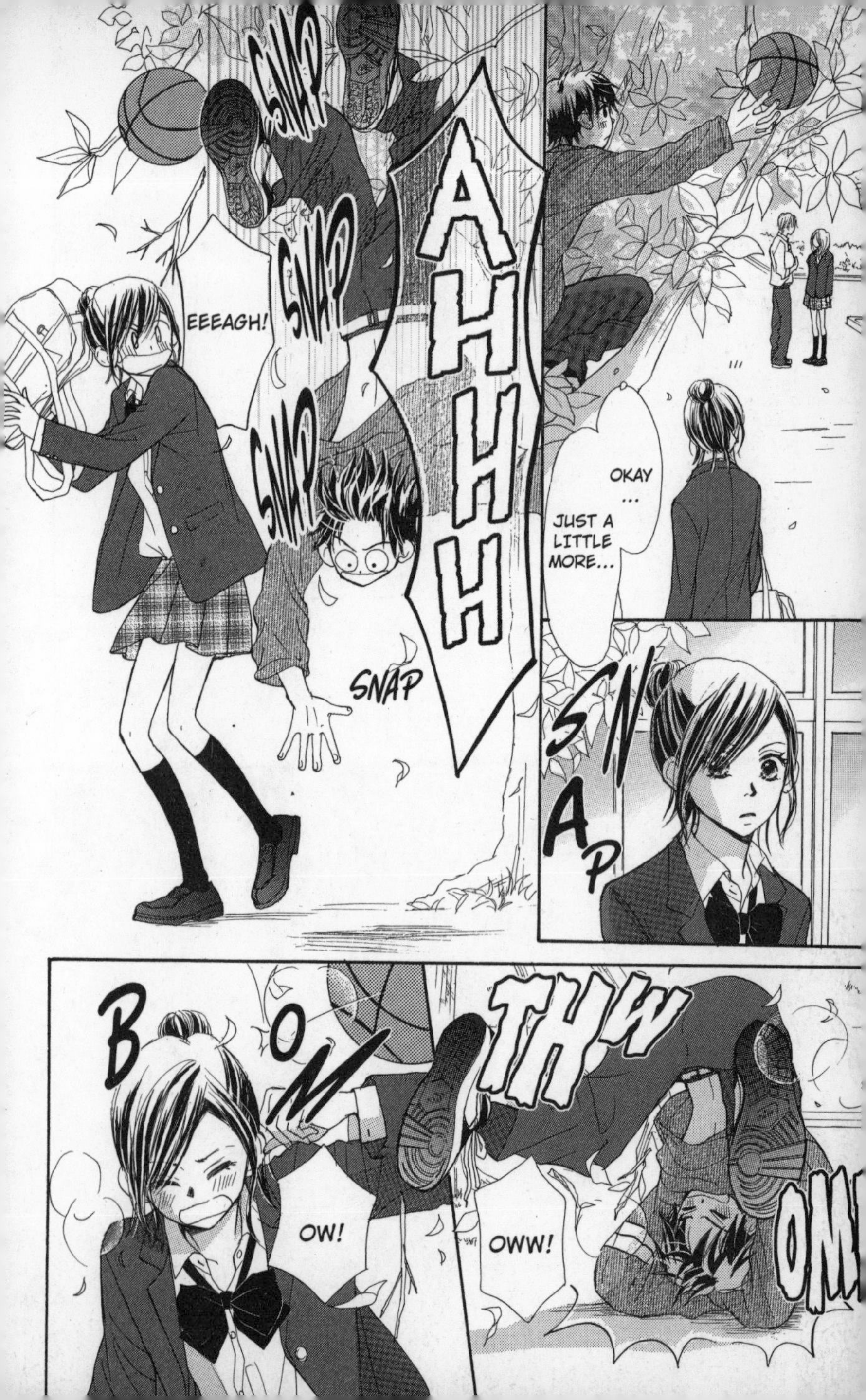
OKAY ... JUST A LITTLE MORE...
SNAP
AHHHH
SNAP
SNAP
SNAP
EEEAGH!
SNAP
OM
THW
OWW!
OW!
BOM

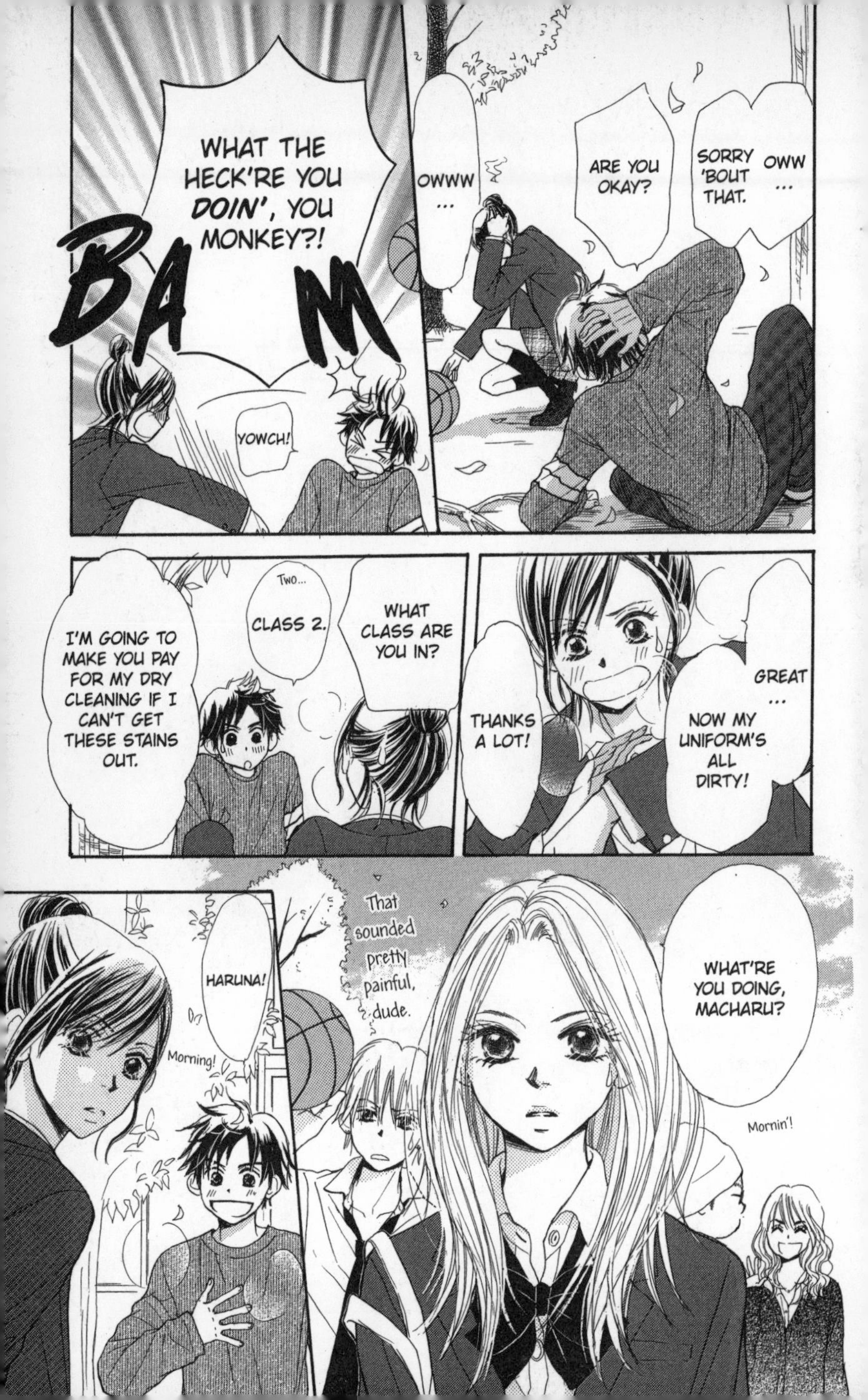
OWW ...
SORRY 'BOUT THAT.
ARE YOU OKAY?
OWWW ...
WHAT THE HECK'RE YOU *DOIN'*, YOU MONKEY?!
BAM
YOWCH!
GREAT ... NOW MY UNIFORM'S ALL DIRTY!
THANKS A LOT!
WHAT CLASS ARE YOU IN?
Two...
CLASS 2.
I'M GOING TO MAKE YOU PAY FOR MY DRY CLEANING IF I CAN'T GET THESE STAINS OUT.
WHAT'RE YOU DOING, MACHARU?
Mornin'!
That sounded pretty painful, dude.
HARUNA!
Morning!

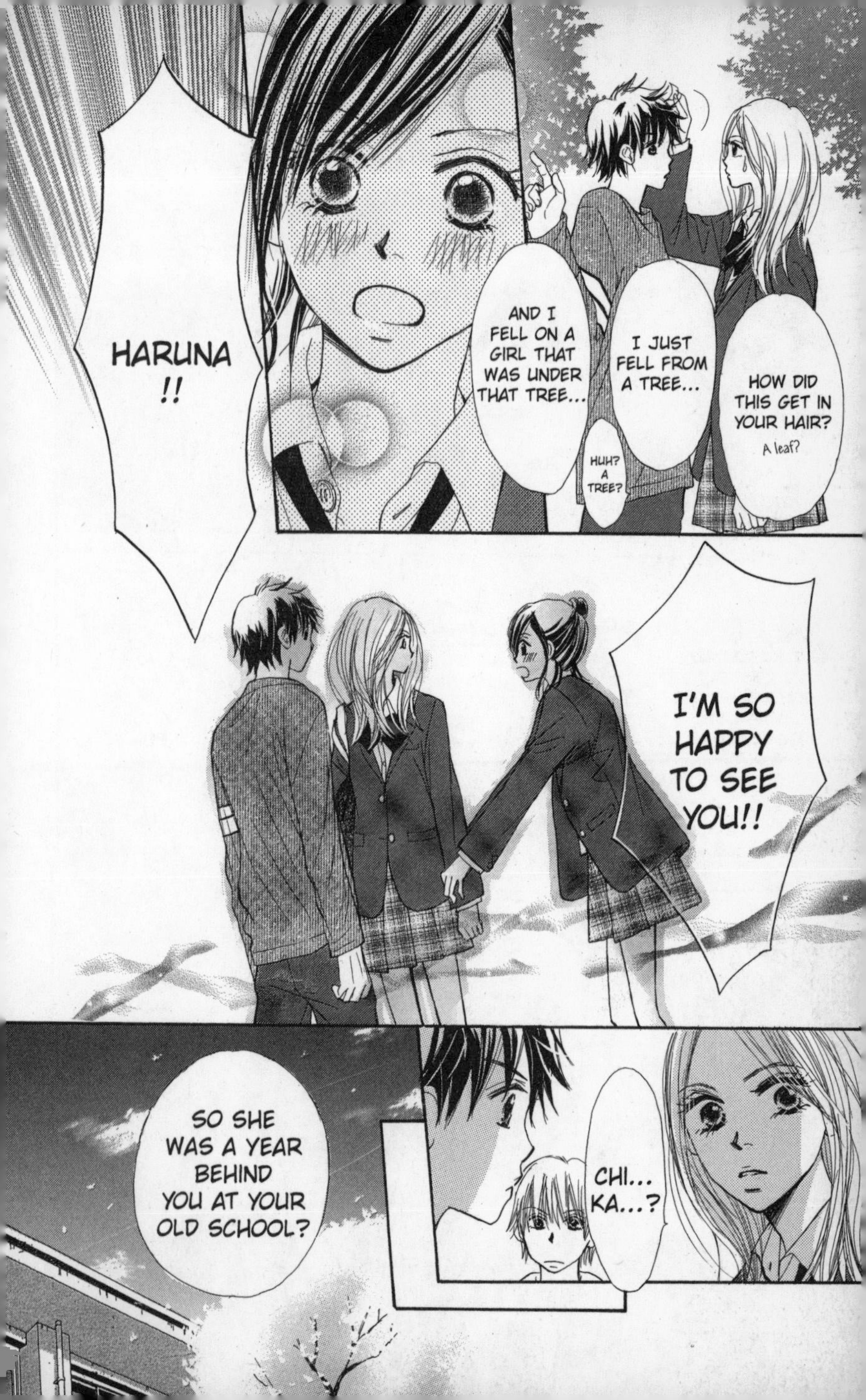
HOW DID THIS GET IN YOUR HAIR?
A leaf?
I JUST FELL FROM A TREE...
HUH? A TREE?
AND I FELL ON A GIRL THAT WAS UNDER THAT TREE...
HARUNA!!
I'M SO HAPPY TO SEE YOU!!
CHI... KA...?
SO SHE WAS A YEAR BEHIND YOU AT YOUR OLD SCHOOL?

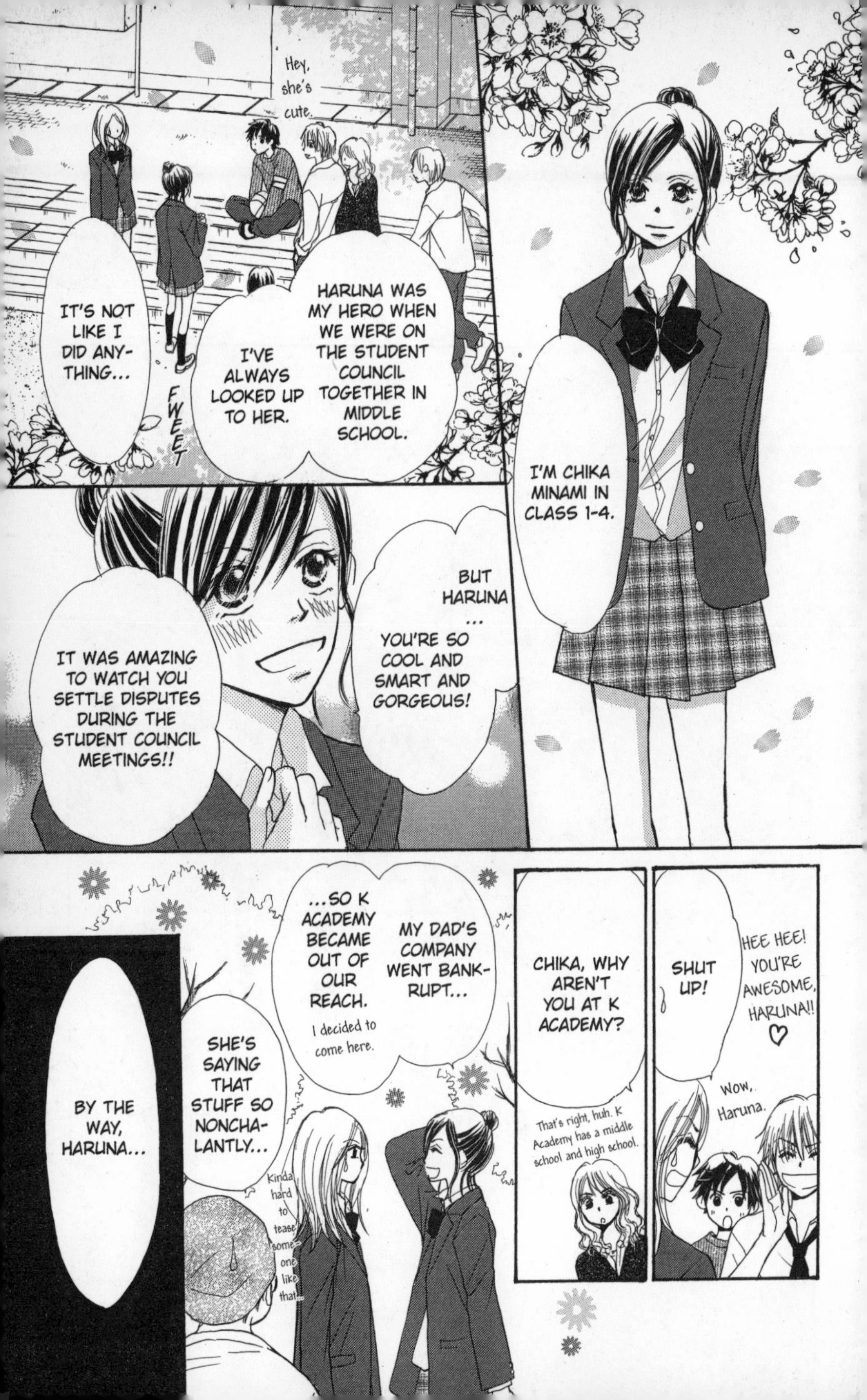
I'M CHIKA MINAMI IN CLASS 1-4.
Hey, she's cute.
HARUNA WAS MY HERO WHEN WE WERE ON THE STUDENT COUNCIL TOGETHER IN MIDDLE SCHOOL.
I'VE ALWAYS LOOKED UP TO HER.
FWEET
IT'S NOT LIKE I DID ANYTHING...
BUT HARUNA... YOU'RE SO COOL AND SMART AND GORGEOUS!
IT WAS AMAZING TO WATCH YOU SETTLE DISPUTES DURING THE STUDENT COUNCIL MEETINGS!!
HEE HEE! YOU'RE AWESOME, HARUNA!! ♡
SHUT UP!
Wow, Haruna.
CHIKA, WHY AREN'T YOU AT K ACADEMY?
That's right, huh. K Academy has a middle school and high school.
MY DAD'S COMPANY WENT BANKRUPT...
...SO K ACADEMY BECAME OUT OF OUR REACH.
I decided to come here.
SHE'S SAYING THAT STUFF SO NONCHALANTLY...
Kinda hard to tease someone like that...
BY THE WAY, HARUNA...

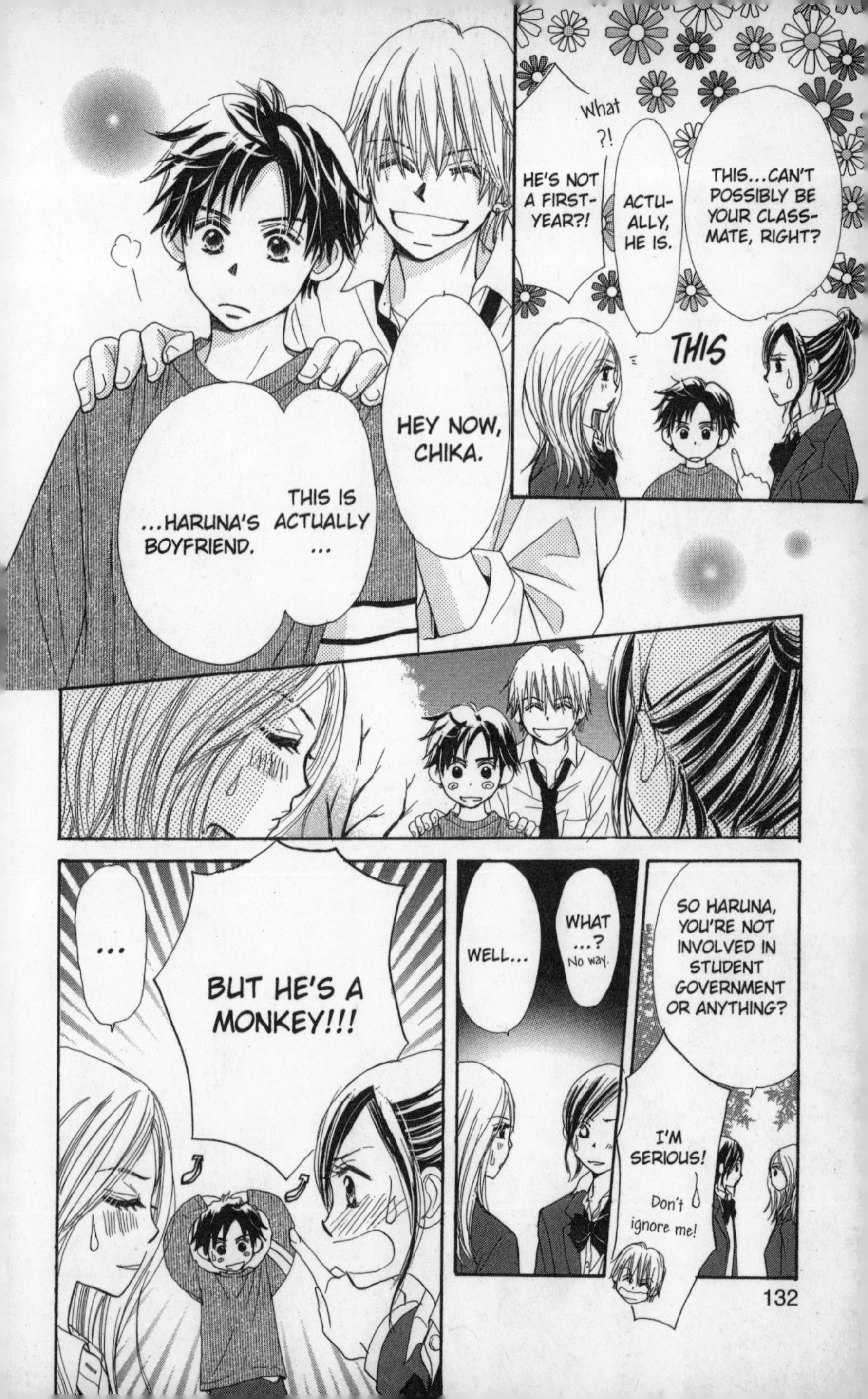
THIS...CAN'T POSSIBLY BE YOUR CLASSMATE, RIGHT?
ACTUALLY, HE IS.
What ?!
HE'S NOT A FIRST-YEAR?!
THIS
HEY NOW, CHIKA.
THIS IS ACTUALLY ...
...HARUNA'S BOYFRIEND.
SO HARUNA, YOU'RE NOT INVOLVED IN STUDENT GOVERNMENT OR ANYTHING?
I'M SERIOUS!
Don't ignore me!
WHAT ...? No way.
WELL...
BUT HE'S A MONKEY!!!
...

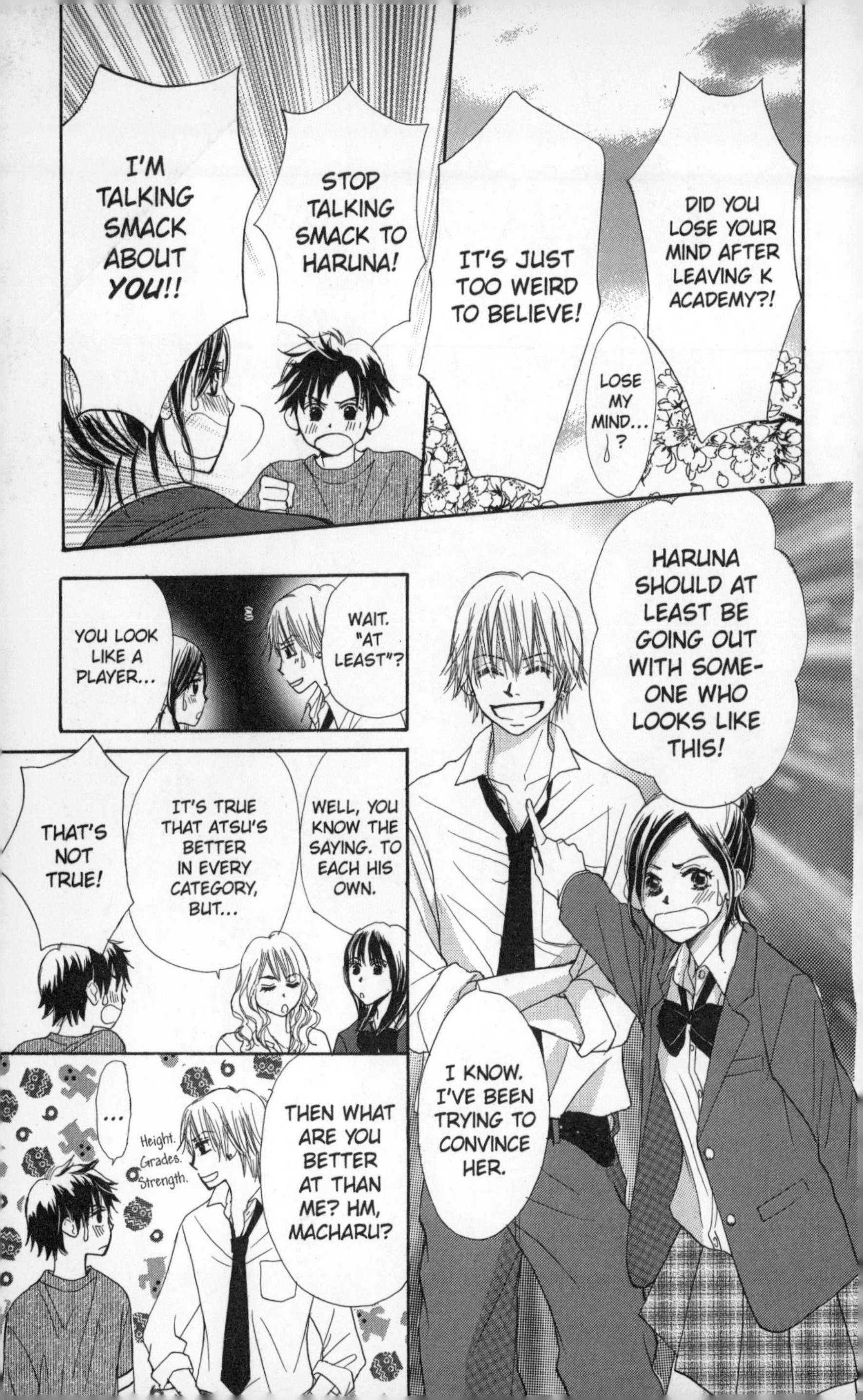

DID YOU LOSE YOUR MIND AFTER LEAVING K ACADEMY?!
IT'S JUST TOO WEIRD TO BELIEVE!
LOSE MY MIND...?
STOP TALKING SMACK TO HARUNA!
I'M TALKING SMACK ABOUT *YOU*!!
HARUNA SHOULD AT LEAST BE GOING OUT WITH SOME-ONE WHO LOOKS LIKE THIS!
I KNOW. I'VE BEEN TRYING TO CONVINCE HER.
WAIT. "AT LEAST"?
YOU LOOK LIKE A PLAYER...
WELL, YOU KNOW THE SAYING. TO EACH HIS OWN.
IT'S TRUE THAT ATSU'S BETTER IN EVERY CATEGORY, BUT...
THAT'S NOT TRUE!
THEN WHAT ARE YOU BETTER AT THAN ME? HM, MACHARU?
...
Height. Grades. Strength.

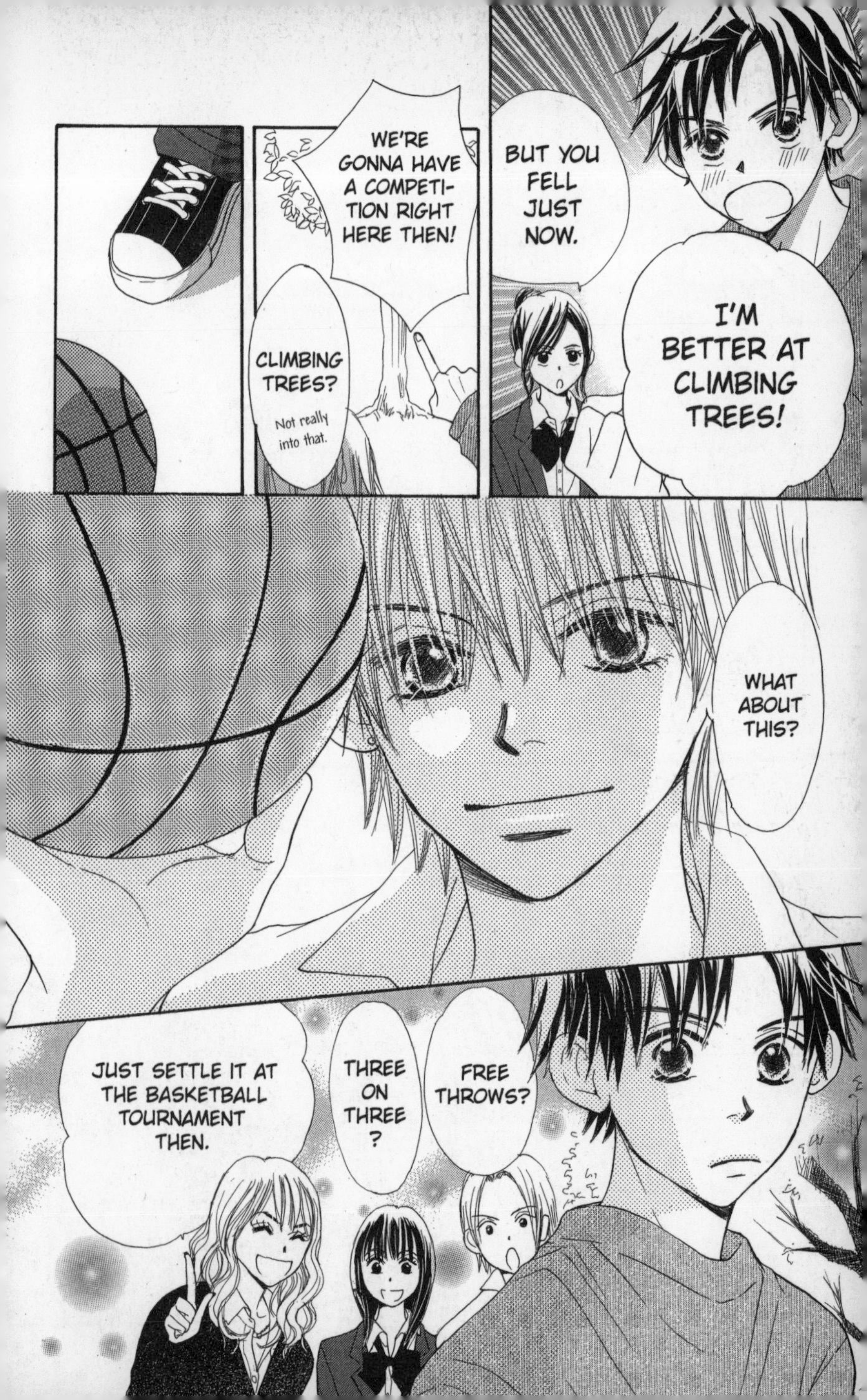
I'M BETTER AT CLIMBING TREES!
BUT YOU FELL JUST NOW.
WE'RE GONNA HAVE A COMPETITION RIGHT HERE THEN!
CLIMBING TREES?
Not really into that.
WHAT ABOUT THIS?
FREE THROWS?
THREE ON THREE?
JUST SETTLE IT AT THE BASKETBALL TOURNAMENT THEN.

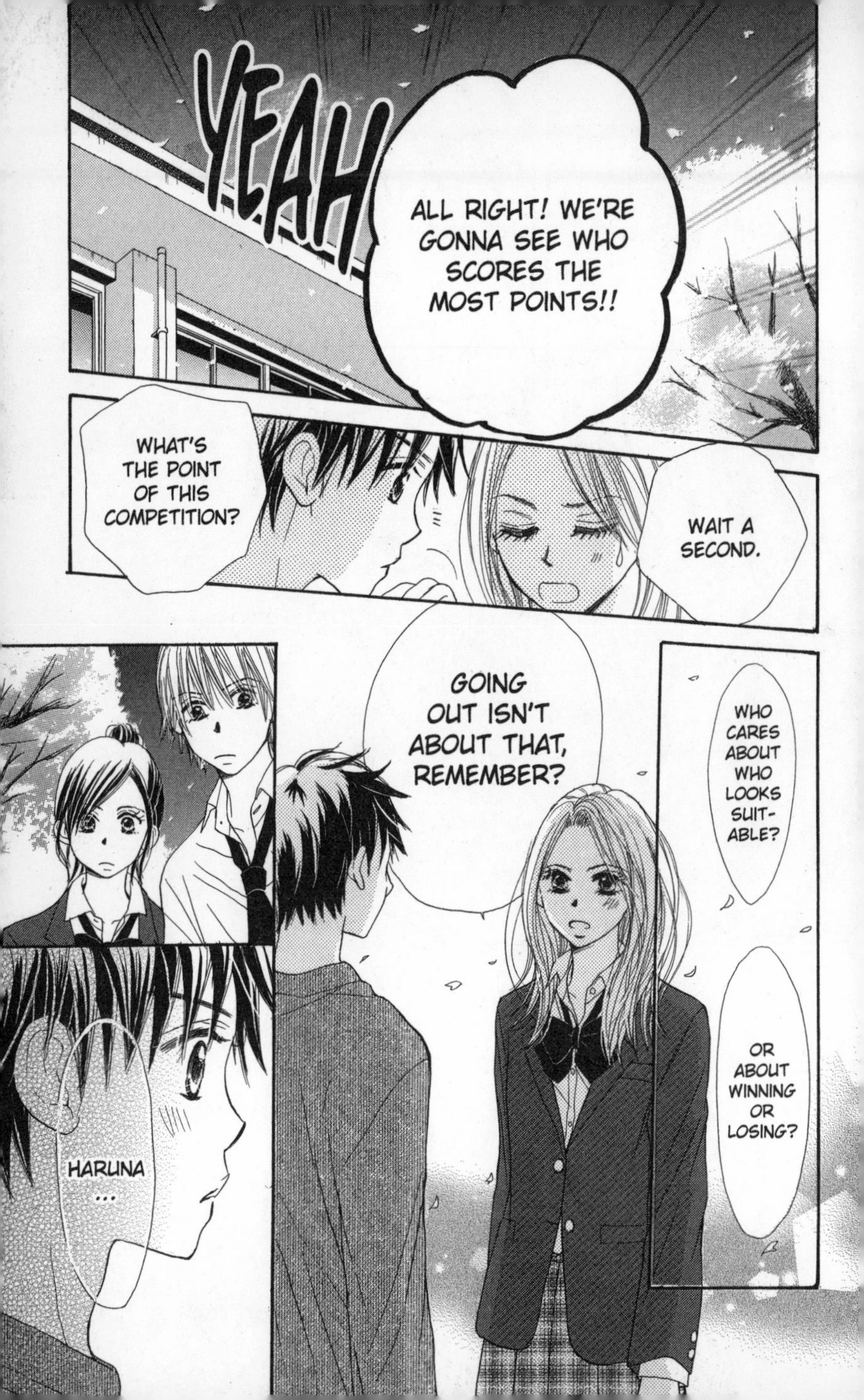
ALL RIGHT! WE'RE GONNA SEE WHO SCORES THE MOST POINTS!!
YEAH
WAIT A SECOND.
WHAT'S THE POINT OF THIS COMPETITION?
WHO CARES ABOUT WHO LOOKS SUIT-ABLE?
OR ABOUT WINNING OR LOSING?
GOING OUT ISN'T ABOUT THAT, REMEMBER?
HARUNA ...

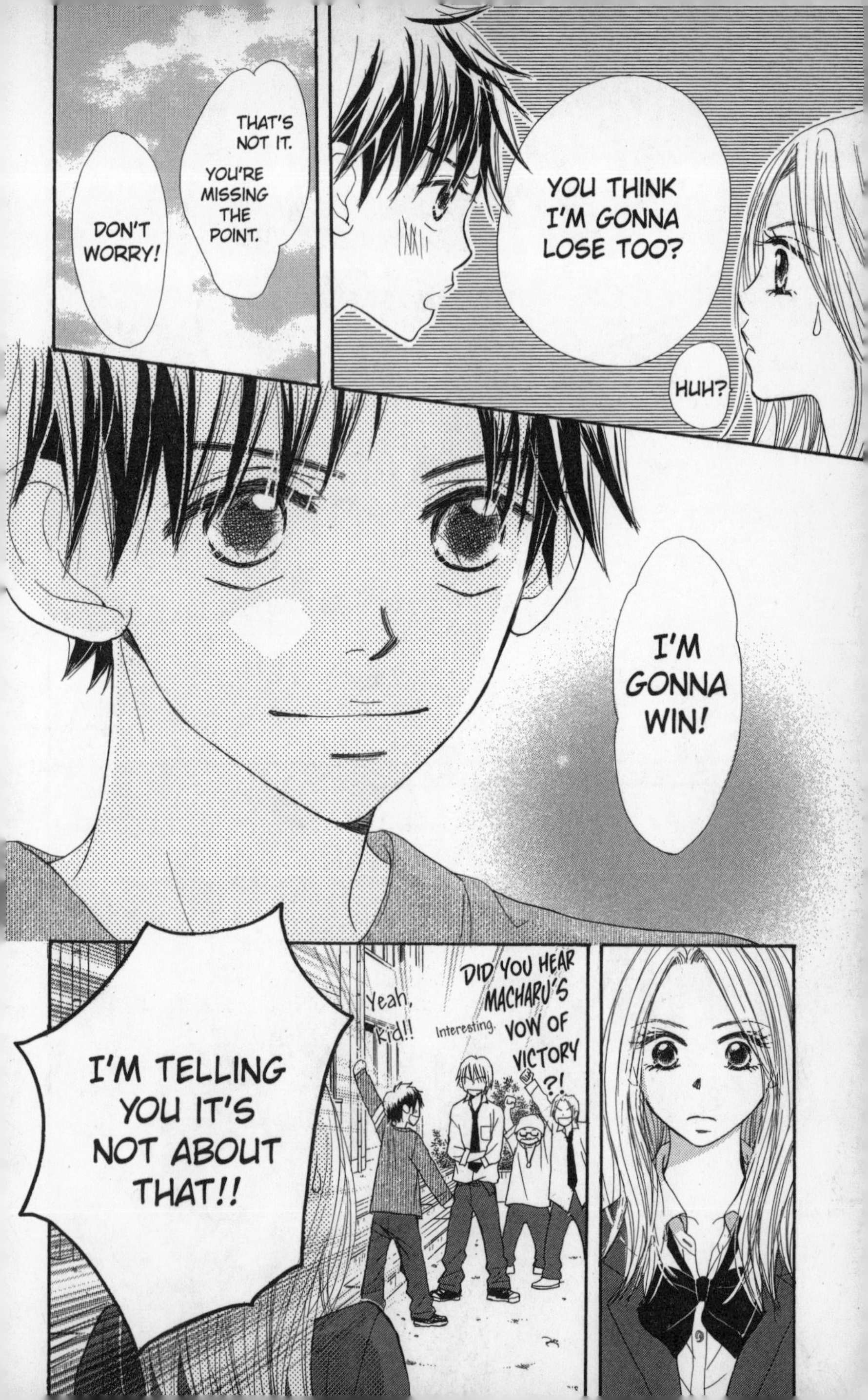
YOU THINK I'M GONNA LOSE TOO?
HUH?
THAT'S NOT IT. YOU'RE MISSING THE POINT.
DON'T WORRY!
I'M GONNA WIN!
DID YOU HEAR MACHARU'S VOW OF VICTORY?!
Interesting.
Yeah, kid!!
I'M TELLING YOU IT'S NOT ABOUT THAT!!

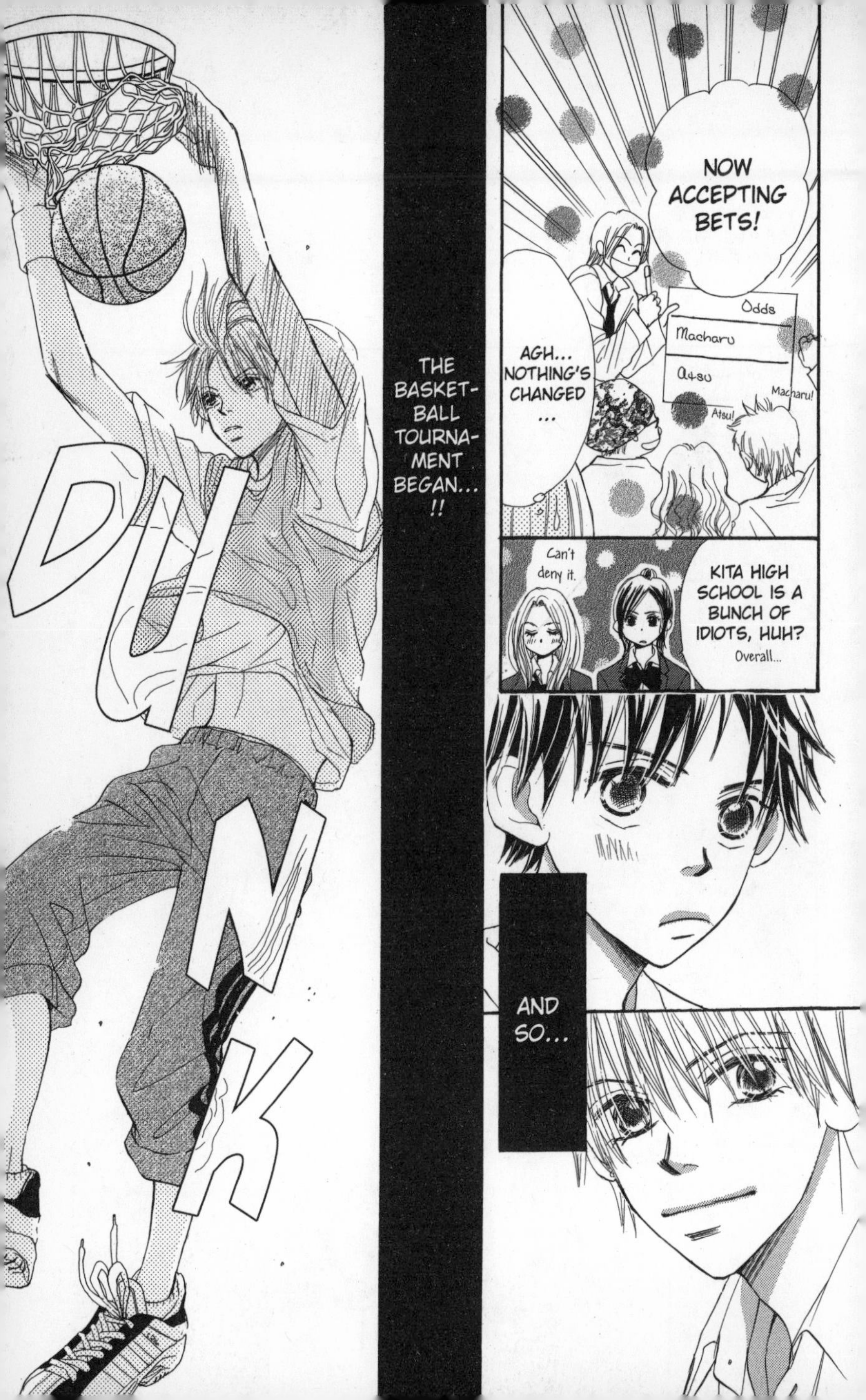
NOW ACCEPTING BETS!
Odds
Macharu
Atsu
Macharu!
Atsu!
AGH... NOTHING'S CHANGED...
KITA HIGH SCHOOL IS A BUNCH OF IDIOTS, HUH?
Overall...
Can't deny it.
AND SO...
THE BASKET-BALL TOURNA-MENT BEGAN... !!
DUNK

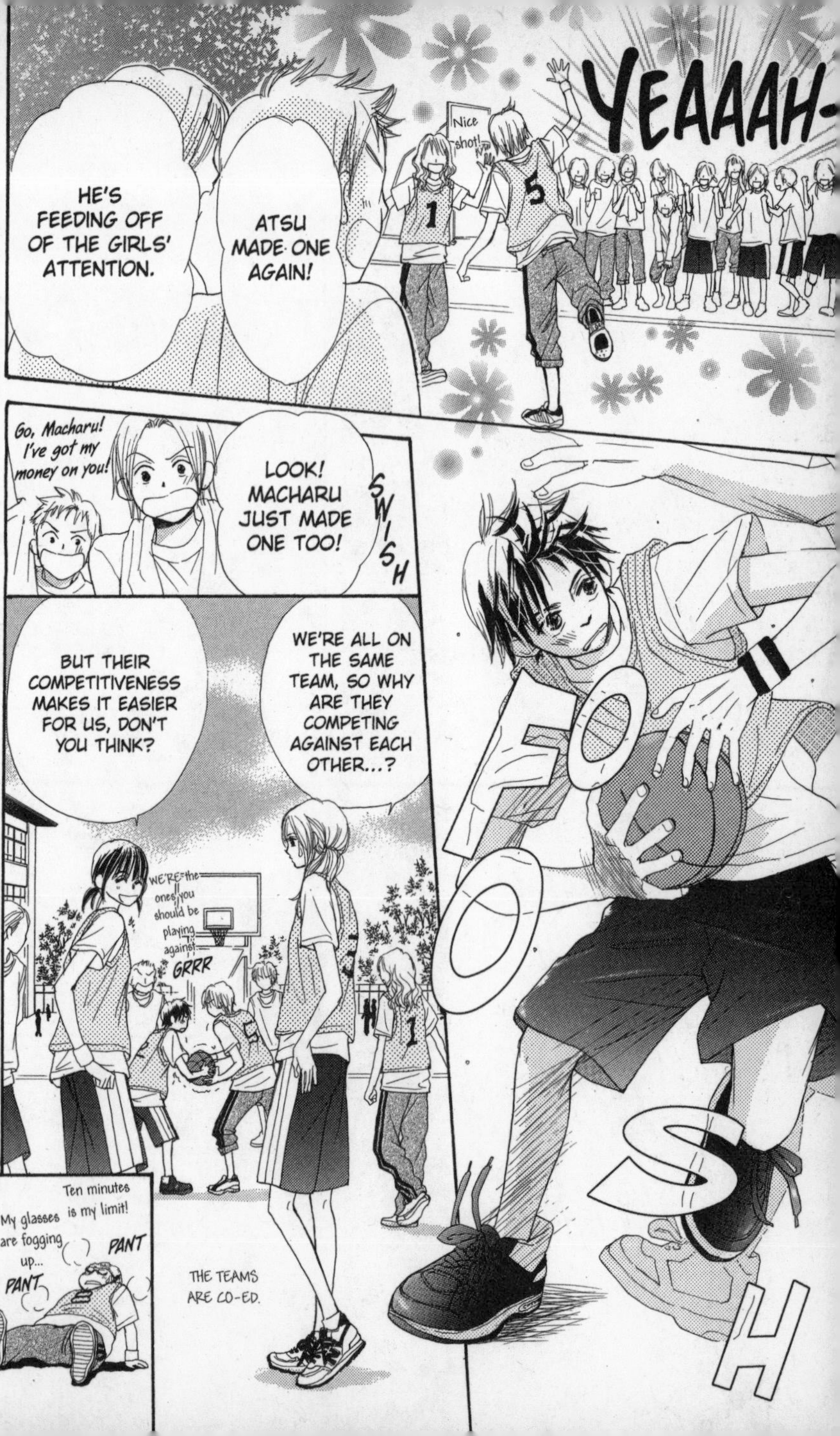
YEAAAH-
Nice shot!
ATSU MADE ONE AGAIN!
HE'S FEEDING OFF OF THE GIRLS' ATTENTION.
FOOSH
LOOK! MACHARU JUST MADE ONE TOO!
SWISH
Go, Macharu! I've got my money on you!
WE'RE ALL ON THE SAME TEAM, SO WHY ARE THEY COMPETING AGAINST EACH OTHER...?
BUT THEIR COMPETITIVENESS MAKES IT EASIER FOR US, DON'T YOU THINK?
WE'RE the ones you should be playing against!
GRRR
THE TEAMS ARE CO-ED.
Ten minutes is my limit!
PANT
My glasses are fogging up...
PANT

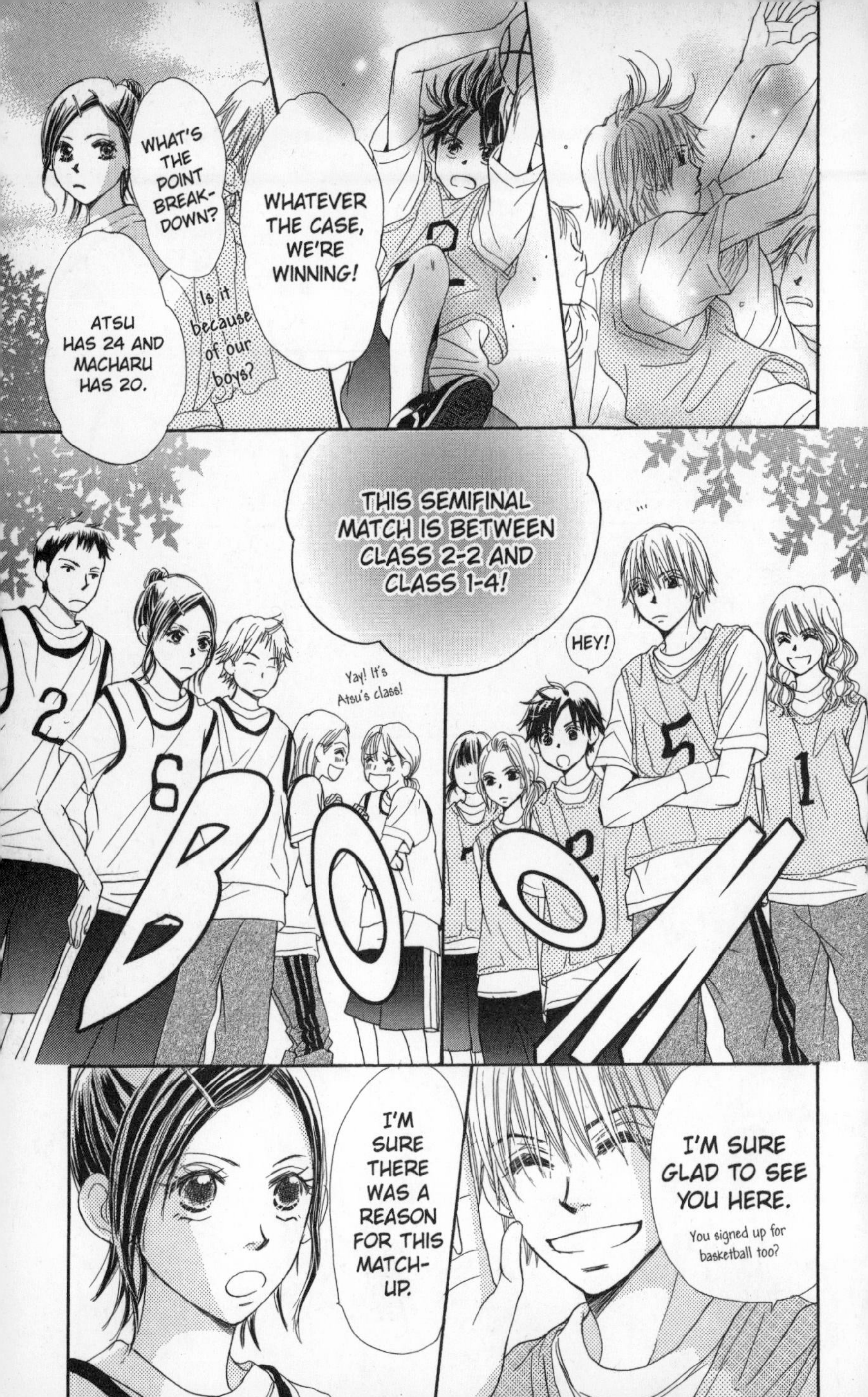
WHATEVER THE CASE, WE'RE WINNING!
WHAT'S THE POINT BREAK-DOWN?
Is it because of our boys?
ATSU HAS 24 AND MACHARU HAS 20.
THIS SEMIFINAL MATCH IS BETWEEN CLASS 2-2 AND CLASS 1-4!
...
HEY!
Yay! It's Atsu's class!
BOO
I'M SURE GLAD TO SEE YOU HERE.
You signed up for basketball too?
I'M SURE THERE WAS A REASON FOR THIS MATCH-UP.

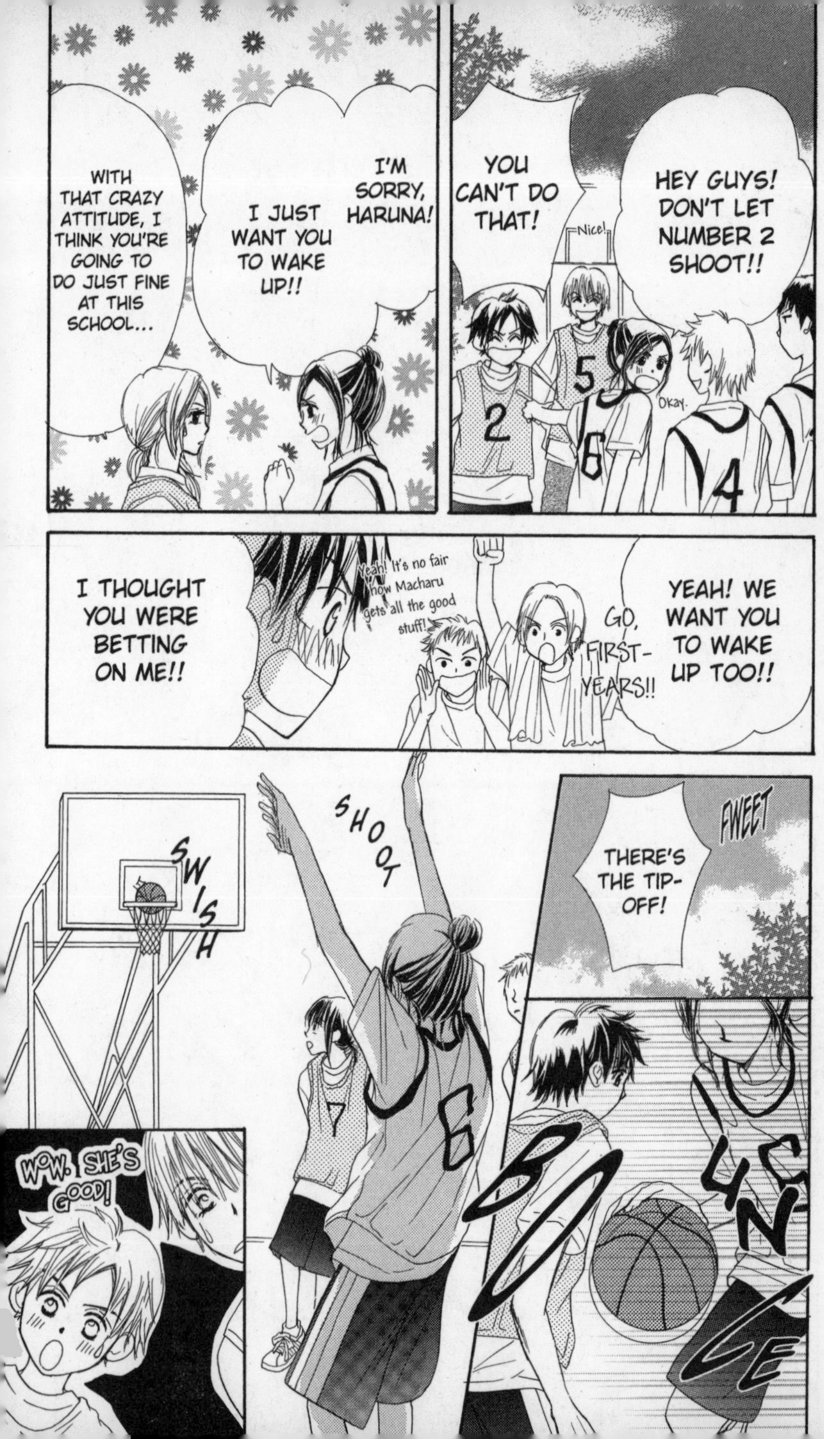
HEY GUYS! DON'T LET NUMBER 2 SHOOT!!
YOU CAN'T DO THAT!
Nice!
Okay.
I'M SORRY, HARUNA!
I JUST WANT YOU TO WAKE UP!!
WITH THAT CRAZY ATTITUDE, I THINK YOU'RE GOING TO DO JUST FINE AT THIS SCHOOL...
YEAH! WE WANT YOU TO WAKE UP TOO!!
GO, FIRST-YEARS!!
Yeah! It's no fair how Macharu gets all the good stuff!
I THOUGHT YOU WERE BETTING ON ME!!
FWEET
THERE'S THE TIP-OFF!
BOUNCE
SHOOT
SWISH
WOW. SHE'S GOOD!

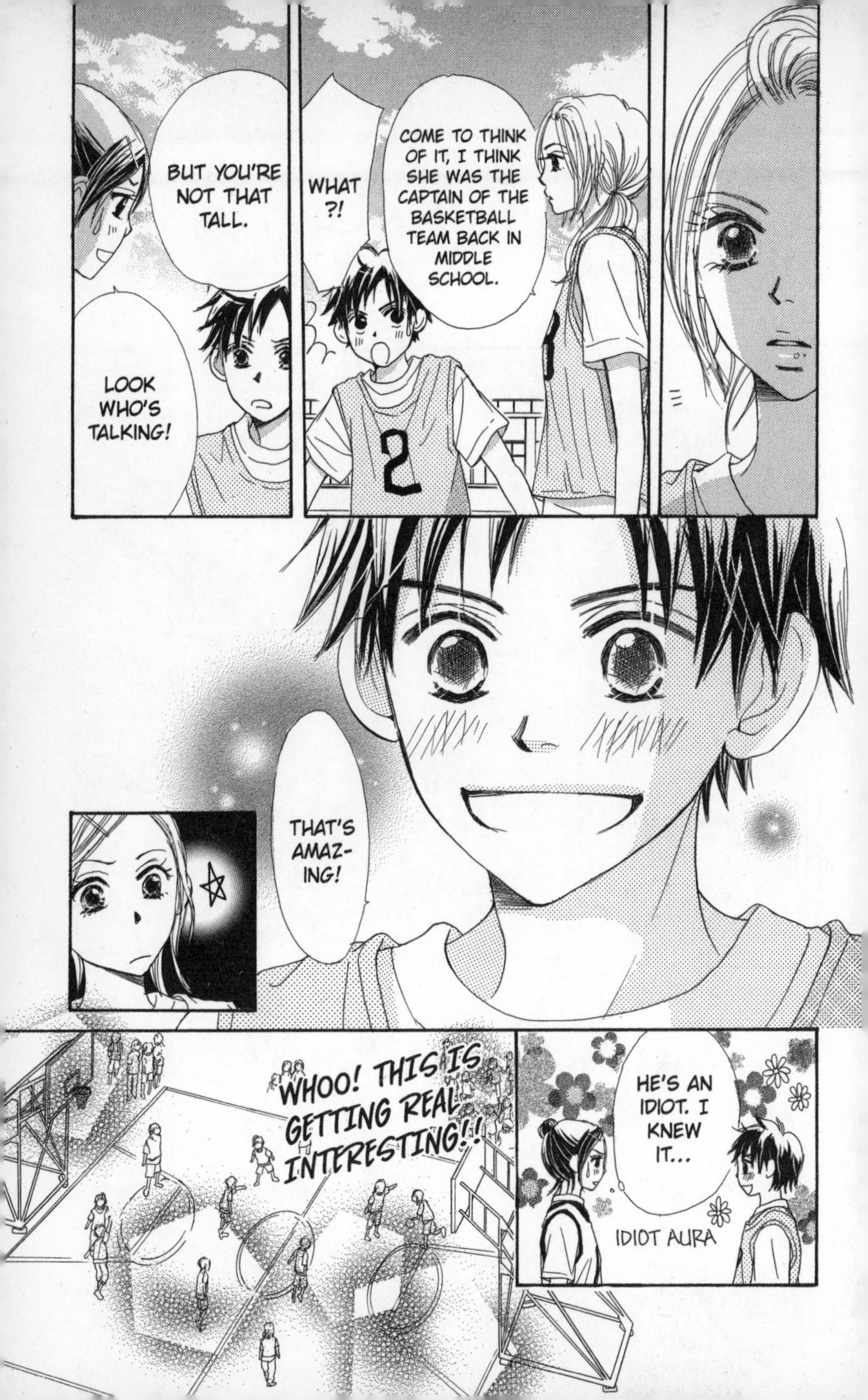
COME TO THINK OF IT, I THINK SHE WAS THE CAPTAIN OF THE BASKETBALL TEAM BACK IN MIDDLE SCHOOL.
WHAT?!
BUT YOU'RE NOT THAT TALL.
LOOK WHO'S TALKING!
THAT'S AMAZ-ING!
HE'S AN IDIOT. I KNEW IT...
IDIOT AURA
WHOO! THIS IS GETTING REAL INTERESTING!!

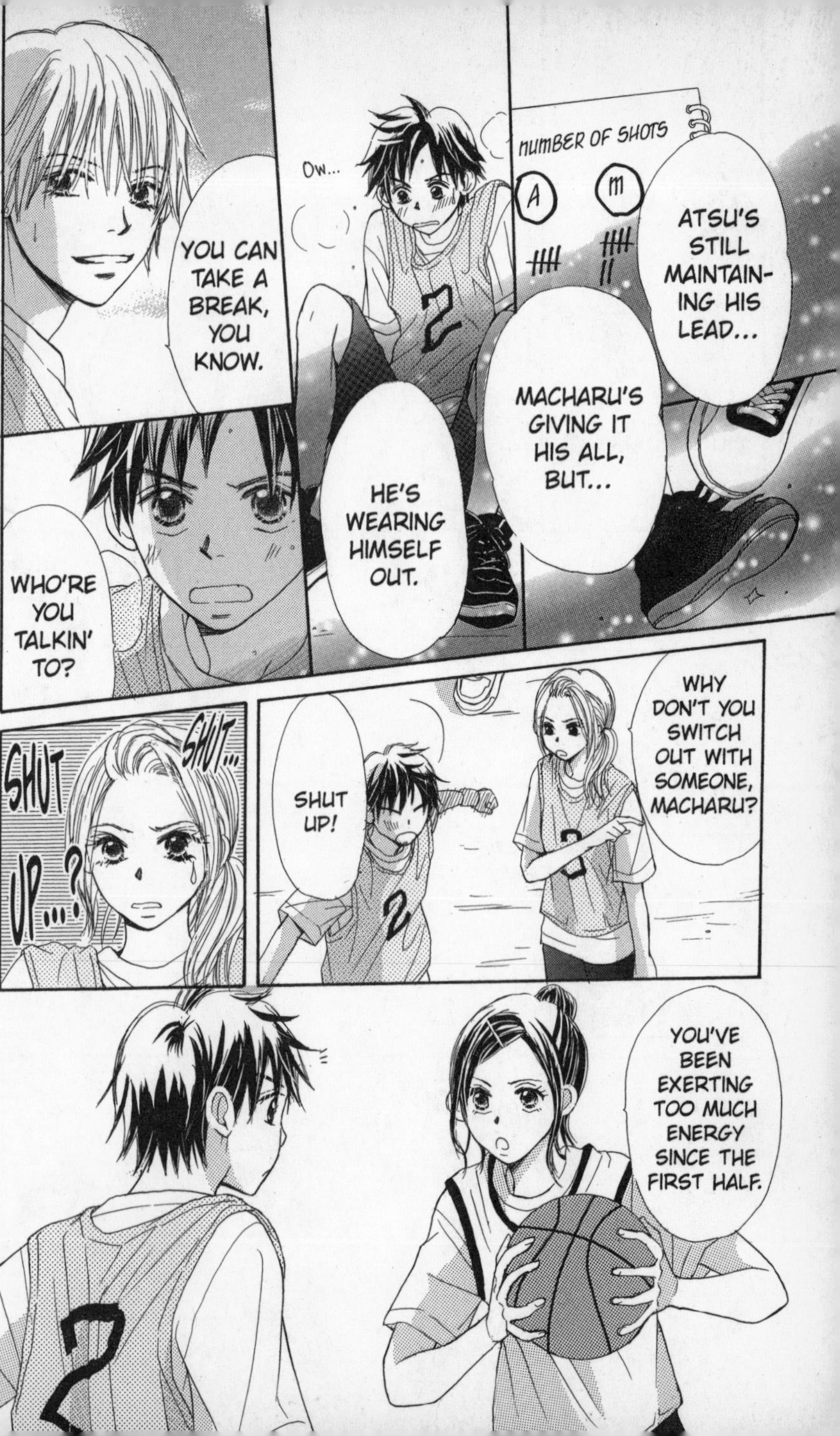
NUMBER OF SHOTS
A
M
ATSU'S STILL MAINTAINING HIS LEAD...
MACHARU'S GIVING IT HIS ALL, BUT...
HE'S WEARING HIMSELF OUT.
OW...
YOU CAN TAKE A BREAK, YOU KNOW.
WHO'RE YOU TALKIN' TO?
WHY DON'T YOU SWITCH OUT WITH SOMEONE, MACHARU?
SHUT UP!
SHUT...
SHUT UP...?
YOU'VE BEEN EXERTING TOO MUCH ENERGY SINCE THE FIRST HALF.

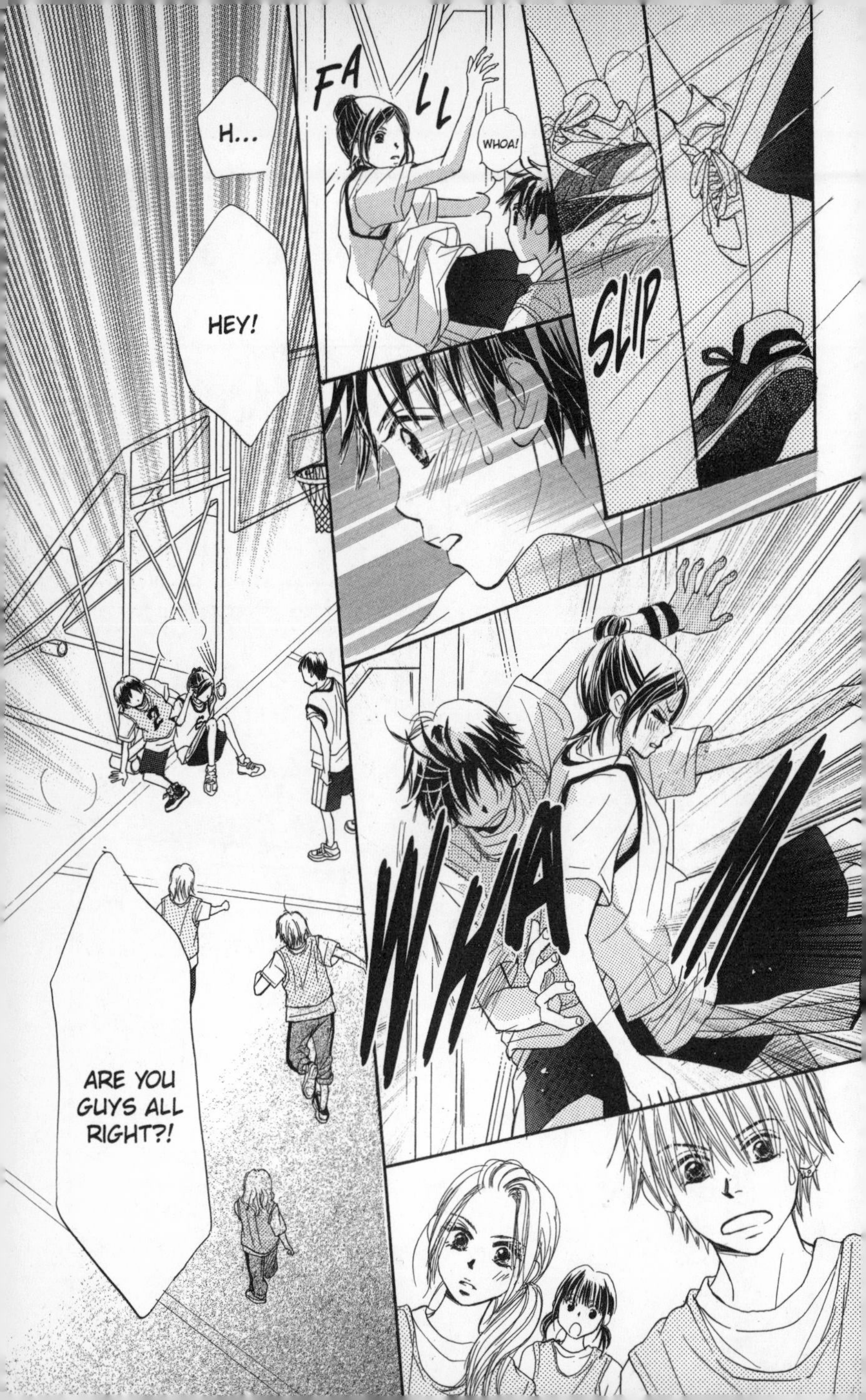
SLIP
FALL
WHOA!
WHAM
H...
HEY!
ARE YOU GUYS ALL RIGHT?!

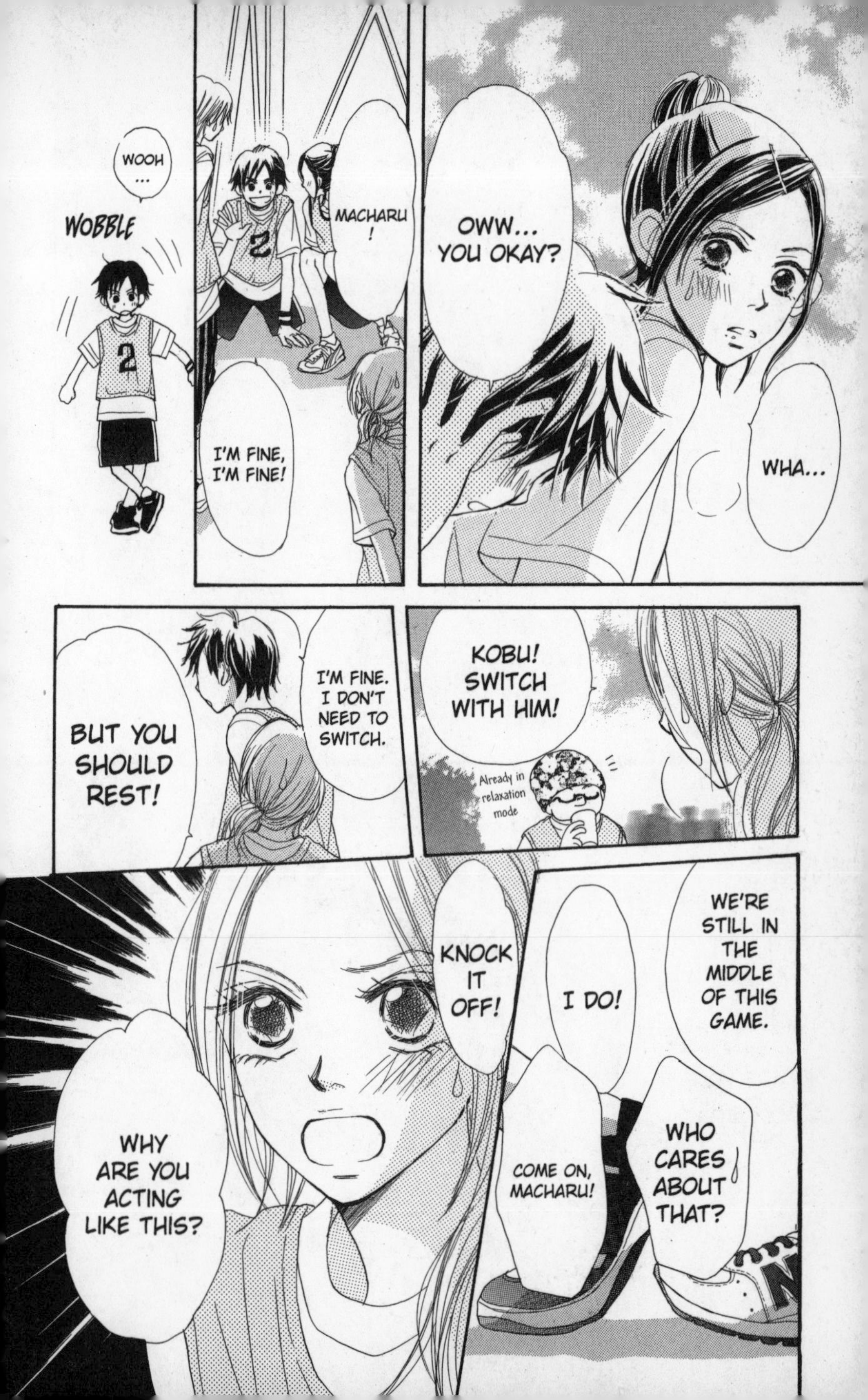
OWW... YOU OKAY?
WHA...
MACHARU!
I'M FINE, I'M FINE!
WOOH...
WOBBLE
KOBU! SWITCH WITH HIM!
Already in relaxation mode
I'M FINE. I DON'T NEED TO SWITCH.
BUT YOU SHOULD REST!
WE'RE STILL IN THE MIDDLE OF THIS GAME.
I DO!
WHO CARES ABOUT THAT?
COME ON, MACHARU!
KNOCK IT OFF!
WHY ARE YOU ACTING LIKE THIS?

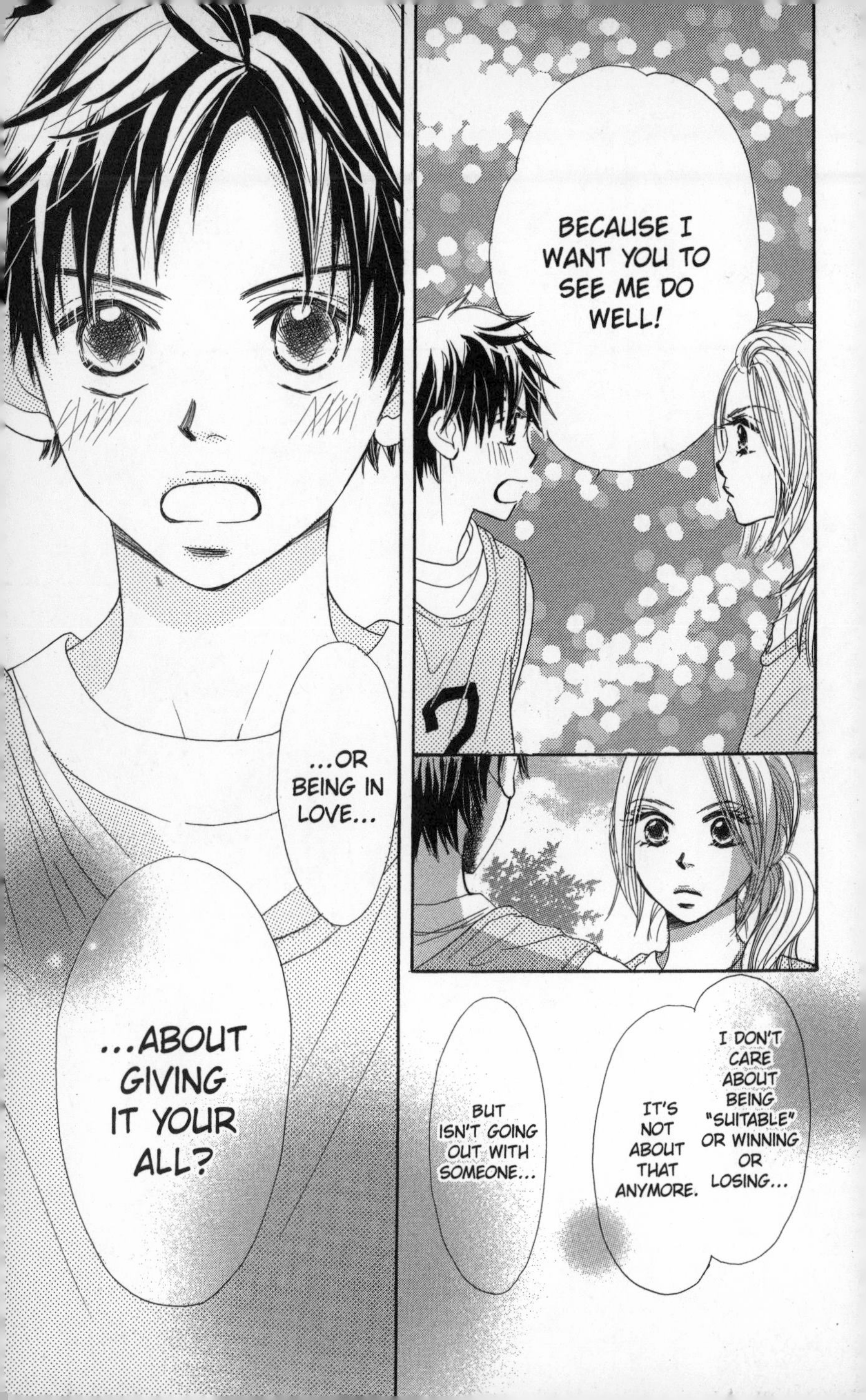
BECAUSE I WANT YOU TO SEE ME DO WELL!
I DON'T CARE ABOUT BEING "SUITABLE" OR WINNING OR LOSING...
IT'S NOT ABOUT THAT ANYMORE.
BUT ISN'T GOING OUT WITH SOMEONE...
...OR BEING IN LOVE...
...ABOUT GIVING IT YOUR ALL?

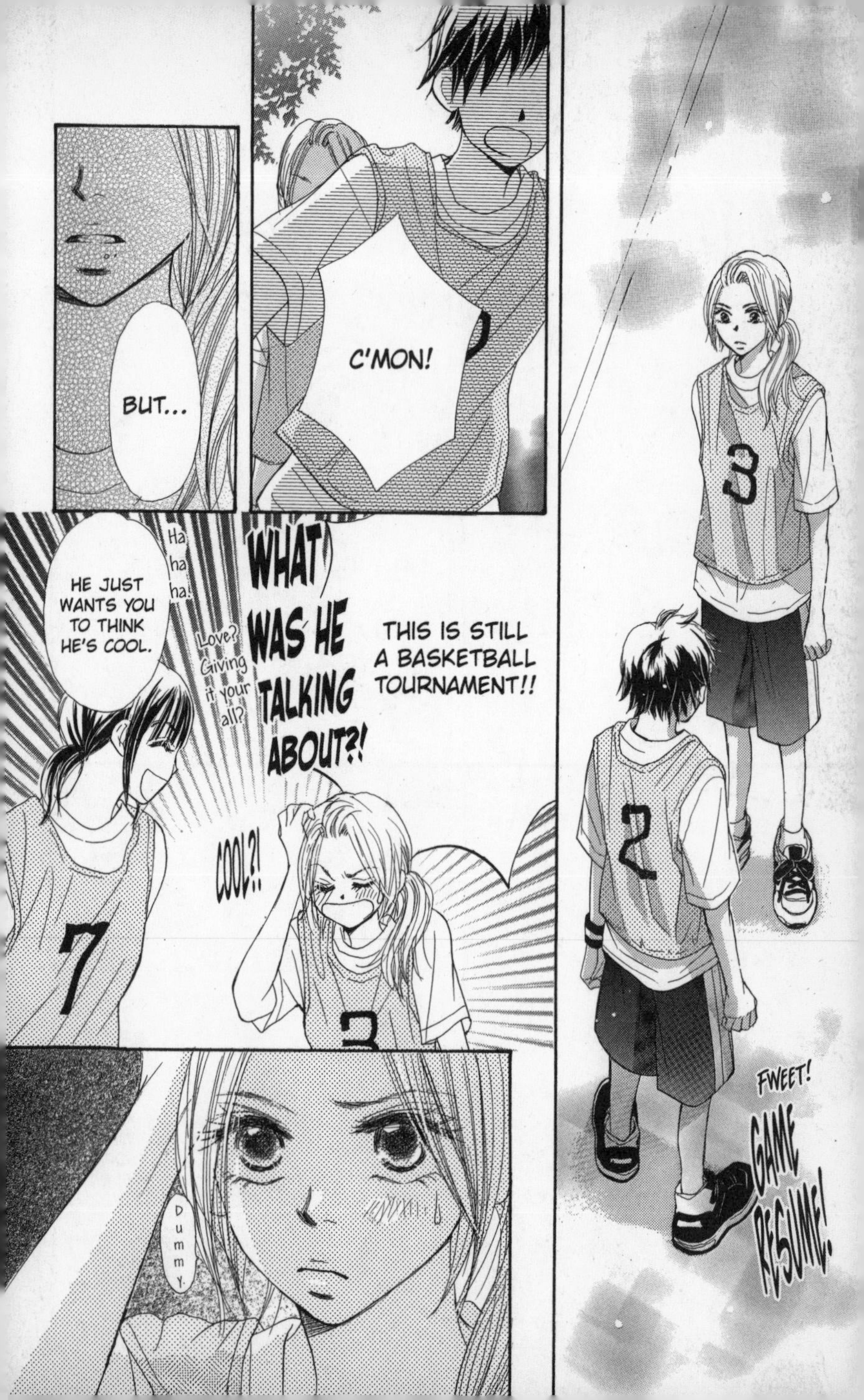
FWEET!
GAME RESUME!
C'MON!
BUT...
THIS IS STILL A BASKETBALL TOURNAMENT!!
WHAT WAS HE TALKING ABOUT?!
Love? Giving it your all?
Ha ha ha!
HE JUST WANTS YOU TO THINK HE'S COOL.
COOL?!
Dummy.

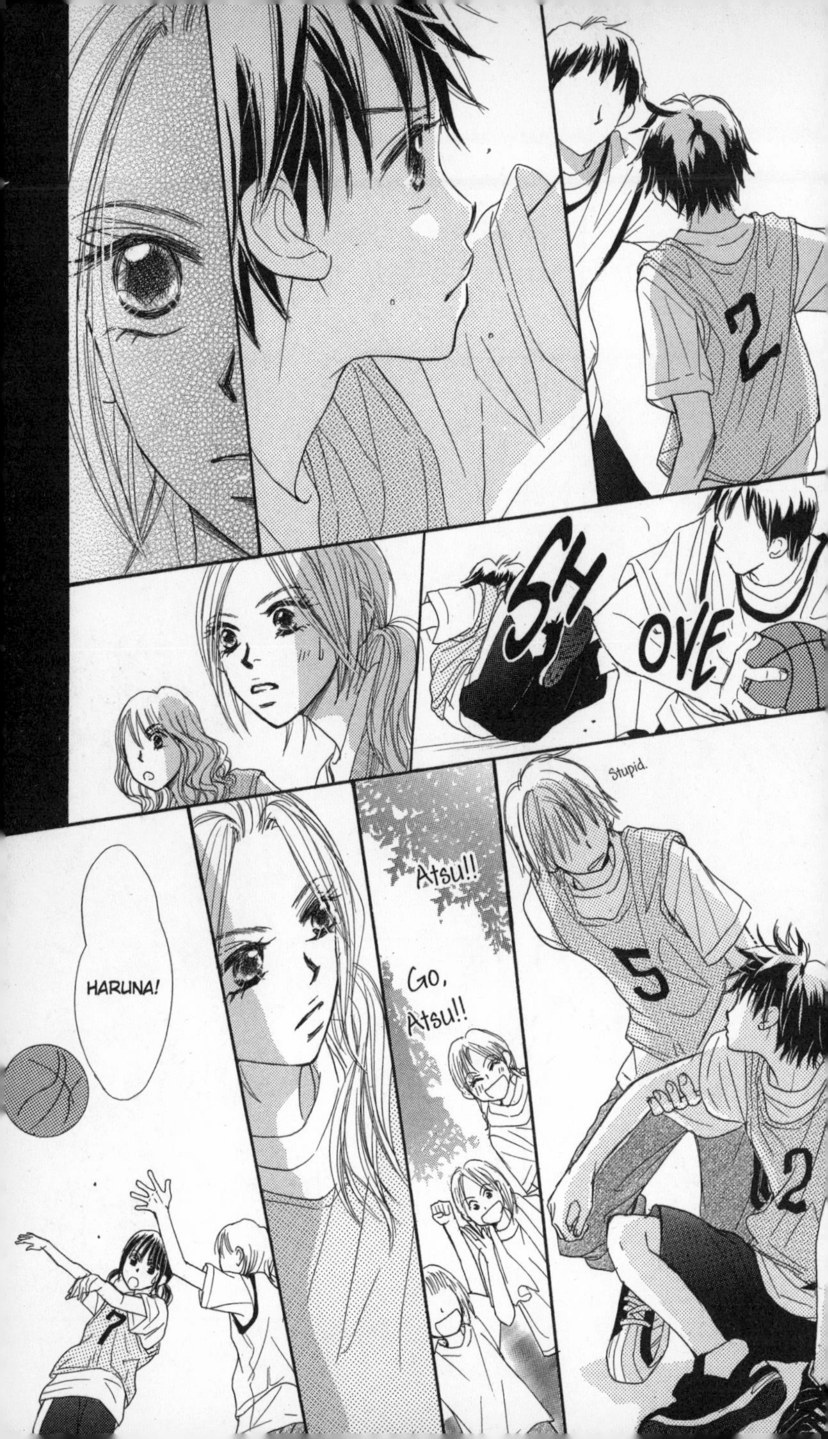
SHOVE
Stupid.
Atsu!!
Go, Atsu!!
HARUNA!

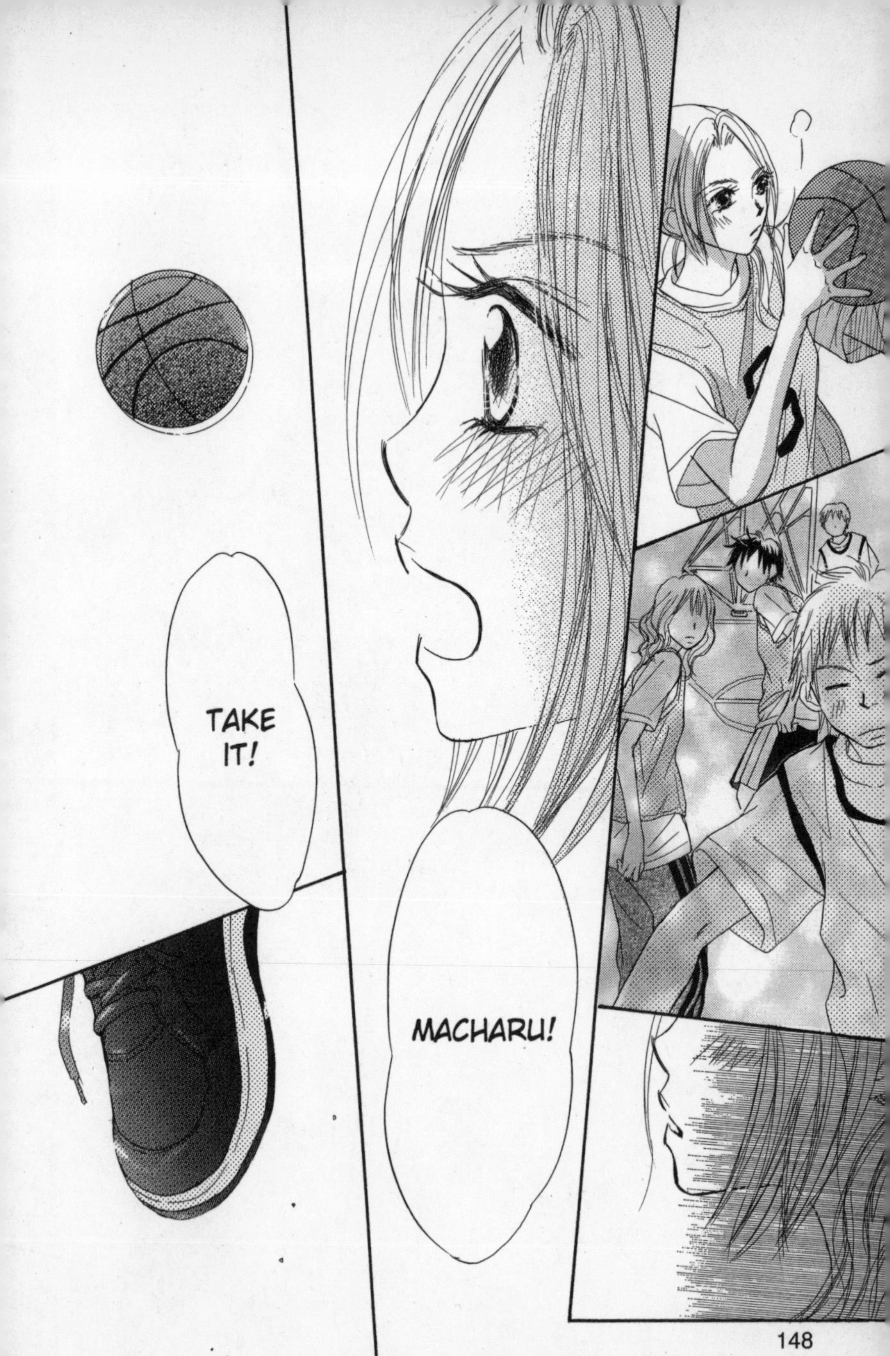
MACHARU!
TAKE IT!

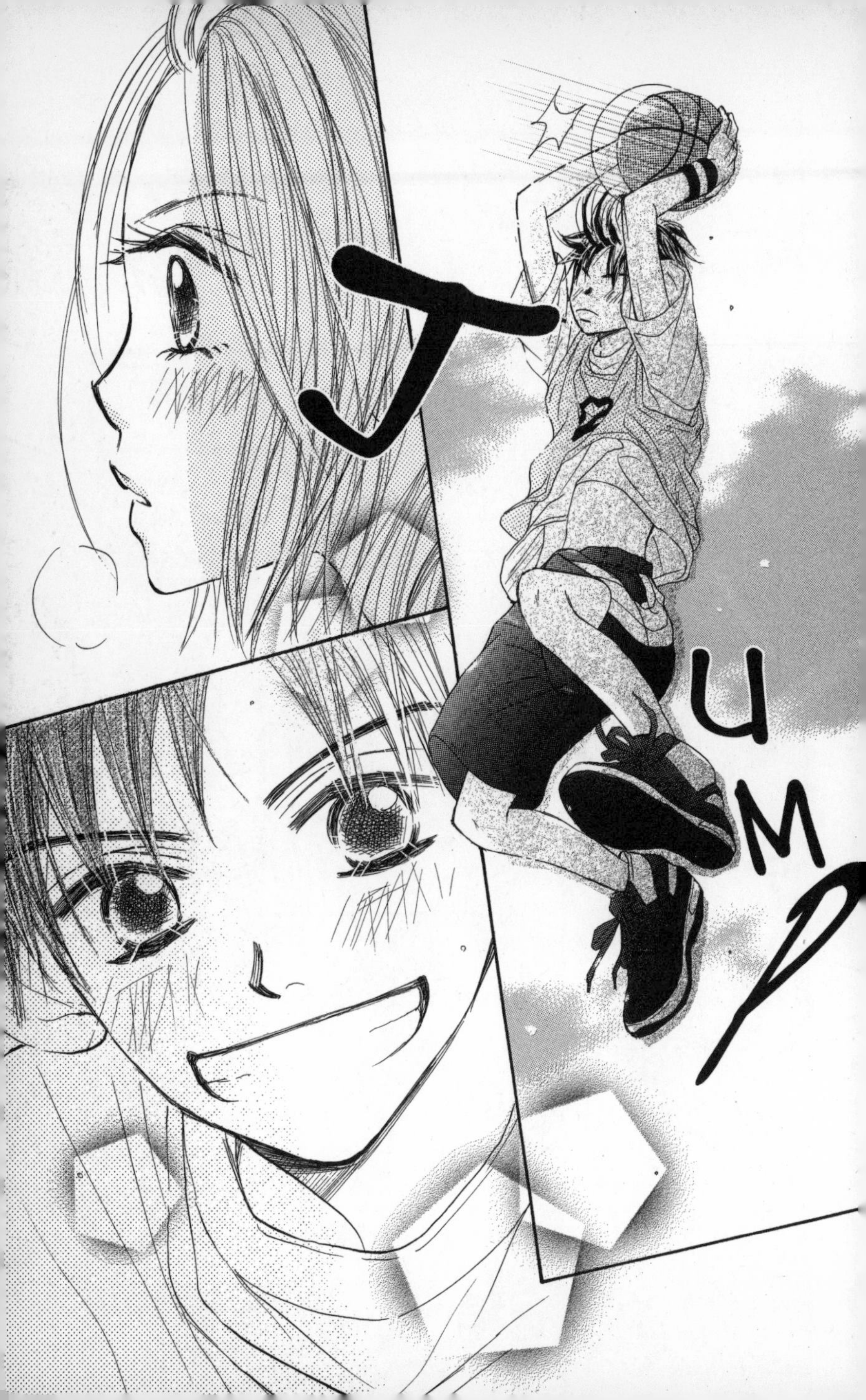
JUMP

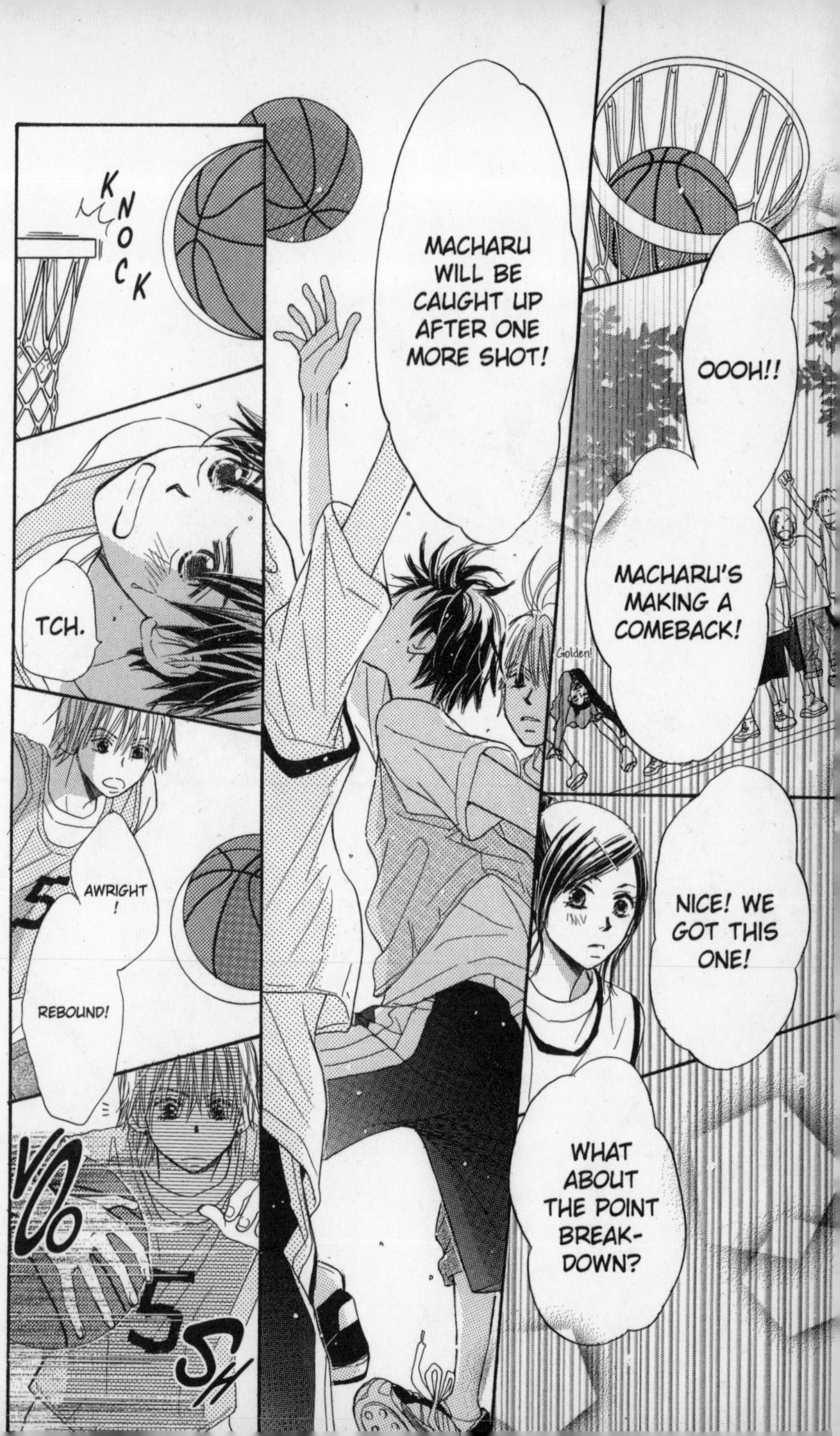
OOOH!!
MACHARU'S MAKING A COMEBACK!
Golden!
NICE! WE GOT THIS ONE!
WHAT ABOUT THE POINT BREAK-DOWN?
MACHARU WILL BE CAUGHT UP AFTER ONE MORE SHOT!
KNOCK
TCH.
AWRIGHT!
REBOUND!
VOOSH

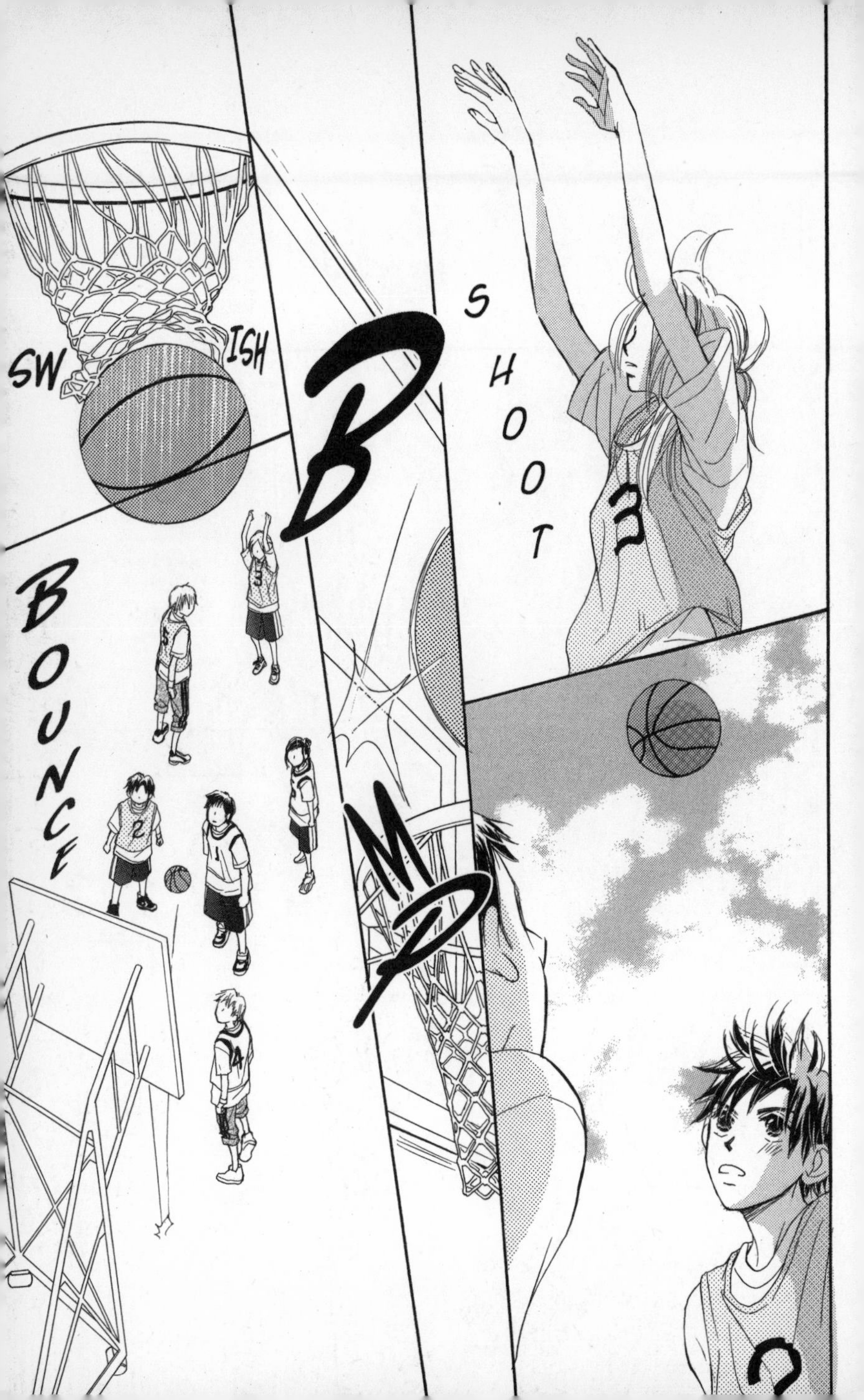
SHOOT
B
MP
SW
ISH
BOUNCE

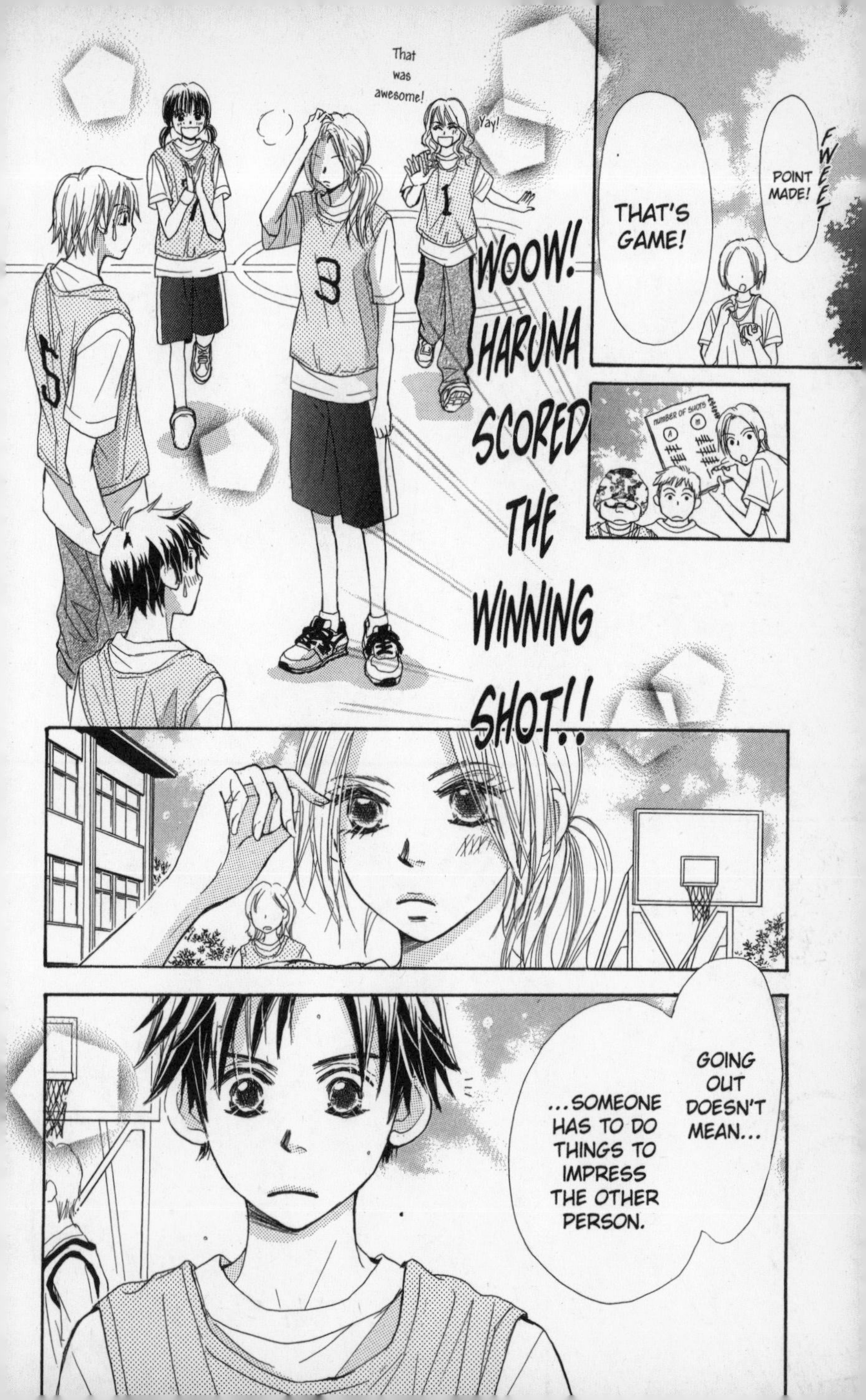
FWEET
POINT MADE!
THAT'S GAME!
NUMBER OF SHOTS
Yay!
That was awesome!
WOOW! HARUNA SCORED THE WINNING SHOT!!
GOING OUT DOESN'T MEAN...
...SOMEONE HAS TO DO THINGS TO IMPRESS THE OTHER PERSON.

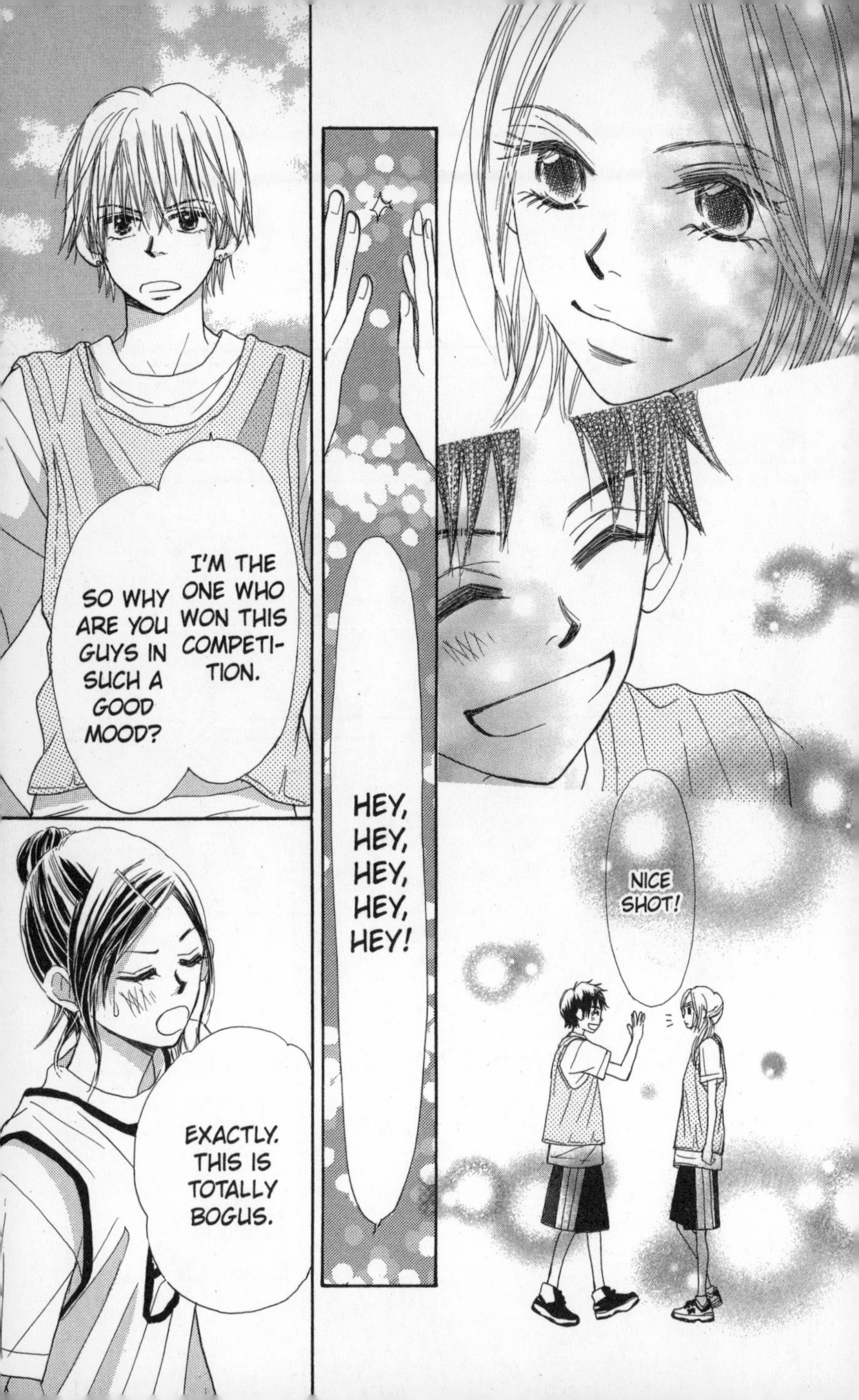
NICE SHOT!
HEY, HEY, HEY, HEY, HEY!
I'M THE ONE WHO WON THIS COMPETITION.
SO WHY ARE YOU GUYS IN SUCH A GOOD MOOD?
EXACTLY. THIS IS TOTALLY BOGUS.

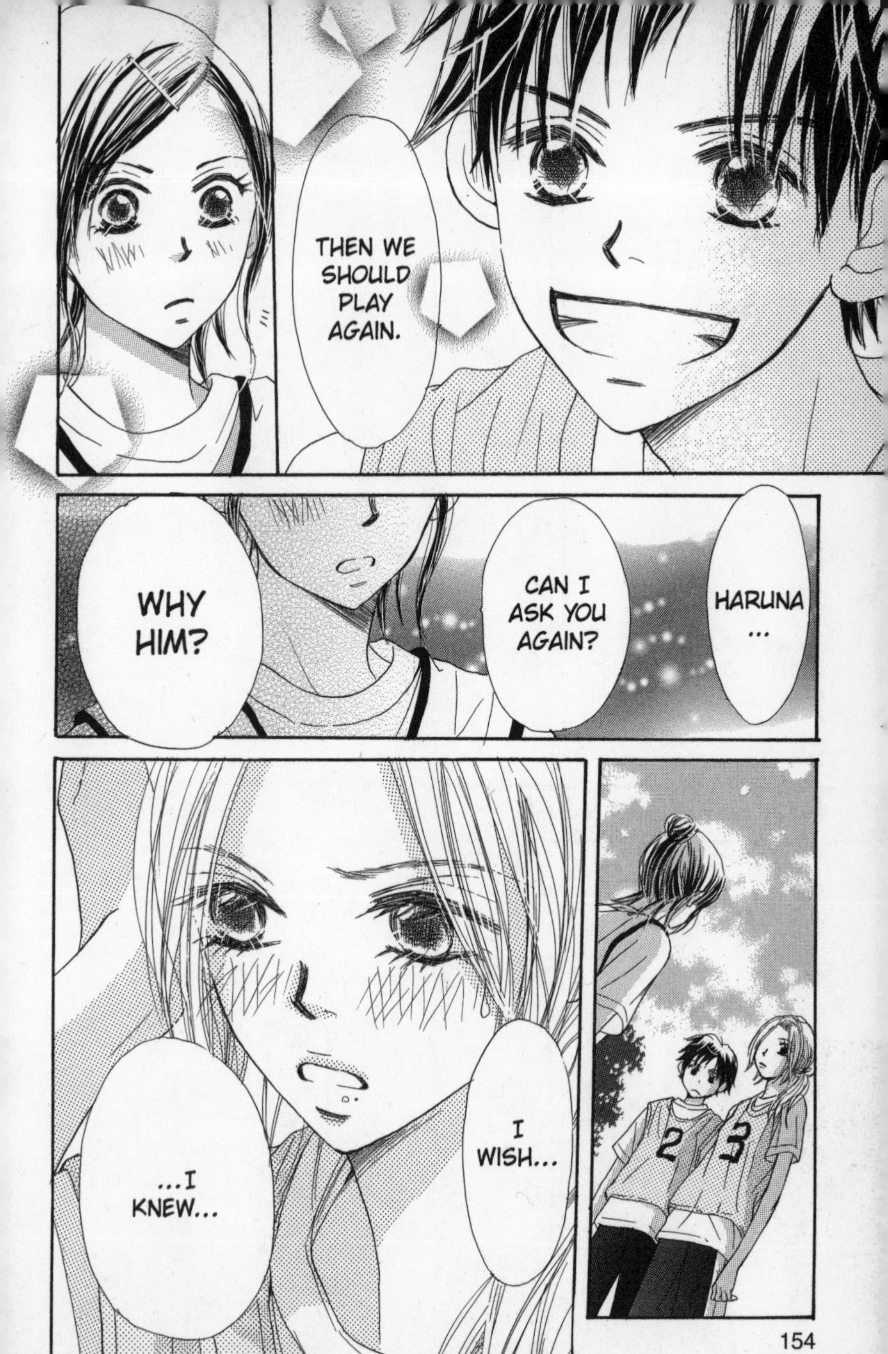
THEN WE SHOULD PLAY AGAIN.
HARUNA...
CAN I ASK YOU AGAIN?
WHY HIM?
I WISH...
...I KNEW...

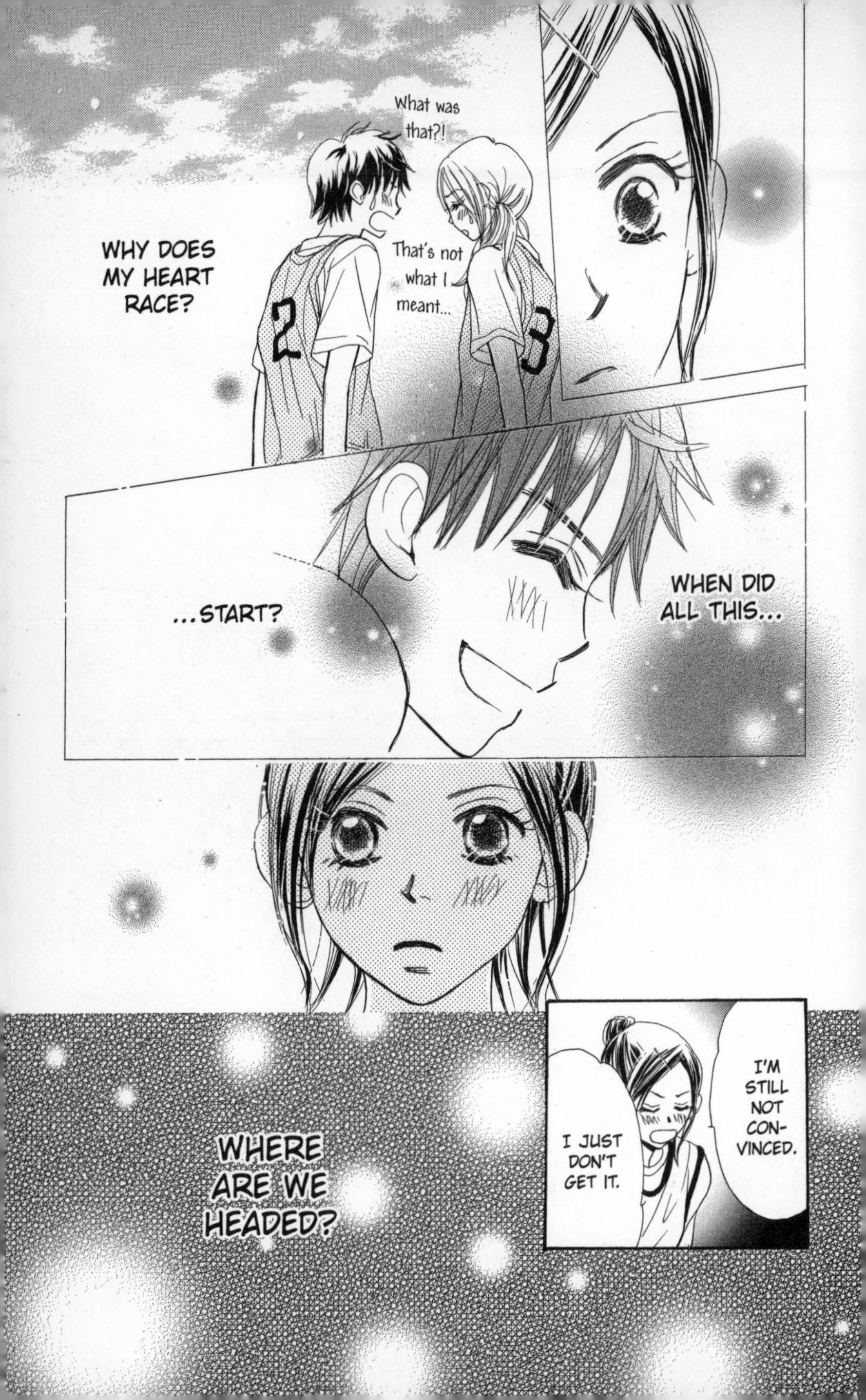
What was that?!
That's not what I meant...
WHY DOES MY HEART RACE?
WHEN DID ALL THIS...
...START?
I'M STILL NOT CON-VINCED.
I JUST DON'T GET IT.
WHERE ARE WE HEADED?

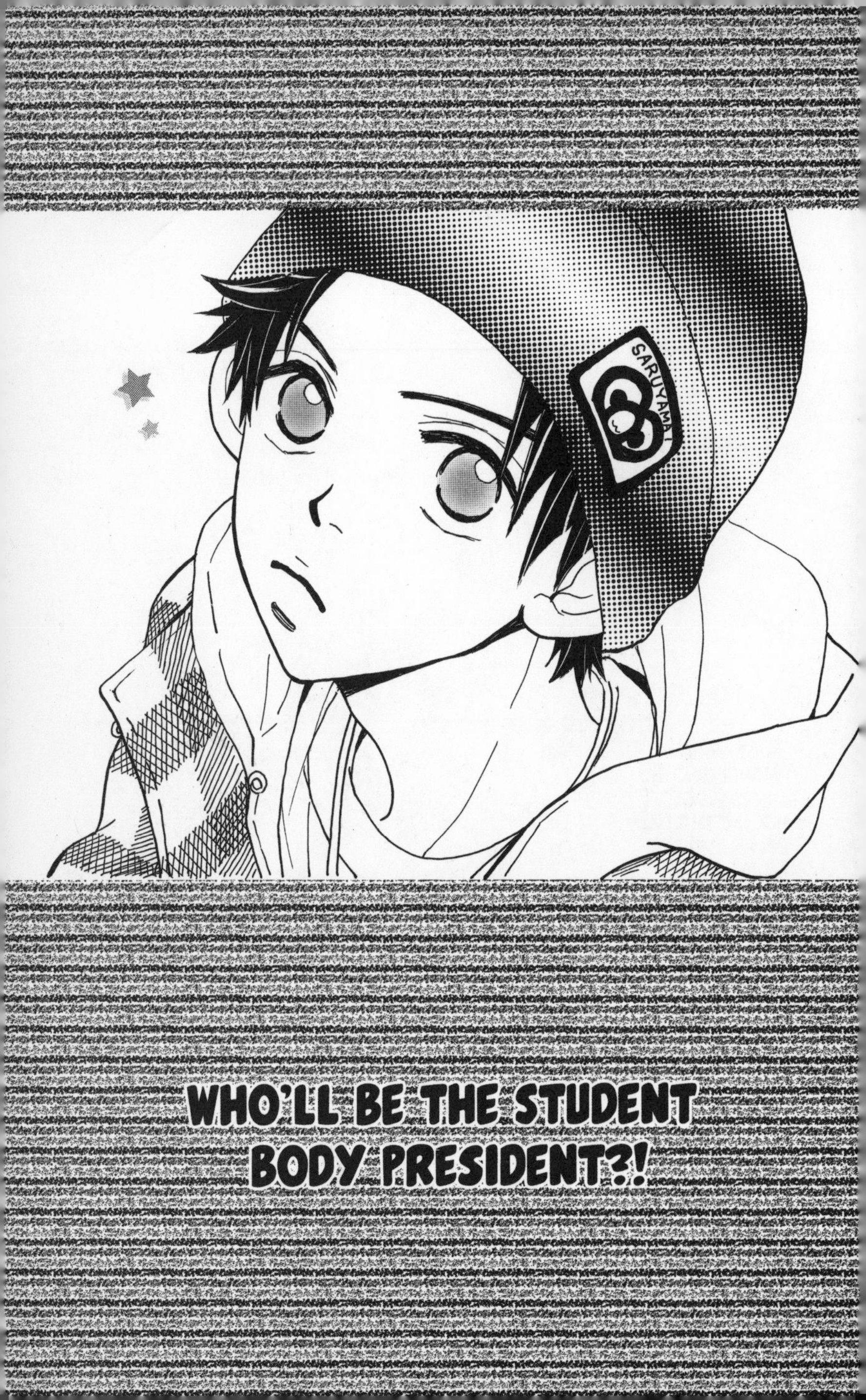
SARUYAMA!

WHO'LL BE THE STUDENT BODY PRESIDENT?!

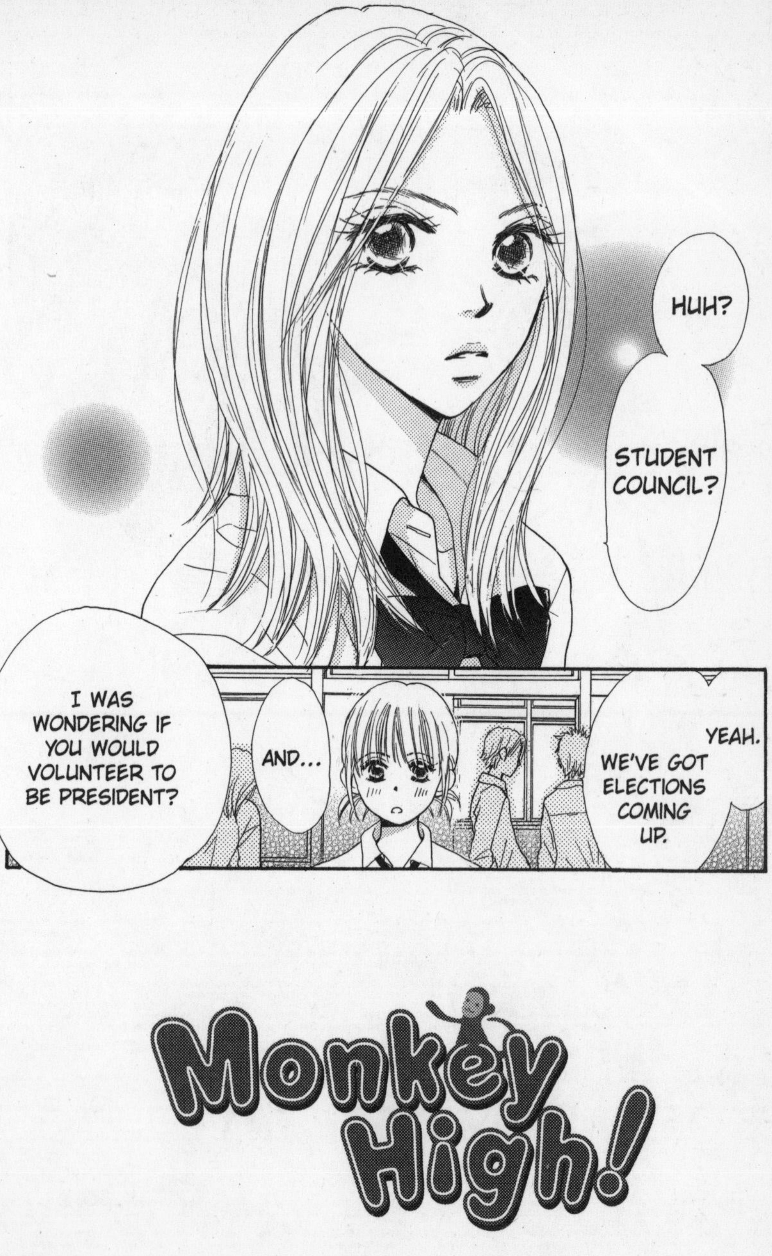
HUH?
STUDENT COUNCIL?
YEAH.
WE'VE GOT ELECTIONS COMING UP.
AND...
I WAS WONDERING IF YOU WOULD VOLUNTEER TO BE PRESIDENT?
Monkey High!

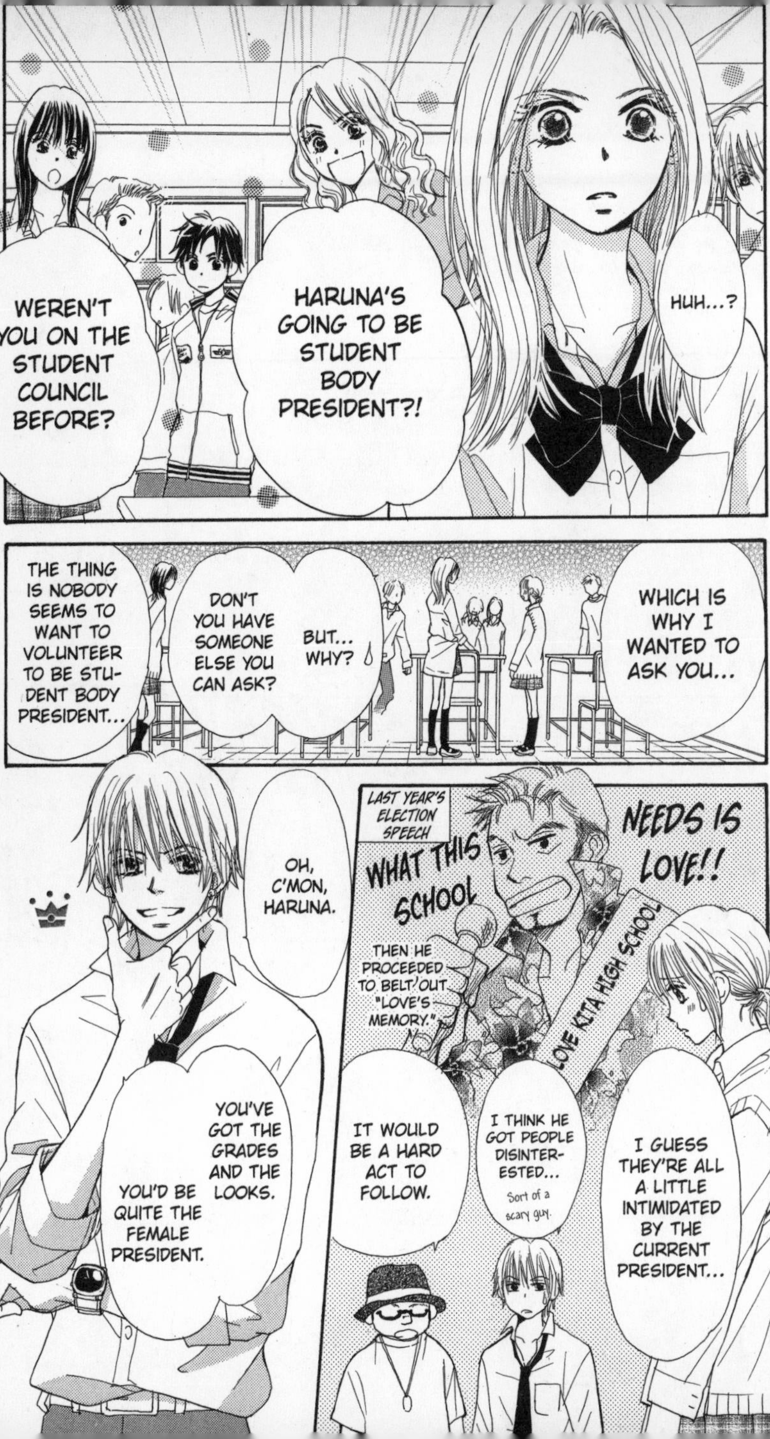
HUH...?
HARUNA'S GOING TO BE STUDENT BODY PRESIDENT?!
WEREN'T YOU ON THE STUDENT COUNCIL BEFORE?
WHICH IS WHY I WANTED TO ASK YOU...
BUT... WHY?
DON'T YOU HAVE SOMEONE ELSE YOU CAN ASK?
THE THING IS NOBODY SEEMS TO WANT TO VOLUNTEER TO BE STU-DENT BODY PRESIDENT...
LAST YEAR'S ELECTION SPEECH
WHAT THIS SCHOOL NEEDS IS LOVE!!
THEN HE PROCEEDED TO BELT OUT "LOVE'S MEMORY."
LOVE KITA HIGH SCHOOL
I GUESS THEY'RE ALL A LITTLE INTIMIDATED BY THE CURRENT PRESIDENT...
I THINK HE GOT PEOPLE DISINTER-ESTED...
Sort of a scary guy.
IT WOULD BE A HARD ACT TO FOLLOW.
OH, C'MON, HARUNA.
YOU'VE GOT THE GRADES AND THE LOOKS.
YOU'D BE QUITE THE FEMALE PRESIDENT.

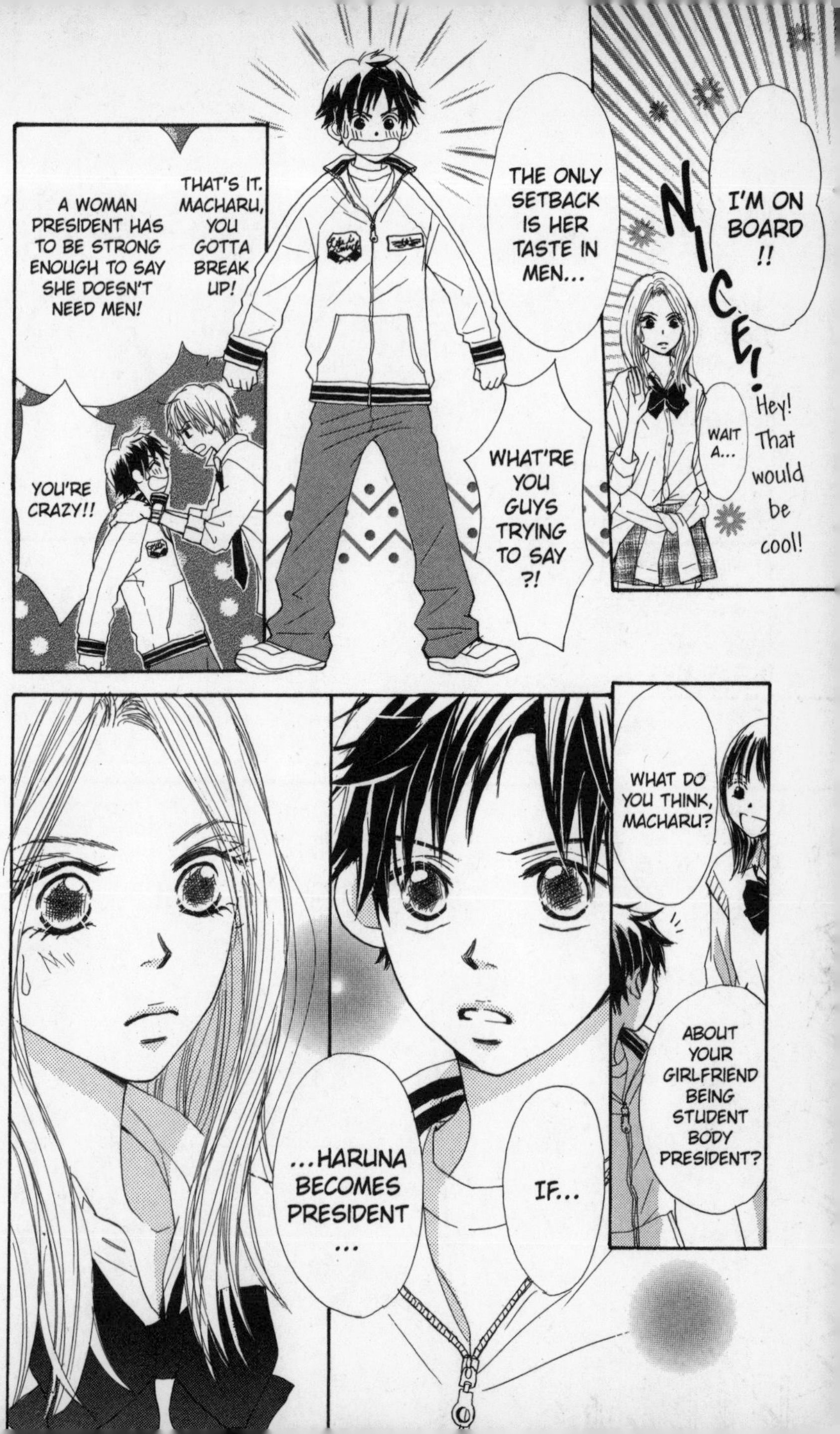
I'M ON BOARD!!
NICE!
WAIT A...
Hey! That would be cool!
THE ONLY SETBACK IS HER TASTE IN MEN...
WHAT'RE YOU GUYS TRYING TO SAY?!
THAT'S IT. MACHARU, YOU GOTTA BREAK UP!
A WOMAN PRESIDENT HAS TO BE STRONG ENOUGH TO SAY SHE DOESN'T NEED MEN!
YOU'RE CRAZY!!
WHAT DO YOU THINK, MACHARU?
ABOUT YOUR GIRLFRIEND BEING STUDENT BODY PRESIDENT?
IF...
...HARUNA BECOMES PRESIDENT...

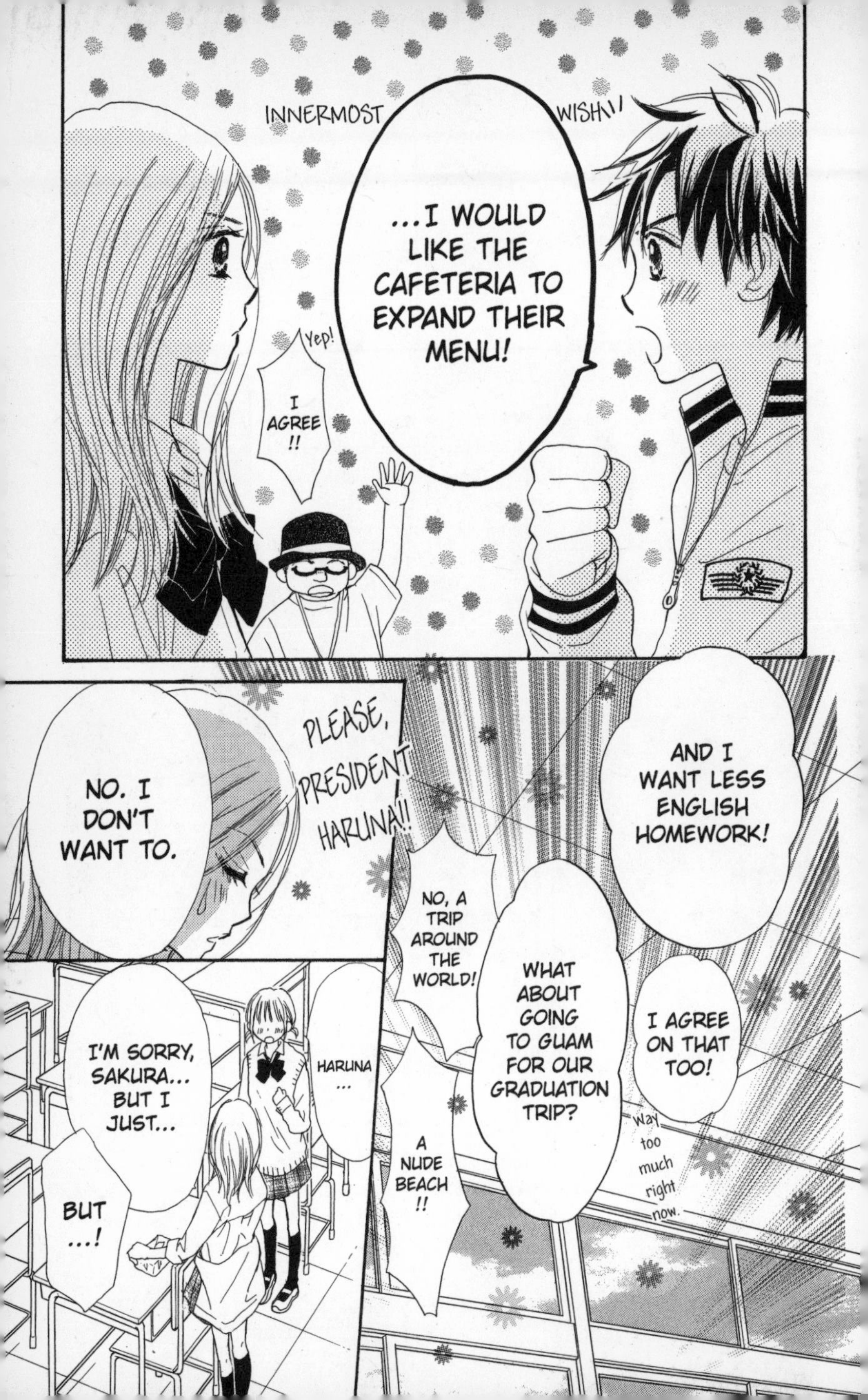
INNERMOST WISH!!
...I WOULD LIKE THE CAFETERIA TO EXPAND THEIR MENU!
Yep!
I AGREE !!
AND I WANT LESS ENGLISH HOMEWORK!
I AGREE ON THAT TOO!
Way too much right now.
WHAT ABOUT GOING TO GUAM FOR OUR GRADUATION TRIP?
NO, A TRIP AROUND THE WORLD!
A NUDE BEACH !!
PLEASE, PRESIDENT HARUNA!!
NO. I DON'T WANT TO.
HARUNA ...
I'M SORRY, SAKURA... BUT I JUST...
BUT ...!

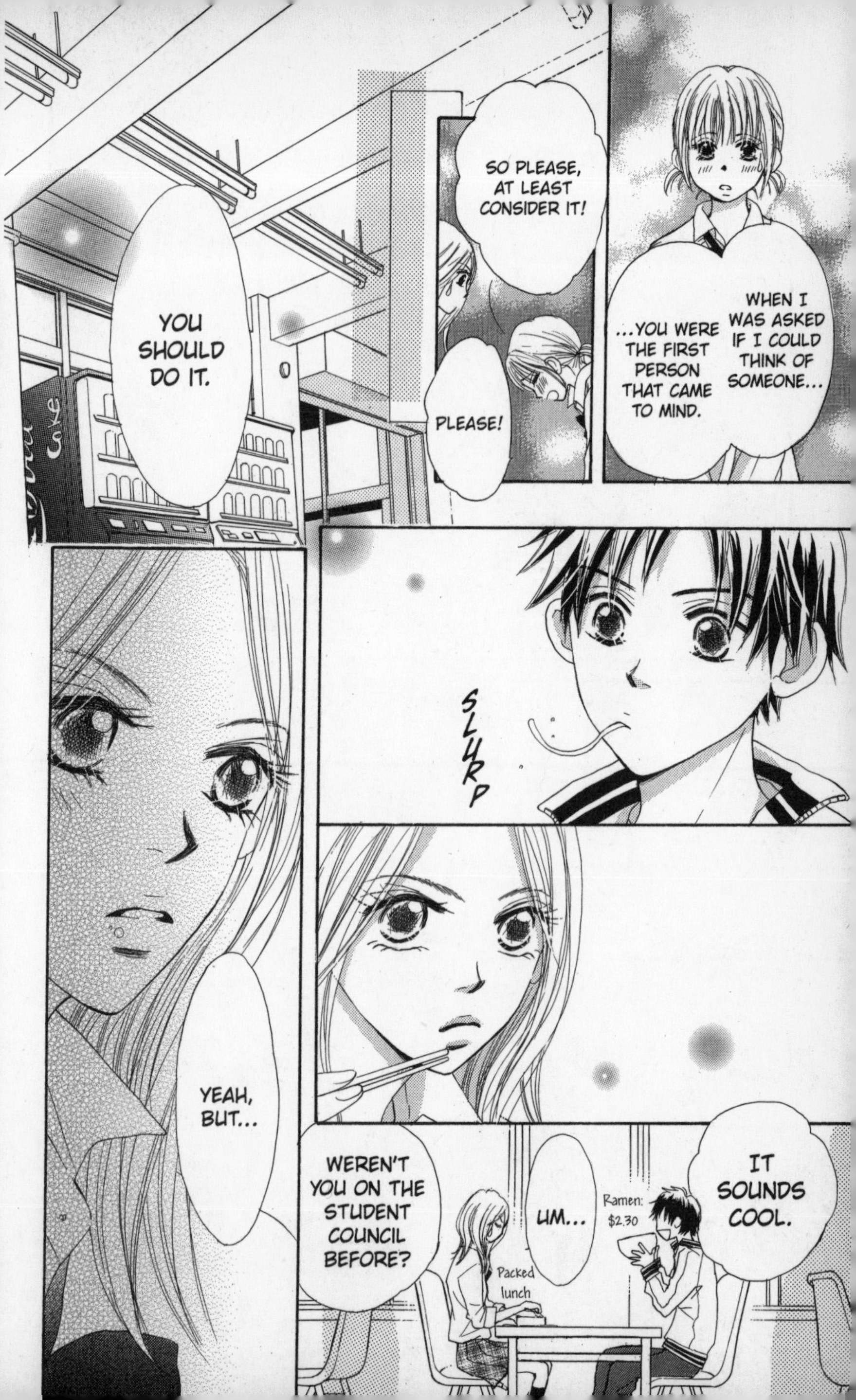
WHEN I WAS ASKED IF I COULD THINK OF SOMEONE...
...YOU WERE THE FIRST PERSON THAT CAME TO MIND.
SO PLEASE, AT LEAST CONSIDER IT!
PLEASE!
YOU SHOULD DO IT.
SLURP
IT SOUNDS COOL.
Ramen: $2.30
UM...
Packed lunch
WEREN'T YOU ON THE STUDENT COUNCIL BEFORE?
YEAH, BUT...

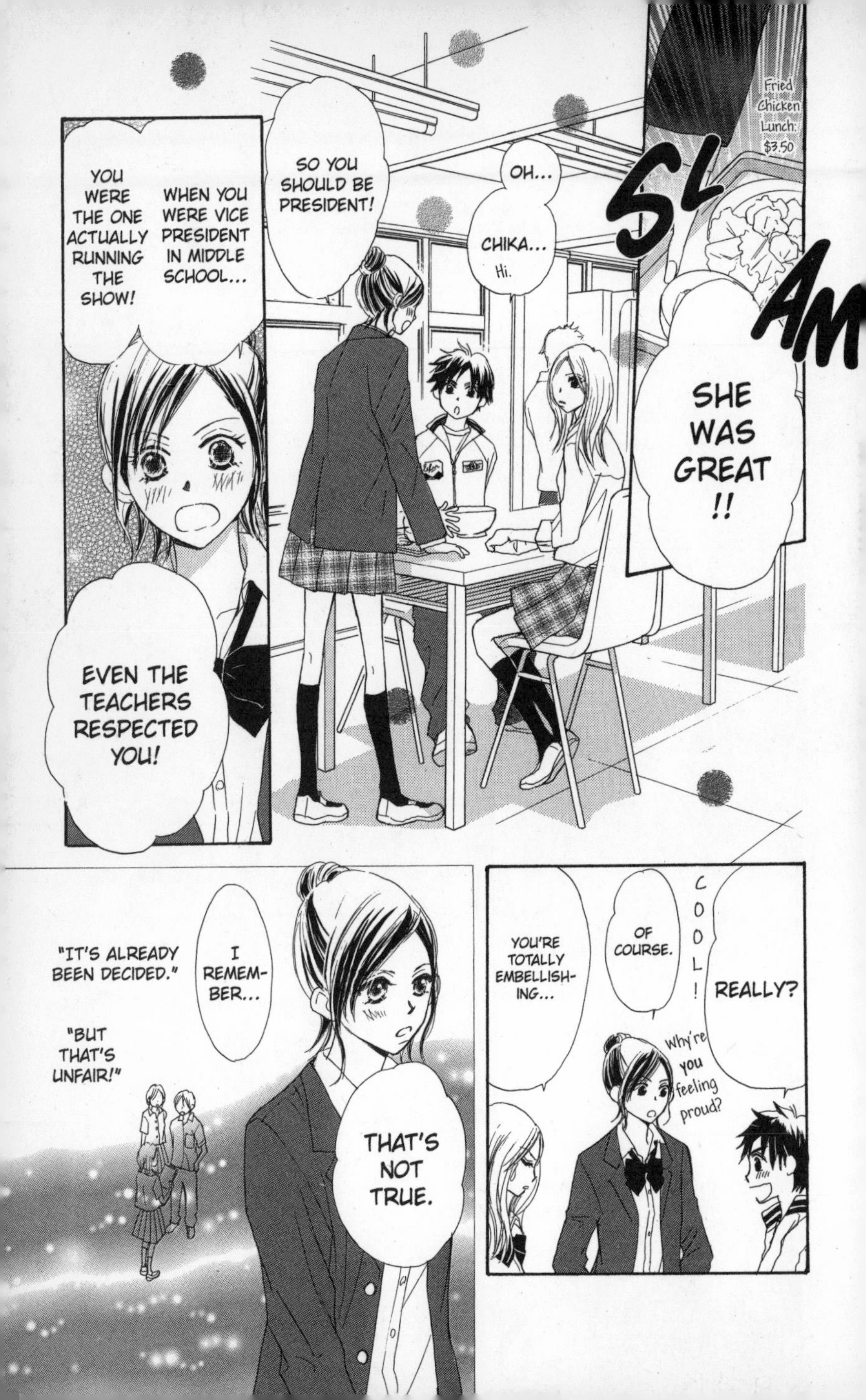

Fried Chicken Lunch: $3.50
SLAM
SHE WAS GREAT!!
OH...
CHIKA...
Hi.
SO YOU SHOULD BE PRESIDENT!
WHEN YOU WERE VICE PRESIDENT IN MIDDLE SCHOOL...
YOU WERE THE ONE ACTUALLY RUNNING THE SHOW!
EVEN THE TEACHERS RESPECTED YOU!
REALLY?
COOL!
Why're you feeling proud?
OF COURSE.
YOU'RE TOTALLY EMBELLISHING...
I REMEMBER...
"IT'S ALREADY BEEN DECIDED."
"BUT THAT'S UNFAIR!"
THAT'S NOT TRUE.

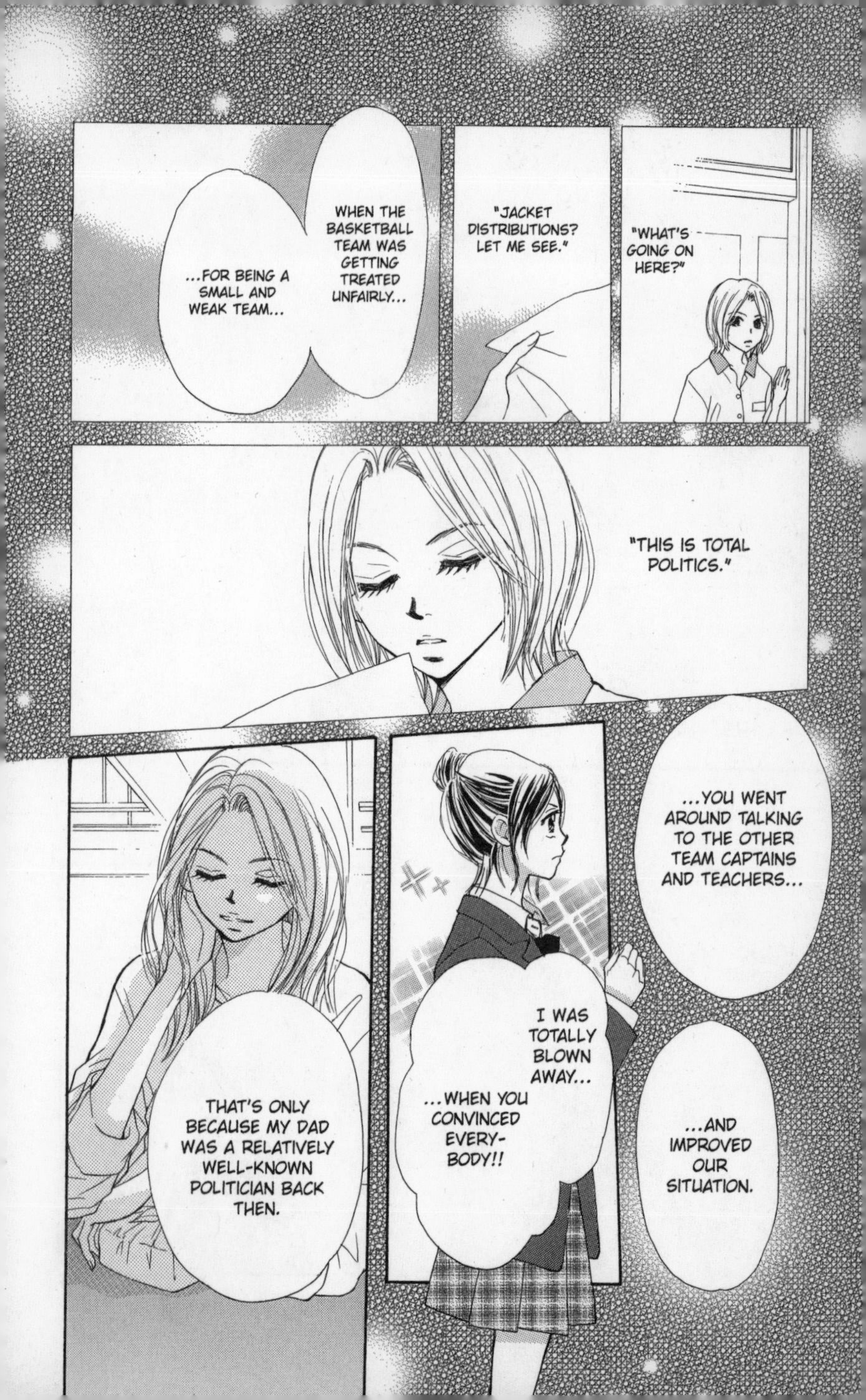
"WHAT'S GOING ON HERE?"
"JACKET DISTRIBUTIONS? LET ME SEE."
WHEN THE BASKETBALL TEAM WAS GETTING TREATED UNFAIRLY...
...FOR BEING A SMALL AND WEAK TEAM...
"THIS IS TOTAL POLITICS."
...YOU WENT AROUND TALKING TO THE OTHER TEAM CAPTAINS AND TEACHERS...
...AND IMPROVED OUR SITUATION.
I WAS TOTALLY BLOWN AWAY...
...WHEN YOU CONVINCED EVERY-BODY!!
THAT'S ONLY BECAUSE MY DAD WAS A RELATIVELY WELL-KNOWN POLITICIAN BACK THEN.

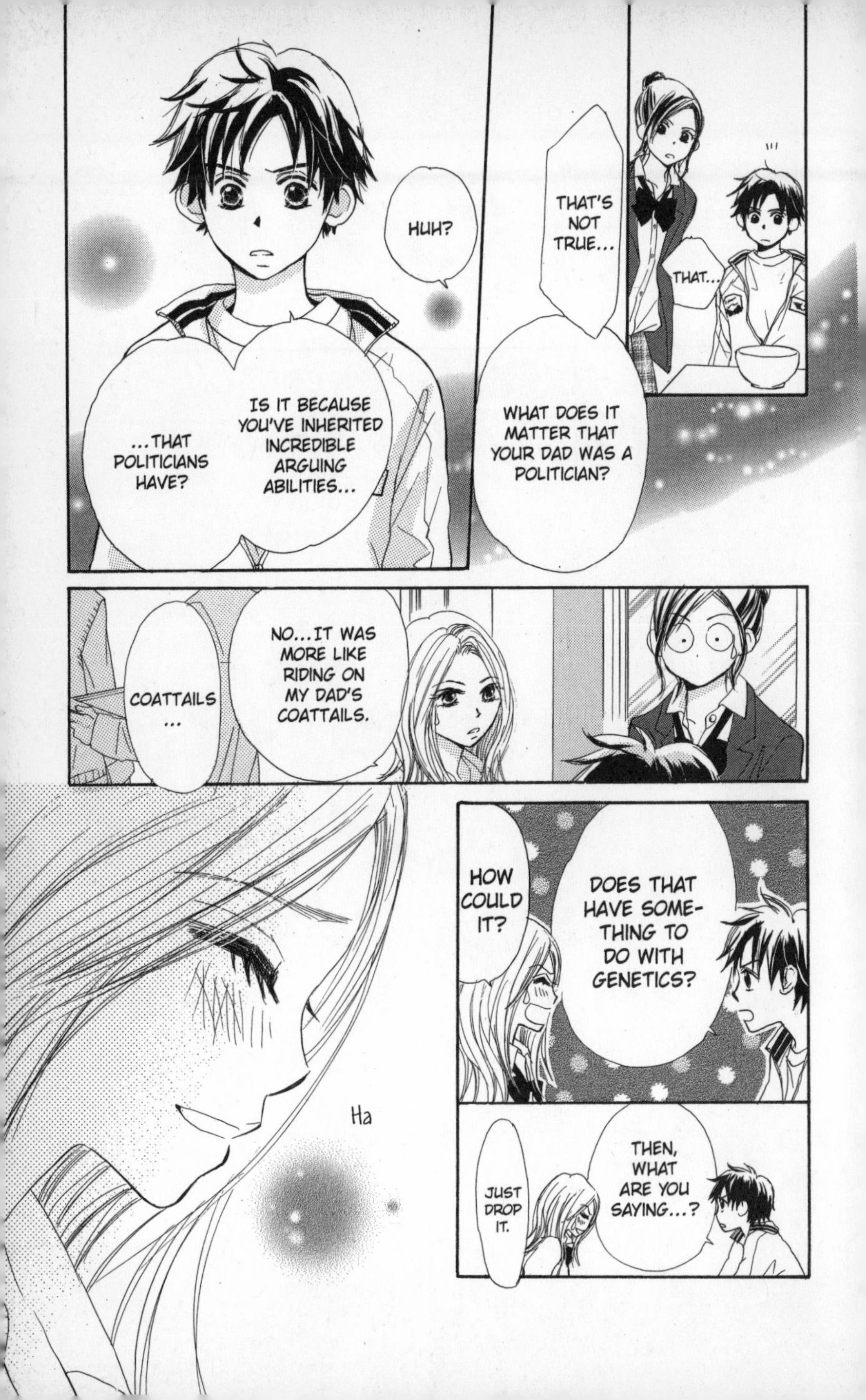
THAT...
THAT'S NOT TRUE...
WHAT DOES IT MATTER THAT YOUR DAD WAS A POLITICIAN?
HUH?
IS IT BECAUSE YOU'VE INHERITED INCREDIBLE ARGUING ABILITIES...
...THAT POLITICIANS HAVE?
NO...IT WAS MORE LIKE RIDING ON MY DAD'S COATTAILS.
COATTAILS ...
DOES THAT HAVE SOME-THING TO DO WITH GENETICS?
HOW COULD IT?
THEN, WHAT ARE YOU SAYING...?
JUST DROP IT.
Ha

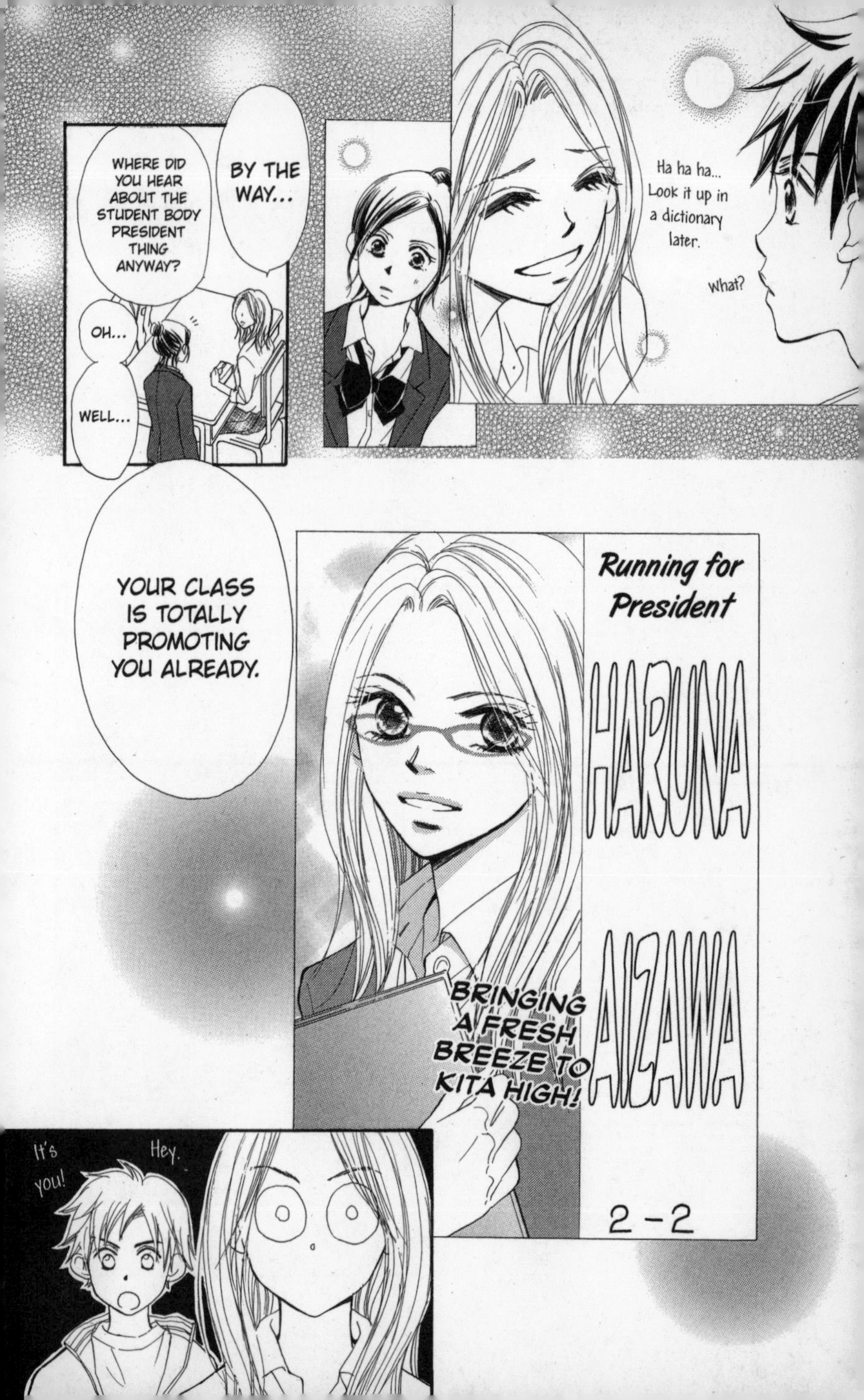
Ha ha ha... Look it up in a dictionary later.
What?
BY THE WAY...
WHERE DID YOU HEAR ABOUT THE STUDENT BODY PRESIDENT THING ANYWAY?
OH...
WELL...
YOUR CLASS IS TOTALLY PROMOTING YOU ALREADY.
Running for President
HARUNA AIZAWA
BRINGING A FRESH BREEZE TO KITA HIGH!
2-2
Hey.
It's you!

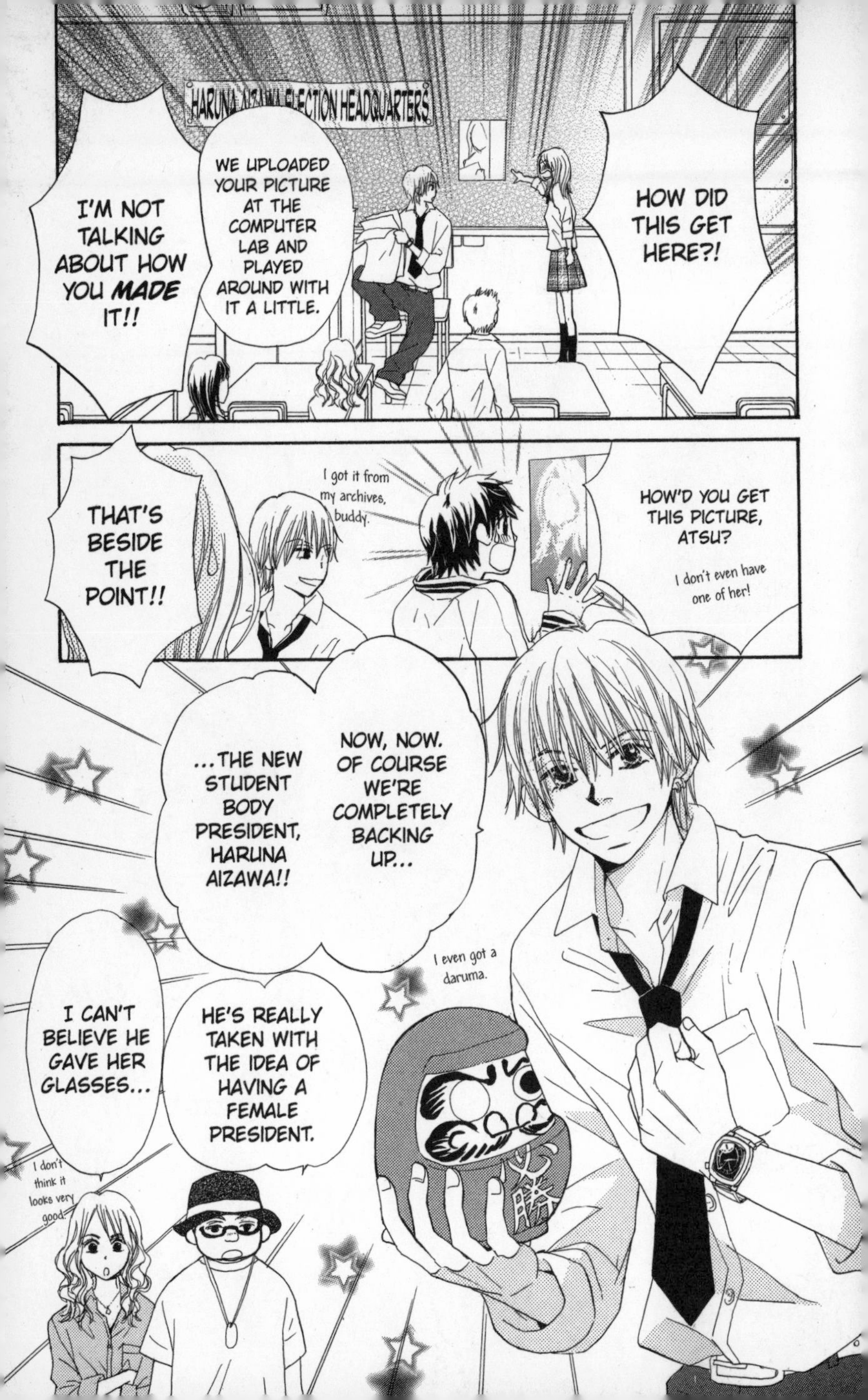
HARUNA AIZAWA ELECTION HEADQUARTERS
HOW DID THIS GET HERE?!
WE UPLOADED YOUR PICTURE AT THE COMPUTER LAB AND PLAYED AROUND WITH IT A LITTLE.
I'M NOT TALKING ABOUT HOW YOU *MADE* IT!!
HOW'D YOU GET THIS PICTURE, ATSU?
I don't even have one of her!
I got it from my archives, buddy.
THAT'S BESIDE THE POINT!!
NOW, NOW. OF COURSE WE'RE COMPLETELY BACKING UP...
...THE NEW STUDENT BODY PRESIDENT, HARUNA AIZAWA!!
I even got a daruma.
HE'S REALLY TAKEN WITH THE IDEA OF HAVING A FEMALE PRESIDENT.
I CAN'T BELIEVE HE GAVE HER GLASSES...
I don't think it looks very good.

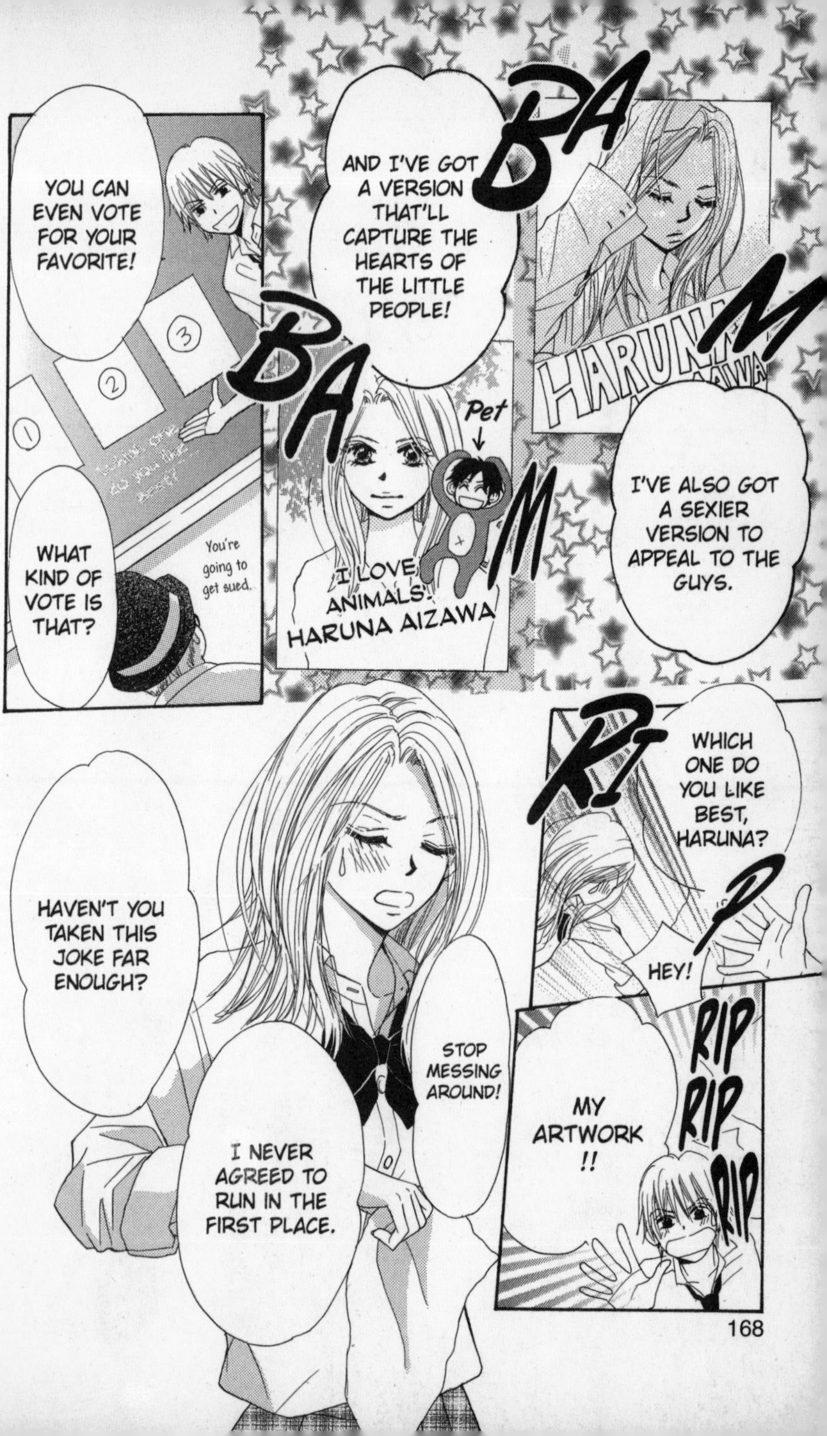
BAM
HARUNA AIZAWA
I'VE ALSO GOT A SEXIER VERSION TO APPEAL TO THE GUYS.
AND I'VE GOT A VERSION THAT'LL CAPTURE THE HEARTS OF THE LITTLE PEOPLE!
BAM
Pet
I LOVE ANIMALS! HARUNA AIZAWA
YOU CAN EVEN VOTE FOR YOUR FAVORITE!
WHAT KIND OF VOTE IS THAT?
You're going to get sued.
RIP
WHICH ONE DO YOU LIKE BEST, HARUNA?
HEY!
RIP RIP RIP
MY ARTWORK!!
STOP MESSING AROUND!
HAVEN'T YOU TAKEN THIS JOKE FAR ENOUGH?
I NEVER AGREED TO RUN IN THE FIRST PLACE.

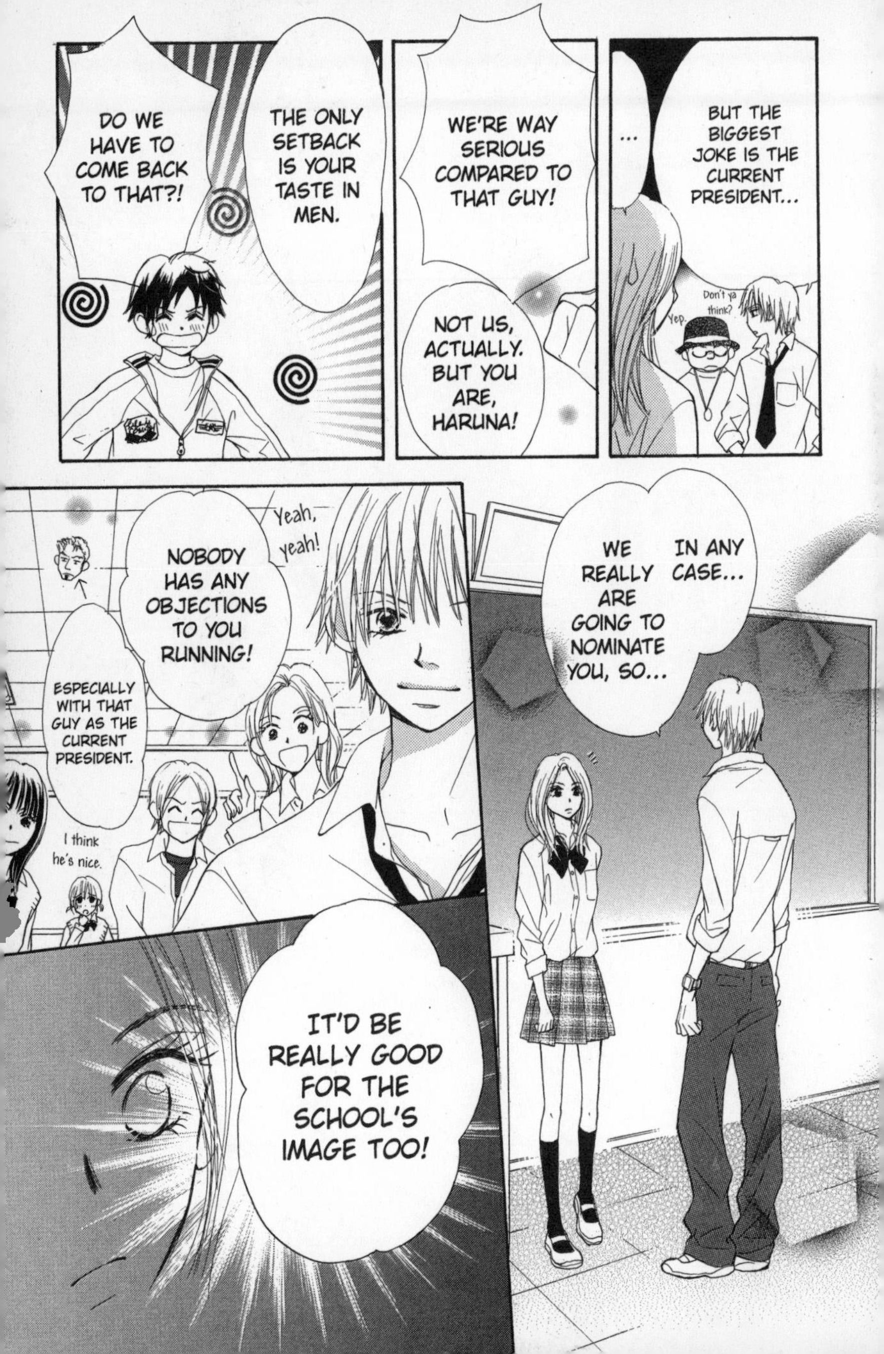
BUT THE BIGGEST JOKE IS THE CURRENT PRESIDENT...
...
Don't ya think?
Yep.
WE'RE WAY SERIOUS COMPARED TO THAT GUY!
NOT US, ACTUALLY. BUT YOU ARE, HARUNA!
THE ONLY SETBACK IS YOUR TASTE IN MEN.
DO WE HAVE TO COME BACK TO THAT?!
IN ANY CASE...
WE REALLY ARE GOING TO NOMINATE YOU, SO...
Yeah, yeah!
NOBODY HAS ANY OBJECTIONS TO YOU RUNNING!
ESPECIALLY WITH THAT GUY AS THE CURRENT PRESIDENT.
I think he's nice.
IT'D BE REALLY GOOD FOR THE SCHOOL'S IMAGE TOO!

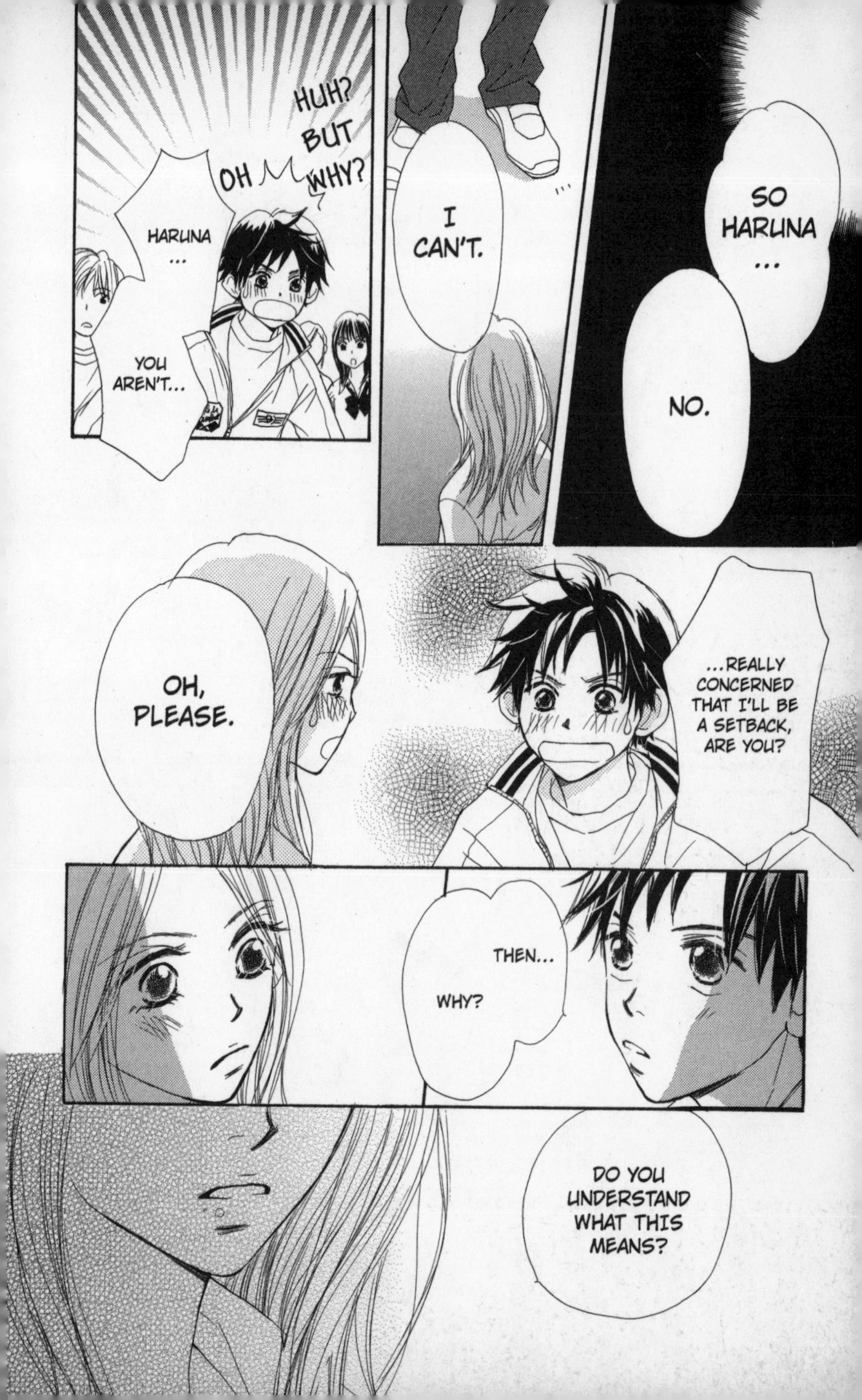
SO HARUNA ...
NO.
I CAN'T.
HUH? BUT WHY?
OH
HARUNA ...
YOU AREN'T...
...REALLY CONCERNED THAT I'LL BE A SETBACK, ARE YOU?
OH, PLEASE.
THEN...
WHY?
DO YOU UNDERSTAND WHAT THIS MEANS?

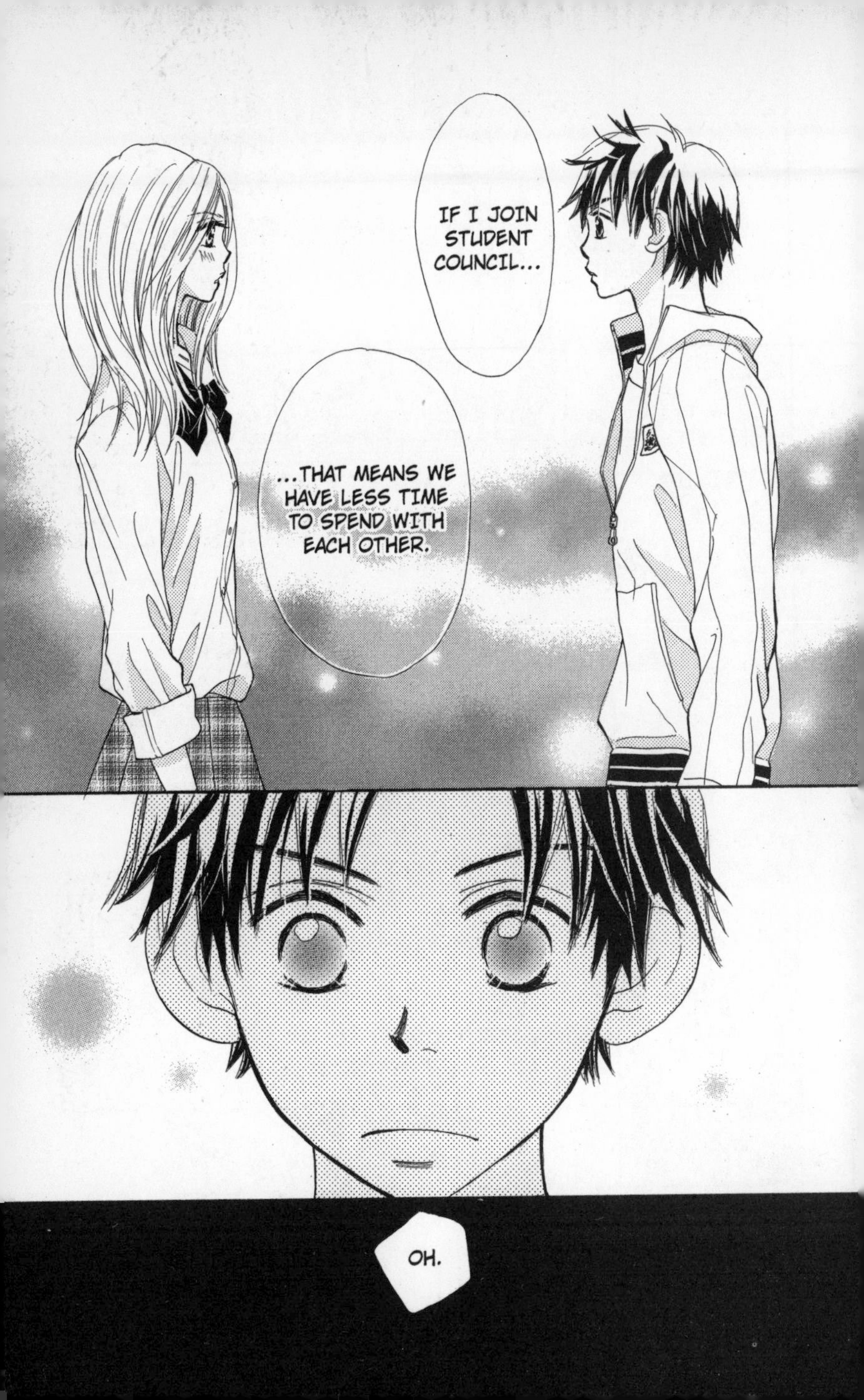
IF I JOIN STUDENT COUNCIL...
...THAT MEANS WE HAVE LESS TIME TO SPEND WITH EACH OTHER.
OH.

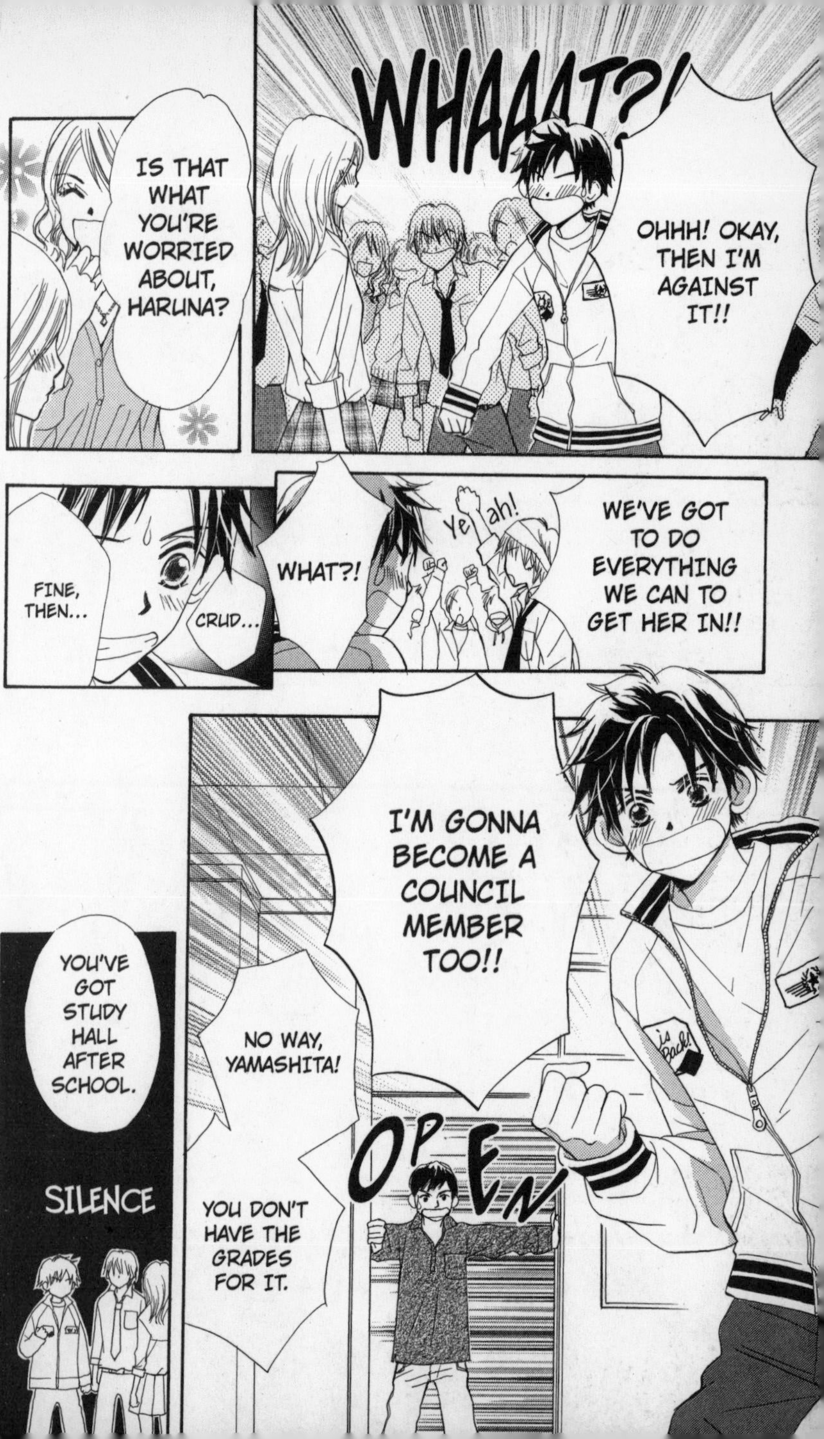
WHAAAT?!
OHHH! OKAY, THEN I'M AGAINST IT!!
IS THAT WHAT YOU'RE WORRIED ABOUT, HARUNA?
WE'VE GOT TO DO EVERYTHING WE CAN TO GET HER IN!!
Yeah!
WHAT?!
CRUD...
FINE, THEN...
I'M GONNA BECOME A COUNCIL MEMBER TOO!!
OPEN
NO WAY, YAMASHITA!
YOU DON'T HAVE THE GRADES FOR IT.
YOU'VE GOT STUDY HALL AFTER SCHOOL.
SILENCE

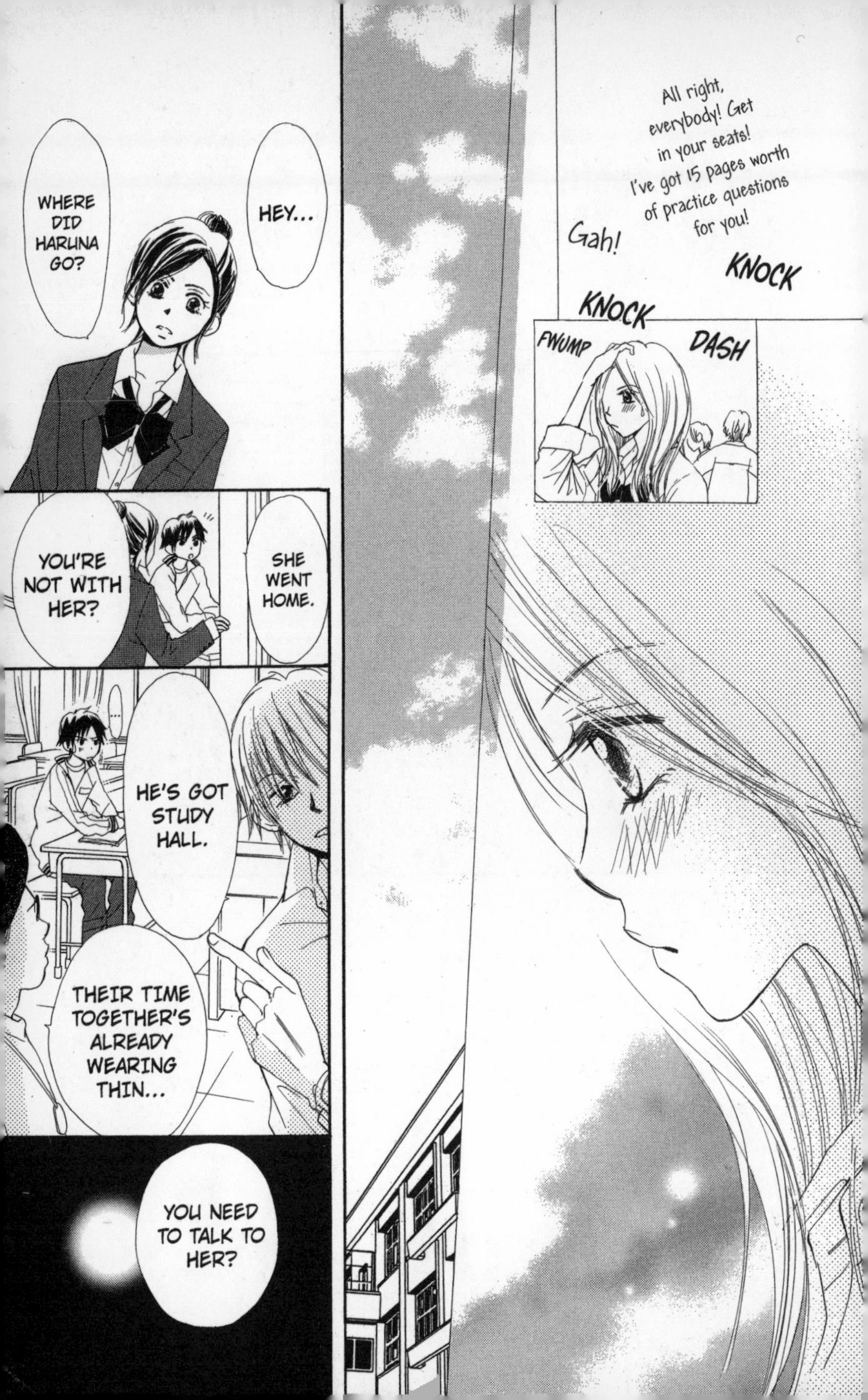
All right, everybody! Get in your seats! I've got 15 pages worth of practice questions for you!
Gah!
KNOCK
KNOCK
DASH
FWUMP
HEY...
WHERE DID HARUNA GO?
SHE WENT HOME.
YOU'RE NOT WITH HER?
HE'S GOT STUDY HALL.
THEIR TIME TOGETHER'S ALREADY WEARING THIN...
YOU NEED TO TALK TO HER?

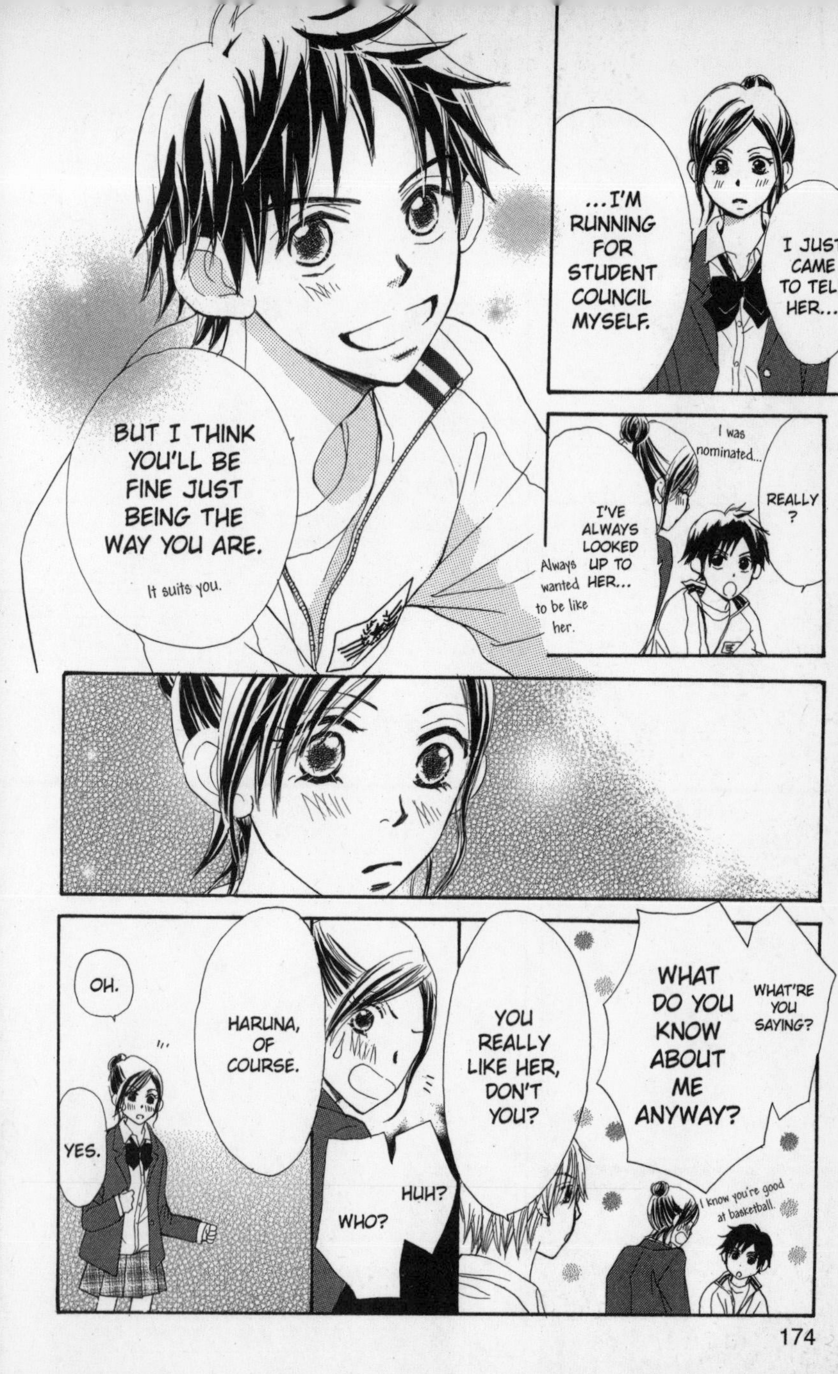
I JUST CAME TO TELL HER...
...I'M RUNNING FOR STUDENT COUNCIL MYSELF.
REALLY?
I was nominated...
I'VE ALWAYS LOOKED UP TO HER...
Always wanted to be like her.
BUT I THINK YOU'LL BE FINE JUST BEING THE WAY YOU ARE.
It suits you.
WHAT'RE YOU SAYING?
WHAT DO YOU KNOW ABOUT ME ANYWAY?
I know you're good at basketball.
YOU REALLY LIKE HER, DON'T YOU?
HUH?
WHO?
HARUNA, OF COURSE.
OH.
YES.

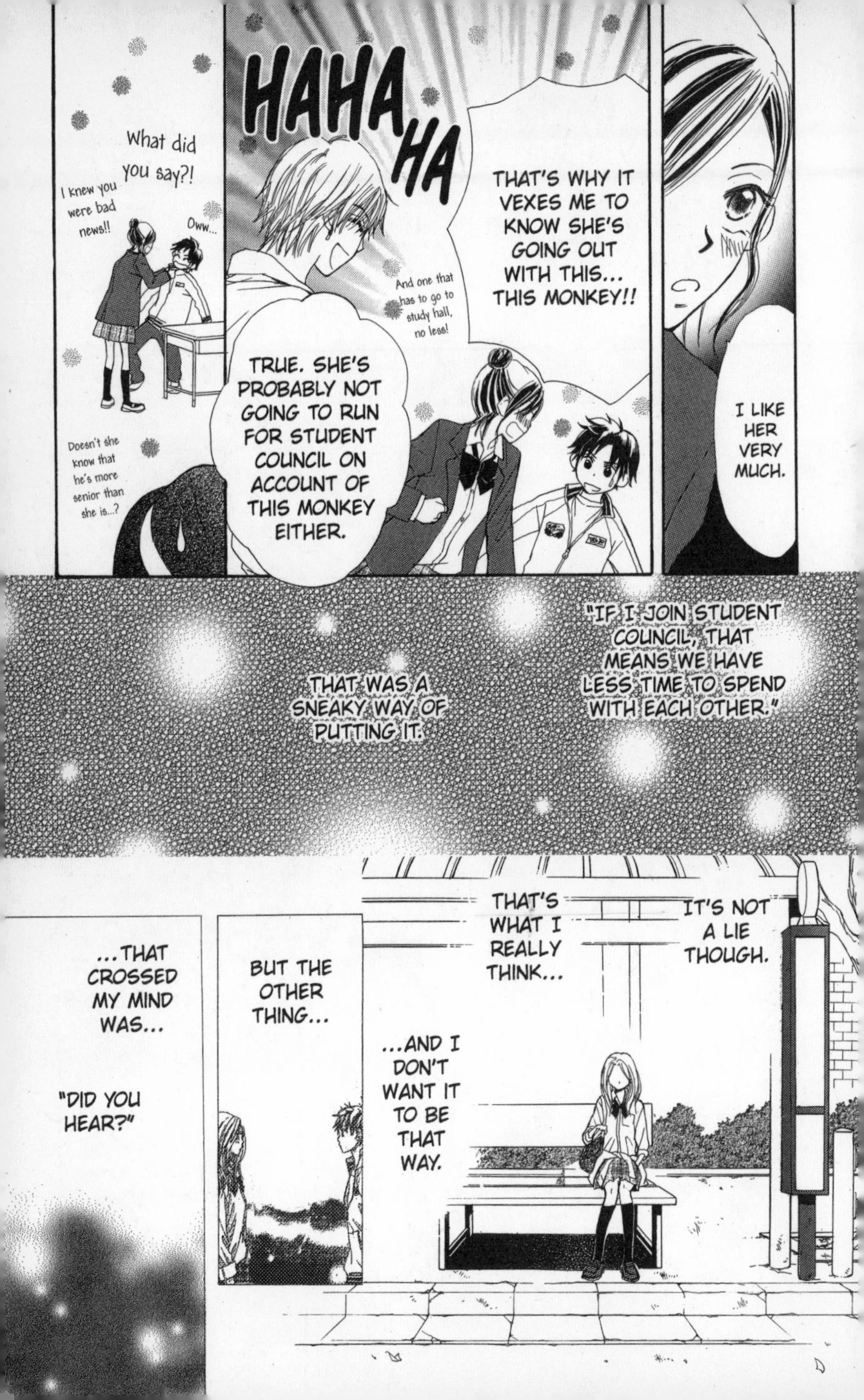
I LIKE HER VERY MUCH.
HAHAHA
THAT'S WHY IT VEXES ME TO KNOW SHE'S GOING OUT WITH THIS... THIS MONKEY!!
And one that has to go to study hall, no less!
TRUE. SHE'S PROBABLY NOT GOING TO RUN FOR STUDENT COUNCIL ON ACCOUNT OF THIS MONKEY EITHER.
What did you say?!
I knew you were bad news!!
Oww...
Doesn't she know that he's more senior than she is...?
"IF I JOIN STUDENT COUNCIL, THAT MEANS WE HAVE LESS TIME TO SPEND WITH EACH OTHER."
THAT WAS A SNEAKY WAY OF PUTTING IT.
IT'S NOT A LIE THOUGH.
THAT'S WHAT I REALLY THINK...
...AND I DON'T WANT IT TO BE THAT WAY.
BUT THE OTHER THING...
...THAT CROSSED MY MIND WAS...
"DID YOU HEAR?"

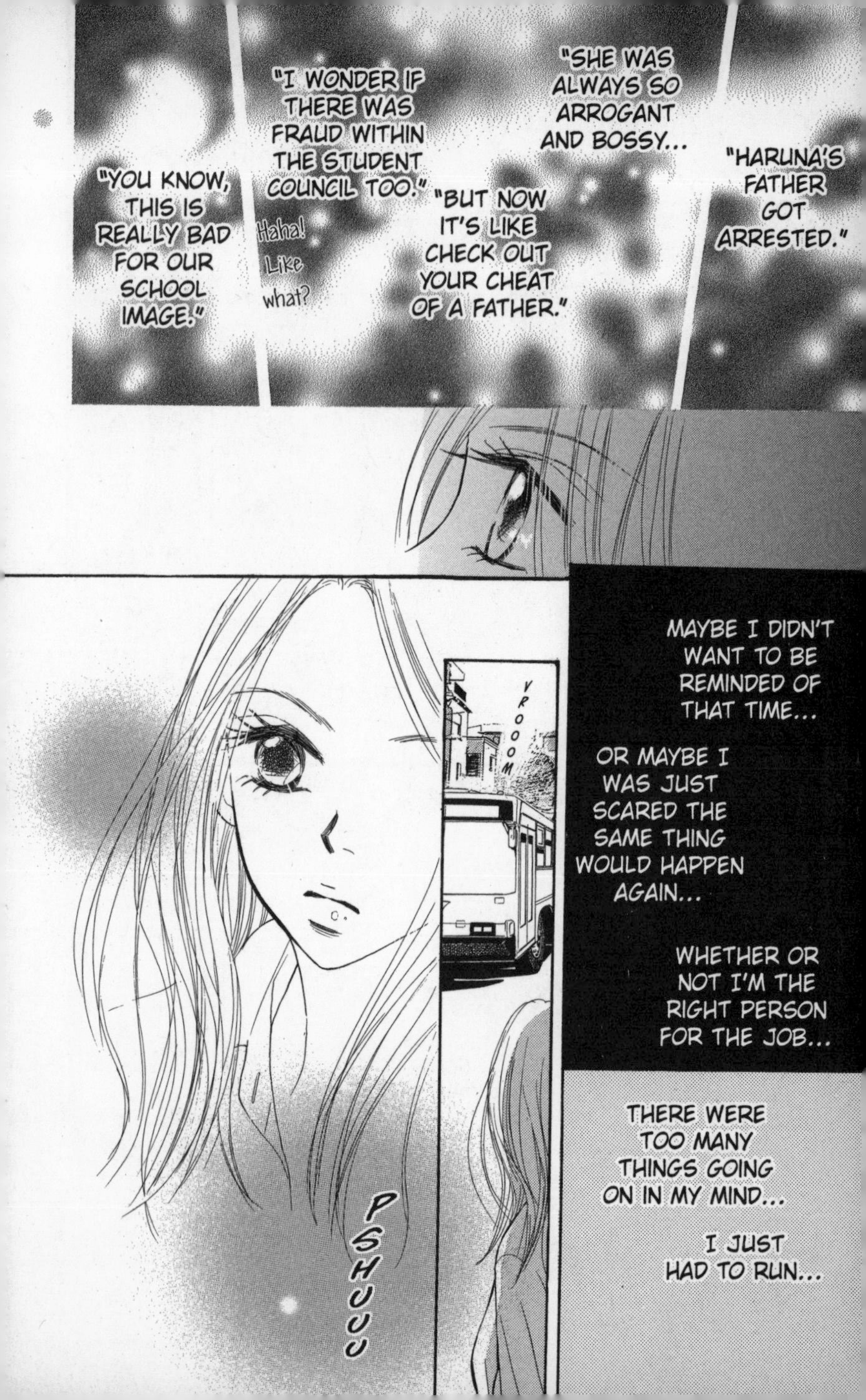
"HARUNA'S FATHER GOT ARRESTED."
"SHE WAS ALWAYS SO ARROGANT AND BOSSY...
"BUT NOW IT'S LIKE CHECK OUT YOUR CHEAT OF A FATHER."
"I WONDER IF THERE WAS FRAUD WITHIN THE STUDENT COUNCIL TOO."
Haha! Like what?
"YOU KNOW, THIS IS REALLY BAD FOR OUR SCHOOL IMAGE."
MAYBE I DIDN'T WANT TO BE REMINDED OF THAT TIME...
OR MAYBE I WAS JUST SCARED THE SAME THING WOULD HAPPEN AGAIN...
WHETHER OR NOT I'M THE RIGHT PERSON FOR THE JOB...
VROOOOM
THERE WERE TOO MANY THINGS GOING ON IN MY MIND...
I JUST HAD TO RUN...
PSHUUU

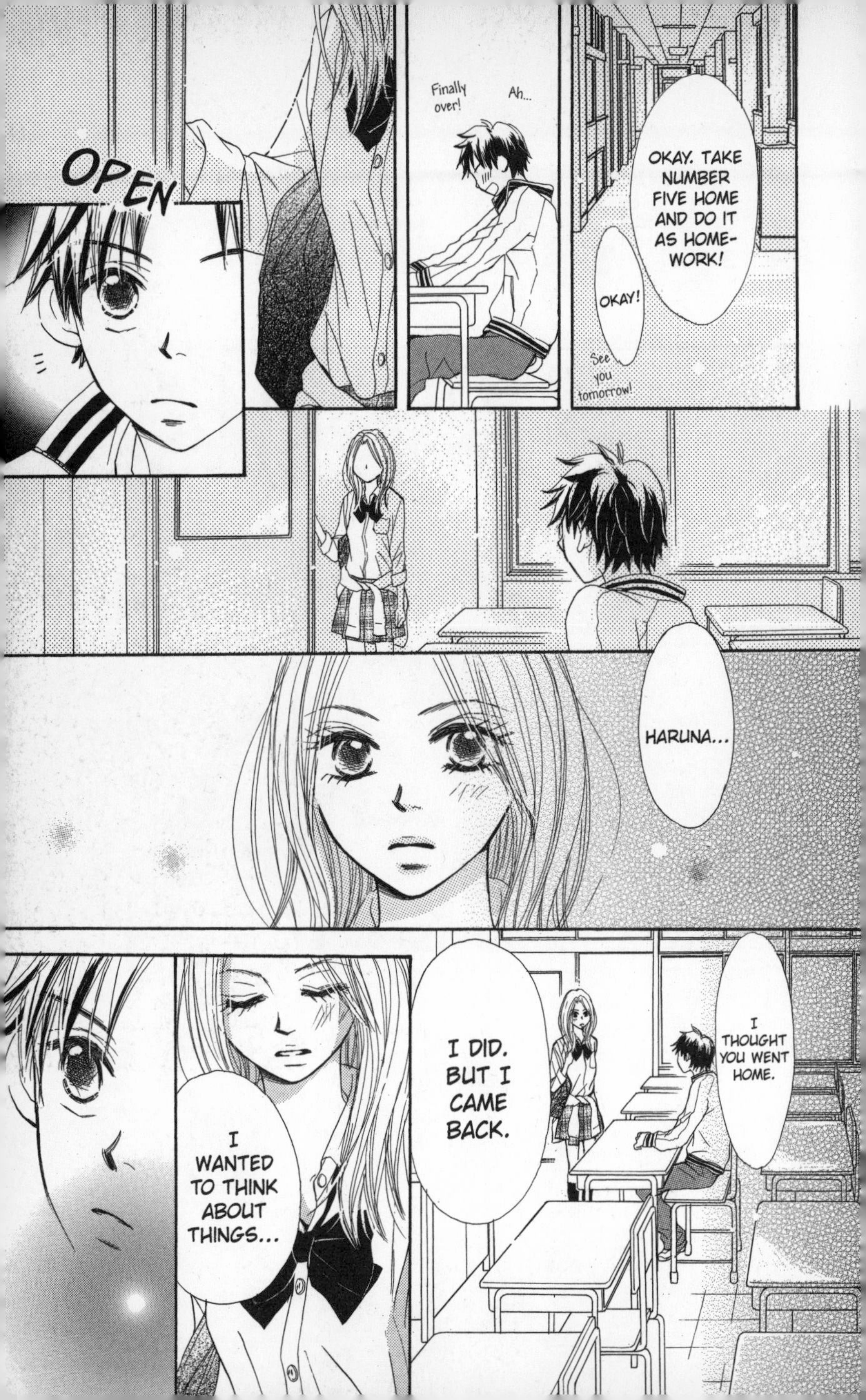
OKAY. TAKE NUMBER FIVE HOME AND DO IT AS HOME-WORK!
OKAY!
See you tomorrow!
Ah...
Finally over!
OPEN
HARUNA...
I THOUGHT YOU WENT HOME.
I DID. BUT I CAME BACK.
I WANTED TO THINK ABOUT THINGS...

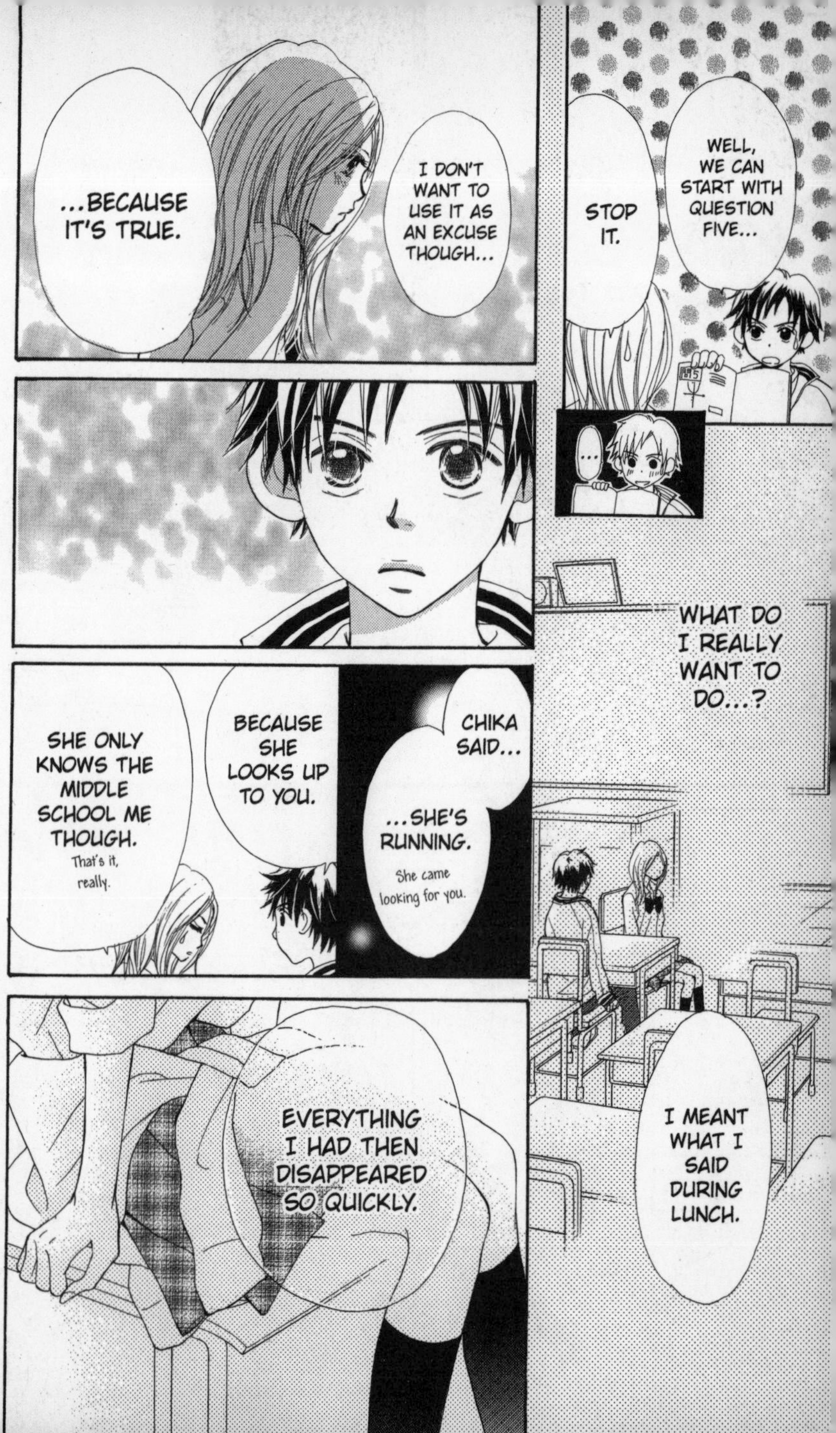
WELL, WE CAN START WITH QUESTION FIVE...
STOP IT.
...
WHAT DO I REALLY WANT TO DO...?
I MEANT WHAT I SAID DURING LUNCH.
I DON'T WANT TO USE IT AS AN EXCUSE THOUGH...
...BECAUSE IT'S TRUE.
CHIKA SAID...
...SHE'S RUNNING.
She came looking for you.
BECAUSE SHE LOOKS UP TO YOU.
SHE ONLY KNOWS THE MIDDLE SCHOOL ME THOUGH.
That's it, really.
EVERYTHING I HAD THEN DISAPPEARED SO QUICKLY.

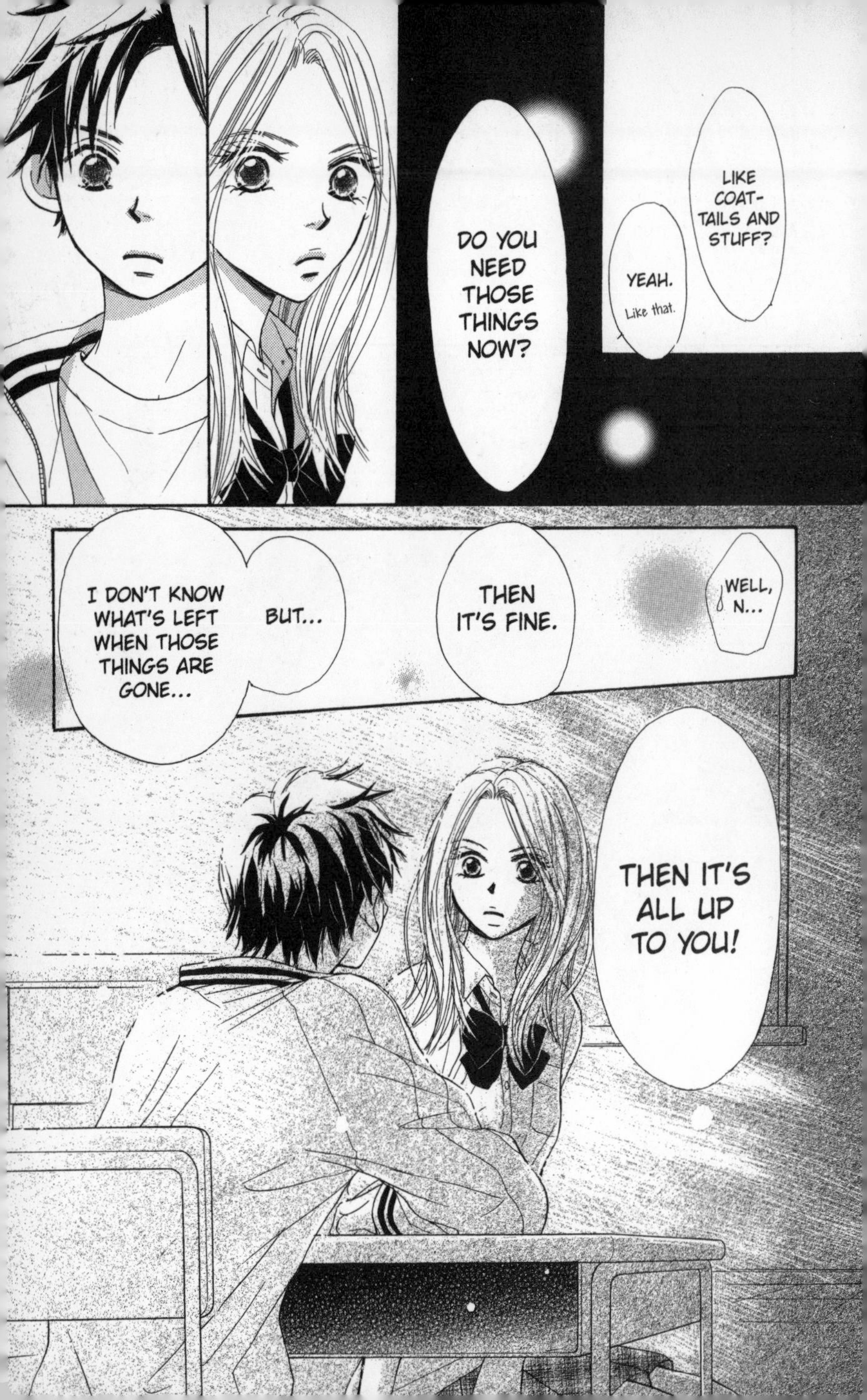
LIKE COAT-TAILS AND STUFF?
YEAH.
Like that.
DO YOU NEED THOSE THINGS NOW?
WELL, N...
THEN IT'S FINE.
BUT...
I DON'T KNOW WHAT'S LEFT WHEN THOSE THINGS ARE GONE...
THEN IT'S ALL UP TO YOU!

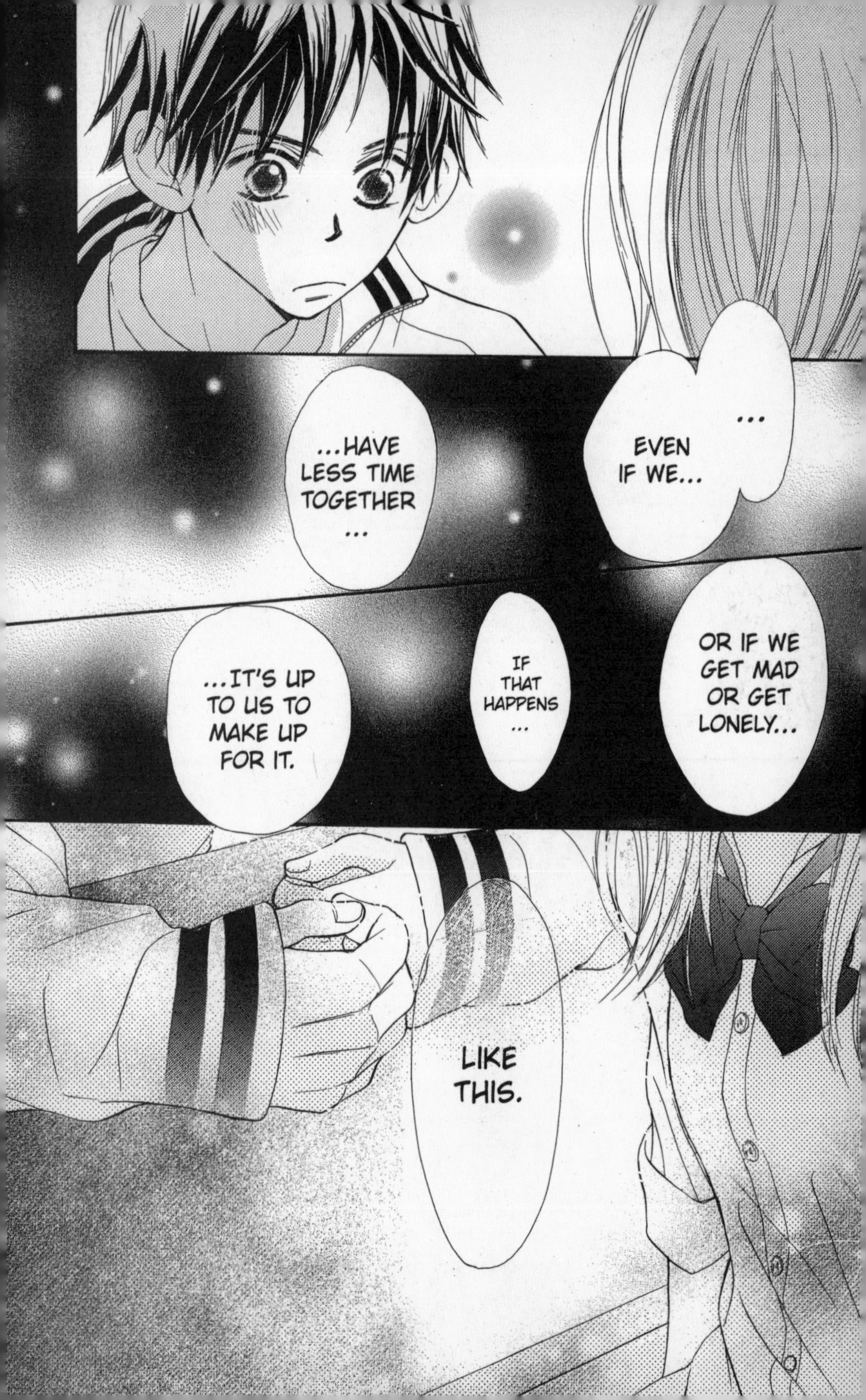
... EVEN IF WE...
...HAVE LESS TIME TOGETHER ...
OR IF WE GET MAD OR GET LONELY...
IF THAT HAPPENS ...
...IT'S UP TO US TO MAKE UP FOR IT.
LIKE THIS.

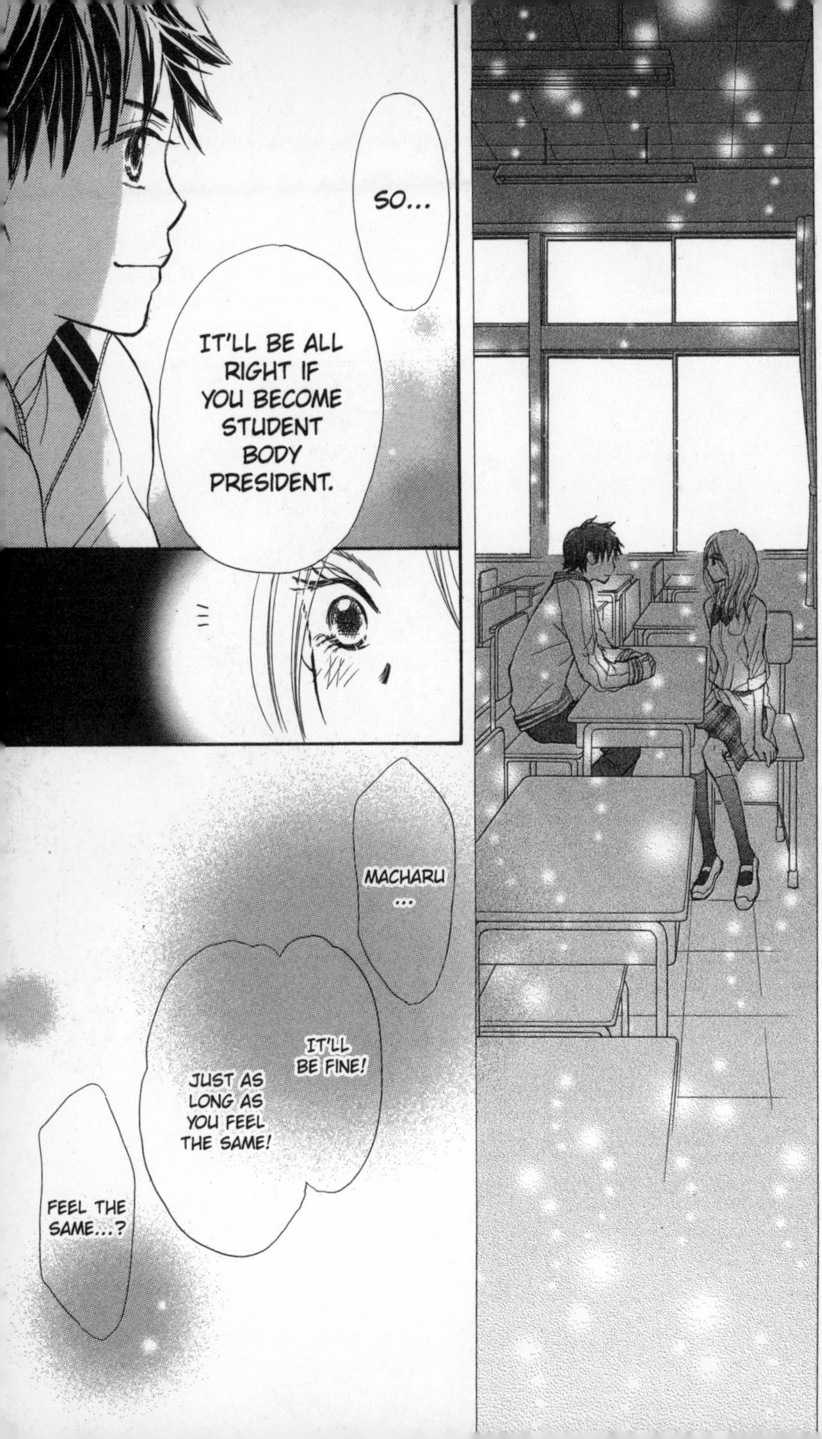
SO...
IT'LL BE ALL RIGHT IF YOU BECOME STUDENT BODY PRESIDENT.
MACHARU ...
IT'LL BE FINE!
JUST AS LONG AS YOU FEEL THE SAME!
FEEL THE SAME...?

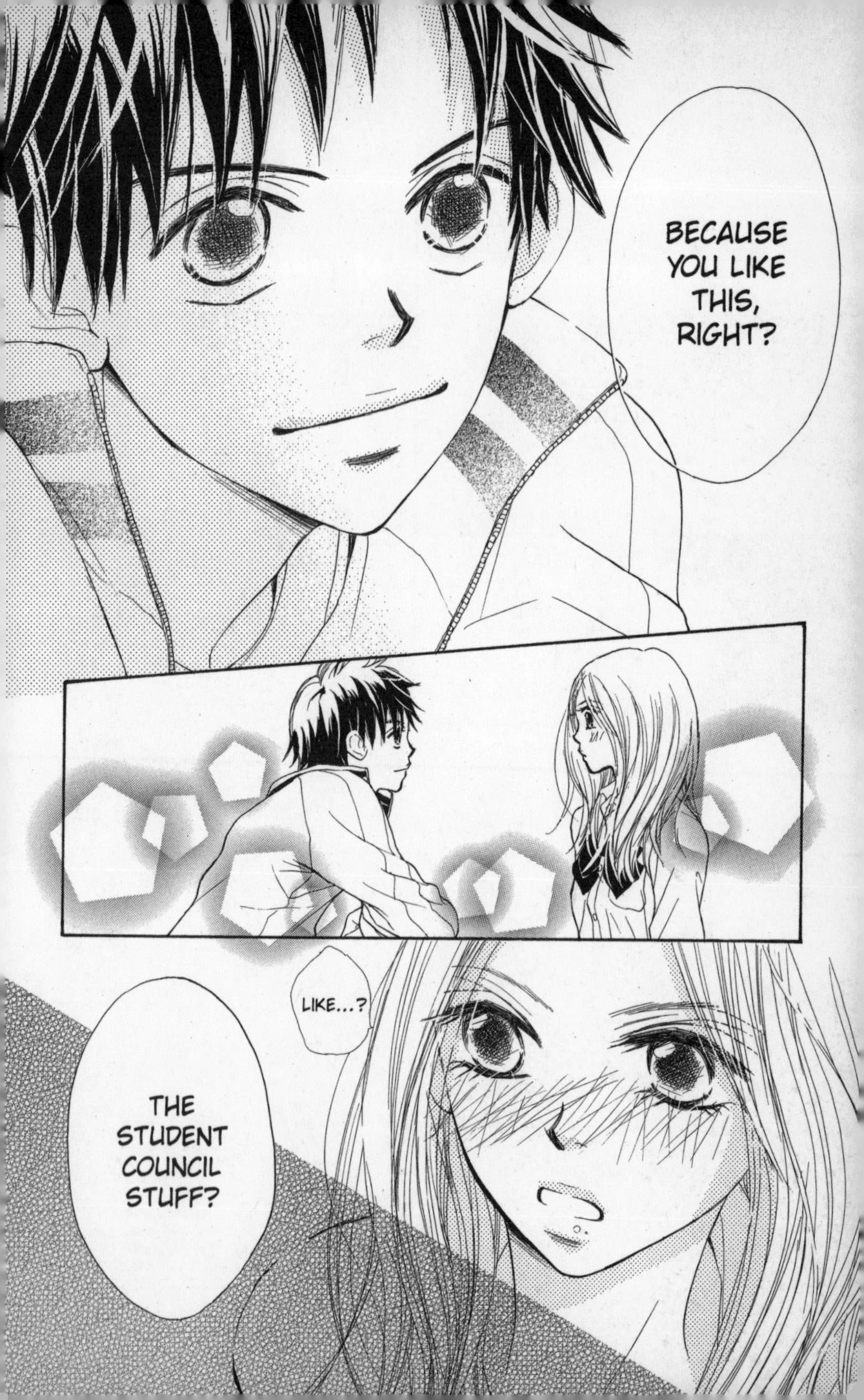
BECAUSE YOU LIKE THIS, RIGHT?
LIKE...?
THE STUDENT COUNCIL STUFF?

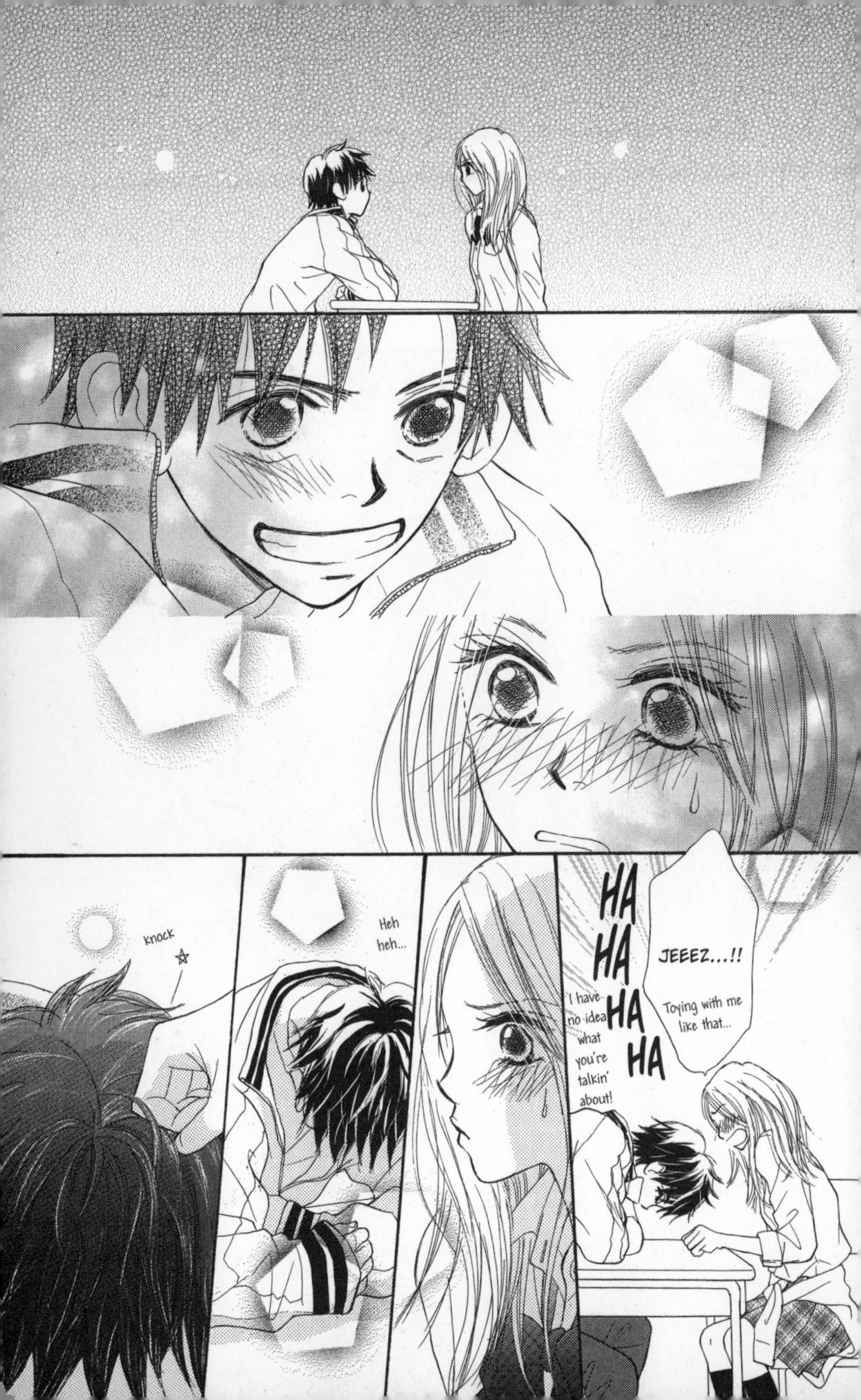
JEEEZ...!! Toying with me like that...
HA HA HA HA HA
I have no idea what you're talkin' about!
Heh heh...
knock ☆

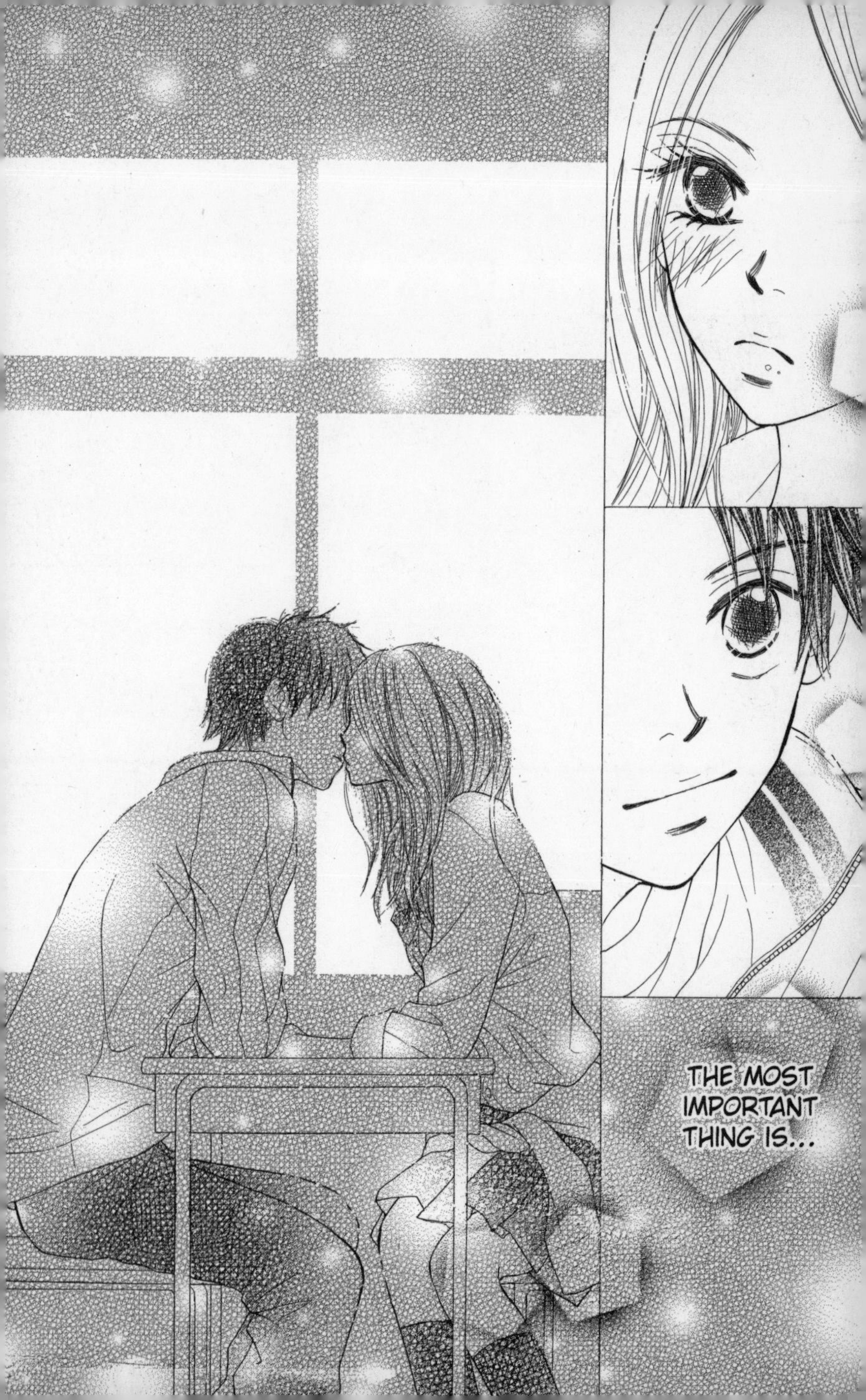
THE MOST IMPORTANT THING IS...

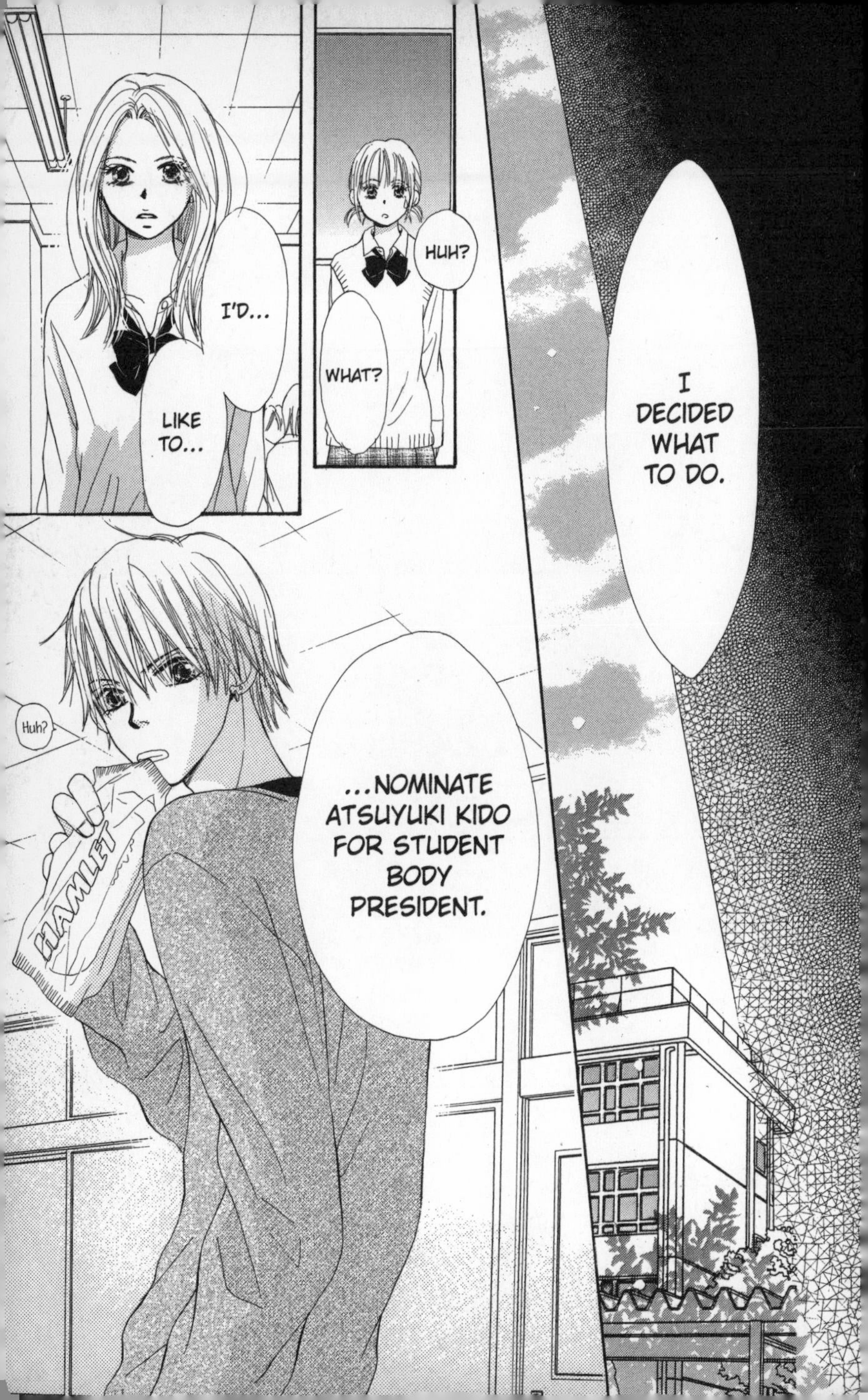
I DECIDED WHAT TO DO.
HUH?
WHAT?
I'D...
LIKE TO...
...NOMINATE ATSUYUKI KIDO FOR STUDENT BODY PRESIDENT.
Huh?

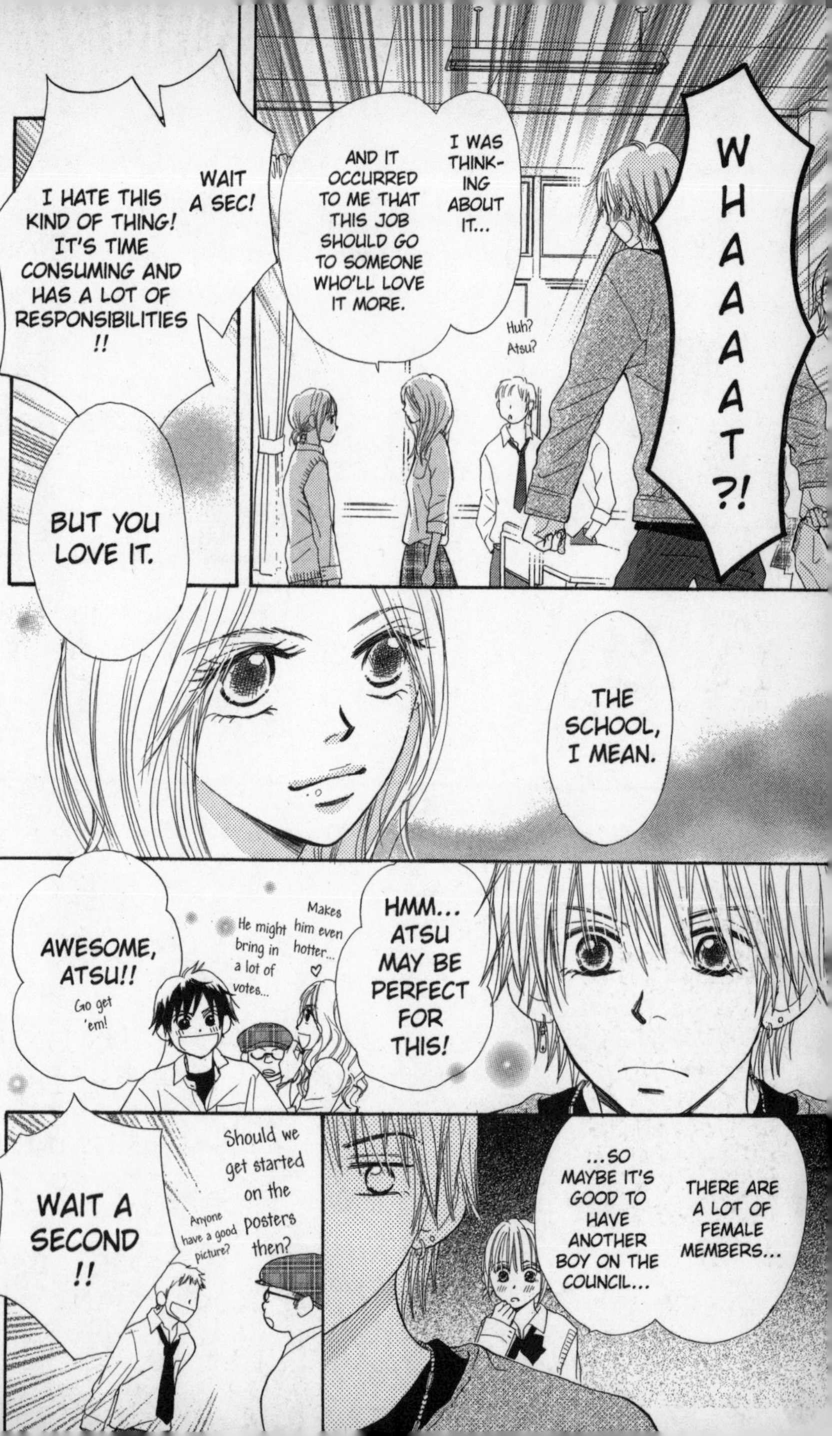
WHAAAAAT?!
I WAS THINKING ABOUT IT...
AND IT OCCURRED TO ME THAT THIS JOB SHOULD GO TO SOMEONE WHO'LL LOVE IT MORE.
Huh? Atsu?
WAIT A SEC!
I HATE THIS KIND OF THING! IT'S TIME CONSUMING AND HAS A LOT OF RESPONSIBILITIES!!
BUT YOU LOVE IT.
THE SCHOOL, I MEAN.
HMM... ATSU MAY BE PERFECT FOR THIS!
Makes him even hotter... ♡
He might bring in a lot of votes...
AWESOME, ATSU!!
Go get 'em!
THERE ARE A LOT OF FEMALE MEMBERS...
...SO MAYBE IT'S GOOD TO HAVE ANOTHER BOY ON THE COUNCIL...
Should we get started on the posters then?
Anyone have a good picture?
WAIT A SECOND!!

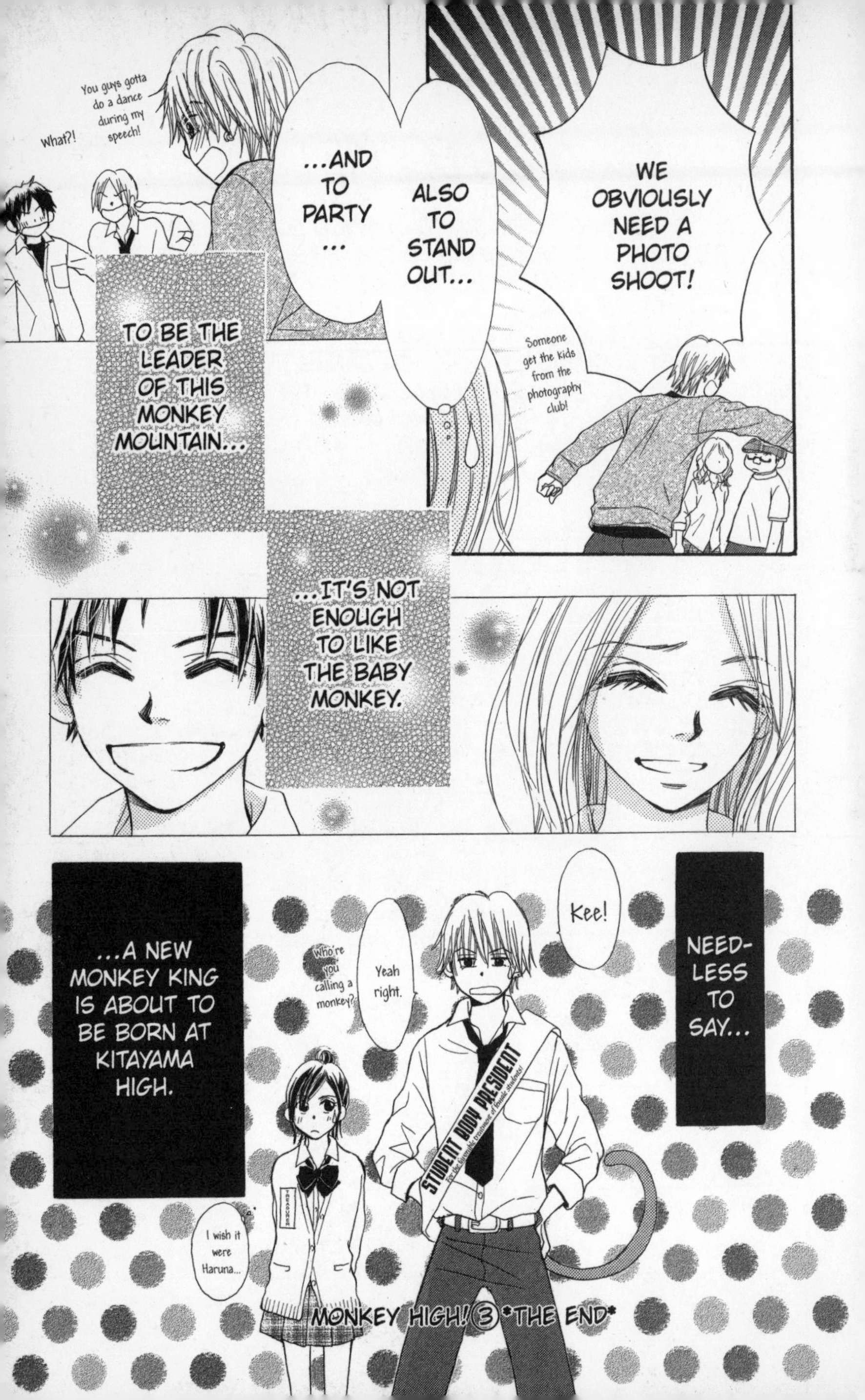
WE OBVIOUSLY NEED A PHOTO SHOOT!
Someone get the kids from the photography club!
ALSO TO STAND OUT...
...AND TO PARTY...
You guys gotta do a dance during my speech!
What?!
TO BE THE LEADER OF THIS MONKEY MOUNTAIN...
...IT'S NOT ENOUGH TO LIKE THE BABY MONKEY.
NEED-LESS TO SAY...
Kee!
Yeah right.
Who're you calling a monkey?!
...A NEW MONKEY KING IS ABOUT TO BE BORN AT KITAYAMA HIGH.
STUDENT BODY PRESIDENT
I wish it were Haruna...
MONKEY HIGH! 3 *THE END*

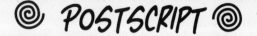

POSTSCRIPT

I'M SHOUKO AKIRA. THANK YOU SO MUCH FOR READING! I CAN'T BELIEVE IT'S ALREADY VOLUME 3! I'VE BEEN DOING THIS FOR A LONG TIME, BUT MOST OF MY COMICS HAVE BEEN SHORT. THEREFORE, THERE'S A DIFFERENT KIND OF SATISFACTION THAT I GET FROM DOING A LONGER SERIES LIKE THIS ONE. HERE'S A BRIEF REFLECTION ON THE STORIES IN THIS VOLUME.

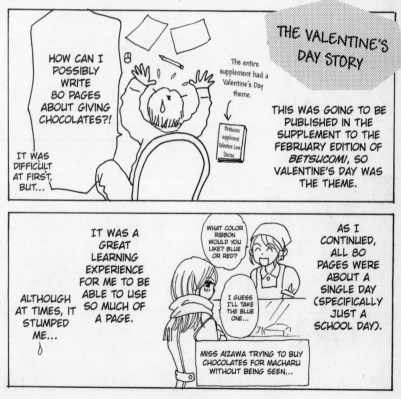

THE VALENTINE'S DAY STORY
The entire supplement had a Valentine's Day theme.
Betsucomi supplement: Valentine Love Stories
THIS WAS GOING TO BE PUBLISHED IN THE SUPPLEMENT TO THE FEBRUARY EDITION OF *BETSUCOMI*, SO VALENTINE'S DAY WAS THE THEME.
HOW CAN I POSSIBLY WRITE 80 PAGES ABOUT GIVING CHOCOLATES?!
IT WAS DIFFICULT AT FIRST, BUT...

AS I CONTINUED, ALL 80 PAGES WERE ABOUT A SINGLE DAY (SPECIFICALLY JUST A SCHOOL DAY).
WHAT COLOR RIBBON WOULD YOU LIKE? BLUE OR RED?
I GUESS I'LL TAKE THE BLUE ONE...
MISS AIZAWA TRYING TO BUY CHOCOLATES FOR MACHARU WITHOUT BEING SEEN...
IT WAS A GREAT LEARNING EXPERIENCE FOR ME TO BE ABLE TO USE SO MUCH OF A PAGE.
ALTHOUGH AT TIMES, IT STUMPED ME...

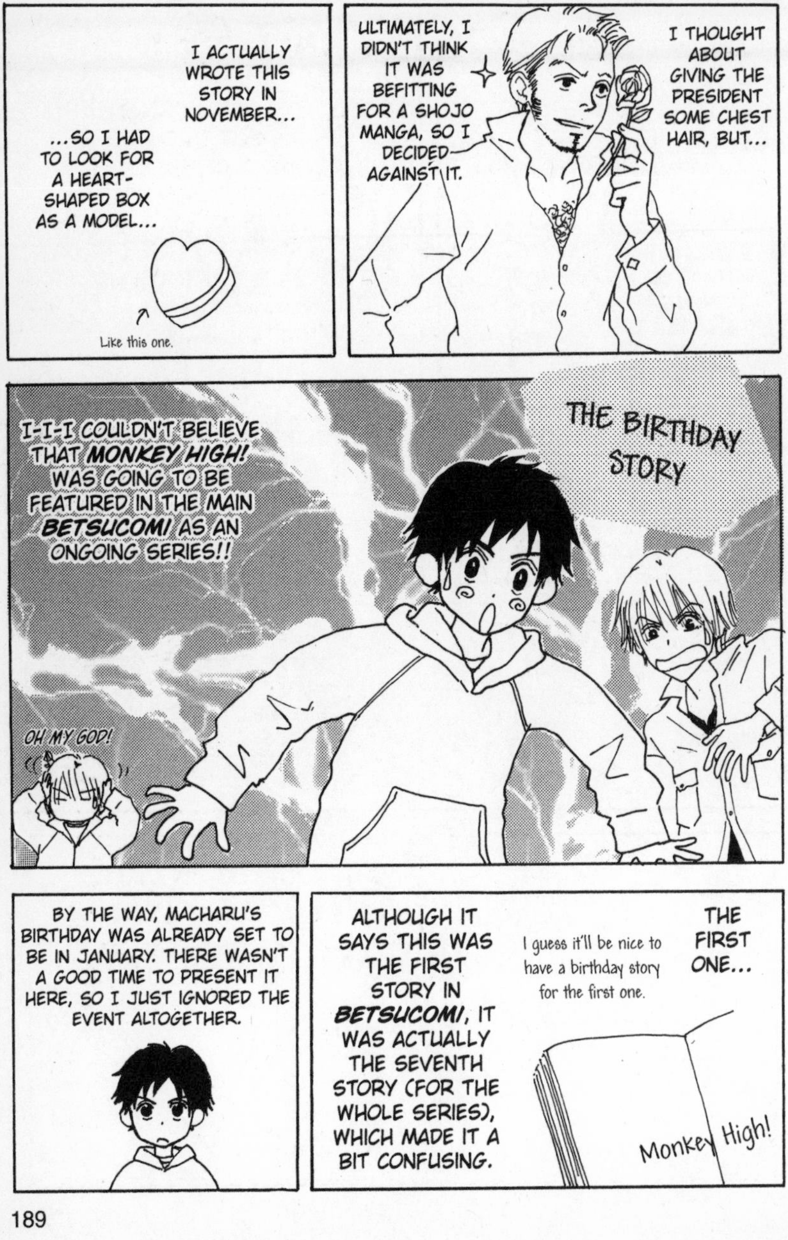

I THOUGHT ABOUT GIVING THE PRESIDENT SOME CHEST HAIR, BUT...
ULTIMATELY, I DIDN'T THINK IT WAS BEFITTING FOR A SHOJO MANGA, SO I DECIDED AGAINST IT.
I ACTUALLY WROTE THIS STORY IN NOVEMBER...
...SO I HAD TO LOOK FOR A HEART-SHAPED BOX AS A MODEL...
Like this one.
THE BIRTHDAY STORY
I-I-I COULDN'T BELIEVE THAT MONKEY HIGH! WAS GOING TO BE FEATURED IN THE MAIN BETSUCOMI AS AN ONGOING SERIES!!
OH MY GOD!
THE FIRST ONE...
I guess it'll be nice to have a birthday story for the first one.
ALTHOUGH IT SAYS THIS WAS THE FIRST STORY IN BETSUCOMI, IT WAS ACTUALLY THE SEVENTH STORY (FOR THE WHOLE SERIES), WHICH MADE IT A BIT CONFUSING.
Monkey High!
BY THE WAY, MACHARU'S BIRTHDAY WAS ALREADY SET TO BE IN JANUARY. THERE WASN'T A GOOD TIME TO PRESENT IT HERE, SO I JUST IGNORED THE EVENT ALTOGETHER.

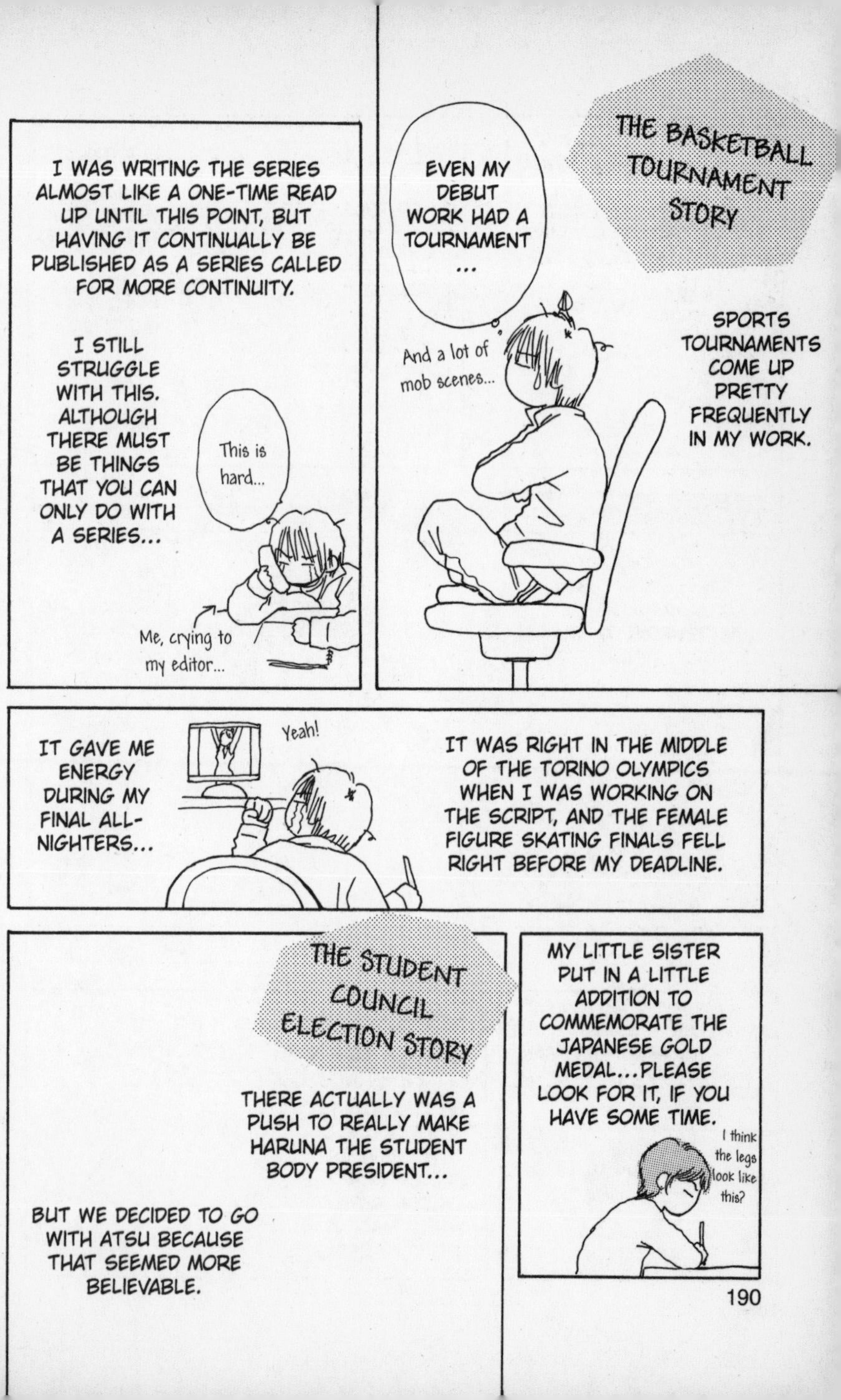
THE BASKETBALL TOURNAMENT STORY
SPORTS TOURNAMENTS COME UP PRETTY FREQUENTLY IN MY WORK.
EVEN MY DEBUT WORK HAD A TOURNAMENT ...
And a lot of mob scenes...
I WAS WRITING THE SERIES ALMOST LIKE A ONE-TIME READ UP UNTIL THIS POINT, BUT HAVING IT CONTINUALLY BE PUBLISHED AS A SERIES CALLED FOR MORE CONTINUITY.
I STILL STRUGGLE WITH THIS. ALTHOUGH THERE MUST BE THINGS THAT YOU CAN ONLY DO WITH A SERIES...
This is hard...
Me, crying to my editor...
IT WAS RIGHT IN THE MIDDLE OF THE TORINO OLYMPICS WHEN I WAS WORKING ON THE SCRIPT, AND THE FEMALE FIGURE SKATING FINALS FELL RIGHT BEFORE MY DEADLINE.
Yeah!
IT GAVE ME ENERGY DURING MY FINAL ALL-NIGHTERS...
MY LITTLE SISTER PUT IN A LITTLE ADDITION TO COMMEMORATE THE JAPANESE GOLD MEDAL...PLEASE LOOK FOR IT, IF YOU HAVE SOME TIME.
I think the legs look like this?
THE STUDENT COUNCIL ELECTION STORY
THERE ACTUALLY WAS A PUSH TO REALLY MAKE HARUNA THE STUDENT BODY PRESIDENT...
BUT WE DECIDED TO GO WITH ATSU BECAUSE THAT SEEMED MORE BELIEVABLE.

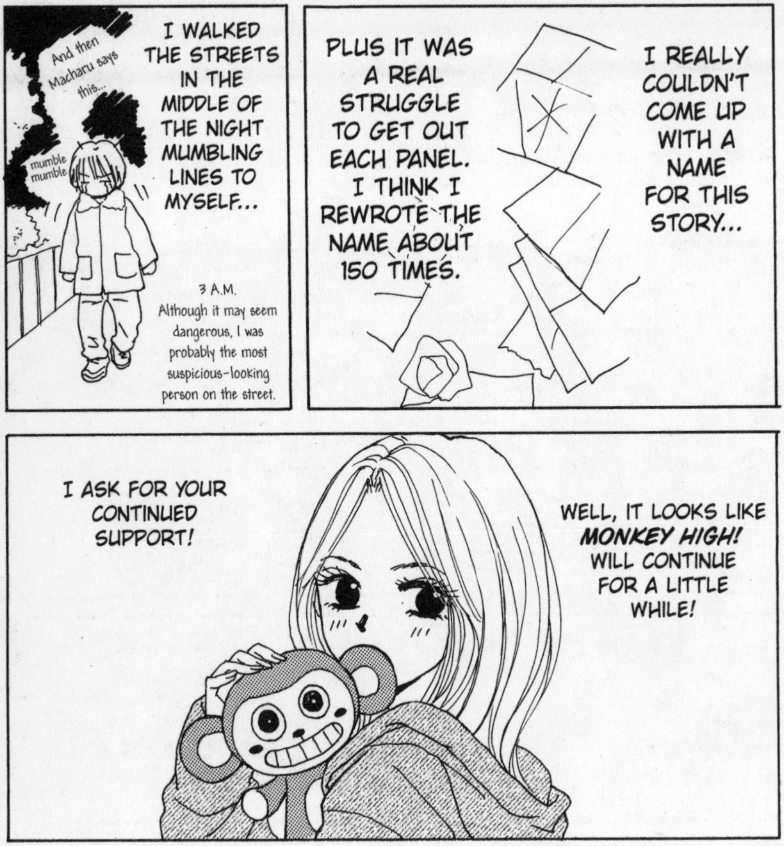
I REALLY COULDN'T COME UP WITH A NAME FOR THIS STORY...
PLUS IT WAS A REAL STRUGGLE TO GET OUT EACH PANEL. I THINK I REWROTE THE NAME ABOUT 150 TIMES.
I WALKED THE STREETS IN THE MIDDLE OF THE NIGHT MUMBLING LINES TO MYSELF...
And then Macharu says this...
mumble mumble
3 A.M. Although it may seem dangerous, I was probably the most suspicious-looking person on the street.
WELL, IT LOOKS LIKE *MONKEY HIGH!* WILL CONTINUE FOR A LITTLE WHILE!
I ASK FOR YOUR CONTINUED SUPPORT!

I'D LIKE TO THANK EVERYBODY WHO HAS HELPED ME—MY EDITOR, MY COORDINATOR, MY DESIGNER, MY FAMILY, FRIENDS AND ALL MY READERS. THANK YOU SO MUCH! I HOPE YOU'LL CONTINUE SUPPORTING ME!

MAY 2006

SHOUKO AKIRA

Slightly confused by all the monkeying around? Here are some notes to help you out!

Page 2: Masaru

Even though everyone refers to him by his nickname, Macharu's real name is "Masaru," which means "superior" in Japanese. Interestingly enough, *saru* by itself means "monkey."

Page 4, panel 1: Valentine's Day

In Japan, it is traditional for girls to give boys chocolates on Valentine's Day. Boys return the favor on March 14, also known as "White Day."

Page 100, panel 6: Takoyaki

Takoyaki are dough balls with pieces of octopus in them. They are made using a hotplate and are often sold at Japanese festivals. *Tako* means "octopus" in Japanese.

Page 167, panel 3: Daruma

A *daruma* is a doll that is used for making wishes. Since its eyes aren't painted in, the wisher fills in the left eye with black ink while thinking of a wish. Should the wish later come true, the right eye is filled in.

Page 188, panel 2: *Betsucomi*

A monthly Japanese *shojo manga* (girls' comics) magazine published by Shogakukan.

I am so grateful that this series has made it to its third volume. It's all thanks to you, my readers. Thank you. I hope you enjoy it...

—Shouko Akira

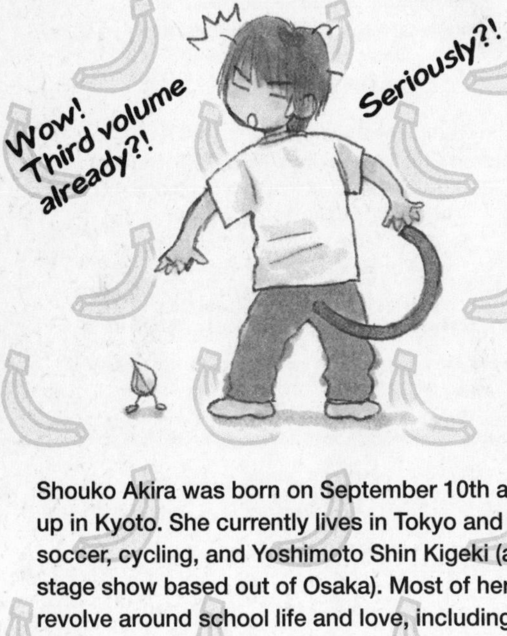
Wow! Third volume already?!
Seriously?!

Shouko Akira was born on September 10th and grew up in Kyoto. She currently lives in Tokyo and loves soccer, cycling, and Yoshimoto Shin Kigeki (a comedy stage show based out of Osaka). Most of her works revolve around school life and love, including *Times Two*, a collection of five romantic short stories.

MONKEY HIGH!
VOL. 3
The Shojo Beat Manga Edition

STORY AND ART BY
SHOUKO AKIRA

Translation & Adaptation/Mai Ihara
Touch-up Art & Lettering/John Hunt
Design/Hidemi Dunn
Editor/Amy Yu

Editor in Chief, Books/Alvin Lu
Editor in Chief, Magazines/Marc Weidenbaum
VP of Publishing Licensing/Rika Inouye
VP of Sales/Gonzalo Ferreyra
Sr. VP of Marketing/Liza Coppola
Publisher/Hyoe Narita

© 2006 Shouko AKIRA/Shogakukan Inc.
First published by Shogakukan Inc. in Japan as "Saruyama!"
All rights reserved.
The stories, characters and incidents mentioned in this publication
are entirely fictional.

Printed in Canada

Published by VIZ Media, LLC
P.O. Box 77010
San Francisco, CA 94107

Shojo Beat Manga Edition
10 9 8 7 6 5 4 3 2 1
First printing, September 2008

www.viz.com

store.viz.com

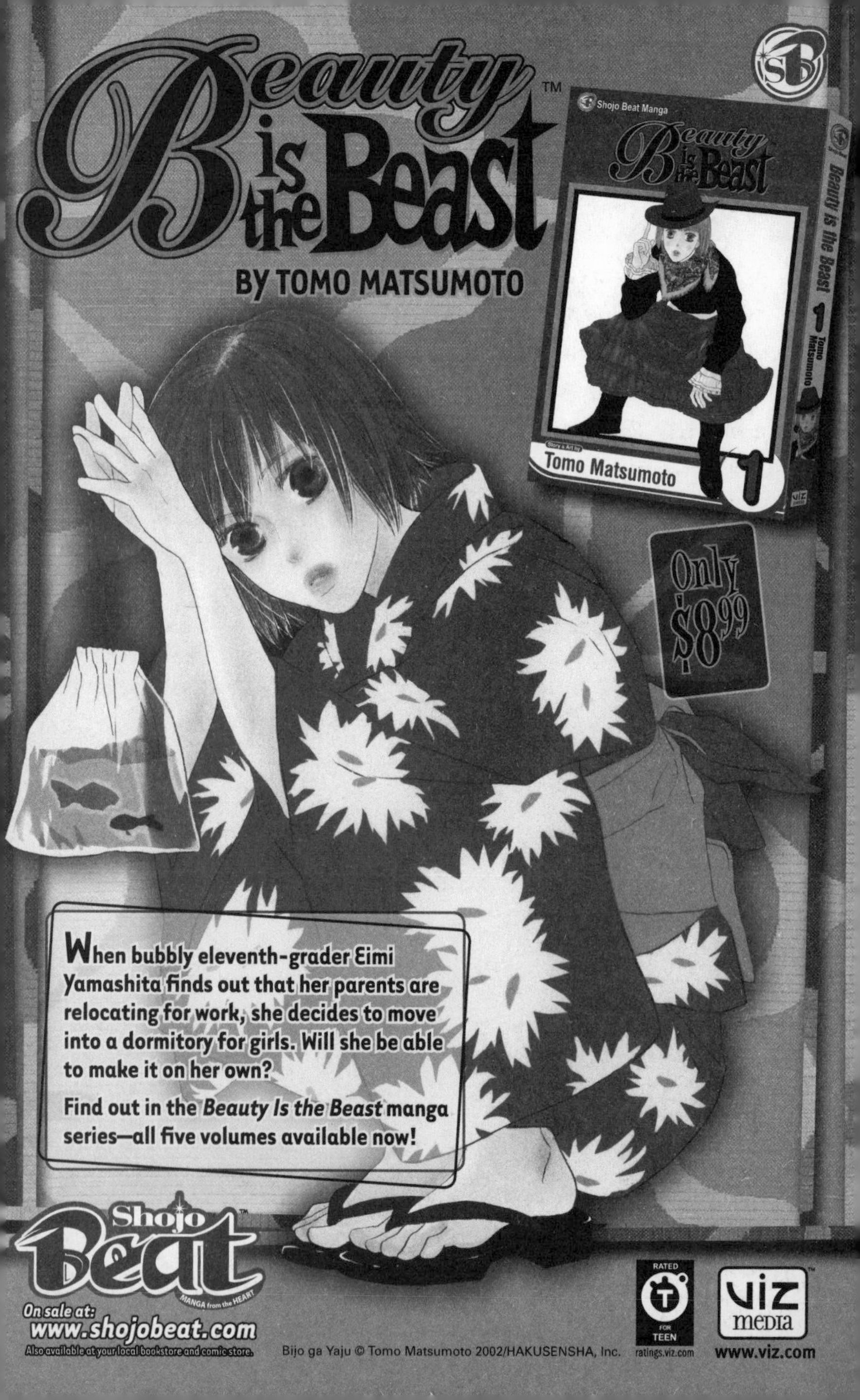
Beauty is the Beast™
BY TOMO MATSUMOTO
Shojo Beat Manga
Beauty is the Beast
Tomo Matsumoto
1
Beauty is the Beast 1 Tomo Matsumoto
Only $8.99
When bubbly eleventh-grader Eimi Yamashita finds out that her parents are relocating for work, she decides to move into a dormitory for girls. Will she be able to make it on her own?
Find out in the *Beauty Is the Beast* manga series—all five volumes available now!
Shojo Beat™
MANGA from the HEART
On sale at:
www.shojobeat.com
Also available at your local bookstore and comic store.
Bijo ga Yaju © Tomo Matsumoto 2002/HAKUSENSHA, Inc.
RATED T FOR TEEN
ratings.viz.com
VIZ media
www.viz.com

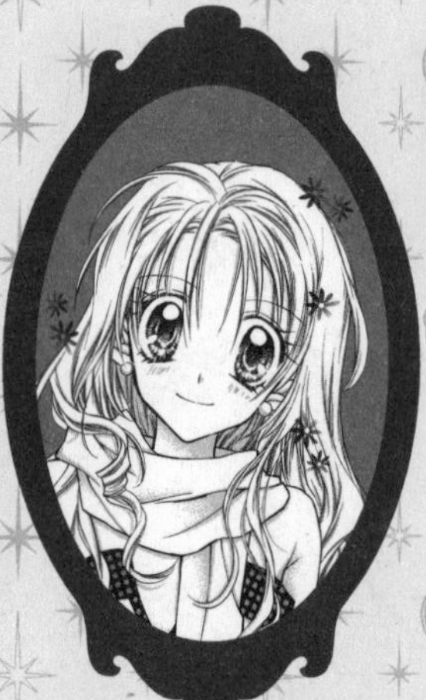

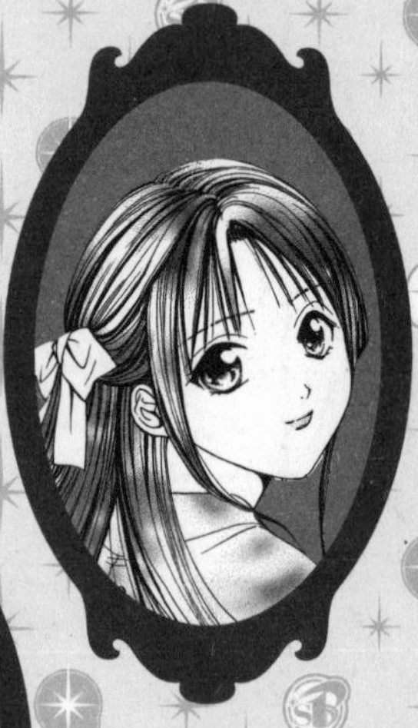

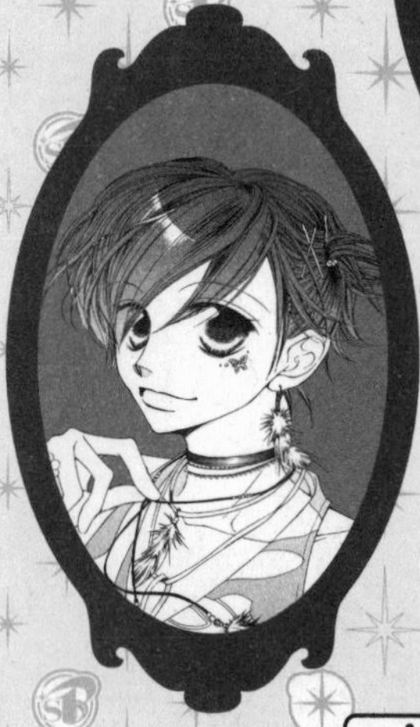